# English Phonology and Pronunciation Teaching

A Companion Website is available at the following address:
http://linguistics.rogersonrevell.continuumbooks.com

Please visit the link and register with us to receive your password and to access these downloadable resources.

If you experience any problems accessing the resources, please contact Continuum at: info@continuumbooks.com

**Also available from Continuum:**

# English Phonology and Pronunciation Teaching

Pamela Rogerson-Revell

continuum

**Continuum International Publishing Group**

| The Tower Building | 80 Maiden Lane |
| 11 York Road | Suite 704 |
| London SE1 7NX | New York NY 10038 |

www.continuumbooks.com

**British Library Cataloguing-in-Publication Data**
A catalogue record for this book is available from the British Library.

ISBN: 978-0-8264-4356-4 (hardcover)
       978-0-8264-2403-7 (paperback)

**Library of Congress Cataloging-in-Publication Data**
A catalog record for this book is available from the Library of Congress.

Typeset by Newgen Imaging Systems Pvt Ltd, Chennai, India
Printed and bound in Great Britain

# Contents

# List of Illustrations

## Figures

# Tables

# About this Book

This book is an accessible introduction to the phonology of English and its practical application to pronunciation teaching. The book assumes no prior knowledge of the subject and is seen as a resource for both newcomers and experienced practitioners in the field of English Language Teaching (ELT) as well as students of Applied Linguistics. It would, for example, be relevant to post-DELTA students or postgraduate TESOL students and experienced English language teachers who want a broad knowledge of phonology and its application to pronunciation teaching. It could also be seen as an introductory text or source of reference for EFL teacher trainers and postgraduate course tutors.

The book aims to provide a clear description of key aspects of English phonology in order to help teachers diagnose and prioritize problem areas in pronunciation. It also aims to develop an awareness of current issues and relevant research in the field to inform teachers' decisions not only about *what* to teach but also *how* to teach pronunciation, particularly in English as an International Language (EIL) contexts.

Specifically, it aims to enable readers to:

- Understand key terms and concepts in phonology and phonetics.
- Become aware of current issues and debates in research and apply these to pronunciation teaching, particularly in EIL contexts.
- Conduct phonological analysis of learner language, including phonemic transcription.
- Diagnose and assess learners' pronunciation difficulties and needs.
- Plan a structured pronunciation syllabus.

The contents are structured and presented in an accessible format that can be used either as a course book or a resource to dip into. It provides clear, straightforward explanations of phonological terms and concepts, emphasizing throughout how an understanding of phonology and phonetics can have a practical application to pronunciation teaching.

The book therefore starts with a general introduction to the nature of phonology and phonetics, and then to the pronunciation of English compared to other major languages. The first section of the book deals systematically with the core features of English phonology: e.g. production of speech, classification of vowels and consonants, phonemes, syllable structure, features of connected speech, stress and intonation, and relates these to 'teaching implications'. The second section of the book applies this knowledge of phonology and speech to specific aspects of pronunciation teaching, such as diagnosing and prioritizing pronunciation difficulties, developing effective teaching techniques, designing an appropriate pronunciation syllabus and assessing pronunciation skills.

An accompanying website hosts the audio files which provide examples of a wide range of native and non-native speaker pronunciation features. The book also provides a range of pronunciation activities and quizzes (with keys) as well as references to further reading, a glossary of technical terms and links to additional online phonology and pronunciation teaching resources.

# Phonology and Pronunciation Learning and Teaching

**1**

## Introduction

Does it matter if the majority of second language (L2) speakers of English do not distinguish between 'ship' and 'sheep'? Is it worth insisting on clear production of consonants at the end of words such as 'what?' if the majority of first language (L1) speakers rarely produce an audible release of such final consonants? Is RP (Received Pronunciation) a relevant model if only 4 per cent of the British population speak it? How is it possible to define the norms and models that are essential to achieve mutual intelligibility among a wide range of non-native[1], and indeed native, speakers of English?

Such questions typify current concerns about how best to approach the teaching and learning of pronunciation. This debate has gathered momentum in recent years, not only because of the natural evolution of the English language but also heightened by the rapid and continuing spread in the use of English as an International Language (EIL). Such concerns may well add to many teachers' uncertainty about how to tackle pronunciation teaching systematically, despite the fact that many students see it as an important area. Lack of time in a busy curriculum or lack of confidence in their own pronunciation or subject knowledge are also long-standing concerns for many English language teachers.

This book aims to provide a clear description of key aspects of English phonology in order to help diagnose and prioritize problem areas in pronunciation teaching and learning. It also aims to develop an awareness of current issues and relevant research in the field to inform teachers' decisions not only about what to teach but also how to teach pronunciation, particularly in EIL contexts.

## The nature of phonology and phonetics

If we hear a unknown language for the first time, we perceive a stream of unidentifiable sounds, that is, an auditory impression, which often form the basis of prejudged reactions about the language. For instance, L1 English speakers often find French 'romantic' or 'sophisticated' while German can be seen as rather 'hard', 'guttural' or 'masculine'.

---

### Activity 1

Can you think of any languages you have heard or know that you (a) like the sound of and (b) don't like the sound of? Try and analyse what exactly you like or dislike about them.

---

Speech sounds are different from other sorts of vocal sounds (**vocalizations**) because they make regular, meaningful patterns. Speech is a series of meaningful sounds and silences and **phonology** is the study of these sound patterns within a particular language, such as Chinese or English, or in a variety of language, such as Cantonese Chinese or Indian English. **Phonetics**, on the other hand, is the scientific description of speech sounds across languages, unrelated to a specific language.

For language teaching, both phonetics and phonology are important. Phonetics enables us to describe the characteristics of individual speech sounds precisely, while phonology helps us explain how such sounds work in patterns within a particular language. To give an example, there is generally a slight difference in the way the sound 'a' is typically pronounced by British and American speakers. The American 'sad' often sounds a bit 'nasalized' to British ears. This is because there is a small difference in tongue position and the distribution of air flowing out through the nose or mouth between the 'a' in the British and American 'sad'.

Nevertheless, both are heard as the same word, so this slight phonetic difference is not phonologically significant. However, there is also a phonetic difference between the first sound in 'thin' and 'tin' (i.e. a small difference in tongue position) but they have a lexically different meaning, that is, they are different words. When a difference in one sound causes different lexical meanings, we say the sound is a **phoneme** of the language and the difference in sound is **phonemic** not just phonetic. Words which can change their lexical meaning by replacing a single phoneme, like 'thin/tin' are called **minimal pairs.**

## Phonology in language learning and teaching

Speech, in all languages is a combination of sounds and each language has its own phonological system. Phonology tries to answer questions such as:

1. How are the sound patterns of one language different from those of another language?
2. Why do L2 learners have particular pronunciation problems?
3. How do the sound patterns of a language change over time or over geographical area?

Phonology forms the basis of all other aspects of language, in the sense that all higher linguistic units (e.g. words, phrases, sentences) can fundamentally be analysed as sounds. Also, phonological differences can signal differences at other levels of language. Here are some examples:

## *Lexical meaning*

For instance, a difference in one vowel sound can signal different word meanings.

bi̱n    ba̱n    bu̱n

## *Grammatical meaning*

Similarly, a small difference in sound can distinguish grammatical categories.
For instance, the difference between [s] and [z] in:

uṣe (noun) vs uṣe (verb);
adviçe (noun) vs adviṣe (verb)

or the difference in 'stress' placement in:

'present (noun) and pre'sent (verb)

## *Discourse meaning*

Phonological differences can also alter the intended meaning of a piece of spoken discourse.
For example:

I thought it was going to **rain** (i.e. it didn't rain)
I **thought** it was going to rain (i.e. and it did rain)

Here, the difference in the amount of emphasis put on different words (e.g. 'rain' and 'thought') in the sentence and differences in the direction of the voice at the end of the utterance can change its meaning.

As well as causing purely linguistic differences, phonology can also differentiate meaning or interpretation of a more social or psychological nature. We manipulate the image we convey to others in many different ways: the way we dress, the way we move, the way we communicate. In particular, the way we speak including our accent conveys a lot about where we come from, and the social groups we belong to or aspire to. In other words, an individual's pronunciation can give important clues about:

personal identity
group identity
emotional state/mood

## Personal identity

It is relatively easy to identify an individual by their voice; everyone has his/her own unique voice quality. People from the same family often have similar voices, and similar physical characteristics, but they are never identical. Even on the telephone, it is possible to get a reasonable idea, for instance, of a person's age group, sex, physical size by his/her voice (Krauss et al. 2002).

### Group identity

Identification with a group can be either (i) geographical or (ii) social:

(i) *geographical* – people from the same geographical region often share identifiable pronunciation patterns while people from different geographical regions may have distinctive regional accents (e.g. New York American, Liverpool English).

(ii) *social* – various types of social groups mark their identification with that group by shared pronunciation patterns, as well as other linguistic patterns. For instance, the common substitution of /θ/ for /f/ (e.g. 'fin' for 'thin') by many English teenagers. Different phonological features may be used as such **group markers**. For instance, the pronunciation of individual sounds, such as 'moor' vs 'more', are the same vowel in southern English but different vowels in many other geographical regions in Britain. In fact, the English short vowel /æ/ has been shown to be an indicator of both geographic and social group identity in both the UK (e.g. 'bath', 'glass') and the US (e.g. 'and', 'can', 'daddy'). Similarly, there may be differences in intonation patterns, for instance in the greeting 'good day', the voice of a standard southern British speaker would probably fall at the end of the word while an Australian speaker's voice would probably rise.

### Emotional state/mood

There is a considerable amount of research suggesting a connection between voice quality and perceptions of mood, attitude or emotions. Various studies have proposed for instance that a 'tense' voice is an indicator of anger and a 'lax' voice suggests boredom or sadness (Scherer 1986).

---

### Activity 2

Do you have a 'telephone voice'. If so, how does it change and why? Can you tell when someone is smiling on the phone?

---

A knowledge of phonology, then, increases our understanding of how many elements of communication work, including grammatical speech, fluent speech and variations in language according to groups and situations. Even if teachers do not teach phonology explicitly, whenever students study the spoken language they are learning its phonology and pronunciation as well.

## Pronunciation teaching and learning – why is it important?

As teachers and as learners of other languages, we all know the crucial impact pronunciation can have not only on assessments of an individual's linguistic ability but also their identity and status. If someone has a 'strong foreign accent' it can be quite easy to guess what their L1 is. If they have little noticeable accent or a 'near native' pronunciation, the reaction is generally one of praise or admiration.

Typically, native speakers (NS) are more sensitive to pronunciation errors than lexical or syntactic ones. According to Mey (1998:47) 'NS are at their most authoritative on matters of phonology, less so on morphology, less still on syntax, and less on semantics. Moreover, this scale corresponds to a scale of the native speakers' tolerance of linguistic deviance: they instinctively abhor phonological deviance, hate the morphological sort, merely dislike the syntactic, and can live with the semantic.'

Similarly, in contexts where English is used as a Lingua Franca between non-native speakers (NNS) of English, research suggests that the majority of communication breakdowns are due to pronunciation errors (Jenkins 2000). Indeed, Jenkins found in her research that of the 40 instances of communication breakdown in her NNS-NNS interactions, the majority (i.e. 27) were due to pronunciation errors with the next largest group being eight lexical errors. Furthermore, all twenty seven pronunciation errors were the result of transfer of L1 sounds.

Jenkins (2000:83) further claims that 'it is in the area of pronunciation that L2 varieties diverge most from each other linguistically and therefore it is this area that most threatens intelligibility' (2000:1). She also concludes from her NNS corpus that 'given speakers' frequent inability to 'say what (they) mean' pronunciation-wise, which is compounded by listeners' seemingly ubiquitous use of bottom-up processing strategies, pronunciation is possibly the greatest single barrier to successful communication' (2000:83). She goes on to say that this is not only a problem for low level learners but 'is still much in evidence when learners are upper-intermediate and beyond' (2000:83).

It is clear then that pronunciation errors can be problematic but there are also some other reasons why pronunciation teaching and learning are important.

## Perceptions of fluency

There are many components of fluency, including the organization of talk and range of vocabulary, but temporal and phonological factors are also important, particularly in language testing and assessment (Hieke 1985). From my own teaching experience, Scandinavian learners, such as Swedes and Danes, are often perceived as being more fluent in English than their French counterparts, even if the French learners are equally, or more, grammatically competent. This seems to relate to the fact that the pronunciation of these Scandinavian languages is relatively closer to English than French (i.e. the 'phonological distance' is smaller) and therefore their pronunciation tends to sound better or at least less heavily accented.

## Acquisition vs learning

It is not obvious that learners, especially adults, will 'pick up' pronunciation naturally themselves. Many factors affect pronunciation learning, including L1, age, exposure, phonetic ability, sense of identity, motivation and attitude and some of these are possibly more important than others.

### Predicting problems

For teachers, a knowledge of the phonology of the target language and the students' first language can help predict some of the problems learners may have as they transfer some of their native language pronunciation to the target language. Obviously, if the teacher shares the same L1 as their learners they could have an advantage here.

### Goals and targets

It is important for learners to have clear models, realistic goals and achievable targets for pronunciation but what exactly should they be? For instance, should the goal be 'comfortable intelligibility' (Abercrombie 1949, Kenworthy 1987) or a near-native command; should the model be RP or a local standard accent?

The first three of these issues will be discussed further in Chapter 2 but we will now consider goals, models and targets more closely.

# Targets, models and goals

## Models

It is generally agreed that teaching and learning pronunciation requires some sort of model for the learner to refer to. The conundrum is choosing a pronunciation model which learners and teachers feel comfortable with and which facilitates successful communication in contexts in which the learner will interact. English has a wide variety of accents from which to choose such a model but traditionally the choice for British English has been the prestige accent 'Received Pronunciation' or 'RP', sometimes equated with 'BBC English' or the 'Queen's English'.

### RP

'Received Pronunciation' is a term coined in the Victorian era to refer to the 'received' or 'socially acceptable' accent of the upper classes. RP is generally recognized as a social rather than regional accent with 'its origins in the public school system and a social elite from London and the Home Counties' (Jenkins 2000:14). According to Crystal (1995) 'pure RP' is spoken by less than 3 per cent of the British population and has been largely replaced by what he calls 'modified RP' which includes some regional features.

Debates have been ongoing about the appropriacy of RP as a model for many decades (e.g. Honey 1989, Widdowson 1994). However, with the growing use of English as an International Language (EIL) or English as a Lingua Franca (ELF) this debate has intensified in recent years/decades.

Many arguments have been forward both 'for' and 'against' the use of RP as a pronunciation model. Some of these are as follows:

## *'For'*

- RP is one of the most extensively documented accents in the world. It has been described in great detail both by sociolinguists and phoneticians over a long period of time.
- The majority of teaching resources for British English, both textbooks and learner dictionaries, are based on RP.
- It is still recognized as a prestige accent and therefore adopting such a model gives learners access to the social status and power related with it.
- Learning a language is about acquiring linguistic proficiency. Having a goal of mastering a native-speaker accent such as RP reflects a concern to achieve a high level of academic and language-learning ability.

## *'Against'*

- RP is a minority accent which perpetuates the norms of an elite minority which few L2 speakers are likely to encounter. Daniels (1995) refers to them as 'phantom speakers of English' to illustrate their scarcity.
- It has been claimed that RP is far from the easiest accent to learn because of features like the non-rhotic /r/, i.e., not pronounced after a vowel, as in 'car' the large number of diphthongs and weak forms. It has been suggested that some other varieties such as Scottish or General American would be easier teaching models (Abercrombie 1988, Modiano 1996).
- RP has changed considerably over time as can be witnessed by comparing older and younger generation RP speakers. Many feel it is 'old fashioned' and 'on the way out' (Abercrombie 1988).
- Adopting an 'alien' accent involves loss or threat to identity – it is 'morally wrong' to change one's pronunciation (Porter and Garvin 1989).
- Assuming a NS accent is an intrusion into a speech community that the NNS is not qualified to join.

---

### Activity 3

Does speaking another language automatically threaten your sense of L1 identity? Is it 'morally wrong' to aim to reduce a learner's L1 accent?

---

Many scholars now conclude that the term 'RP' is outmoded and embodies negative connotations regarding social class and elitism. Various alternative terms have been suggested, including for example, 'BBC pronunciation/English', 'Estuary English',[2] 'Non-Regional Pronunciation' (Collins and Mees 2003) and 'Standard Southern English'. All such terms strive to reflect the phonetic changes which traditional RP has undergone over recent decades and the general social and geographical spread of the accent, although arguably this is still a prestige accent of educated southern English speakers.

The term adopted here, as an alternative to 'RP', is **BBC pronunciation'**, in line with Roach (2000), Trudgill (1999), Ladefoged (2001) and as used in the Daniel Jones Pronunciation Dictionary (15th edition 1997). As Roach (2000) points out, this is not because all BBC presenters use this accent or because the organization enforces its use but because it is still relatively easy for teachers and learners to find examples of this accent from the BBC media.

'BBC pronunciation' is also the accent used as the main model throughout this book, although a range of both native and non-native varieties will be presented. Again, the argument here is that at some point teachers and learners need a clear, unambiguous reference point from which to practice sounds and other pronunciation features. It is little help to learners to suggest they can choose to pronounce 'go' as /gəʊ/, gou/ or [gœ] even if all three would be readily intelligible to many NS. Obviously, it can be useful, at a later stage perhaps, for learners to be aware of this flexibility but this degree of choice does not help in the early or intermediate stages of pronunciation production.

Again, choosing this as the main model for production, does not assume that it is the 'best' accent. As many others have pointed out, there are several alternative accents, such as some Scottish or Irish accents which could be easier to learn because of the closer link between sound and spelling and the fewer number of vowel sounds. In fact, there are a wide variety of NS and NNS accents which would provide a suitable model and preferably learners would be exposed to a large selection of both.

This leads to a further point regarding models. Normally, the main pronunciation model for learners, is the class teacher together with any available audio materials. If the teacher is an L1 English speaker who does not speak with a BBC accent (for instance, they may have a Scottish, or American or Australian accent), they will have to be aware of points where their own accent deviates from this model and decide which of the two to choose as the main teaching model. If the teacher is an L2 English speaker, they will need to decide similarly if BBC pronunciation or some standard L2 model (such as Singaporian or Indian English) is more appropriate for their learners' needs. Regardless of whether the teacher is an L1 or L2 English speaker, they will have to provide consistent examples of the main model as well as examples of other appropriate models for later stages of learning.

A final point about models is that there is often confusion between the terms 'model' and 'goal'. A 'model' is a set of standard pronunciation forms for a particular accent which can be used a point of reference or guideline with which to measure pronunciation appropriacy or accuracy. Inevitably, a model provides examples of normal pronunciation for a particular accent, for example, the use of /ɑ:/ is the normal phoneme in 'grass' using an RP model.

## Goals

There is a difference between the reference points or model we use for guidance in pronunciation teaching and learning and the target we set as an achievable goal or aim. The 'goal' is the level which a learner's pronunciation aims to reach in order to facilitate effective communication. The goal may vary depending on the particular contexts in which the learner needs to communicate, for instance, someone intending to work in an international CALL centre may require a target of near native proficiency while a person who will interact primarily with other L2 speakers may be comfortably intelligible with a limited degree of pronunciation competence, as outlined for instance in Jenkins' 'Lingua Franca Core' (which is described later in this chapter).

### Intelligibility

Increasingly, the goal of '**intelligibility**' is seen as more achievable and appropriate for many learners. The term has been interpreted in different ways with a distinction sometimes made between intelligibility as recognition of words and utterances (Smith and Nelson 1982) and a broader concept which includes the understanding and interpretation of words and messages, sometimes referred to as '**comprehensibilty**' (James 1998).

There have also been differences in the way the goal of intelligibility is conceived.

For instance, the concept of '**comfortable intelligibility**' (Abercrombie 1949, Kenworthy 1987) takes into account the role of the listener as well as the speaker in intelligibility. Understanding someone who makes frequent pronunciation errors requires a lot of effort on the part of the listener and can be uncomfortable in the sense that it can cause irritation and confusion. Kenworthy therefore sees 'comfortable intelligibility' as a pronunciation goal where speaker and listener can communicate effectively without undue stress or effort.

Similarly, Jenkins (2000) notion of 'international intelligibility' raises the question of intelligible to whom? She claims that whereas intelligibility has traditionally been viewed from the standpoint of the NS listener, in EIL contexts it can also be considered from the point of view of both NS and NNS listeners and in English spoken as a Lingua Franca (ELF) contexts it is important to consider mutual intelligibility between NNS speakers and listeners.

There is a common belief that foreign accent is the cause of unintelligibility and is necessarily a learner 'problem'. It obviously can be, depending on the degree of accent and the context but so can a native accent such as Glaswegian or Geordie (from Newcastle in the north of England) to those unfamiliar with such varieties. The issue is deciding if and when an accent can be problematic to intelligibility.

## Learner and teacher pronunciation competence

While there is little disagreement over the importance of intelligibility as a key goal in pronunciation teaching and learning, debates continue over what level of competence learners and teachers should aim for.

### Teacher competence

Most teachers would agree that they need a higher level of competence than the average student. However, there is some discussion regarding what exactly constitutes this competence, as reflected in the following quotes from some key experts in the field:

'Is it really necessary for most language learners to acquire a perfect pronunciation? Intending secret agents and intending teachers have to, of course, but most other language learners need no more than a comfortably intelligible pronunciation (and by "comfortably intelligible" I mean a pronunciation which can be understood with little or no conscious effort on the part of the listener).' (Abercrombie 1965, in Brown 1991:93)

'For the teacher, however, easy intelligibility is not enough. He has the added responsibility of serving as a model for his pupils, who, if they are young, will imitate equally well a correct or a faulty pronunciation. His aim therefore must be perfection in respect of all aspects of pronunciation.' (Gimson 1977:56)

'Learners who plan to become teachers of English will want to approximate a native accent and, depending on their future teaching situations, may want to be familiar with several major accents of English in the world.' (Kenworthy 1987:3)

'However, for the immediate future, ELT students will also need to acquire the non-core areas receptively in order to be able to understand "NSs" face-to-face (for example, in British American, or Australian universities) or, more likely, in the media. In effect, this means that pronunciation teacher education should cover the full range of phonological features of at least one of the main "NS" varieties of English – even though teachers will not thence be expected to pass this on to their students for productive use.' (Jenkins 2000:202)

There seems to be some agreement therefore that pronunciation teachers need to provide a clear, consistent pronunciation model and they should also have at least receptive competence in one or more standard NS varieties. Which variety will depend on the teacher's own linguistic background and on the needs of the learners.

### Learner competence

While many learners may be happy to aim for comfortable intelligibility, some prefer to go beyond this to a higher level of competence. As Jenkins says, 'it is important not to patronize those learners who wish to work towards the goal of a NS accent by telling them they have no need to do so' (2000:101).

Nevertheless, increasing acceptance of the goal of intelligibility has led to a renewed focus on the level of competence required by learners and what pronunciation features need to be mastered to achieve this.

The continuing growth of English as a global language means that the number of people who use it as a second language or lingua franca far outweighs the number of first language speakers. Many of these users have little realistic possibility or need to acquire a native-like level of competence as the majority of their communication will not be with L1 speakers. The acceptance of this fact has led to various suggested alternative goals for such L2 learners.

### 'Amalgum English' and 'International English'

These terms were introduced in the seventh edition of 'Gimson's Pronunciation of English' (2008 revised by Alan Cruttenden), in recognition of the changes that English has undergone since the first edition appeared in 1962. In it, the terms '**Amalgum English**' and '**International English**' are introduced. The former refers to the goal which would be relevant to learners who use English 'as an L2 and/or lingua franca within their own country (and maybe including neighbouring countries) and who may only have limited meetings with L1 speakers'.

The latter refers to speakers who use English 'as a lingua franca on a more international basis and need a minimum standard for occasional communication (e.g. non-English speaking businessmen who use English as the common language between them)' (Cruttenden 2008:317).

A summary[3] is provided here (Figures 1.1 and 1.2) of the core pronunciation features of both 'Amalgum English' and 'International English' (Cruttenden 2008:329 and 333).

---

*'Amalgum English'*
(1) General aim: easy intelligibility by native speakers
(2) Consonants:
    I. Insist on aspirated plosives but allow dental or retroflex /t,d/ and palatal /k,g/
    II. Insist on /f,v, s,z/ but allow conflation of /ʃ ʒ/ and /θ ð/. /h/ required but allow velar/uvualr replacements
    III. Insist on / ʧ , ʤ/ distinct from /tr, dr/
    IV. Allow any variety of /l/. Allow prepausal and pre-consonantal /r/ and /r/ = [ɽ].
        Allow insertion of /g/ following /ŋ/. Discourage /w/ = [ʊ]
    V. Insist on consonantal clusters (apart from usual reductions allowable in RP.
(3) Vowels: a possible reduced inventory:
    I. Short vowels /ɪ, e, æ, ʊ, ə/
    II. Long vowels /i:, e:, ɑ:, ɔ:, ɜ:, o:, u:/
    III. Diphthongs /aɪ, aʊ (ɔɪ)/
(4) Connected speech:
    I. Insist on nucleus movement and basic tunes

**Figure 1.1** 'Amalgum English' (from Cruttenden 2008:329)

---

*'International English'*
(1) General aim: minimal intelligibility in the use of English in international lingua franca situations.
(2) Consonants:
    I. Allow voicing distinctions to be made using different features than those used by native speakers.
    II. All forms of /r/ and /l/ are allowed but distinction between the two to be given high priority (even for those speakers from Asia who find it difficult, eg Japanese and some Chinese). As for Amalgum English /r/ should follow the spelling and any sort of /r/ allowed.
    III. Distinction between /v/ and /w/ should be insisted on; use of /ʊ/ for either or both discouraged.
(3) Vowels:
    I. A reduction in the vowel inventory to five short and five long vowels is allowable (it will be used naturally by many learners, for example, Bantu speakers).
(4) Connected speech:
    I. Some attempt should be made to place the accent on the usual syllable of polysyllablic words, that is, no reduction to /ə/ need be made.
    II. No effort need be made to learn native intonation patterns of English.

**Figure 1.2** 'International English' (from Cruttenden 2008:333)

### The Lingua Franca Core (LFC)

Jenkins' (2000) research on ELF, that is, between NNS of English led her to conclude that it is neither feasible nor necessary to try to teach a full set of phonological contrasts to learners who use English in ELF contexts. She suggests instead a restricted set of contrasts which she refers to as the Lingua Franca Core.

Jenkins suggests we need 'some sort of international core for phonological intelligibility; a set of unifying features which, at the very least, has the potential to guarantee that pronunciation will not impede successful communication in EIL settings' (2000:95). This core then would prioritize those pronunciation features which are key to mutual intelligibility in international communication contexts. Jenkins claims that such as core would 'scale down the phonological task for the majority of learners' (2000:95) and would provide more realistic and achievable classroom teaching priorities.

The main features of the Lingua Franca Core are:

- All the consonants are important except for /δ/ sounds as in 'thin' and 'this'.
- Consonant clusters are important at the beginning and in the middle of words. For example, the cluster in the word 'string' cannot be simplified to 'sting' or 'tring' and remain intelligible.
- The contrast between long and short vowels is important. For example, the difference between the vowel sounds in 'sit' and 'seat'.
- Nuclear (or tonic) stress is also essential. This is the stress on the most important word (or syllable) in a group of words. For example, there is a difference in meaning between 'My son uses a computer' which is a neutral statement of fact and 'My SON uses a computer', where there is an added meaning (such as that another person known to the speaker and listener does not use a computer).

According to Jenkins, other phonological features, which appear outside this core, and which are regularly taught on English pronunciation courses appear not to be essential for intelligibility in EIL interactions. These are:

- The /δ/ sounds (see above).
- Vowel quality, that is, the difference between vowel sounds where length is not involved, for example, a German speaker may pronounce the 'e' in the word 'chess' more like an 'a' as in the word 'cat'.
- Weak forms such as the words 'to', 'of' and 'from' whose vowels are often pronounced as schwa instead of with their full quality.
- Other features of connected speech such as assimilation, where the final sound of a word alters to make it more like the first sound of the next word, so that, for example, 'red paint' becomes 'reb paint'.
- Word stress.
- Pitch movement.
- Stress timing.

Jenkins emphasizes that the Lingua Franca Core relates to EIL contexts and not to situations where communication occurs between native and NNS of English.

There have been other attempts to establish a common core of pronunciation features to ensure international intelligibility. For instance, Ogden's BASIC (British American Scientific

Intercultural Commercial) in the 1930s was an attempt to facilitate international communication and reduce cultural influences. Similarly, Crystal described the emergence of an international variety of English, World Standard Spoken English (WSSE), influenced more by American than British English. He also predicted that 'as the balance of speakers changes, there is no reason for L2 features not to become part of WSSE' (1997:138).

## Some criticisms of the LFC

Jenkins' LFC has led to considerable lively debate, partly on the appropriateness of the pedagogic content. For example, can word stress be dismissed as unteachable (Dauer 2005) and, at a more political level, whether the LFC implies some sort of inverted discrimination whereby NNS are not given access to the complete phonological repertoire in order to maintain their status and phonological identity as NNS.

Others have argued that Jenkins and others concern for the socio-political nature of pronunciation models and goals is overplayed. For instance, Gikes[4] recently suggested on the IATEFL pronunciation SIG forum that 'Jenkins' concerns about 'native speakerism' apply more to other areas of language teaching, such as the sociolinguistic examples I gave above. In other words, if we make a prescriptive statement that a particular pronunciation of a segment should be the global 'norm', we are just delineating an area of phonological space. To English learners, it is just a statement about articulatory behaviour: it is irrelevant that the norm comes from a particular 'native' variety.

Interestingly, much of the ELF debate suggests strong support for non-standard/non-native models by NS teachers and researchers and less from NNS counterparts (e.g. Kuo I-Chun 2006). Also, as some teachers and researchers have pointed out (Hartle 2008, Kuo I-Chun 2006), many learners still value NS norms and models.

Nevertheless, many argue that Jenkin's Lingua Franca Core or Gimson's 'Amalgum English' and 'International English' are sensible initial goals for the majority of pronunciation learners. Even if learners then want to go on to a higher level of pronunciation mastery, none of these features need to be unlearned or are unnecessary. However, even if such targets are seen as a useful starting point, there is still the question of which model is appropriate. The features of such core targets do not, understandably, relate to any one specific accent. They are broad enough to describe standard American, Scottish or many competent NNS accents. The main point is that there are numerous NS or NNS varieties which would provide a suitable model and preferably learners would be exposed to a wide range of both.

## Activity 4

How do you feel about Jenkins 'Lingua Franca Core' or Gimson's 'Amalgum' and 'International English' targets? What impact, if any, would they have on your pronunciation teaching?

The issue of models and goals has been considered in some depth here because of its importance to pronunciation teachers and learners, particularly with the increasing use of English as an International Language and the growing role of NNS of English in ELT.

# Key points

- The application of a knowledge of phonetics and phonology is important for language learning and teaching because a knowledge of the 'building blocks' (i.e. phonetics) and the 'system' (i.e. phonology) underlying pronunciation can help the teacher:

  (1) predict the needs and likely difficulties of learners.
  (2) diagnose errors and find the most efficient solutions to correct them.
  (3) evaluate teaching materials and select or adapt as appropriate for your learners.

- This knowledge includes (a) an awareness of differences between L1 and L2 phonological systems and (b) the ability to identify, in phonetic and phonological terms, the nature of a pronunciation problem.
- An understanding of some of the current issues and debates regarding pronunciation teaching, such as choice of pronunciation model and goals, should also help teachers make informed decisions about what aspects of pronunciation to teach and how to prioritize these.

---

### Activity 5

Consider your own views about pronunciation teaching and learning by answering the following questions.

1. How important is pronunciation in overall English language learning?
2. Is pronunciation difficult to teach and learn and, if so, why?
3. What is your goal in pronunciation teaching?
4. What model of pronunciation would you use and why?
5. How important is the learner's L1 in L2 pronunciation acquisition?
6. Are you aware of any research into L2 pronunciation acquisition?
7. 'Pronunciation is a more sensitive area of language than the other linguistic levels' (Setter and Jenkins 2005:6). Do you agree with this?
8. 'Losing your L1 accent implies losing your L1 identity' – do you agree with this statement?

# Notes

1 There has been increasing debate over the use of the terms 'native speaker' (NS) and 'non-native speaker' (NNS) in recent years, relating partly to the growing complexity of the users and uses of English and partly to growing sensitivity to the possible ethnic and political connotations behind the terms. The general debate has been described in detail by Davies (2003) and with particular reference to pronunciation by Jenkins (2000). Unfortunately however, no simple or satisfactory alternative forms have been widely accepted to date but the slightly more neutral terms 'L1 speaker' and 'L2 speaker' will be used wherever possible.

2 The variety of English spoken in London and, more generally, in the southeast of England – around the river Thames and its estuary.

3 As this summary necessarily includes phonemic symbols, you may want to return to it after reading later chapters covering the phonemes of English, i.e. chapters 4–6).

4 from IATEFL Pronunciation SIG member Stephanie Gikes retreived online on 04.06.09.

# Further reading

Bex, T. and Watts, R. (eds) (1999) *Standard English: The Widening Debate*. London: Routledge.

Abercrombie, D. (1988) 'RP R.I.P', *Applied Linguistics*, 9 (2), 115–24.

Dauer, R. (2005) 'The lingua franca core: A new model for pronunciation instruction?' *TESOL Quarterly*, 39 (3), 543–50.

Derwing, T. and Munro, M. (2005) 'Second language accent and pronunciation teaching: A research-based approach', *TESOL Quarterly*, 39 (3), 379–97.

Jenkins, J. (1998) 'Which pronunciation norms and models for English as an international language?,' *ELT Journal*, 52 (2), 119–26.

Jenkins, J. (2002) 'A sociolinguistically based, empirically researched pronunciation syllabus for English as an international language', *Applied Linguistics*, 23, 83–103.

Kuo, I-Chun. (2006) 'Addressing the issue of teaching English as a lingua franca', *ELT Journal*, 60 (3), 213–21.

Levis, J. (2005) 'Changing contexts and shifting paradigms in pronunciation teaching', *TESOL Quarterly*, 39 (3), 369–78.

Widdowson, H. (1994) 'The ownership of English', *TESOL Quarterly*, 28, 377–89.

# 2 Research and L2 Phonological Acquisition

## Introduction

Although many teachers are convinced of the importance of pronunciation for their learners, it remains a relatively marginalized area in applied linguistics. For instance, while there is a growing body of research in phonetics and phonology, there is currently no dedicated journal applying such research to pronunciation teaching. As a result, there is little connection between research findings and teaching materials; as Derwing and Munro (2005:383) state: 'this situation thus creates a twofold problem: relatively little published research on pronunciation teaching and very little reliance on the research that exists'.

One of the main aims of this book is to help teachers and students prioritize key areas of pronunciation learning. As well as developing a deeper knowledge of phonology and phonetics, one way of doing this is through an understanding of current issues and relevant research in the field.

One area of research which is particularly relevant to pronunciation teaching and learning is L2 phonological acquisition, that is, studies which investigate the factors which influence pronunciation achievement and the processes by which learners master various aspects of L2 pronunciation. Understanding some of these factors and processes should help teachers and learners make decisions about which aspects of pronunciation to concentrate on and how to go about teaching and learning them.

## Key factors in pronunciation achievement

Many factors have been proposed as influential in L2 phonological acquisition, such as age, exposure to the target language, attitude and motivation, aptitude and the role of the L1. Some of these factors will be considered in further detail here.

### Age

Recurrent claims have been made for a 'critical period' in language learning and indeed in pronunciation learning. The Critical Period Hypothesis, originally proposed by Lenneberg (1967), states that the ability to achieve native-like speech is impaired after puberty, largely due to neurological changes in the brain. Although there is a considerable body of scientific research (e.g. Flege 1987, Long 1990) as well as anecdotal evidence to support this claim, there is also some evidence that adults can achieve native-like L2 pronunciation after the critical period (Ioup et al. 1994). It has been argued that adults have the same ability as children to discriminate speech sounds (Schneiderman et al. 1988), but they perceive new sounds in terms of the categories of their first language (Best 1994, Polka 1995). So, while there is some support for the Critical Period Hypothesis, it is unclear exactly why many adults find it harder to achieve native-like L2 accents. It could be that social and linguistic factors such as sense of identity and interference from L1 phonological systems are as important as neurological factors.

---

### Activity 1

What age were you when you started to learn your first foreign language? How proficient have you become in terms of pronunciation? Do you think age was significant in your own case?

---

## Personality

It is unclear how important personality is in L2 acquisition. Earlier research suggested a link between the personality characteristics of introversion and extroversion and language learning (Dewaele and Furnham 1999). It seems reasonable to assume that confident, outgoing types may be willing to take more risks and therefore have more opportunity for practice through interaction. However, Suter (1976) saw this as a relatively minor factor in L2 pronunciation achievement, suggesting that an individual's motivation and belief in the importance of pronunciation was far more important. For teachers, however, it is obviously important to bear in mind personality differences and to make the classroom environment as interesting and conducive to participation as possible.

---

### Activity 2

Do you think personality is important in pronunciation learning? Do you think the 'introversion/extroversion' dimension is significant?

---

## Sociocultural factors

This is an area that researchers increasingly suggest is important for L2 phonological acquisition. Pronunciation, much more so than grammar and vocabulary, is inextricably bound up with identity and attitude. Accent can convey a lot about who we are and where we are from and some researchers suggest that developing an L2 accent can be seen as a threat to L1 identity (Daniels 1995). The importance of accent to cultural identity can be seen not only in foreign accent retention but also with native English speakers who speak different varieties, such as Australian, Scottish or Jamaican. For some such speakers, retaining their 'accent' is a strong marker of social identity.

Traditionally, it has been suggested that the more a learner identifies with the target culture, the more likely they are to try to acquire a target language accent. Conversely, a strong desire to preserve their own cultural identity would reduce the motivation to lose their 'foreign accent'. However, the growth of IEL may query this argument somewhat, as the target culture of such an international language community is less clear cut. As Jenkins and Setter state: '. . . motivation is no longer a straightforward concept involving the learner's orientation to the accent of the language's native speaker community' (Jenkins and Setter 2005:6). Nevertheless, it is important for pronunciation teachers to be aware of the complexity of sociocultural factors underlying phonological acquisition and how these may influence their learners and their goals.

---

### Activity 3

In your own language learning or teaching experience, do you know cases of people who have become fluent in a foreign language while maintaining a strong L1 accent? Why do you think this is?

---

## Aptitude

Individual aptitude as well as the ability to mimic have been seen as possible predictors of second language pronunciation performance (Purcell and Suter 1980). However, it has also been claimed (Suter 1976) that the concept of individual ability or aptitude is much less important than other factors in L2 pronunciation learning.

Although teachers and learners often refer intuitively to the notion of 'a good ear' in terms of pronunciation learning, little research has been done to investigate this phenomenon or its possible role in phonological acquisition. Some research (Ellis 1994) suggests that a good phonological short term memory may help vocabulary learning and the repetition of new utterances. Also, Carroll's (1962) research on language aptitude suggests that learners with weak phonetic coding ability (i.e. the capacity to discriminate and code foreign sounds) would have more difficulty producing readily intelligible pronunciation than those with high aptitude in this area.

---

### Activity 4

Do you think there is such a thing as having 'a good ear' for languages?

## Exposure

According to language learning theories such as Krashen's (1982), learners acquire language mainly from the input they receive and they require large amounts of 'comprehensible input' before being expected to speak. On this basis, exposure to the target language would be a critical factor in pronunciation acquisition. Indeed, Suter (1976) claimed that conversation with native speakers was the third most important factor in pronunciation achievement. Nowadays, this claim is more likely to be modified to include 'proficient', rather than 'native', speakers of the L2, including the non-native class teacher. It could also include 'comprehensible input' via a variety of multimedia channels such as TV, radio, DVD or synchronous online chat rather than simply face-to-face conversation.

## Role of the L1

Each language has its own sounds system: its own set of sounds and rules that govern how sounds can be combined into words and which stress and intonation patterns are meaningful. The errors that emerge in L2 pronunciation are rarely random attempts to produce unfamiliar sounds but reflect the underlying patterns and rules of the L1 phonological system. It is often easy for L1 speakers to detect foreign accents, so for instance an L1 English speaker would commonly recognize Spanish or Russian accented English.

Transfer from the first language, that is, the notion that a learner's L1 habits and knowledge influence the acquisition of an L2, is generally recognized as playing an important role in second language pronunciation, both at the segmental (i.e. individual sounds) and suprasegmental levels (i.e. stress and intonation) (Major 1987, Ellis 1994). Indeed, Suter (1976) suggested that this was the most important factor in determining L2 pronunciation achievement. It has also been noted (Ioup 1984) that phonetic transfer is more significant than transfer at other linguistic levels and that the pronunciations of second language learners who share the same native language exhibit common features.

The concept of L1 transfer underlay the Contrastive Analysis Hypothesis proposed by Robert Lado in the 1950s. According to Lado, 'the student who comes in contact with a foreign language [will find that] those elements that are similar to his native language will be simple for him and those elements that are different will be difficult' (Lado 1957:2). More recent studies have revealed that this is an oversimplification and that in terms of the production of sounds, the reverse may even be the case (Selinker 1992). For instance, some research suggests that sounds which are new are more likely to be acquired correctly than sounds that have a similar counterpart in the L1. In contrast, L2 sounds that are similar to L1 sounds will tend to be categorized as the same. This can also lead to intelligibility problems, for instance if a Japanese learner pronounces 'who' as [ɸuː] instead of /huː/ (Flege and Hillenbrand 1984:177).

On the other hand, studies have shown that similarities between the L1 and L2 can lead to positive transfer regarding the perception of sounds or features. For example, Broselow et al. (1987) found positive transfer of the falling pitch tone, familiar to English speakers, when learning tones in Mandarin Chinese. Similarly, Jenkins (2000) also concluded that perception of contrastive stress in English relates to similarity or difference of this feature in the learner's L1. So, it appears that while L1-L2 similarity may facilitate pronunciation perception, it may also handicap the accurate production of L2 sounds and features. Indeed, the notion of 'transfer' came into disrepute in SLA theories for some years based on a rejection of the view that L1 interference simply involved the removal of bad L1 'habits'; often referred to in phonological terms as 'accent reduction'. More recently, the importance of L1 transfer has regained credibility although the processes involved appear more complex than initially assumed.

There are several ways in which the L1 sound system can influence L2 pronunciation acquisition. First, if a sound or feature does not exist in the L1, the learner will need to develop new muscular habits to produce new articulations. Given enough time and practice, this is possible for learners to do. Secondly, a sound may exist in both the L1 and the L2 (such as /tʃ/ in English and Cantonese) but the rules for how and where such sounds are used in words may differ. Therefore, although the learner is able to hear the sound, it is as if it is heard through a first language 'filter' which gets in the way of accurate L2 sound perception and production.

Thirdly, a sound may exist in the L1 which is similar but not identical to the sound in the L2 such as /u/ in French 'tu' and /uː/ in English 'two'. So the learner replaces the L2 sound with the similar L1 sound or feature. This can result in the perception simply of a 'foreign accent' but can also lead to intelligibility problems. A fourth issue is that differences between the L1 and L2 stress and intonation patterns can either result in the incorrect transfer of L1 patterns or the need for the learner to learn new, unfamiliar patterns.

The production of speech sounds involves the formation of automatic motor skills and this results in ingrained L1 speech habits which are hard to remove in the L2. This can give rise to positive transfer with L1 sounds corresponding to L2 sounds being automatically transferred to the L2 repertoire. However, lack of an L1 sound and lack of equivalent articulatory motor skills can make it very hard to acquire an L2 sound (e.g. German /X/ in 'buch' for some English speakers). Similarly, it can be very difficult to remove incorrectly transferred sounds.

A further consideration relating to the role of the L1 is the notion of *phonological distance*, that is, the degree of difference between two phonological systems. Typically, languages from the same family or root, such as French and Spanish or German and Dutch are seen as easier to acquire. The sound system of English is closer to Dutch than to Cantonese so it is predictable that it would be more difficult for a Cantonese speaker to acquire English pronunciation than for a Dutch speaker. While there may be some truth in this hypothesis (Broselow et al. 1987), phonological distance is not the only factor affecting L2 pronunciation acquisition. As we see in this chapter, there are many other factors involved and learners' needs must ultimately be diagnosed on an individual basis.

## Activity 5

Can you think of any instances where similarities between the L1 and L2 sound system has (a) helped and (b) hindered L2 pronunciation acquisition?

# Processes involved in L2 pronunciation acquisition

The acquisition of second language pronunciation involves complex and dynamic processes which are inevitably influenced by the context and conditions in which the language is learned. In this section, we will consider some of these processes and their relation to pronunciation learning and teaching.

## Phonological universals

Much of the research into L2 pronunciation acquisition relates to the concept of 'phonological universals'. There are universal linguistic processes which are thought to play a part in L1 and L2 phonological acquisition. One such example in phonology is the universal tendency to simplify groups of consonants, that is, consonant clusters. This is illustrated in L1 English acquisition when children systematically reduce clusters such as 'crumbs' to 'come' and its continuation in to adult speech with regular consonant deletion in final clusters such as 'last thing'. This tendency to simplify clusters is traced to a universal phonological preference for open syllables (i.e. ending in a vowel such as 'me'), whereby the complex, and often closed syllable structure of English (i.e. ending in a final consonant such as 'meet') is quite distinctive or 'marked'. This preference may account for the strategy employed by some L2 English learners, for instance Japanese learners, to insert an additional schwa to some word final consonants so that 'log' would become 'logger' / lɒgə/. A further universal preference is for devoiced word final consonants, so that some L2 learners, for instance German learners, will pronounce 'dog' as 'dock' /dɒk/, following German pronunciation rules, with a final /k/. While L1 English speakers also devoice some final consonants (e.g. 'bed', 'cab') they maintain the preceding vowel length to avoid confusion with 'bet' and 'cap'.

## Markedness

This concept relates to the degree of difference or distinctiveness of linguistic contrasts in a language in relation to universal preferences. So, for example, final voiced consonants, such as /d/ in 'read' or /z/ in 'rise', are common in English but marked universally, as most languages do not permit this phenomenon. The concept of markedness has been used to explain or predict the degree of difficulty that L2 learners may have with particular L2 linguistic features. For instance, Eckman's 'Markedness Differential Hypothesis' (1977) suggests that a difference between the L1 and L2 is only likely to cause difficulty if the feature in the L2 system is more marked than the L1. This could explain, for example why German learners of English find it harder to produce final voiced consonants as in 'dog' than English learners of German producing devoiced final consonants as in 'tag'.

## Developmental processes

While the concept of phonological transfer and universals are very important processes in the consideration of pronunciation acquisition, other 'developmental processes' are also significant. These processes refer to the way L2 pronunciation systems develop regardless of the learner's L1. According to de Bot (1986:113) the concept of L2 developmental errors is supported by 'the numerous observations have shown that certain types of errors are made by nearly all learners of a given language, irrespective of their mother tongue'. An example of this is the difficulty that many learners have with the English 'th' sounds (for 'thin' and 'this') regardless of their L1, Schmidt suggests that this might be explained by the fact that these are 'the sounds mastered last and substituted most frequently by English native speakers' (1977:367). Jenkins gives another example of the difficulty of trying to teach pitch patterns to L2 learners. She argues that because pitch movement is one of the earliest phonological features to be acquired in all first languages (acquisition even starts in the womb according to Locke 1993), it is so deeply ingrained in the L1 to be unteachable to adult L2 learners (Jenkins 2000:108).

Research suggests that transfer errors occur before developmental errors. Wenk for instance found that beginner French learners impose French rhythm features on English but many advanced learners can correct this (1986). Major's Ontogeny Model (1987) explains this by suggesting transfer errors predominate in early stages of L2 learning but are replaced by developmental errors at later stages, and that both decline over time.

---

### Activity 6

In your own experience learning a foreign language, can you remember any particular pronunciation features or sounds that you had difficulties with or acquired later than others? Why do you think that was?

---

## How can research help pronunciation teaching?

There seems to be growing recognition of the gap between phonological research and pronunciation teaching. This is highlighted in Derwing and Munro's recent article (2005) where they call for much greater application of research to pedagogy. They claim that the study of pronunciation has been marginalized within the field of applied linguistics and that much less research has been carried out on L2 pronunciation than other skills such as grammar and vocabulary (Derwing and Munro 2005). As mentioned earlier, this is evidenced in the lack of dedicated teacher-oriented journals on pronunciation teaching. Although there is a considerable body of L2 speech research published in well-established journals such as the Journal of the Acoustical Society of America and Language and Speech, Derwing and Munro (2005) suggest that such publications are not aimed at a language teaching audience and therefore these findings do not feed down into pronunciation teaching or teaching textbooks. As Levis points out, 'present international research is almost completely divorced from modern language teaching and is rarely reflected in teaching materials' (1999:37). The result of this is that teachers have intuitively decided which features have the greatest effect on clarity and which are learnable in a classroom setting (Levis, 2005).

One of the key aims of this book is to help teachers prioritize key areas of pronunciation teaching not only by developing a deeper knowledge of phonology and phonetics but also by understanding current issues and relevant research in the field. Throughout the following chapters reference will be made to research into the various topics so that the necessary links can be made between such studies and actual teaching and learning contexts.

### Revisiting some 'old-fashioned' notions in pronunciation teaching

One way that research findings can help is by enabling us to revisit long-established beliefs or approaches to pronunciation teaching. In some cases this may mean revising or rejecting such beliefs in light of new findings while in others it may result in reviving notions that were considered 'old-fashioned'. Here are some examples.

### Drilling

Given that motor skills and automaticity are key to learning sounds, the importance of drilling new sounds needs to be recognized. This may seem an 'old-fashioned' notion particularly within a Communicative Language Teaching (CLT) paradigm, however the articulation of new L2 sounds requires the formation of new muscular habits. Given time and practice, such habits can be acquired but they can also slip if the learner's attention is deviated, for instance to a focus on content rather than form.

### Dictation

Dictation has a long history in language teaching methodology but fell out of favour with many with the advent of CLT. However, the value of this traditional approach seems to be regaining strength in pronunciation teaching as witnessed in research (Pennington 1989, Brown 2001) as well as teaching materials (Rogerson and Gilbert 1990).

### Noticing – focus on form

Again, research suggests that acquiring pronunciation is no different from acquiring syntax in the sense that students need help noticing what they are doing (Flege and Wang 1989). Just as students learning certain grammar points benefit from being explicitly instructed to notice the difference between their own productions and those of L1 speakers (Spada 1997), students learning L2 pronunciation benefit from being explicitly taught phonological form to help them notice the differences between their own productions and those of proficient speakers in the L2 community.

### Phonetics/ear training

Again, spending classroom time on listening to phonetic details may seem outdated and unnecessary. However, specific phonetic training has generally been found to be positively associated with phonetic development in a second language (Neufeld and Schneiderman

1980, Cenoz and Lecumberri 1999). Similarly, Jenkins (2000) calls for more phonetic training of specific sounds and particular allophonic features (such as aspiration) to facilitate possible transfer, rather than blanket coverage of all phonemes. McCarthy goes further, suggesting that without fundamental auditory and articulatory training, 'any teaching of pronunciation is so ineffective as to be largely a waste of time' (McCarthy in Brown 1991:299). The main point McCarthy and others are making is that learners need to learn how to listen accurately, that is, to notice what is relevant in the stream of speech before being able to proceed to other aspects of pronunciation learning.

Caudwell and Hewings (1996) makes a similar claim about the importance of listening to and analyzing fluent connected speech in detail. They suggest that not enough attention is given to helping learners decode the minutiae of fast everyday speech, what they refer to as the 'acoustic blur'. They suggest that learners need to spend more time in class listening to authentic recordings and observing and imitating features of fluent, connected speech. They believe that this sort of training can avoid the common dilemma of many learners who feel they 'know words' but in fact are unable to recognize them in fluent speech.

## Stress-timing

We will see in Chapter 10 that the concept of 'stress-timing' (i.e., that speech rhythm reflects the regular occurrence of stressed syllables in speech) in a rigid sense is hard to support with research and yet it remains a popular notion in pronunciation teaching. Marks (1999:198) argues that the use of rhythmical materials in class is justifiable as it 'provides a convenient framework for the perception and production of a number of characteristic features of English pronunciation which are often found to be problematic for learners: stress/unstress (and therefore the basis of intonation), vowel length, vowel reduction, elision, compression, pause'. So, perhaps this is a case of teachers needing to recognize the theoretical limitations of a concept while continuing to refer to those aspects of it which are pedagogically useful.

## Intonation patterns

We will also consider, in Chapter 11, the traditional view that specific intonation patterns can be associated with certain sentence types, for instance, 'yes/no' questions and rising pitch. Research into authentic discourse suggests that such clear links are unfounded (Caudwell and Hewings 1996, Brazil 1997). Setter and Jenkins (2005:12) suggest that 'teachers, teacher trainers and materials developers should be ready to take this on board and develop curricula which make use of this information'.

# Key points

- Transfer of L1 phonological features is a major influence on L2 and phonological acquisition.
- L1 phonological transfer is much more influential than L1 syntactic or lexical transfer. Learners instinctively try to categories L2 sounds using their L1 system (Jenkins 2000:104). It is important therefore for teachers to consider: (a) which L1 features affect intelligibility and (b) which are teachable.

- It may well be that features that do not occur in L1 phonology or are acquired late in the L1 (e.g. interdental fricatives such as /θ' in 'teeth') are unteachable.
- Similarity between the L1 and L2 may help L2 pronunciation in terms of perception but hinder pronunciation production.
- More transfer errors occur in informal speech than formal speech (Major 1987).
- If a sound such as /θ/ /ð/ is infrequent in the world's languages, it may by implication be difficult to acquire and therefore a waste of time to try to teach it, unless the learner is highly motivated to learn them.
- Learners need to learn not only new L2 articulations but also become aware of gaps and overlaps in L1/L2 phonological systems (e.g. the distinction between the /l/ in 'low' and the /ɫ/ in 'full' is allophonic[1] in English but they are different phonemes in Russian. Similarly, /l/ and /n/ are different phonemes in English but allophones in Japanese).
- Interlanguage phonology may help predict L2 learner difficulties, for example, markedness and syllabification. It may also help plan the sequence of teaching, for example, initial /s/ clusters are most marked and therefore may be the most difficult to teach (Carlisle 2001).
- Consonants in final position are the most difficult to acquire (Eckman and Iveson 1994) as they are phonologically marked.
- Given the range of L2 pronunciation proficiency, the pronunciation teacher obviously has a considerable role to play in facilitating pronunciation achievement.
- Research into pronunciation teaching and learning can help teachers update and revise their pedagogic approach and ensure that teaching priorities are relevant and effective.

## Note

1   This concept will be discussed in detail in Chapter Six.

## Further reading

Flege, J., Munro, M. and MacKay, R. (1995) 'Factors affecting strength of perceived foreign accent in a second language', *Journal of the Acoustical Society of America*, 97, 3125–34.

Gatbonton, E., Trofimovich, P. and Magid, M. (2005) '"Learners" ethnic group affiliation and L2 pronunciation accuracy: A sociolinguistic comparison', *TESOL Quarterly*, 39 (3), 489–511.

Jenkins, J. (2005) 'Implementing an international approach to English pronunciation: The role of teacher attitudes and identity', *TESOL Quarterly*, 39, 535–43.

Leather, J. (1999) 'Second-language speech research: An introduction', *Language Learning*, 49 (1), 1–37.

Major, R. C. (1994) 'Chronological and stylistic aspects of second language acquisition of consonant clusters', *Language Learning*, 44 (4), 655–80.

Moyer, A. (1999) 'Ultimate attainment in L2 phonology: The critical factors of age, motivation and instruction', *Studies in Second language Acquisition*, 21, 81–108.

Pennington, M. C. (1994) 'Recent research in L2 phonology: Implications for practice', in Morely, J. (ed.) *Pronunciation Pedagogy and Theory: New Views, New Directions*. Alexandria, VA: TESOL, pp. 94–108.

Purcell, E. and Suter, R. (1980) 'Predictors of pronunciation accuracy: A reexamination', *Language Learning*, 30, 271–87.

Smit, U. and Dalton, C. (2000) 'Motivation in advanced EFL pronunciation learners', *International Review of Applied Linguistics*, 40, 89–116.

# 3 Speech Sounds

## Introduction

Speech sounds are different from other sorts of vocalizations in that they make regular, meaningful patterns and speech is composed of a series of sounds that we can segment into meaningful words and utterances. We have already seen that phonology is the study of these sound patterns within a particular language, like English, while phonetics focuses on describing how sounds are made in general, unrelated to a specific language. Before discussing the sound system of English, we therefore need to consider how sounds are actually produced and this involves covering some basic concepts in phonetics.

For teachers to diagnose and remedy learners' pronunciation problems effectively, they need some understanding of phonetics. Indeed, as we saw in Chapter 2 it has been suggested that phonetics training should be an area of key concern for pronunciation teachers (Jenkins 2000). This knowledge will help explain why a particular student, for example, has a problem producing an English 't' sound or why the word 'bat' sounds like 'bet'. Understanding how sounds are articulated will also enable teachers to guide their students towards correct L2 articulations. First of all, however, it is necessary to make a clear distinction between the English sound system and the English spelling system.

## Sounds and spelling

Unlike many languages, the English spelling system is quite complicated because there is not always a direct correspondence between sounds and letters. Different letters may represent the same sound, as in 'two', 'too', 'to', 'shoe', 'few', 'through' and 'threw' where the same vowel sound is represented by seven different spellings. Also, the same letter, for example, 'a', may represent different sounds, as in 'can', 'cake', 'many', 'ball' and 'sofa'. Similarly, the letter 's' can be pronounced in various ways, as in 'measure', 'see' and 'design'. In some cases, a combination of letters represents a single sound, as in 'rough', 'photo' and 'head'. In others, a letter or letters may not be pronounced at all, as in 'lamb', 'knee' and 'through'. Speakers of many other languages in which the sounds and the letters are more closely connected have a much easier time learning to spell in their L1 than native speakers of English have learning to spell in theirs.

Nevertheless, despite these complexities, there are rules and patterns governing English spelling and it is important that L2 learners are aware of these. Generally speaking, there is a more consistent relationship between letters and the consonant sounds they represent than between letters and vowels. This is partly because there are many more vowels in English than there are letters in the Roman alphabet and also because, historically, pronunciations have changed considerably. So letters such as 'b', 'm' and 'n' have a single pronunciation, unless they are silent. When some consonants occur in combination, they may have a different but stable pronunciation, such as 'ph' representing /f/ in 'photo'. Others may have two different pronunciations, depending on the following vowel, such as 'c' and 'g'. The pattern here is that preceding the letters 'i', 'e' and 'y' (sometimes taught to children as 'thin' vowels), the letter 'c' is pronounced as 's' (as in 'cinema' and 'cyclamen') and the letter 'g' as /dʒ/ (as in 'ginger' and 'gyrate'). Preceding the other letters, 'a', 'o' and 'u' (sometimes referred to as 'fat' vowels), 'c' is pronounced as /k/ (as in 'cat' and 'local') and 'g' is pronounced as /g/ (as in 'gap' and 'legal').

Nevertheless, there are some generalizations that can be made regarding sound-spelling correspondences with vowels. One of these involves the traditional division of vowels into two categories, that is, 'long' and 'short' vowels (although 'long' and 'short' are misnomers in phonetic terms as they do not reflect the actual length of these sounds). When they appear in words ending in 'e', vowels are typically pronounced in their 'long' form (e.g. 'mate', 'home', 'shine'), otherwise, they are 'short'. So, for example, we have:

| | | |
|---|---|---|
| Pete | pet | petrify |
| hide | hid | hideous |

Another pattern that can be pointed out to learners is that the pronunciation of vowels in longer words can be predicted by counting the number of consonants after the vowel. One consonant after a vowel results in a 'long' vowel sound while two results in a 'short' sound. So, for instance, 'completion' will have a 'long' 'e' while 'congestion' will have a 'short' 'e'. Kenworthy (1987) claims that this rule is very useful for learners as it is effective more than 99 per cent of the time.

There are obviously links between spelling and word stress rules as well and these will be discussed later on, in Chapter 9.

---

### Activity 1

Consider the sound/spelling correspondences for a language other than English but based on the Roman alphabet. What difficulties would you predict a learner of that L1 to have with English spelling/pronunciation rules?

# Producing speech sounds

Human speech is a combination of sounds and silences. All speech begins as a silent breath of air, created by muscular activity in the chest. Starting with the muscles in the chest and lungs (the respiratory system) which cause a flow of air up through the throat (the phonatory system), where muscles in the larynx can modify the airflow. The air then continues upwards along what is called the **vocal tract,** between the larynx and the mouth or nose (the articulatory system) and is finally expelled as a sound wave, either through the mouth or nose. Various sets of muscles in the vocal tract can further change the shape of the airstream resulting in the perception of different speech sounds. These **speech organs** (otherwise known as the **speech mechanism)** can be categorized into three parts, the respiratory organs, the phonatory organs and the articulatory organs.

Basically, the speech mechanism has four components: muscular activity, air, some type of resistance or obstruction to the air which causes some sort of sound to be made, and amplification to make the sound loud enough to be heard. When we speak, organs in the various parts of the speech mechanism modify the air expelled from the lungs on its way through the throat, mouth and nose. It is important that teachers of pronunciation have a reasonably detailed knowledge of how these modifications occur.

So, as can be seen in Figure 3.1, air starts off in the lungs, flows up through the trachea (or windpipe), through the larynx, past the epiglottis and through the pharynx. From there, the air can go either through the mouth or nose.

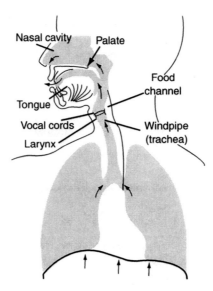

**Figure 3.1** The speech mechanism

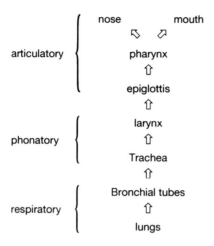

**Figure 3.2** Simplified model of the speech mechanism

The speech mechanism can be divided into three parts (see Figure 3.2); the lower section, the chest, involves the respiratory organs; the middle section, the throat, involves the phonatory organs; and the upper section, between the throat and the nose or mouth, involves the articulatory organs.

## The respiratory organs

Air expelled from the lungs travels up through the bronchial tubes to the throat or trachea. For the production of English sounds, the airflow outwards from the lungs is described as **egressive.** Although the egressive pulmonic airstream is the most commonly used in the articulation of most languages, other airstreams are possible. For example, there are some languages which use an inward or **ingressive** airflow occasionally, such as 'oui' ('yes') in French which can be said in this way. There are other languages, such as the southern African languages, Xhosa and Zulu, where sounds called 'clicks', made with an ingressive airflow, represent distinct, meaningful sounds. However, these airstreams are not generally used in English, except involuntarily, for instance if you try speaking when out of breath or while sobbing.

---

### Activity 2

(1) Try speaking while breathing in, rather than out. How does it sound? How long can you talk on one continuous intake of breath?

### Activity 2—Cont'd

(2) Speech is a disturbance of air pressure which a speaker brings about by moving various parts of the speech mechanism. Try these exercises to feel the air moving through the various organs:

(a) Take a deep breath and say 'aaah!'

(b) Take another deep breath, hold your breath and, *still holding your breath*, say 'aaah!' again. (Impossible'!)

(c) If you made a noise the second time, you were not really holding your breath (unless you have sprung a puncture).

(d) As you say 'aaah', feel your chest 'deflating'. In order to speak, it is necessary to get the air in your body moving. This can be done just be breathing out.

(e) Can you say 'aaah' while breathing in?

(f) As you say 'aaah', feel your throat, around the area of the larynx ('Adam's apple'). Can you feel the vocal cords 'buzzing'.

(g) Now try *whispering* 'aaah'. Do the vocal cords buzz? The vocal cords modify the flow of air coming out of your lungs, but this modification is not necessary in order for you to hear 'aaah'. (Whispering is audible, after all.)

(h) Where does the air leave your body? Does it come out of your mouth? (Try holding your lips shut tight as you say 'aaah!'. Is it possible?) Try holding your nose shut? (pinch the nostrils.) How does this affect the sound?

(i) Now say 'bah!' a few times. Concentrate on the 'b'. Is there any airflow out of your mouth and/ or nose during the time in which your lips are closed for the 'b'?

(j) Can you say 'bah' while breathing in?

## The phonatory organs

The upper end of the bronchial tubes forms the windpipe or **trachea** and at the top of this is the **larynx** or voice box, the upper end of which connects to the pharynx. The larynx is the main phonatory organ and has a key role in many speech sounds.

The larynx consists mainly of cartilage (soft flexible matter intermediate between muscle and bone). The front of the larynx comes to a point at the front of the neck. This can be felt particularly easily in men and is commonly known as the 'Adam's Apple'. Inside the larynx are two thick flaps of muscle. When swallowing the muscles are completely closed, to avoid food 'going down the wrong way'. These muscles are called the **vocal folds or vocal cords** (Figure 3.3). They are about 1 cm long and ½ cm wide and look like two thick pieces of elastic. The muscles can open and close and vibrate, causing a weak sound. Tightening the muscles raises the pitch of the voice and loosening the muscles lowers the voice pitch. If the cords are too tight, the voice becomes tight and pinched and eventually voice may be lost completely. If the cords are too loose, there will be no voice either, because the cords are too slack to sustain vibration. The gap or opening between the vocal folds is called the **glottis** (Figure 3.3).

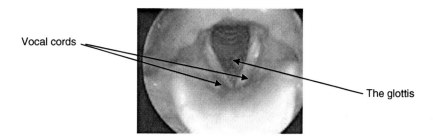

**Figure 3.3** The vocal cords and the glottis (Image of normal vocal cords, courtesy of the Milton J. Dance Jr. Head and Neck Centre at the Greater Baltimore Medical Centre, Baltimore (retrieved 13 July 2009 from www.udel.edu/PR/UDaily/2008/jul/vocal073107.html)

The size and shape of the glottis can change considerably. When the vocal cords are held wide apart, as in relaxed breathing, air passes through freely producing **voiceless** sounds. When the vocal cords are close together and air passes through them, the cords vibrate rapidly, this vibration (or **phonation**) produces a **voiced** sound. As we shall see later, voicing is an important phonological variable in English, and many other languages.

If the cords are tightly closed (i.e. the glottis is tightly shut) a stop sound can be produced when pent up air behind the closure is suddenly released. The **glottal stop** /ʔ/ functions as a phoneme in some languages, such as Arabic and Farsi and can occur in English, for example, in Cockney speech. It also occurs as a replacement for /p/ /t/ /k/ as in butter, pronounced /bʌʔə/ instead of /bʌtə/. The sound is called glottal because it is articulated behind a closure in the glottis. When the glottis is suddenly opened, there is a sudden release or plosion of air. As a result, a glottal stop is called a **plosive** or **stop** consonant.

The speed of vibration of the vocal folds changes considerably but is generally faster in women than in men with an average of 130 times per second for men and 230 times per second for women, this is because larger vocal folds produce slower vibrations. The speed of vibration is known as **frequency.** The higher the frequency of vibration of the vocal folds, the higher the perceived **pitch** of the voice, so typically women are perceived as having higher voices than men.

The vocal folds can be used to create a variety of other phonetic characteristics which are features of speech. For instance, creaky voice is created by a succession of glottal stops (rather like an old door opening slowly) combined with vocal fold vibration. **Creaky voice** is a feature of voice quality (which is discussed later in this chapter) and is common in some accents of British and American English. In some languages, such as Danish, it is also used to distinguish phonemes, and therefore word meaning.

Another phonetic characteristic created with the vocal folds is **whisper,** where the folds are brought close together but without vibration. Sometimes whisper is combined with voicing to create **breathy voice.** Breathy voice is commonly used by female singers in English (such as Marianne Faithfull and Marilyn Monroe) but is also used as a phonemic contrast in some Indian languages, such as Hindi.

---

### Activity 3

Can you think of anyone who employs 'breathy voice'? How do you think they sound?

---

## The articulatory organs

The third part of the speech mechanism, above the larynx (i.e. **supralaryngeal**), is known as the **vocal tract** and the organs within it are the **articulatory organs** or articulators. The articulators are the different parts of the vocal tract that can change the shape of the air flow as it escapes either through the mouth or nose.

There are three sections or cavities in the vocal tract (Figure 3.4), one for the throat or pharynx (the **pharyngeal cavity**), one for the mouth (the **oral cavity**) and one for the nose (the **nasal cavity**).

The size and shape of these cavities can be altered by movements of the various articulatory organs, resulting in changes to the sound of the escaping airstream, similar to the way a

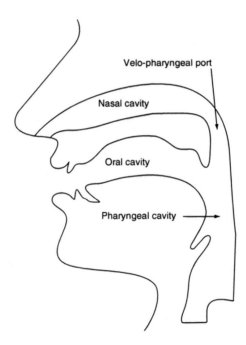

**Figure 3.4** Cavities in the vocal tract (retrieved 21 September 2009 from http://www.asel.udel.edu/speech/tutorials/production/cavity.htm)

musician can adjust the sound produced by a wind instrument such as a flute. Air can, for instance, be blocked momentarily by the articulators creating a small popping sound or explosion or it can be forced through a narrow stricture creating a hissing sound because of friction.

## The Vocal Tract

We will now look at each of the articulators in the vocal tract. The vocal tract is represented in Figure 3.5 in diagrammatic form.

### Pharynx / ˈfærɪŋks/ (adj. pharyngeal)
This is a tube, about 7–8 cm long, which begins just above the larynx and divides into two cavities, that is the mouth (oral) and the nose (nasal).

### Velum, or soft palate / ˈviːləm/ (adj. velar)
The velum can move up or down, switching the airflow to either the oral or nasal cavity. It can be touched by the tongue. If the velum is raised (i.e. velic closure), it blocks off air to the nasal cavity and air flows out through the mouth producing an oral sound. If the velum is lowered, air can flow through the nose creating nasal sounds. Most speech sounds are oral but many languages also have nasal consonants, such as 'm' and 'n'. Some languages also have nasal vowels, such as the vowel sounds in the French words 'Mont Blanc'. The back of the tongue can also be placed against the velum to produce velar sounds, such as /g/ and /k/ in English.

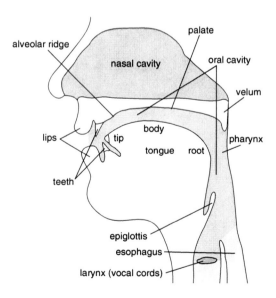

**Figure 3.5**  The vocal tract (retrieved 22 September 2009 from http://www.indiana.edu/~hlw/PhonUnits/vowels.html)

### Uvula / ˈjuːvjələ/ (adj. uvular)

This is the soft, fleshy hanging tip that falls from the base of the soft palate. It is not directly involved in the articulation of English sounds (although it is used by some speakers with Geordie accents (i.e. from the North East of England). It is used in French for production of French 'r' (a difficult sound for English speakers to produce when they learn French).

---

**Activity 4**

Can you produce a uvular 'r'? If not, it is similar to the sound you make when gargling or pretending someone is trying to strangle you!

---

### Hard palate (roof of the mouth) (adj. palatal)

This is the smooth, curved surface on the roof of the mouth. The hard concave gum area between the soft palate and the teeth ridge. It can be touched by the tongue. The term palatal means the centre of the tongue touches the hard palate.

### Alveolar ridge /ælviˈəʊlə/ (adj. alveolar)

This is found immediately behind the top front teeth. It is the hard ridge of gum located directly behind the teeth before rising to the hard palate in the roof of the mouth. Alveolar sounds are produced when the tongue is in contact or near contact with the alveolar ridge. Many English consonants are alveolar.

### Tongue (adj. lingual)

The tongue is composed of very mobile muscular tissue and it is a very important articulator. For phonetic purposes it can be divided into areas, that is, 'tip', 'blade', 'front', 'back' and 'root' (Figure 3.6).

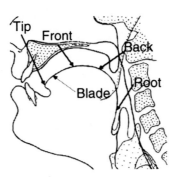

**Figure 3.6** Parts of the tongue (from Laver 1994)

The centre of the tongue is divided into the 'front' and 'back' portions which are raised or arched during vowel sounds. The sides of the tongue can also be lowered for some sounds called 'laterals, such as "l"'. Also, the middle of the tongue can be depressed making a groove, for sounds like 's' and 'z'.

---

### Activity 5

Try saying 'sam' and then 'lamb' in succession. Can you feel the tongue arching up and down?
　　Say 'l' and then continue the sound while breathing in. Can you feel the cold airflow along the sides of the tongue?

---

## Teeth (adj. dental)

The teeth are used in many sounds. The tongue can be in contact with the side teeth (as in /s/ or /z/) or just behind the top teeth (as in /θ/) or the upper front teeth can be in contact with the lower lip (as in /f/).

---

### Activity 6

Try saying 'sin', 'fin', 'thin' in succession. Can you feel the contact between tongue and teeth in different positions?

---

## Lips (adj labial)

The lips can come together to produce bilabial sounds such as 'm' or 'b'. Alternatively, the lower lip can make contact with the upper teeth making a labio-dental sound such as 'f' or 'v'. Lips can also be rounded (as in the vowel in 'ought' and consonant in 'we'). They can be spread (as in the vowel in 'see') or wide apart (as when yawning).

---

### Activity 7

Why do we ask people to say 'cheese' before taking a photograph?

---

## Jaw

The jaw is not theoretically considered an 'articulator', but the position of the jaw, and cheeks, are very important for the articulation of speech sounds.

---

### Activity 8

(a) In your own mouth, make sure that you can locate
   (i) the alveolar ridge
   (ii) the hard palate
   (iii) the velum
   (iv) the uvula

---

A common distinction in the production of sounds is between what we call 'vowels' and 'consonants'. Typically, we say that for consonant sounds there is some obstruction of the air flow by one or other of the articulators, as with the sounds /t/ or /m/, while for vowel sounds the air flows unobstructed, as when the doctor asks us to say 'ah' to examine the throat. However, when we look as speech sounds phonetically, it is not quite so clear cut and it is not always easy to decide whether sounds should be classed as consonants or vowels. For instance, the initial sounds in 'you' or 'way' do not involve an obstruction of the airflow but are classed as consonants in English. Similarly, the first sound in 'red' is classed as a consonant in English but is treated as a vowel in some Chinese dialects.

---

### Activity 9

Try saying 'map' several times. Can you feel the obstruction of the airflow at the beginning and end of the word but not in the middle?

---

# Articulatory Settings/Voice Quality

A knowledge of speech production and articulations is very helpful for teachers to enable them to understand the problems learners may have trying to produce L2 sounds and the differences between some L1 and L2 articulations. Also, although there is probably very little value in trying to explain these differences in technical terms to learners, this knowledge can enable the teacher to provide appropriate activities or exercises to remedy articulation problems.

An aspect of speech production that can be of direct interest to pronunciation learners and one that has largely been overlooked in many pronunciation teaching materials, is the area of **articulatory settings** or **voice quality**. It is this concept that we are referring to intuitively when we make informal observations or remarks about the characteristics of a language or of how an individual speaker talks. For instance, it is not uncommon for learners of English to remark that the English 'don't open their mouths when they speak' or 'mumble';

## Activity 10

Try and label the different organs of speech in Figure 3.7.

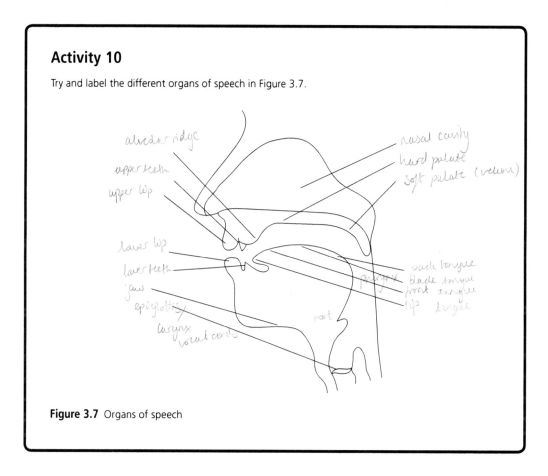

**Figure 3.7** Organs of speech

that the Danes speak 'as if they had a hot potato in their mouths' (referring to the 'creaky' voice which is characteristic of Danish). Such observations reveal an underlying phenomenon which has received relatively little attention either in phonological studies or in pronunciation teaching. It is referred to as articulatory setting (Honikman 1964) or vocal setting or, more broadly, voice quality (Trask 1996).

Voice quality is defined by Trask (1996:381) as the characteristic auditory colouring of an individual's voice, derived from a variety of laryngeal and supralaryngeal features and running continuously through the individual's speech. The natural and distinctive tone of speech sounds produced by a particular person yields a particular voice.

Thus, voice quality settings refer to the characteristic or long-term positioning of articulators by individuals or groups of speakers of a particular language, that is, the 'general differences in tension, in tongue shape, in pressure of the articulators, in lip and cheek and jaw posture and movement, which run through the whole articulatory process' (O'Connor 1973:289). These articulatory settings can account for the characteristic 'accent' of speakers of different languages or of the 'voice quality' of individual speakers of the same language.

Differences in L2 articulatory settings involving movements of the tongue, lips and velum (soft palate), as well as in the degree of tension and muscularity in the cheeks and jaw, can cause learners difficulties. According to Honikman,

> . . . the greater part of English articulation takes place behind (loosely) closed jaws. It is this feature of English, no doubt, which helps to give foreigners the impression that we do not move or open our mouths when we speak. (Honikman 1964 in Laver 1980)

Honikman (1964) divides articulatory settings into 'external' and 'internal' settings. External articulatory settings refer to those articulations which can be observed externally, that is, of the jaw, lips and mouth. For example, she suggests that if you watch speakers in French, English and Russian films, you will notice differences such as considerable mobility and rounding of the lips in French, which contrasts with Russian where the lips are mostly stretched and spread while in English, the lips are more neutral, that is, neither very stretched or rounded and less mobile and there is little jaw movement. Internal articulatory settings refer to the characteristic positioning of the internal articulatory organs, particularly the tongue. Honikman claims that these internal settings are a reflection of the most common sounds and sound combinations in a language. So, for example, in English, there is frequent tapping of the tongue tip against the alveolar ridge (because of the high proportion of alveolar consonants). In contrast, in French, the tongue tip is barely noticeable and much less active than the blade and front and the constantly mobile (rounding and spreading) lips.

As Honikman (1964:81) says, the impression that English speakers do not seem to open or move their mouths when speaking, reflects the characteristic articulatory settings, including:

- the general lack of muscularity of articulations, particularly the 'laxness' of English consonants,
- the neutral character of lip movements with little lip rounding, spreading or protrusion.
- the preference for centralized vowels (e.g. 'about' 'butter').
- the prevalence of articulations where the tongue tip is on the alveolar ridge (e.g. 't' 'd' 'l'), unlike many other languages.
- the frequent return to a rest position between articulations.

There are notable differences between languages regarding articulatory settings. For instance, O'Connor compares the articulatory settings of English and French:

> 'in English the lips and jaw move little, in French they move much more, with vigorous lip-rounding and speading: the cheeks are relaxed in English but tensed in French: the tongue-tip is tenser in English and more used than in French, where the blade is dominant, and so on'. (O'Connor 1973:289)

Similarly, the characteristic articulatory settings of individual languages have been described, such as Chinese:

1 close jaw
2 nasal voice
3 dentalized or alveolar tongue body position (Esling and Wong 1983) and American English:

> . . . in the United States, a broad model of voice quality setting might include the following features:

1 spread lips
2 open jaw
3 palatalized tongue body position
4 retroflex articulation
5 nasal voice
6 lowered larynx
7 creaky voice (Esling and Wong 1983:91)

Indeed, differences in voice quality have been associated with various varieties of English. For instance, according to Pennington, tense voice is a characteristic of Hong Kong English while 'lax voice, a narrow jaw opening and a retroflex tongue position characterizes Indian English' (1996:162). Similarly, a nasal vocal quality is seen as prestigious by some social groups (such as RP and Edinburgh English) but as an undesirable feature when associated with other accents (Esling 1994).

When an articulatory setting which is significant in the L1 is not present or significant in the L2, it may create misunderstanding or misinterpretation. For example, the use of breathy voice in English can be associated either with weakness or sexiness, whereas breathy voice is used as a signal of vowel contrasts in some languages such as Gujarati (Laver 1994:22).

Many scholars, as long ago as Sweet in the nineteenth century but more recently Honikman (1964), O'Connor (1973) and Thornbury (1993), have claimed the importance of acquiring L2 articulatory settings to facilitate pronunciation learning. O'Connor, for instance, advised that, 'better results are achieved when the learner gets the basis of articulation right rather than trying for the foreign sound sequences from the basis of his own language' (1973:298). Indeed, Honikman goes so far as to assert that 'where two languages are disparate in articulatory setting, it is not possible to master the pronunciation of one whilst maintaining the articulatory setting of the other' (1964 in Taylor 1993:13).

Concern for the importance of articulatory settings in L2 language learning is reflected in calls to make voice quality the starting point of L2 pronunciation training. As we have already seen, our first experience of an unknown language is an auditory impression of how it sounds. As Jones and Evans say, 'This perception is usually a learner's first conscious contact with the phonology of the second language: students are often able to describe or imitate the way a language "sounds" before they are actually able to speak it' (1995:245).

Other reasons have been proposed to make voice quality a starting point. Brown, for instance, argues that 'If a learner can be trained to abandon the long-term settings of his or her native language and switch to those of L2 (to "get into gear" as Honikman (1964) called it), then this large-scale adjustment will facilitate small-scale changes needed in the articulation of the particular vowels and consonants of the language' (1992:13 in Dalton and Seidlhofer 1994:140). Jones and Evans claim 'it gives students a chance to experience pronunciation on intuitive and communicative levels before moving on to a more analytical exploration of specific elements of phonology. Finally, work in voice quality can help students to improve their image when they speak English, and thus increase their confidence' (1995:245–6).

# Teaching implications

## Sounds and spelling

An understanding of the sound/spelling system in English and other learner languages can help both the teacher and learner diagnose pronunciation problems related to the written word. Exercises designed for students to discover some of the sound/spelling rules themselves can be very helpful. For instance, giving learners words to group based on a spelling rule, such as dividing the words below into two groups, one group for 'soft c' and one for 'hard c':

cycle, cot, cell, certificate, catch, call, local, cake, cinema, acid

Other exercise types could include crossword completion exercises and marking nonsense words which break English spelling rules, as in:

monr, linhg, hwalp, kcoll, fitch, lowh, qeep, jhisking

Learners need to be proficient in saying the letters of the English alphabet, so teachers should give sufficient time to practice this, preferably using realistic communicative activities such as spelling their own, or others', name and address. As well as helping to decode print, spelling aloud is a good way to correct a communication breakdown.

Learners need to be aware of English sound/spelling regularities. Teachers should aim to familiarize themselves with any differences between the sound/spelling system of English and their learners' L1s. For example, German learners of English may pronounce /v/ as /f/ as in German, so that 'van' would sound like 'fan'.

Some learners may have an L1 which is not alphabetic, such as Japanese where for instance a symbol represents a syllable, or like Arabic where vowels may be omitted in certain types of script.

Learners whose L1 is strictly 'phonetic', that is, where one letter represents one sound, such as Spanish or Italian, may expect English to work in the same way. Speakers of languages which, like English, do not have a strictly phonetic system, such as French, may have fewer problems in this area.

## Speech production

A knowledge of speech production and articulations is very helpful for teachers to enable them to understand the problems learners may have trying to produce L2 sounds and the differences between some L1 and L2 articulations. Also, although there is probably very little value in trying to explain these differences in technical terms to learners, this knowledge can enable the teacher to provide appropriate activities or exercises to remedy articulation problems. If we can accurately describe how sounds are made, we should be able to teach them more effectively and understand more readily the kind of problems that our learners face.

## Voice quality

The differences in articulatory settings between languages can make it hard for L2 learners to master L2 sounds and can therefore hinder intelligibility. Articulatory settings act as a link between the production of segmental and suprasegmental features. We have seen there is an argument for introducing voice quality work early on in pronunciation training as a way of getting learners to use their intuitive knowledge of what makes a foreign language different and to help them 'get their tongues around' new sounds.

## Further reading

Acton, W. (1984) 'Changing fossilized pronunciation', *TESOL Quarterly*, 18 (1), 71–85.

Esling, J. (1978) 'The identification of features of voice quality in social groups', *Journal of the International Phonetic Association*, 7, 18–23.

Esling, J. and Wong, R. (1983) 'Voice quality settings and the teaching of pronunciation', *TESOL Quarterly*, 17 (1), 89–95.

Honikman, B. (1964) 'Articulatory settings', in Brown, A. (ed.), *Teaching English Pronunciation: A Book of Readings* (1991). London: Routledge.

Jones, R. and Evans, S. (1995) 'Teaching pronunciation through voice quality', *ELT Journal*, 49 (3), 244–51.

Kenworthy, J. (1987) *Teaching English Pronunciation*, Chapter 5. Harlow, U.K.: Longman.

Laver, J. (1980) *The Phonetic Description of Voice Quality*. Cambridge: Cambridge University Press.

Thornbury, S. (1993) 'Having a good jaw: Voice setting phonology', *ELT Journal*, 47 (2), 126–31.

# 4 Consonants

We will now concentrate on identifying the production of the 24 consonant phonemes in British English and how they can be classified.

## The production of consonants

Normally, we describe the formation of consonant sounds in terms of:

1. the *place* of articulation – that is, where the sounds are produced in the vocal tract
2. the *manner* of articulation – that is, how they are produced
3. the presence or absence of *voicing* – that is, whether or not there is vibration of the vocal cords.

### Place of Articulation

Sounds are labelled according to their principal point or points of articulation in the voice tract. The principal points are represented diagrammatically in Figure 4.1.

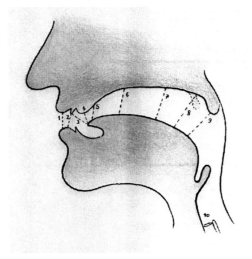

1 bilabial

2 labio-dental

3 dental

4 alveolar

5 post-alveolar

6 palato-alveolar

7 palatal

8 velar

9 uvular

10 glottal

**Figure 4.1** Points of articulation

The chief points of articulation, with special reference to English sounds are as follows:

**1. bilabial** – upper lip ( lower lip)

## Activity 1

◀ Listen and repeat the examples – (/p/ in 'pin', /b/ in 'bin', /m/ in 'mit') (Figure 4.2).

**Figure 4.2** /p/

**2. labio-dental** – lower lip (upper teeth)

## Activity 2

◀ Listen and repeat the examples – (/f/ in 'fat', /v/ in 'vat') (Figure 4.3).

**Figure 4.3** /f/

3. **dental** – tongue tip (behind or between teeth)

---

## Activity 3

◀ Listen and repeat the examples – /θ/ in 'thin', 'with', /ð/ in 'this', 'breathe' (Figure 4.4).

---

**Figure 4.4** /θ/

4. **alveolar** – tongue tip (alveolar ridge)

---

## Activity 4

◀ Listen and repeat the examples – /t/ in 'tin', /s/ in 'sip', /d/ in 'dip' (Figure 4.5).

---

**Figure 4.5** /t/

**5. post (palatal)-alveolar** – tongue blade/front (back of alveolar ridge/front of hard palate)

> ### Activity 5
>
> ◀ Listen and repeat the examples – /ʃ/ in 'shed', /ʒ/ in 'vision' /tʃ/ in 'chips', 'rich' /dʒ/ in 'judge','urge' (Figure 4.6).

**Figure 4.6** /ʃ/

**6. palatal** – front of tongue (hard palate)

> ### Activity 6
>
> ◀ Listen and repeat the examples – /j/ in 'yes', 'yawn', 'layer' (Figure 4.7).

**Figure 4.7** /j/

7. **velar** – back of tongue (soft palate)

## Activity 7

◀ Listen and repeat the examples – /k/ in 'cat', 'lock', /g/ in 'go', 'log', /ŋ/ in 'sing' (Figure 4.8).

**Figure 4.8** /k/

8. **glottal** – glottis

## Activity 8

◀ Listen and repeat the examples – (/h/ in 'home', 'ahead') (Figure 4.9).

**Figure 4.9** /h/

Articulations can occur at two points in the vocal tract as with /w/ in wet which is articulated at the lips (labial) and the velum (velar) so is termed labio-velar.

Other 'non-English' consonant sounds exist. For example, the 'r' sound is produced with a **retroflex** articulation in some varieties of English, such as West Country accents, with the tip of the tongue curled back on to the hard palate. Similarly, the 'r' sounds can be **uvular** in some North East English accents (as it is in French) where the back of the tongue is against the uvula.

In English then, consonant sounds can be described as bilabial (both lips), labio-dental (lips and teeth), dental, alveolar, post-alveolar, palato-alveolar, velar and glottal according to their point of articulation.

---

### Activity 9

Say these words, paying attention to the place of articulation of the consonants underlined:

| | | | |
|---|---|---|---|
| ma̱p | Bilabial | c̱harge | palato-alveolar |
| f̱ive | labio-dental | y̱es | palatal |
| the ten̲th | Dental | ki̱ng | velar |
| si̱de | Alveolar | ẖome | glottal |
| ṟan | post-alveolar | | |

---

The tip or blade of the tongue is the organ most frequently called into action to produce the consonant sounds. The tip of the tongue is involved in the production of dental, alveolar and post-alveolar consonant sounds, while the back of the tongue is used to articulate velar consonants. Vowel sounds involve the front, central or back part of the tongue.

Consonant sounds are thus distinguished by their point of articulation, that is to say, the place of the most significant obstruction to the passage of air through the vocal tract.

## Manner of Articulation

As well as knowing where sounds are made, we also need to be able to describe the manner in which they are made. Just as there are different places of articulation, there are different 'types' of articulation, that is, different types of stricture (narrowing) or contact between the articulators. These are (a) complete closure, (b) partial closure and (c) approximation.

(a) Complete closure
   This involves a complete 'stop' of the air flow somewhere in the vocal tract:
   e.g.  bilabial plosive /p/ (as in 'pin')
       velar plosive /k/ (as in 'kit')

(b)  Partial closure

Here there is a narrowing or partial closure of air stream:

(a)  narrowing causes friction between articulators, producing fricatives:

e.g.  labio-dental fricatives /f/ (as in 'fan')
dental fricatives /θ/ (as in 'thin')

(b)  partial closure causes the air to 'go round' the closure, producing laterals and nasals:
e.g.  alveolar lateral /l/ (as in 'lip') – the air passes along the sides of the tongue
bilabial nasal /m/ (as in 'man') – the air passes through the nasal cavity

(c)  Approximants

This involves proximity of the articulators without them being sufficiently close to touch each other:

e.g.  the alveolar approximant /r/ (as in 'ran')
bilabial approximant /w/ (as in 'wet')
palatal approximant /j/ (as in 'yes')

The phonemes /w/ and /j/ are sometimes called 'semi-vowels', as they act phonetically like vowels but phonologically like consonants.[1]

## Presence or absence of voicing

A third way of classifying articulation is in terms of the presence or absence of 'voicing', which you will recall is vibration of the air flowing through the vocal cords when the cords are in close contact. For **voiceless** sounds, air passes through the open glottis with no vibration. For **voiced** sounds, the vocal cords are close together and tightened.

e.g.  voiceless bilabial plosive p (as in 'pin')
voiced velar plosive g (as in 'give')

To recap then, a consonant is a speech sound which obstructs the flow of air through the vocal tract. Some consonants do this a lot and some do it very little: the ones that make maximum obstruction (i.e. **plosives**, which make a complete stoppage of air stream) are the most consonantal. **Nasal** consonants are less obstructive than plosives as they stop the air completely in the oral cavity but allow it to escape through the nasal cavity. **Fricatives** obstruct the air flow considerably, causing friction, but do not involve total closure. **Laterals** obstruct the air flow only in the centre of the mouth, not the sides, so the obstruction is slight. Some other sounds, classed as **approximants**, obstruct the air flow so little that they could almost be classed as vowels (e.g. /w/ or /j/).

The term '**consonant**' is a phonological one, referring to the way such sounds function in the language. For instance, consonants are typically found at the beginning and ends of syllables while vowels are typically found in the middle. If we want to be more precise we can use the phonetic terms '**contoid**' to describe those sounds which produce a significant obstruction to the flow of air through the vocal tract and '**vocoid**' for sounds that do not obstruct the air flow. So, sounds like /w/ and /j/ are vocoids but they function as consonants.

# The classification of consonants

There are 24 consonants in British English. They are plotted on the chart in Table 4.1.

**Table 4.1** Chart of English consonant phonemes

| Place of articulation | | Bilabial | labiodental | dental | Alveolar | Palato-alveolar | Palatal | Velar | Glottal |
|---|---|---|---|---|---|---|---|---|---|
| Manner of articulation | PLOSIVE | p b | | | t d | | | k g | |
| | FRICATIVE | | f v | θ ð | s z | ʃ ʒ | | | h |
| | AFFRICATE | | | | | tʃ dʒ | | | |
| | NASAL | m | | | n | | | ŋ | |
| | LATERAL | | | | l | | | | |
| | APPROXIMANT | ω | | | | r | j | | |

As we have seen, the most important criteria for the classification of consonants in English are the place and manner of articulation, together with presence or absence of voicing. In Table 4.1, the two axes represent the place and the manner of articulation and the pairs of phonemes in a single cell represent a voicing contrast (i.e. a minimal pair of voiced/voiceless phonemes). The majority of the consonant phonemes in English consist of such voiced/voiceless pairs. We will now look at how we can classify and describe consonants in more detail using these categories.

## Plosives

Some consonants involve a complete closure of the airflow caused by one of the articulators, usually the lips or the tongue, blocking off the air momentarily at some point along the vocal tract. Consonants that stop the airstream in this way are called **stops** or **plosives**. Plosives have four phases of articulation:

(i) closure phase – articulators come together
(ii) hold phase – air pressure builds up
(iii) release phase – articulators come apart
(iv) post-release phase – air flow after the movement of the articulators, that is, 'plosion'.

Plosive sounds are not **continuants** because air is stopped at some point and not allowed to continue before it is released in plosion.

---

### Activity 10

Try and make a /p/ sound in slow motion so that you can feel the phases of articulation.

---

## Syllable initial plosives

The initial sounds of words like 'pin' and 'bin', 'tin' and 'din', and 'kill' and 'gill' are all stop consonants but the stoppage of the airflow occurs at different points in the vocal tract for each of the three pairs. For 'pin' and 'bin', the air is stopped by the two lips coming together (i.e. they are bilabial plosives), for 'tin' and 'din', it is stopped by the tongue tip touching the alveolar ridge (i.e. they are alveolar plosives) and for 'kill' and 'gill', the air is stopped by the back of the tongue reaching the soft palate (i.e. they are velar plosives). Also, what distinguishes the initial consonants in each of the pairs is that the first one is voiceless and the second is voiced:

|  | Voiceless | Voiced |
|---|---|---|
| Biabial | /p/ | /b/ |
| Alveolar | /t/ | /d/ |
| Velar | /k/ | /g/ |

Some phonemes involve an auditory plosion where the air can be heard passing through the glottis after the release phase. Such phonemes are said to be **aspirated**, for example, initial /p/, /t/, /k/ in 'pie', 'tie', 'cat'. The voiceless pairs /b/, /d/ /g/ are not aspirated in initial position, for example 'buy', 'die', 'gate'; this difference in aspiration is more significant that the absence or lack of voicing.

## Syllable final plosives

The plosives /p/ /t/ /k/ are of course not voiced in final position and final /b/ /d/ /g/ have little voicing as well. Furthermore, these sounds are regularly unexploded in this position, or only partly exploded. The primary distinguishing factor between /p/ /t/ /k/ and /b/ /d/ /g/ in final position is that vowels preceding /p/ /t/ /k/ are generally much shorter than before /b/ /d/ /g/, as for example in pairs such as 'rip vs rib' or 'rick vs rig'.

## Inter-vocalic mid-word plosives

In contrasts like 'rapid' vs 'rabid', 'whiter' vs 'wider', 'mucky' vs 'muggy', there will be slight aspiration on the mid-word voiceless plosives /p/ /k/ /t/. However, the voiceless vs voiced distinction is much clearer in these cases as the vocal cords vibrate right the way through the closure and hold phases of the production. Also, as with syllable final plosives, the added vowel length before the voiced plosives (e.g. 'rabid', 'wider', 'muggy') is distinctive in such cases.

## Fortis and Lenis

The terms voiced and voiceless are sometimes replaced by the terms **lenis** (Latin for 'weak') and **fortis** (Latin for 'strong'). The voiceless consonants /p/ /t/ /k/ are uttered with greater breath force and muscular tension than /b/ /d/ /g/. So, the following classification is sometimes used:

| Fortis | Lenis |
|--------|-------|
| p | b |
| t | d |
| k | g |

In English, all fortis consonants are voiceless and lenis consonants can potentially be voiced (but are not in some positions, as you will see in Chapter 5).

## Activity 11

Say 'park – bark' several times. Can you hear that the /p/ in park has a more energetic, stronger articulation? Can you hear the slight puff of air after the release of /p/ but not after /b/?

## Activity 12

◀ Listen and then repeat the following words with fortis plosives, noticing the aspiration:

| pear | care |
|------|------|
| car | tar |
| pie | tie |
| tea | key |

◀ Now listen and repeat the following words with lenis plosives and notice the lack of aspiration:

| go | dough |
|------|------|
| bear | dare |
| gear | dear |

## Fricatives

All languages have fricatives. They are the largest group of consonant sounds in English (there are nine). In contrast to plosives, fricatives are continuants in that the air escapes through a narrow passage, making a hissing sound. The hissing is so marked in some of the fricatives that they are referred to as **sibilants** (as in /s, z, ʃ, ʒ/). There are five places of articulation for fricatives and at each point of articulation there is a voiced/voiceless pair (+v/-v) (apart from the glottal fricative /h/).

| | | | |
|---|---|---|---|
| 1 labio-dental | /f/ fan (-v) | /v/ van (+v) | |
| 2 dental | /θ/thin (-v) | /ð/ this (+v) | |
| 3 alveolar | /s/ sip (-v) | /z/ zip (+v) | } sibilants |
| 4 palato-alveolar | /ʃ / mesh (-v) | /ʒ/ measure (+v) | } sibilants |
| 5 glottal | /h/ home | | |

Voiceless fricatives can also be termed fortis (because there is more friction involved) and voiced fricatives can be termed lenis (because there is less friction involved).

Phonetically [h] is a vocoid which assumes the quality of the vowel that follows it, while phonologically, /h/ is a consonant. /h/ is always characterized by friction in the glottis but is usually voiceless. It is voiced in inter-vocalic position as in 'ahoy', 'ahead', 'behalf', 'behold' etc. In other positions, the devoiced allophone is used.

### Syllable Initial Fricatives

Traditionally, the voiceless /f, θ, s, ʃ/ and voiced /v, ð, z, ʒ/ distinction is applied. However, in initial position, the so-called voiced fricatives are hardly voiced at all so the greater energy of /f, θ, s, ʃ/ actually serves to distinguish them from /v, ð, z, ʒ/, therefore the fortis/lenis classification is preferable.

## Affricates

Affricates are combinations of two sounds, a stop and a fricative. There are two affricates in English:

v-    / tʃ/ palato-alveolar affricate – chin /tʃɪn/
v+    /dʒ/ palato-alveolar affricate – gin /dʒɪn/

These palato-alveolar affricates follow the same sorts of distinctions as the fricatives above. They begin as plosives and end as fricatives.

### Word-initial affricates

In this position the fortis /tʃ/ has greater friction than the lenis /dʒ/.

Examples include:

cheers  /tʃɪəz/  vs  jeers  /dʒɪəz/
chop   /tʃɒp/  vs  judge  /dʒʌdʒ/

---

## Activity 13

◀ Listen and repeat the following words containing fricatives and affricates:

| f | fan | offer | laugh |
|---|-----|-------|-------|
| v | van | oven | leave |
| θ | thin | method | breath |
| ð | this | other | breathe |
| s | son | lesson | less |
| z | zip | lazy | lose |
| ʃ | sheep | wishing | wish |
| ʒ | | leisure | beige |
| h | hot | ahead | |

---

## Nasals

Nasals are also continuants, but they are not fricatives, as the velum is lowered and air passes freely out through the nasal cavity. They are characterized by this escape of air through the nose.

There are three nasal phonemes in English:

/m/ voiced bilabial nasal    – sum
/n/ voiced alveolar nasal    – sun
/ŋ/ voiced velar nasal      – sung

The consonant /ŋ/ is very unusual and may cause difficulty for learners. It never occurs in initial position. It is difficult to describe its phonology because it is not easy to describe the contexts in which it is found. In final position as above it is always /ŋ/ but words like 'linger', 'longer', 'anger' have the cluster /ŋg/ in medial position.[2]

## Laterals

Laterals are consonants where the air does not flow in the usual way across the centre of the tongue, but rather round the sides (laterally), as the centre of the tongue is in contact with the alveolar ridge. There is only one lateral phoneme is English:

/l/ alveolar lateral    e.g. 'light'

To make the English /l/ phoneme, the blade of the tongue is in contact with the alveolar ridge as for /t/ or /d/ but the sides of the tongue are lowered to allow air to pass over.

If you say dldldldldldl you can feel the sides of the tongue moving up and down.

## Approximants

Approximants are not 'truly' consonants as the articulators get close to, or approximate each other, but do not touch. The three approximants in English are:

/r/ post alveolar approximant
/j/ palatal approximant
/w/ bilabial approximant

There are many differences in the articulation and pronunciation of the English /r/ across accents and dialects. However, if we describe the BBC English /r/, it is a post-alveolar approximant. The tongue tip is close to the alveolar ridge, as for /t/ or /d/, but not touching it. The tongue is also slightly curled back with the tip raised, producing a retroflex shape.

If you say drdrdrdrdrdrd you should feel the tip of the tongue moving backwards and forwards.

Some phoneticians classify /j/ and /w/ as approximants but many writers have classified them as semi-vowels. The reason, as we have seen before, is that /j/ and /w/ are phonetically like vowels but they function in the language like consonants.

So, /j/ is a voiced, palatal approximant while /w/ is a voiced, labio-velar approximant. But, /j/ can be described in vowel-like terms as being unrounded, front and close, like a very short /iː/. The articulation of /j/ is almost the same as for the front close vowel /iː/. If you say the word 'yet' and hold the /j/ for a long time you will hear this. It occurs in yes, you, tulip, pure, news. However, there is a tendency for it to be lost, for example, in suit.

Similarly, the articulation of /w/ is almost the same as for the back close vowel /uː/. If you say the word 'wet' and hold the /w/ you will hear this. /w/ is rounded, back and close, like a very short /uː/.

If these approximants follow a definite or indefinite article, they take the /ə/, not /ən/ form and /ðə/ not /ðiː/ form:

| e.g. | the way | /ðə weɪ/ | a way | /ə weɪ/ |
|------|---------|----------|-------|---------|
|      | the year | /ðə jɪə/ | a year | /ə jɪə/ |
|      | the apple | /ðiː æpəl/ | an apple | /ən æpəl/ |
|      | the orange | /ðiː ɒrəndʒ/ | an orange | /ən ɒrəndʒ/ |

**Table 4.2** Summary of English consonant articulations

| | |
|---|---|
| **Plosive** (or stop sound) | This involves a complete closure of the airway, with compression building up so that the release involves plosion. Plosives are not continuants<br>English plosives are /p/, /b/ /t/, /d/ /k/, /g/<br>In addition, the glottal stop /ʔ/ may be heard in the speech of many native speakers |
| **Fricative** | The obstruction is not quite complete, such that air escapes through the mouth with friction as in /f/, /v/, /θ/, /ð/, /s/, /z/, /ʃ/, /ʒ/, /h/. Fricatives are continuants, unlike plosives |
| **Affricate** | This is a homorganic sequence of a plosive and a fricative, produced at the same point of articulation. In English, the affricates are palato-alveolar (or sometimes grouped as post-alveolar) as in /tʃ/ for example church, /dʒ/ for example jade |
| **Nasal** | Nasal sounds are produced by stopping or blocking up the mouth and lowering the soft palate to allow air to escape through the nose. Sounds already described above allow air through the middle of the mouth, but nasals, /m/, /n/, allow it through the nose. These sounds are described as continuants |
| **Lateral approximant** | Lateral sounds allow air to pass along the sides of the mouth as in /l/ where the tongue touches the alveolar ridge but air escapes by the side of the tongue |
| **Approximants** or **glides** | These sounds involve a closure just short of that necessary to create friction as in the production of English /r/, a post-alveolar frictionless sound. /r/ is a quick, smooth non-friction glide towards a following vowel sound. /r/ can also be described as a frictionless continuant |
| **Semi-vowels** or **Semi-consonants** | These sounds are also **approximants**, phonetically like vowels but they function in syllables as consonants, as in /w/, wet, /j/ yet. The two sounds /w/, /j/ can be said to consist of a quick, smooth, non-friction glide towards a following vowel sound. So /j/ is a quick glide from the position of the vowel /i/ to any following vowel and /w/ from /u/ to a following vowel, for example, /j/ in 'youth' and /w/ in 'war' |

## Activity 14

◄ Listen and repeat the following words containing nasals, laterals and continuants:

| m | man | remain | ram |
|---|---|---|---|
| n | now | renew | ran |
| ŋ | | singer | sing |
| l | low | below | roll |
| r | rim | mirror | |
| j | you | | |
| w | wet | reward | |

# Teaching implications

According to Gimson (1977) consonants rather than vowels carry the message at segmental level. Also, generally speaking, consonant sounds can be easier to teach or correct than vowel sounds because the articulation of at least some consonants can be easily seen. This is true of consonants produced in the front of the mouth (such as /m/ and /f/) but less so of consonants produced in the middle or back of the mouth (such as /ʒ/ or /ŋ/). So, it might be best for morale to teach learners some of the 'front' consonants first.

Both BBC English and General American have 24 common consonants. Jenkins suggests that the majority of these are essential for L2 learners to master within the Lingua Franca Core. Jenkins claims that the consonants which can be omitted are the /ð/ /θ/ distinction, which does not cause intelligibility problems in her research data. It is also a contrast which does not exist in some regional dialects, such as Dublin Irish. Many languages have a /t/ /d/ opposition and it is suggested that this could be an acceptable substitute for the /ð/ /θ/ contrast. Particularly as the /t/ /d/ is dental in many cases.

An alternative argument is that although the /ð/ /θ/ distinction is not always essential for intelligibility, the phonemes are relatively easy to teach because they are articulated at the front of the mouth. Also, although the /ð/ sound is relatively uncommon, it is used in a lot of frequently used words, such as 'this', 'those', then', 'other', 'either'.

---

### Activity 15

Where do you stand in this argument?

---

For teaching purposes, it can be useful to make a distinction between 'stops' and 'continuants', explaining to students that, unlike a stop sound, you can make a continuant sound for as long as you have breath, as the air continues to flow out. Rogerson and Gilbert (1990) take this approach (see chapter 20).

Given the subtlety of the voiced vs voiceless distinction for plosives, learners may benefit from focusing on other features like aspiration and the fortis/lenis contrast.

The existence of final voiced consonants in English is marked, as most languages do not permit this phenomenon. In English, syllable final voiced consonants are common. This could explain why, for instance, German learners of English find it hard to produce final voiced plosives like /g/ in 'dog' and Polish learners have difficulty distinguishing between 'leave' and 'leaf'.

In many languages there is no lenis/fortis contrast in word final consonants. So, for example, in Dutch 'hout' (wood) and 'houd' (hold) are pronounced the same and in German 'wirt' (host) and 'wird' (become) are pronounced the same. This means that learners with these or similar L1s may have considerable difficulty making the contrast in English pairs such as 'rice' 'rise' and 'light' 'lied'.

Fricatives is the group of consonants which is acquired late by native speaking children (Gimson 1994:165). Also, fricatives and affricates are marked, in that they are relatively rare across languages, especially in final position. They can be a source of difficulty for foreign learners as the distinctions are quite sophisticated, involving the five places of articulation listed above and the tip or blade of the tongue.

For /f/ /v/, the position of the teeth and lips is demonstrable. For /θ/ and /ð/, there is similarly the possibility of demonstrating the tongue position (though there may be issues of cultural sensitivity to take account of!).

# Key points

- The majority of 24 BBC English consonants are essential for intelligibility with native speakers of English.
- The distinctive feature of aspiration should be taught to contrast the initial voiceless plosives /p/ /t/ and /k/ from their voiced counterparts, /b/ /d/ and /g/ as the distinction using voice alone will cause confusion.

However, Gimson (1994), similarly to Jenkins (2000), makes the following caveats about the targets for learners in EIL contexts:

- The distinctions between the different points of articulation of fricatives should be maintained. However, Gimson agrees with Jenkins that the distinctions between /θ/ and /ð/ and between /ʃ/ and /ʒ/ are unnecessary for EIL targets, because of their low functional load, and that the /θ/ and /ð/ pair can be replaced with /t/ /d/.
- The fricatives /f/ /v/ /s/ z/ should be distinct but /ʃ/ and /ʒ/ can be conflated, as can /θ/ and /ð/.
- The distinction between the pairs /tʃ/ and /ʤ/ and /tr/ and /dr/ should be maintained as they distinguish many minimal pairs.
- The distinction between /v/ and /w/ ('veal' vs 'wheel') should be maintained.
- The contrast between /l/ and /r/ is high priority for both near native speaker and EIL targets, although any phonetic forms of /l/ and /r/ are permissible.
- /r/ can be pronounced in all positions in which it occurs in writing (i.e. both rhotic and non-rhotic). The argument being that this 'may indeed reflect a majority pronunciation among the total number of native speakers and will ease learning for many learners' (Cruttenden 2008:326).
- Lip-rounded or vocalic /ʊ/ realization of dark /ɫ/ should be avoided before vowels to avoid confusion with English /w/ but such variants are acceptable in post-vocalic position (e.g. 'bull' /bʌʊ/ ).

Table 4.2 summarizes how consonant sounds are made, that is, the manner in which they are articulated.

# Consonant Practice Activities

## Activity 1

(1) Place the consonants of English on the chart below. Post-alveolar and palato-alveolar consonants are placed in the same line of the grid.

| | Bilabial | Labio-dental | Dental | Alveolar | Palato-alveolar | Palatal | Velar | Glottal |
|---|---|---|---|---|---|---|---|---|
| Plosive | p b | | | t d | | | k g | |
| Fricative | | f v | θ ð | s z | ʃ ʒ | | | h |
| Affricate | | | | | tʃ dʒ | | | |
| Nasal | m | | | n | | ŋ | | |
| Lateral Approximant | | | | l | | | | |
| Approximant | w | | | r | j | | | |

## Activity 2

(2) ◀ Listen and underline the words beginning with,

(i)  a voiced, bilabial plosive
   pit  sit  hit  <u>bit</u>  lit

(ii)  a voiced labio-dental fricative
   beer  fear  tear  <u>dearveer</u>

(iii)  a voiceless palato-alveolar affricate
   gin  tin  sin  <u>chin</u>  shin

(iv)  a voiceless alveolar plosive
   <u>tight</u>  bite  sight  height  right

(v)  a voiced bilabial nasal
   night  <u>might</u>  height  kite  fight

(vi)  a voiced bilabial approximant
   tear  <u>weir</u>  rear  year  near

(vii)  a voiceless labio-dental fricative
   bare  care  dare  <u>fare</u>  hair

(viii)  a voiced dental fricative
   den  Ben  men  <u>then</u>  zen

(ix)  a voiceless palato-alveolar fricative
   dour  poor  fewer  <u>sure</u>  cure

(x)  a voiced velar plosive
   cot  hot  pot  lot  <u>got</u>

## Activity 3

(3) ◀ Listen and then describe the underlined sounds, for example, bo<u>dy</u> = voiced alveolar plosive

    (i) televi<u>si</u>on *voiced palato alveolar fricative*   (vi) pu<u>sh</u>ing *voiceless palato alveolar fricative*
    (ii) sha<u>k</u>ing *voiceless velar plosive*  (vii) so<u>l</u>id *alveolar lateral approximant*
    (iii) ba<u>dg</u>er *voiced palato alveolar affricate*  (viii) re<u>g</u>ard *voiced velar plosive*
    (iv) fa<u>th</u>er *voiced dental fricative*  (ix) pat<u>ch</u>y *voiceless palato alveolar affricate*
    (v) du<u>ng</u> *palatal nasal*  (x) re<u>v</u>eal *voiced labio dental fricative.*

## Activity 4

Write the symbols for the consonants in the following words:

| White | clock | edge |
|---|---|---|
| pull | through | vision |
| chalk | shell | finger |
| boxes | fifth | wrong |
| queue | cares | anger |

## Activity 5

◀ Listen and underline the /ð/ and /θ/ sounds in the following text:

Then, the three young boys hid in the bushes until their pursuers passed by. At one point, the youngest began to groan in fear. The other two threw themselves on top of him and smothered the noise. The danger passed.

## Activity 6

How do the following consonants work phonologically in English, that is, in which positions can they occur in words?

    /ŋ/ /r/ /h/ /ʒ/

## Notes

1   See Chapter Seven 'The Syllable' for more on this.
2   'Some accents of English use /ŋg/ in preference to /ŋ/ in words like 'singer'.

## Further reading

Gill, S. (1997) 'Vite volves and wegetarian wampires', *Modern English Teacher,* 6 (3), 45–6.

Scott, I. (1988) 'Betty Botter vs Peter Piper: A plosive encounter', *Modern English Teacher,* 15 (3), 13–17.

# Vowels 5

## Introduction

Most of the world's languages have twice as many consonants as vowels. English is distinctive or 'marked' in that it has 24 consonants and up to 20 vowels. Consequently, it is unsurprising that the English vowel system can be problematic for learners. To make the matter more difficult, there is a great deal of variation in the production of vowels among native speakers, which can be caused by a variety of factors including geographical region, age, gender or social or educational background. The vowels described here are those of BBC English, although we will occasionally point out some accent variations. As explained in Chapter 1, it is important to recognize that your own vowel system may diverge from this model.

We cannot describe vowels in the same way as consonants. Vowels are different from consonants in that air passes relatively unrestricted between the articulators, so that all vowels are approximants. Also, vowels are typically voiced, so there are no meaningful voiced/voiceless or lenis/fortis contrasts.

Alternatively, vowel sounds can be classified in terms of:

> *a. The position of the articulators*
> *b. The duration of the sound*

## a. The position of the articulators

The main articulators involved in the production of vowel sounds are the tongue, lips and jaw. The tongue is very mobile, sections of it can be raised or lowered to produce different sounds, for example, 'tea' 'two', 'teen' 'tan'. Vowels where the front part of the tongue is raised (as in 'tea' and 'tan') are called **front vowels**. Vowels where the back part of the tongue is raised (as in 'two' and 'tar') are called **back vowels**.

> The lips can be **spread** ('eel'), **rounded** ('few') or **neutral** ('er..').
> The jaw can be **closed** ('eat') or **open** ('arm'), or somewhere between the two ('egg').

Vowels which are produced with an open jaw position ('hat') are called open vowels and vowels produced with a closed jaw position ('heat') are called close vowels.

|  | Front | Back |
|---|---|---|
| **Close** | tea | few |
| **Open** | tan | far |

## b. The duration of the sound

Differences in vowel length are an important part of English phonology and are a significant factor in the distinctive rhythm of the language. Some vowels are much shorter than others and vowels are sometimes referred to as 'long' ('bead', 'bird') and 'short' ('bat', 'hot').

# The classification of vowels

To recap, vowels are different from consonants in that there is no complete obstruction by the articulators in the vocal tract, that is, they have a relatively open aperture of articulation. All vowels in English are voiced, unless you whisper (in which case they are voiceless). And all vowels are produced in the oral tract, but they may be **nasalized** if they occur before a nasal consonant, such as 'and' (and especially in American accents). Vowels are **sonorants**, that is, the sonority of a sound is its inherent loudness or strength. Vowels are also continuants because they can be lengthened and continued. As vowels are louder than consonants and can be prolonged, they form the core or **nucleus** of syllables in most languages.

There are, however, some difficulties in trying to distinguish vowels and consonants on a purely phonetic basis, as some English 'consonants' are phonetically more like vowels (e.g. /w/, /j/, /r/). In some ways, it may be easier to classify vowels in terms of their distribution in syllables and words, rather than their articulation. Despite these theoretical issues, for practical teaching purposes we will assume there is a clear distinction between vowels and consonants.

As we said earlier, vowels can also be classified in terms of:

*(i) Tongue position and shape*
*(ii) Degree of lip-rounding*

### (i) Tongue position and shape

Vowels are produced by changing the position of the tongue in ways which do not generally involve it touching the roof of the mouth. They are voiced sounds, with the air passing through the mouth in a continual stream without obstruction or audible friction.

It is very difficult for us to report or describe how we change the shape of the tongue to produce vowels. Explaining such changes to students, for example, would only give them very rough, imprecise guidance on the production of the vowels. However, we do need to come up with some **stylized** way of classifying these sounds.

In the production of vowels, the tongue is usually convex in the mouth and vowels are classified as **front**, **back** or **central**, according to which part of the tongue that is raised highest in the mouth. The tip and the blade of the tongue are not directly involved in the articulation of vowel sounds.

### Activity 1

◀ Listen and say these sounds and classify them into front, back or central.

  1. /u:/ as in f**oo**l, r**u**de   *back*
  2. / i:/ as in t**ea**, s**ee**, r**ea**d   *front*
  3. /ə/ as in butt**er**, **a**lone   *central*

Making the sounds in Activity 1, you should be able to feel the following distinctions. The sound /u:/ in 'fool' and 'rude' has the back of the tongue raised to the highest point in respect of the roof of the mouth (as in Figure 5.1).

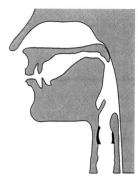

**Figure 5.1** Tongue position for /u:/

So, the sounds in (1) are back vowels. /i:/ has the front of the tongue raised, so the sound in (2) is front (as in Figure 5.2).

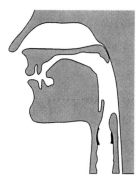

**Figure 5.2** Tongue position for /i:/

For /ə/, the middle of the tongue is raised highest. This leads to the classification:

| Front | Central | Back |
|-------|---------|------|
| i: | ə | u: |

The **12** simple vowels of English can all be classified as front, back or central.

---

### Activity 2

Listen and say the following vowels, then try to classify them as front, back or central in your articulation. Try to feel where the highest part of the tongue is.

| /i:/ meat | /ɪ/ sit | /ɜ:/ fur | /e/ pen | /ʊ/ put |
|-----------|---------|----------|---------|---------|
| / æ / bat | /ɔ:/ short | /ʌ/ done | /ɒ/ pot | /u:/ rule |
| /ɑ:/ father | /ə/ again | | | |

| Front | Central | Back |
|-------|---------|------|
| /i:/ɪ/e/æ/ | /ə/ ʌ /ɜ:/ | /ʊ/ ɑ:/ɔ:/ɒ/ |

---

Vowels are also classified in relation to the height of the tongue and jaw. When the tongue is raised as close as possible to the roof of the mouth, the vowel is said to be **close** or high, as in 'tea' (as in Figure 5.2). You can also remember the term close in association with the jaw being closed.

When the tongue is lowered and the jaw is as open as possible the vowel is said to be **open** or low, as in 'tap' (as in Figure 5.3). To consider the difference between **close** and **open** vowels,

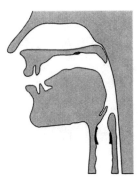

**Figure 5.3** Tongue height for /æ/ in 'tap'

articulate /iː/ and /æ/. When making /iː/, the tongue is close to the roof of the mouth. With /æ/, as in h<u>a</u>t, it is much lower. Therefore, we classify it as a relatively open vowel. With /iː/ the degree of openness is much less, the tongue being very close to the roof of the mouth. So, /iː/ is classified as close.

Vowels which are articulated somewhere between the two extreme heights are termed **mid**, that is, close-mid, as in 'leg' or open-mid, as in 'hut'.

In making the two vowel sounds in 'tea' and 'tap', the front of the tongue is raised, so we classify these as relatively **front vowels**. However, if we say 'tea' and then 'two' the back of the tongue is raised for the second vowel, so we can say the vowel in 'two' is relatively **back**. Similarly, if we say 'tap' and then 'tar' the back of the tongue is similarly raised on 'tar'. So, we can distinguish between the vowels in 'tea', 'tap', 'two' and 'tar' in the following way:

|  | Front | Back |
|---|---|---|
| **Close** | iː 'tea' | uː 'two' |
| **Open** | æ 'tap' | ɑː 'tar' |

Figure 5.4 shows how we can categorize vowels for their open/close and front/back qualities.

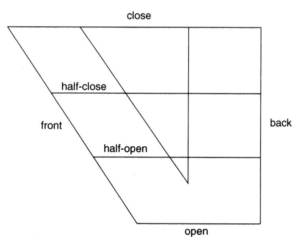

**Figure 5.4** Vowel chart categories

Such a diagram helps us to plot the relative degree of opening and closing in the mouth, that is, the extent to which the highest part of the tongue is raised towards the roof of the mouth. Also, in order to help understand the location of vowel articulations, we can see how the vowel chart relates to the space within the oral cavity, as in Figure 5.5.

In general, we can only really talk of vowels in approximate terms. It is very difficult to be exact about the point of articulation. Nevertheless, the front/back, close/open distinctions are helpful.

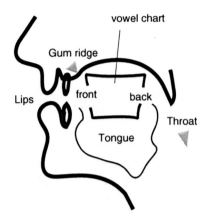

**Figure 5.5** Vowel space in relation to the mouth

---

## Activity 3

◀ Listen and try to classify the following vowels for their relative degrees of open or closeness and plot them on the diagram, Figure 5.4.

| /iː/ | /ɪ/ | /e/ | /æ/ | (front vowels) |
| /uː/ | /ʊ/ | /ɔː/ | /ɒ/ | (back vowels) |
| /ə/ | | | | |

---

### (ii) Degree of lip-rounding

The second important aspect of vowel articulation is the position of the lips (Figure 5.6) and, in particular, the degree of lip-rounding. The degree of lip-rounding affects the shape of the resonance chamber in the mouth. There are basically three possibilities, (a) *rounded* (b) *spread* or (c) *neutral*.

Usually, the closer the vowel is, the more spread, less rounded are the lips. However, /uː/ is close but it also has lip-rounding. Unrounded lips can be spread as in /iː/ in 'meet', a close vowel. The open vowel /æ/ as in 'hat' has unrounded neutral lips. Rounded lips occur in the

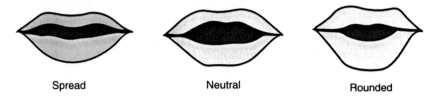

Spread                    Neutral                    Rounded

**Figure 5.6** Position of lips for vowels

articulation of the close vowel /u:/ where the lip-rounding is said to be close-rounding and in the open vowel /ɒ/ as in 'got', where the rounding is more open.

Individual vowels can be identified fairly easily by lip position alone, as lip-reading can verify. Generally, front vowels have a more spread position and back vowels have a more rounded position (consider the back vowels in 'put', 'got', 'law'). This is true of English but also of many of the world's languages.

## The English vowel system

The relatively large vowel system of English (with 20 vowels in BBC English and 15 in American English) is characteristic of Germanic languages (Swedish has even more vowels). There are seven short vowels, five long vowels and eight diphthongs. The 12 short and long vowels are shown in Figure 5.7.

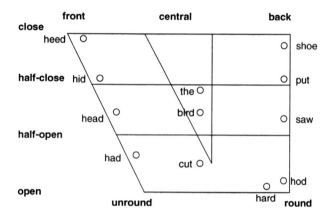

**Figure 5.7** The English long and short vowels

We will now look at the articulation of the vowels by locating them on the vowel chart (Figure 5.8) which shows their corresponding phonemic symbols.

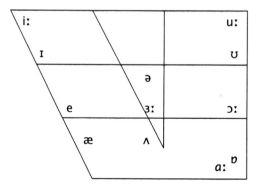

**Figure 5.8** Phonemic symbols of English vowels

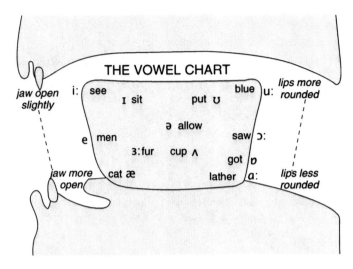

**Figure 5.9** Position of vowel chart in oral cavity

The shape of the chart is modelled on the shape of the **phonetic space**, that is, the shape of the oral cavity produced by various positions of the tongue (Figure 5.9).

For English, because of where the vowels are made, the phonetic space is represented as a trapezoid (but some languages would be represented by a triangle). The vowel system for English is usually classified as containing four front vowels, three central vowels, five back vowels and eight diphthongs.

## Tense and lax vowels

Some vowels involve greater muscular tension to produce than others:

> e.g. **tense**        **lax**
> /iː/ beat        bit /ɪ/
> /uː/ boot        book /ʊ/
> /eɪ/ bait        bet /e/

The vowels in the left hand column, which require more musculatory effort, are sometimes called **tense** vowels, while the right-hand vowels are called **lax** vowels. It is possible to feel that the facial muscles are more tense when we say 'beat' than when we say 'bit'. Some writers give the label 'tense' to long vowels and 'lax' to short vowels (Jackobson and Halle 1964).

## Dialectal variations

The dialect of English will determine how some of these vowels are pronounced:

> e.g. bath, grass, after, hat, span

Some accents of English (particularly northern ones) and most Americans would say all of these words with the same open front vowel /æ/. However, BBC English speakers would use a different vowel, that is, an open back vowel /ɑː/, for the first three words.

English speakers from New Zealand, South Africa and the Southern States of America would pronounce the vowels in the two words 'pin', 'pen' the same, that is, mid close front /ɜ/. Whereas for most British speakers the pairs of words 'cot', 'caught' have different vowels, for many Americans the vowels in the pair are synonomous, that is, [kɔt].

Generally, many American accents use a lot more nasalization in vowel articulation than British speakers, for example, 'fought', 'fork'. For BBC English speakers, the vowels in these words would be the same, that is, a back, mid open rounded vowel /ɔː/. However, many accents, including Scottish English and American would pronounce the /r/ in fork, such accents are called **rhotic** (NB /r/ pronounced after a vowel is called a **post-vocalic** /r/).

## The short and long vowels in English

It is important for teachers to be able to recognize the vowel sounds of English and respond to learner difficulties in perception and production. To assist with that, a description of the vowel sounds follows. These descriptions should, if possible, be read in conjunction with the recordings of English vowels that are provided.

How vowels are analyzed in English is a matter of great debate and unfortunately there is no neat pattern. What is presented here is a compromise, generally accepted view that is of use to teachers. In general, there is little variation in vowel qualities in BBC English, but an immense amount of dialectal variation.

Both length and quality help to distinguish the vowel phonemes in English.

## 'Long' and 'short' vowels

The concept of long and short vowels can be a useful distinction for learners of English pronunciation. However, not all transcription systems use the length marks used here to distinguish vowels. This is because length variation between vowels such as /ɪ/ in 'ship' and /iː/ in 'sheep' is dependent on context and there are also differences in quality between the two vowels, which is why the two vowels are represented with different symbols as well as with a length mark.

## Short vowels in English

There are seven short vowels in English, as shown in Figure 5.10.

Seven Short Vowels /ɪ/ /e/ /æ/ /ə/ /ʌ/ /ʊ/ /ɒ/

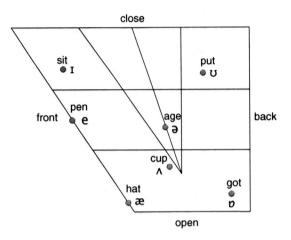

**Figure 5.10** English short vowels

---

## Activity 4

/ɪ/ ◄ Listen and repeat the examples: 'w<u>o</u>m<u>e</u>n', 'b<u>u</u>s<u>y</u>', 'b<u>i</u>t', 'f<u>i</u>t', 'p<u>i</u>t<u>y</u>' (Figure 5.11)

---

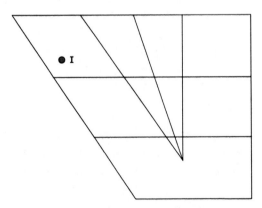

**Figure 5.11** /ɪ/

This is a front, close vowel, with the lips lightly spread.

There is a perceptual difficulty for some native speakers who feel that the final sound in busy is intermediate between long /iː/ and short /ɪ/. In this unit, we do not focus on this perception as it is not phonemically distinctive (see Chapter 6 for guidance on phonemic distinctions).

## Activity 5

/e/ ◀ (Listen and repeat the examples:   'p<u>e</u>n', 'fr<u>ie</u>nd', 'h<u>ea</u>d', 'said') (Figure 5.12)

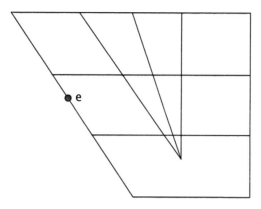

**Figure 5.12** /e/

This is a front vowel, produced with the tongue half-raised in the mouth so that it is between half-close and half-open. It is only found in closed syllables, that is, it cannot be the final element in a syllable (it can be initial or medial as in end or pet).

## Activity 6

/æ/ ◀ (Listen and repeat the examples:   'h<u>a</u>t'; 'm<u>a</u>tter'; 'c<u>a</u>t', '<u>a</u>pple') (Figure 5.13)

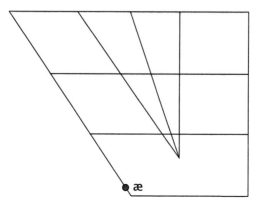

**Figure 5.13** /æ/

This is a front, open vowel with lips slightly spread. Again, it is found in closed syllables. This vowel is traditionally put with the short vowels but it tends to be longer than the others in this group.

---

**Activity 7**

/ə/ ◀ Listen and repeat the examples: 'ago', 'about', 'persist', 'women' (Figure 5.14)

---

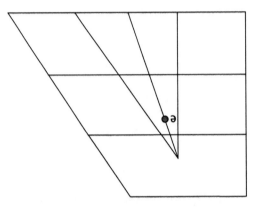

**Figure 5.14** /ə/

This sound is called **schwa** and it is the most frequently occurring vowel in English. It only occurs in unstressed syllables (e.g. ago /əgəʊ/ and plays a major role in the English stress system. It occurs in the so-called weak forms, for example:

> They <u>were</u> playing all day
> /wə/

> Those plants <u>are</u> beautiful
> /ə/

It is a central, half-open vowel, without lip-rounding, that is, with lips neutral and can occur in initial, medial and final position in the syllable.

---

**Activity 8**

/ʌ/ ◀ Listen and repeat the examples: 'cut', 'tough', 'flush', 'comfort' (Figure 5.15)

---

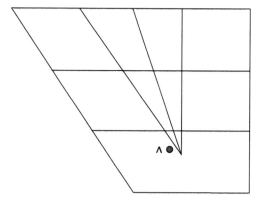

**Figure 5.15** /ʌ/

This vowel is only found in closed syllables, as in the examples above, and in syllable initial position as in 'up', 'utter', 'until'.

It is a central, half-open vowel with neutral lips. In some varieties of English this sound is infrequently used, for example, in parts of Northern England.

**Activity 9**

/ɒ/ ◄ Listen and repeat the examples:  'd<u>o</u>t', 'c<u>ou</u>gh', 'fr<u>o</u>st', 'l<u>o</u>ng') (Figure 5.16)

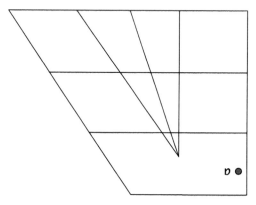

**Figure 5.16** /ɒ/

The sound is a back, open vowel with lips slightly rounded. It is used in closedsyllables and it can be found in initial position in the syllable as in 'ostrich', 'offal', 'on'.

---

**Activity 10**

/ʊ/ ◀ (Listen and repeat the examples:   'p<u>u</u>t', 'f<u>u</u>ll', 's<u>oo</u>t') (Figure 5.17)

---

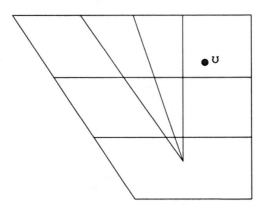

**Figure 5.17** /ʊ/

This is a close, back vowel with lips rounded. However, its position is close to being half-open and central. The lips are more rounded in this case than for the other short back vowel /ɒ/. It occurs in closed syllables, not being found in final position.

Perceptions about the shortness of vowels vary from language to language. As a result, the short vowels may cause difficulties for learners. For instance, some learners may have difficulty in producing the short vowel /ɪ/ in 'bit' in a way that distinguishes it convincingly from 'beat'.

## Long vowels in English

There are five long vowels in English, as shown in Figure 5.18.

---

**Activity 11**

/iː/ ◀ Listen and repeat the examples: 'b<u>ea</u>t', 'p<u>eo</u>ple', 'm<u>ee</u>t', 'm<u>e</u>ter' (Figure 5.19)

---

Five Long Vowels /iː/ /uː/ /ɜː/ /ɔː/ /aː/

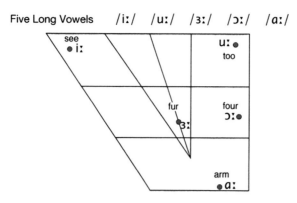

**Figure 5.18** English long vowels

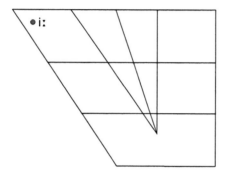

**Figure 5.19** /iː/

This sound is a close, front vowel made with the lips slightly spread. It is more close and more front than the short vowel /ɪ/.

## Activity 12

/ɜː/ ◀ Listen and repeat the examples: 'bi̲rd', 'rehe̲arse', 'shi̲rt', 'wo̲rk' (Figure 5.20)

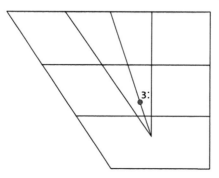

**Figure 5.20** /ɜː/

This is a central vowel made with lips in a neutral position. Many English speakers in the UK use this sound when they hesitate ('er . . .').

***

### Activity 13

/ɑ:/ ◀ Listen and repeat the examples: 'f<u>a</u>ther', 'c<u>a</u>lm', 'c<u>ar</u>', 'p<u>a</u>rt' (Figure 5.21)

***

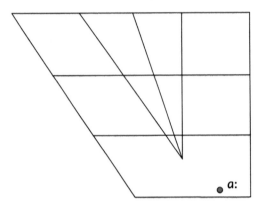

**Figure 5.21** /ɑ:/

This is an open back vowel, made with lips in a neutral position. With this vowel the tongue is at its lowest position, which is why doctors ask patients to say it when they want to look inside the mouth.

There is significant regional variation in the use of this vowel. The following generalizations in Table 5.1 illustrate how it is replaced by the short vowel /æ/ before some double consonants, in some varieties of English.

**Table 5.1** Short and long 'a' in English

| Word | Phonetic Transcription | | |
|------|------------------|------------------|------------------------|
|      | Southern England | Northern England | US (General American) |
| bath | bɑːθ | bæθ | bæθ |
| gasp | gɑːsp | gæsp | gæsp |
| pass | pɑːs | pæs | pæs |

***

### Activity 14

/ɔ:/ ◀ Listen and repeat the examples: 's<u>aw</u>', 'l<u>or</u>d', 'f<u>or</u>ce', 'sw<u>or</u>d' (Figure 5.22)

***

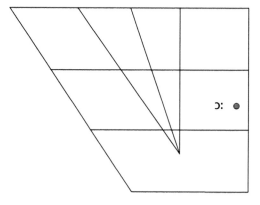

**Figure 5.22** /ɔ:/

This is a back vowel, between half-open and half-close positions in the mouth, with quite a pronounced degree of lip-rounding.

---

### Activity 15

/u:/ ◀ Listen and repeat the examples:   'soon', 'boot', 'lose', 'tune' (Figure 5.23)

---

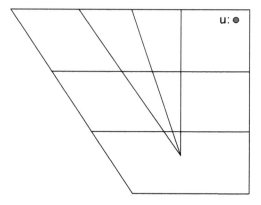

**Figure 5.23** /u:/

This is a close, back vowel which is made with the lips fully rounded.

The length marks [:] are not always used with the phonemic symbols for these vowels. These marks are used here as a reminder of the length difference. However, it is important to remember that the differences are not just of length but also of quality. If we compare the short and long vowels:

| /ɪ/ | with | /iː/ |
|-----|------|------|
| /ʊ/ | with | /uː/ |
| /æ/ | with | /ɑː/ |

In each case, the different symbol represents not just differences of length, but also differences in tongue position and degree of lip-rounding or spreading.

The long vowels also have a tendency to become slight diphthongs, with some teachers of English possibly presenting them as such for learners. For example, you may know speakers who vary the pronunciation of:

soon from /suːn/ to /suːən/
school from /skuːl/ to /skuːəl/
cord from /kɔːd/ to /kɔːəd/

Usually, the diphthongization (or glide from one vowel to another so that they are pronounced as one phoneme) involves a move to the schwa position, the central unstressed vowel which is very common in English.

## Monophthongs, diphthongs and triphthongs

The English vowel system includes **monophthongs**, or **pure** vowels, as we have just seen, as well as **diphthongs and triphthongs.** For monophthongs, the tongue remains in a relatively stable position throughout the articulation. In diphthongs, however, the tongue moves from one position to another. Diphthongs require two articulations, a **nucleus** and a **glide,** while triphthongs require three, a nucleus and two glides. The nucleus is the central part of the

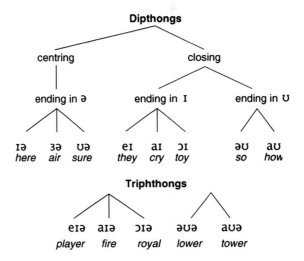

**Figure 5.24** English diphthongs and triphthongs (Davis, 1995)

vowel – the part that is sustained longest; the glide is a transient sound leading either into or out of the nucleus. In English, the nucleus always comes first and the glide is a transition out of the nucleus. In some languages, the glide and nucleus are reversed.

BBC English has eight diphthongs (but many other English accents, including American, have fewer). As diphthongs are all at least as long as long vowels, and because the second part is a glide, they probably contribute to the perception of English as sounding 'drawling'.

It is important to make the first part of the vowel longer and stronger than the second. The easiest way to remember the diphthongs is in terms of three groups, that is, (a) centring to /ə/ (b) closing to /ɪ/ and (c) closing to /ʊ/, while triphthongs form two groups, that is, (a) those ending in /ɪə/ and (b) those ending in /ʊə/, as shown in Figure 5.24.

## Diphthongs in English

Diphthongs have similar length to long vowels. They consist of a glide from one vowel to the position of another.

> Three diphthongs end in /ɪ/ (closing diphthongs)
> Two diphthongs end in /ʊ/ (closing diphthongs)
> Three diphthongs end in /ə/ (centring diphthongs)

**Closing diphthongs** ending in /ɪ/: /eɪ//aɪ//ɔɪ/ are represented together in Figure 5.25. Each one is then explained in turn.

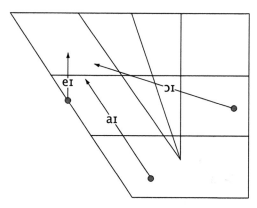

**Figure 5.25** /eɪ/ /aɪ/ /ɔɪ/

---

### Activity 16

/eɪ/ ◀ Listen and repeat the examples: 'p<u>ai</u>n'; 'pl<u>ay</u>'; 'd<u>a</u>te', 'm<u>a</u>le' (Figure 5.26)

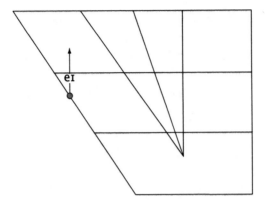

**Figure 5.26** /eɪ/

This vowel begins at the point of the /e/ as in pen sound and glides to /ɪ/. The glide takes the diphthong to a slightly more close position.

**Activity 17**

/aɪ/ ◀ Listen and repeat the examples: 'r<u>i</u>de', 't<u>ie</u>', 'fl<u>y</u>', 's<u>i</u>gh' (Figure 5.27)

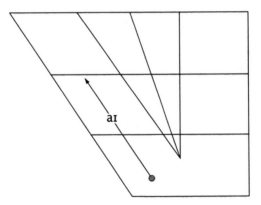

**Figure 5.27** /aɪ/

The glide to a close position is more pronounced with this diphthong as it moves from an open to half-close position in the mouth.

### Activity 18

/ɔɪ/ ◀ Listen and repeat the examples: 'b<u>oy</u>', 't<u>oy</u>', 'c<u>oi</u>l', 's<u>oi</u>l' (Figure 5.28)

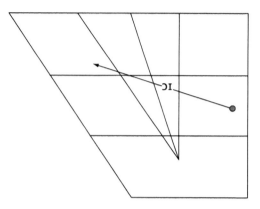

**Figure 5.28** /ɔɪ/

This glide moves gently to a half-close position from ɔ to ɪ.

**Closing diphthongs** ending in /ʊ/:    /əʊ/    /aʊ/

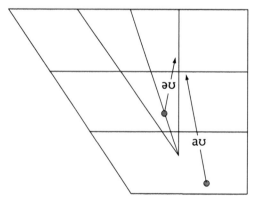

**Figure 5.29** /əʊ/ /aʊ/

The two diphthongs end in /ʊ/ are represented in Figure 5.29.

### Activity 19

/əʊ/ ◀ Listen and repeat the examples: 'h<u>o</u>me', 'r<u>oa</u>m', 'd<u>o</u>me', 'c<u>o</u>mb' (Figure 5.30)

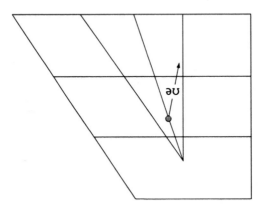

**Figure 5.30** /əʊ/

The nucleus of this diphthong is the schwa vowel /ə/ as in the word 'ago'. The glide is accompanied by quite pronounced lip-rounding as it closes to /ʊ/.

Listen carefully to the tape-recording of the diphthongs as these often cause difficulties for learners who may more readily perceive a pure vowel.

### Activity 20

/aʊ/ ◀ Listen and repeat the examples: 'n<u>ow</u>', 't<u>ow</u>n', 'fr<u>ow</u>n', 'm<u>ou</u>nd' (Figure 5.31)

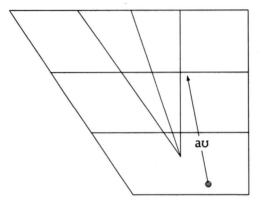

**Figure 5.31** /aʊ/

This closing diphthong moves from a position near the articulation of /ɑ:/, withslight lip-rounding to a position near /ʊ/. The end of the glide is somewhere between half-open and half-close. The lip-rounding may be more pronounced by the end of the glide.

**Centring diphthongs** ending in /ə/: /ɪə/ /eə/ /ʊə/ (Figure 5.32)

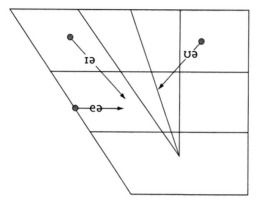

**Figure 5.32** /ɪə/ /eə/ /ʊə/

The centring diphthongs all glide towards the schwa vowel.

**Activity 21**

/ɪə/ ◀ Listen and repeat the examples: 'h<u>e</u>re', 'd<u>ee</u>r', 'cl<u>ea</u>r', 'b<u>ea</u>rd' (Figure 5.33)

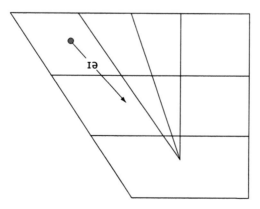

**Figure 5.33** /ɪə/

This glide begins at a closer position than /ɪ/ as in 'pit' and moves to /ə/.

**Activity 22**

/eə/ ◀ Listen and repeat the examples: 'th<u>ere</u>', 'r<u>are</u>', 'f<u>air</u>', 'sh<u>are</u>' (Figure 5.34)

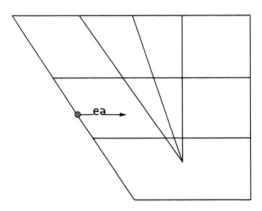

**Figure 5.34** /eə/

This glide begins at the /e/ sound as in pen and moves back to a central position at /ə/. Typically this diphthong is being replaced in present day BBC English by a long monophthong, a bit like a long /e:/, as in 'square' /skwe:/ or 'hair' /he:/.

**Activity 23**

/ʊə/ ◀ Listen and repeat the examples: 'sure'; 'lure'; 'dour' (Figure 5.35)

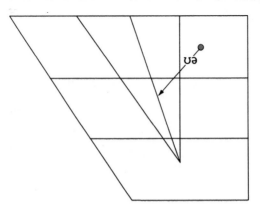

**Figure 5.35** /ʊə/

The starting point for this glide is a little closer than /ʊ/ in put. It then centres to /ə/. This diphthong is subject to significant regional variety with many UK English speakers using

/ɔː/ instead of /ʊə/, for example, in their production of 'poor' as /p ɔːr/.

## Triphthongs

These are the most complex group of vowels in English, being a composite of three sounds, a rapid glide from one sound to another and then to a third. The five triphthongs of English can be thought of as composed of the five closing diphthongs with schwa added on the end.

---

### Activity 24

◄ Listen and repeat the examples:

eɪ+ ə = eɪə (player)
a ɪ+ ə = aɪə (fire)
ɔɪ+ ə = ɔɪə (royal)
əʊ+ ə = əʊə (lower)
aʊ+ ə = aʊə (hour)

---

However, the use of some diphthongs and triphthongs in English is rather unstable at present and some seem to be disappearing in standard southern English (e.g. Ireland -/ɑːlənd/, moor) – /mɔː/). Also, the vowel movement within the triphthongs can be very small and difficult to hear, except in careful speech. In particular, the middle vowel, that is the /ə/ or /ʊ/ sound, can be hard to distinguish, so that in some cases it is argued that a word like 'player' has two syllables with a consonant /j/ in the middle /pleɪjə/ rather than a single syllable with a triphthong /pleɪə/.

## Cardinal vowels

So far we have been looking at English vowels, that is, English vowel phonemes, but there is also a way of describing vowels irrespective of language, that is, phonetically. A system of such vowel reference positions was developed by phonetician Daniel Jones in 1917 and is called the cardinal vowel system. Just as the International Date Line is a reference point to locate the exact time in different geographical zones, so the primary cardinal vowels can be used to plot the exact location of vowels in any specific language (Figure 5.36). The standard is permanent and internationally agreed. According to Roach (2000:14). 'They are extremes of vowel quality', so they sound somewhat odd to many listeners. They are represented as follows.

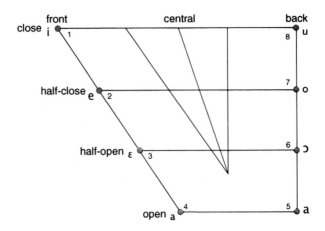

**Figure 5.36** Cardinal vowels

Vowel number 1 [i] is as close and as front as it is possible to produce a vowel. Any further closing or fronting would result in audible friction or hissing. Cardinal vowel 4 is fully open and front, as extremely open and front as it is possible to be. With this idealized reference grid, we are able to classify English vowels: for example,

> the English vowel /æ/ (the vowel in 'cat') is not as open as cardinal vowel number 4 [a].
> (Roach 2000:14)

Teachers of English may wonder whether such a classification is useful but they can act as an important reference point for an understanding of the vowel similarities and contrasts between languages and between varieties of English.[1]

## Summary

Vowels are characterized by a lack of audible friction, by a relatively unhindered passage of the airstream through the vocal tract.

In BBC English there are:

| | |
|---|---|
| five long vowels: | /iː/; /ɜː/; /ɑː/; /ɔː/; /uː/; |
| seven short vowels: | /ɪ/; /e/; /æ/; /ʌ/; /ɒ/; /ʊ/; /ə/; |
| eight diphthongs: | /ɪə/; /eə/; /ʊə/; /eɪ/; /aɪ/; /ɔɪ/; /əʊ/; /aʊ/; |

Distinctions applying to vowels involve the relative degree of openness or closeness depending on the raising of the highest point of the tongue. In addition, vowels are classified as **front**, **central** or **back** depending upon the part of the tongue which is raised.

**Activity 25**

To check your knowledge of the English vowel system, place all the vowels on the chart below, plotting the positions of articulation:

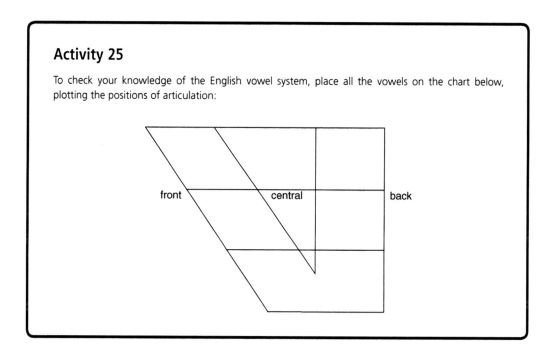

# Teaching implications

It appears that accurate vowel sounds are harder to learn than consonants, possibly because there is no tongue contact to act as a reference point, unlike consonants. This distinction between vowels and consonants may be why consonants tend to be acquired more efficiently through speaking tasks, whereas vowel distinctions may be more efficiently accomplished through listening tasks (Fucci et al. 1977, Leather 1983, Chun 2002).

The two key distinguishing characteristics of vowels are quality and quantity; quality relates to the position of the tongue and lips while quantity relates to the duration of the sound. While quantity is relatively stable across varieties of English, there are considerable variations in quality. So, for instance, 'shut' might be pronounced /ʃʌt/ in BBC English and /ʃʊt/ in northern varieties. Similarly, 'late' might be pronounced /leɪt/ in BBC English and /laɪt/ in South London accents.

Some phonologists therefore, such as Jenkins (2000) and Jenner (1995), suggest that English language teachers concentrate on the quantity dimension rather than quality, in other words, make sure learners distinguish clearly between long and short vowels rather than worrying too much about the accuracy of articulations. On the other hand, others claim that the quality of each vowel should take precedence over their intrinsic length and some research (Hillenbrand and Clark 2000) suggests, for instance, that North American English speakers distinguish between /ɪ/ and /iː/ (e.g. bit and beat) primarily on the basis of vowel quality rather than difference in vowel length.

Similarly, there is some debate regarding the value of teaching diphthongs. Many languages and some varieties of English have pure vowels where BBC English has diphthongs (e.g. 'here' can be /hɪə/ in BBC English and /hiːr/ in Scottish varieties). In fact, Jenner (1995) claims that only the three closing diphthongs /aʊ/ /aɪ/ and /ɔɪ/ are common across all native speaker varieties, concluding that diphthongs in general should not be given high priority in L2 teaching.

> ### Activity 26
>
> Jenkins (2000) goes even further, suggesting that diphthongs be excluded from the Lingua Franca Core, as long as the long vowel length is maintained.
> Do you agree? Is it worth teaching diphthongs?

Figure 5.37 illustrates a ten vowel system predicted by Cruttenden (2008) as tolerable for learners of English as an International Language. We can see that in this description, some of the vowel quality contrasts, such as /ɪ/ /iː/ and /æ/ /ɑː/ have been replaced by simpler differences in vowel length (e.g. /i/ /iː/ and /e/ /eː/. We also see that there are no central vowels, including schwa.

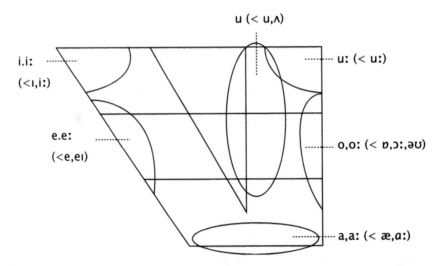

**Figure 5.37** Cruttenden's 10-vowel system for International English (from Cruttenden 2008:332)

Jenkins (2000) also omits the schwa from the Lingua Franca Core, seeing it as non-essential for intelligibility in EIL contexts (i.e. between NNS), although she does see it as important for EFL interaction. Many others do not make the EFL/ELF distinction (e.g. Avery and Ehrlich 1987) and see the acquisition of schwa as essential because of its frequency and its role in distinguishing unstressed syllables.

---

**Activity 27**

Where do you fit into this argument? How important is it to teach Schwa?

---

There are many more vowel sounds than vowel letters in the English alphabet, so phonemic symbols rarely correspond to English spelling, so all work on vowels should be reinforced by referring to sound/spelling correspondences.

The tense vowels are found more frequently in stressed syllables than the lax or 'short' vowels (ɪ, æ, e, ʊ, ʌ). Also, these short vowels are the most difficult to correct.

# Key points

- Accurate vowel sounds are harder to learn than consonants. However, vowel contrasts in general appear to play a less crucial role in intelligibiltiy than consonant contrasts.
- According to Cruttenden (2008) the 20 vowel phonemes (i.e. 12 monophthongs and 8 diphthongs) of BBC English should be the ultimate target of a learner aiming at achieving a near native English accent. However, both Cruttenden and Jenkins agree that a major simplification of the vowel system is possible if L2 learners are aiming at an EIL target and the number of vowels and vowel contrasts can be reduced considerably. These could consist of 5 short vowels (/ɪ/ /e/ /æ/ /ʊ/ /ɒ/) and five long BBC English vowels (/ɑː/ /iː/ /uː/ /ɔː/ /ɜː/) or of Cruttenden's revised set (see Figure 5.37).
- The correct use of schwa /ə/ is considered high priority by many because of its role in reduced syllables, weak forms, rhythm and stress. However, both Jenkins and Gimson believe it is dispensable for international English targets.
- /ʊ/ can be conflated with /ʌ/ as it carries a low functional load. So, 'luck' and 'look' could be pronounced similarly as they are in many northern English accents.
- Only the three closing diphthongs /aʊ/ /aɪ/ and /ɔɪ/ are common across all native speaker varieties and therefore merit attention for L2 learners. Many diphthongs either vary considerably across regional dialects or are changing across generations. In particular, /ɔɪ/ /ʊə/ and /eə/ are unstable; /ʊə/ is increasingly replaced by /ɔː/ (e.g. 'poor') and /eə/ by /eː/ (e.g. 'square').
- Contrasts between /ɪ, iː/ (e.g. 'ship', 'sheep') and /æ, ʌ/ ('hat', 'hut') should have high priority because they carry a high functional load and distinguish many minimal pairs.
- It is important to distinguish the phoneme /ɜː/ from /ɑː/ for both native speaker and EIL targets as an overlap can lead to lexical confusions such as 'curtain' vs 'carton' and 'birth' vs 'bath'.

# Note

1   An original recording of Daniel Jones reading the cardinal vowels can be found at http://www.youtube.com/watch?v=6UIAe4p2I74 and http://www.let.uu.nl/~audiufon/data/e_cardinal_vowels.html

# Further reading

Chen, Y., Robb, M., Gilbert, H. and Lerman, J. (2001) 'Vowel production by Mandarin speakers of English', *Clinical Linguistics & Phonetics, 15*, 427–40.

Cruttenden, A. (2008) *Gimson's Pronunciation of English*, 7th edition, Chapters 4 and 8. London: Hodder Education.

Ladefoged, P. and Maddieson, I. (1990) 'Vowels of the world languages', *Journal of Phonetics, 18*, 93–122.

Leather, J. (1999) 'Second language speech research: An introduction', *Language Learning, 49* (1), 1–56.

O'Connor, J. D. (1980) *Better English Pronunciation*, Chapter 5, Cambridge: Cambridge University Press.

Roach, P. (2000) *English Phonetics and Phonology*, 3rd edition, Chapters 2 and 3, Cambridge: Cambridge University Press.

Rogerson, P. and Gilbert, J. (1990) *Speaking Clearly.* Chapters 23 & 24 on Sound Contrasts. Cambridge: Cambridge University Press.

Underhill, A. (1994) *Sound Foundations.* Oxford: Hienemann. Section on 'Working with individual sounds' (pp. 96–102).

# Vowel practice activities

## Activity 1

Say the following vowel sounds and give a word that exemplifies each:

/ɒ/  /ɪ/  / i:/  / ɔ:/  /æ/  /eɪ/  /əʊ/  /ɑ:/  /ʊ/  /u:/  /ʌ/  /ə/

/ɜ:/  /aɪ/  /ɔɪ/  /ɪə/  /eə/  /e/  /aʊ/  /ʊə/

## Activity 2

◀ Listen and repeat the short vowel contrasts:

| ɪ | e | e | æ | æ | ʌ |
|------|------|------|------|------|------|
| bit | bet | met | mat | lack | luck |
| fill | fell | said | sad | ran | run |

| ʌ | ɒ | ɒ | ʊ |
|------|------|------|------|
| luck | lock | lock | look |
| dug | dog | pot | put |

## Activity 3

◀ Listen and pick out the vowel sound that is different from the rest. Choose A, B, C or D.

| | A | B | C | D |
|---------|------|------|--------|------|
| Example | bean | bean | bun (c) | bean |

| | A | B | C | D |
|----|---|---|---|---|
| 1 | | | | |
| 2 | | | | |
| 3 | | | | |
| 4 | | | | |
| 5 | | | | |
| 6 | | | | |
| 7 | | | | |
| 8 | | | | |
| 9 | | | | |
| 10 | | | | |
| 11 | | | | |
| 12 | | | | |
| 13 | | | | |
| 14 | | | | |
| 15 | | | | |
| 16 | | | | |
| 17 | | | | |
| 18 | | | | |
| 19 | | | | |
| 20 | | | | |

Now listen again and repeat all the words.

## Activity 4

Identify the vowel sounds occurring in the following words and write the phonemic symbol, for example:

| sack | suck | sock |
|------|------|------|
| /æ/ | /ʌ/ | /ɒ/ |

Only if necessary, refer back to the phonemic symbols.

| | | | | |
|----|------|-------|---------------|-----|
| 1 | hot | hate | hit | |
| 2 | cup | cap | cop | |
| 3 | fill | file | full | |
| 4 | dawn | darn | den | |
| 5 | dirt | dart | debt | |
| 6 | food | fed | fade | |
| 7 | beer | boy | bow (tie a bow) | |
| 8 | tie | toy | tea | |
| 9 | kite | coat | Kate | |
| 10 | point | paint | pint | |
| 11 | hat | heart | hoot | hut |
| 12 | rest | roast | wrist | |
| 13 | horde | herd | hard | |
| 14 | sit | seat | sort | |
| 15 | poor | pear | pier | |

## Activity 5

a. ◀ Listen to the following words and then write the symbols for the vowels only:

| cat | seal | cool |
|-------|-------|------|
| share | hill | beer |
| walk | feel | bin |
| sank | fur | why |
| far | bird | shot |
| broad | shore | cut |
| send | few | pull |

b. Give the articulatory description (in terms of quality and duration) for each of the following vowel sounds:

e.g.          cat – /æ/     short, open, front, unrounded/neutral vowel

1. /uː/ in 'soon'
2. /ɪ/ in 'hill'
3. /ɒ/ in 'hot'
4. /ɜː/ in 'work'
5. /iː/ in 'feet'

## Activity 6

◄ Now listen to the following words and then write the symbols for each of the vowels:

| | | |
|---|---|---|
| window | roses | information |
| woman | apples | tower |
| women | usual | fire |
| gentlemen | secretary | idea |

## Activity 7

Now listen to the following words and then write the symbols for the diphthongs:

a. dive /aɪ /   e. pain /ɛɪ/
b. coin /ɔɪ/   f. near /ɪə/
c. hair /eə/   g. pure /ʊə/
d. now /aʊ/   h. home /əʊ/

# 6 Phonemes in Context

This chapter explores the concept of the phoneme: the smallest distinctive speech sound in a specific language; we consider how phonemes vary depending on their contextual environment and why this is important to pronunciation teaching.

## The phoneme

Natural speech is a continuous stream of sounds which we 'segment' into pieces and a **phoneme** is the smallest, linguistically meaningful segment of speech.

So, the words

```
m a n
p a n
```

can each be segmented into three sounds or phonemes and what distinguishes the meaning of one word from the other is the different initial phoneme /m/ or /b/. Both these phonemes have features in common, that is, they are both bilabial but /m/ is a bilabial nasal while /p/ is a bilabial plosive.

Phonemes are abstractions, they are not auditory realities. In the same way, the letters of the alphabet are representations, that is, just as we can write letter 'b' in various ways and it is still understood as representing a 'b'.

**b  B  Ƀ  ɓ  ƀ  *b***

We can say the sound 'a' in various ways in the same word and it is still understood as representing the phoneme /æ/, for example, stag. The different phonetic realizations of the phoneme are called **allophones**.

### Allophones

If we were to try to classify all the possible variations in an explanation of the sound system, the classification would become impractical. Languages tolerate a significant level of sound variation before comprehension is affected. Consider the variation that might occur in the pronunciation of the phoneme /r/.

Typically, in BBC English, this is pronounced as a post-alveolar approximant in words like 'three' or 'run'. However, there are considerable differences in the production of the /r/, depending on its position in words, that is, **positional variation**. For instance, the degree of lip rounding will vary depending on the following vowel (e.g. 'room' vs 'rim') and /r/ will be devoiced following a voiceless plosive (e.g. 'price', 'cream'). There is also considerable **regional variation** in the articulation of /r/ with many Scottish speakers producing a trill (a succession of taps by the tip of the tongue on the alveolar ridge) and some speakers (of rural North East England and Southern Scotland) producing a uvular sound similar to French /r/. Nevertheless, we typically tolerate such variations as representing the same sound. In other words, these different phonetic realizations are seen as allophones of the phoneme /r/.

Even apparently identical sounds may vary according to their position in a word or in a connected utterance as they are affected by the sounds that occur around them. This positional variation can be explored by comparing the /l/ sounds in

l̲ip   and   fil̲l̲

where the quality of the consonant is different. In the first word, the /l/ is made by the tip of the tongue touching the alveolar ridge but the back of the tongue is lowered. This is called clear 'l'. In the second case, alveolar contact is again made by the tip of the tongue but the back of the tongue is higher, raised towards the soft palate or velum. This is called dark 'l'. However, there is no meaningful difference in our understanding of the sound. There are no pairs of words where the only difference is dark or light 'l'. If someone used a dark 'l' in place of a clear 'l' the result might sound strange to our ears but we would still understand what was being said.

Similarly, levels of aspiration can be measured by placing a piece of paper in front of your mouth and saying

p̲ot
sp̲ot
top̲
top̲s

The movement of the paper should vary as each /p/ is released. In English, an initial /p/ will be aspirated while a medial or final /p/ will be relatively unaspirated. However, the difference between them is non-distinctive. As a result, /p/ is presented as one basic sound, a phoneme of English and the variations in its production are considered allophonic variations rather than as different phonemes.

When one allophone or variation of a phoneme occurs where another does not, it is said that the allophones are in **complementary distribution** – that is, there is a strict separation of where a particular variant can occur and one cannot replace the other. So, in English the clear 'l' allophone occurs before vowels (as in 'lift'), while dark 'l' occurs in other positions (as in 'fill'). Aspirated and unaspirated /p/ occur in different positions, not randomly.

When one allophone can be substituted for another without changing the meaning they are said to be in **free variation**, for example, /ɪ/ in 'di'vide' may be pronounced as a weak, lax vowel or as a strong, tense vowel. Similarly, as we have seen, /r/ in English may, for instance, be a voiced post-alveolar approximant or a voiced alveolar tap. The variations in the production of 'r' in English are not significant so they are said to be allophones and are not meaningful in any way.

## Assigning sounds to phonemes

So, the phoneme is recognized as the minimum distinctive unit of sound that we classify in the sound system but how do we establish the phonemes of English?

Traditionally, **minimal pair** contrasts have been used to justify the identification of a sound as a phoneme. If sounds occurring in identical environments produce a difference in meaning, for example:

'curl' vs 'girl' /k/ v /g/
'toy' vs 'tie' /ɔɪ/ v /aɪ/

those particular sounds are meaningful, that is, they are phonemes in that language. So, despite many similarities in the way they are made, /k/ and /g/ are considered distinctive in English. Similarly, /d/ and /t/, as in 'god' and 'got', are separate phonemes. The feature that distinguishes them is presence or absence of voicing.

Some contrasts are considered sufficient to distinguish phonemes, even though they are not found in exactly identical environments. These near-identical contrasts are accepted where there is an absence of minimal pairs. This type of contrast differentiates the sounds for instance in:

'remission' /ʃ/ and 'revision' /ʒ/

### Activity 1

Which of the following pairs of words are minimal pairs? If they are minimal pairs, which phonemes do they distinguish?

| chop | ship |
|------|------|
| right | rat |
| muggy | mucky |
| leisure | lesser |
| pool | pull |
| other | author |

There is a problem for the foreign language learner who will inevitably have a different range of phonemes and allophones in their own language. Allophones of English (e.g. aspirated /p/ and unaspirated /p/) may be separate phonemes in another language. For instance, a Spanish learner of English may not easily distinguish between /b/ and /v/ in English or between /d/ or /ð/ because in Spanish, these sounds do not distinguish meaning. They are in complementary distribution with /d/ occurring word initially and /ð/ medially, so for example, 'de nada' (don't mention it) is said as /de naða/. Similarly, we have seen that variants in the production of /r/ in English are allophonic that is, non-meaningul, however, in Spanish there are two variants (a rolled [r] and flapped [ɾ]), which distinguish words, as in 'perro' [pero] meaning 'dog' and 'pero' [peɾo] meanging 'but'.

# Distinctive features

The phonemes distinguished by minimal pairs like 'pat' vs 'bat' have both identical characteristics and differences. The sounds /p/, /b/, for example, parallel one another but stay apart due to a similar phonetic feature to that which distinguishes, that is, presence or lack of voice (+/- voice):

| /t/ | from | /d/ |
|-----|------|-----|
| /k/ | from | /g/ |
| /s/ | from | /z/ |

where a phonetic feature of this type operates to separate and identify a number of contrasting units of sound, we are said to be dealing with a **distinctive feature**. So, we can conclude that the feature of voice may be considered distinctive. In other languages, voice could be allophonic and therefore not distinctive, for example, in Tamil, a southern Indian language, changing from /p/ to /b/ does not result in a change in meaning (Cruttenden 2008:43).

All the allophones of a phoneme have the same distinctive features that distinguish it from all other phonemes, for example, /p/ may be aspirated, unaspirated, exploded in initial position, unexploded in final position but it is usually a voiceless, bilabial, plosive. As a result, we can say that /p/ is distinguished because it is:

> bilabial
> voiceless and
> plosive.

Its voiced counterpart /b/ is always:

> bilabial
> voiced and
> plosive

Similarly, we can say that /t/ is:

> alveolar
> voiceless and
> plosive

and /d/ is:

> alveolar
> voiced and
> plosive

and /k/ is:

> velar
> voiceless and
> plosive

This leads to the confirmation of three dimensions of distinctive features in English:

> voice vs unvoice
> oral vs nasal
> labial vs lingual (alveolar, labiodental, dental etc.)

For instance,

> /n/ is alveolar, voiced and nasal
> /ŋ/ is velar, voiced and nasal

This three-level set of descriptors is sufficient in English to give an accurate, distinctive classification of each consonant phoneme. Other languages may have more or fewer than three dimensions. For instance, in some languages of Northern parts of the Indian sub-continent, for example, Hindi, aspiration is distinctive while in English it only accounts for allophones of /p/ /t/ /k/. So, distinctive features in Hindi occur at four levels rather than three.

Distinctive feature analysis allows us to describe phonemes with regard to sets of characteristics or features rather than a simple binary opposition as we do with minimal pairs. It can therefore be useful for describing consonants. However, it is rarely applied to the description of vowels as the classification is much less straightforward and therefore less helpful.

# The role of phonemic distinctions

Some phonemic distinctions carry a greater burden in the language than others. This is referred to as their **functional load** and relates to the amount of work two phonemes do to distinguish word meaning (King 1967), in other words the frequency of occurrence of minimal pair contrasts. For instance, the /p/, /b/ distinction is used much more frequently than the /ʃ/ /ʒ/ contrast or /θ/ /ð/ contrast, where minimal pairs are almost non-existent ('thigh' vs 'thy', 'teeth' vs 'teethe', 'leash' vs 'liege').

Various ranking scales have been developed (see Catford 1987, Brown 1991). Ranking is based on the frequency of occurrence of minimal pairs and the stability of contrasts across regional varieties. For example, the /l/ /n/ distinction occurs frequently in both initial and final position in minimal pairs (e.g. 'light' vs 'night' and 'sill' vs 'sin') and is not subject to regional variation. This contrast would therefore be afforded a 'high' functional load. However, the /ð/ /d/ contrast distinguishes relatively few minimal pairs and does not occur in some regional accents (such as Dublin Irish). It would therefore be considered a 'low' functional load contrast.

However, it is difficult to determine which distinctions are most frequent in everyday English. Word counts are not necessarily representative. /ð/ might appear to be a fairly rare sound if you could count all English words. It does not occur in nearly as many words as /t/ and /d/, yet, it is one of the most frequently occurring sounds in function words such as *the*, *this*, *that*, *them*, *there*, *than*, *those*, *these*, *their*, *then*, *therefore*.

# Phonemic and phonetic transcription

If we want to represent speech sounds in writing we can transcribe the sounds using either:

(a) phonemic symbols / / (in slanted brackets)
(b) phonetic symbols [ ] (in square brackets)

**(a)** **phonemic symbols** represent the phonemes of English – for example /ʊ/. They are generalizations, not auditory realities. There are 44 phonemes in BBC English.
**(b)** **phonetic symbols** represent auditory realities and are not related to a specific language: they are international (**IPA** = International Phonetic Alphabet).

**Phonetic transcription** is much more precise than phonemic transcription. A **broad** phonetic transcription gives some more information than phonemic transcription and a **narrow** transcription gives much more information than phonemic transcription. Most of the transcriptions in this book use phonemic symbols as they represent the phonemes of English but occasionally, if we want to show more detail about contextual variations, we may use phonetic symbols as well (as in this chapter).

**Diacritics** are symbols used to add more, precise information to phonetic symbols, for example, the symbol [ ~ ] shows that a sound is nasalized.

Phonemic transcription does not represent precise phonetic qualities and therefore there are several possible symbols to represent one phoneme. Unfortunately, this means that different books on RP use different symbols. We will follow the IPA consonants and use length marks for vowels (as in Roach 2000, Wells 2008), that is, recognizing qualitative and quantitative differences.

# Context effects on consonants

Like vowels, consonant phonemes vary either due to contextual distribution or accent differences. The contexts in which phonemes occur are termed (a) **initial** (b) **medial** and (c) **final**. Each consonant has a pattern of distribution or occurrence which may include all or some of these positions:

|  |  | Initial | Medial | Final |
|---|---|---|---|---|
| e.g. | /g/ velar plosive | got | jogging | jog |
|  | /n/ alveolar  nasal | net | sinner | sin |

Most consonants have positional variants but the variation is often slight and not considered significant phonologically, therefore such variants are classed as allophonic variants rather than different phonemes. We will consider some of the most common contextual effects here.

## Positional effects on plosives

In initial stressed position, voiceless plosives (/p/,/t/,/k/) are generally strongly **aspirated** (aspiration is marked by the diacritic [ʰ]):

e.g.  pʰ in      [pʰ ɪn]
      pʰ an      [pʰ æn]
      pʰ ot      [pʰ ɒt]

However, /p/ /t/ and /k/ preceded by /s/, that is, in initial consonant clusters, are **unaspirated**:

e.g.  spin [spɪn]
      span [spæn]
      spot [spɒt]

After /s/ voiceless plosives have a very similar sound quality to /b/ /d/ and /g/. In initial position, the distinction between /p/, /t/ and /k/ and /b/, /d/ and /g/ is largely due to aspiration rather than voicing.

We can test for aspiration by holding a piece of paper in front of the mouth and saying 'pin, pan, pot'. The paper should move noticeably. If we then say 'spin, span, spot', the paper should move less or not at all.

Also, in final position, voiceless plosives are regularly unexploded, or only partly exploded. As a result, the release stage may be inaudible in distinctions like:

rip vs rib   writ vs rid;   rick vs rig

This lack of release is marked by the diacritic [ˀ]:

e.g.  cut     [kʌtˀ]
      kit     [kɪtˀ]

---

## Activity 2

◄ Listen and see if you notice any difference in the articulation of the /k/ sound in these words. Try holding the palm of your hand in front of your mouth when you say them.

a. <u>k</u>it
b. s<u>k</u>ip
c. ti<u>ck</u>
d. so<u>ck</u>s

---

This lack of audible release can also occur in plosive clusters, such as:

ba<u>gp</u>ipe; sui<u>tc</u>ase; co<u>ckp</u>it; rece<u>pt</u>ive; fa<u>ct</u>or; tra<u>ct</u>or; produ<u>ct</u>ive

If the first consonant in the cluster involves the same point of articulation as the second (i.e. it is homorganic), we get an **overlapping stop**, that is, the first plosive is unexploded as the second begins before plosion can occur in the first.

These homorganic plosive sequences tend to occur across word boundaries as in:

cu<u>t d</u>own, thi<u>ck g</u>lue, pu<u>b b</u>eer, col<u>d t</u>ea

but they are also found within words as in:

bac<u>kg</u>round, bac<u>kg</u>ammon

This can confuse some learners if their first language explodes all plosives whatever their position. It also means it is difficult to hear the difference between phrases such as 'dropped back' and 'drop back' as it is typically only the last plosive in the cluster which is audibly released (drɒpˀ <u>b</u>æk).

---

## Activity 3

◄ Listen and underline the consonant that has no audible release in these words.

fitness; midday; tractor; picnic, hot dog

### Activity 3—Cont'd

◀ Listen and practice saying the following phrases. The main difference between them is that the three consonant cluster is longer than the two consonant cluster:

| Column 1 | | Column 2 | |
|---|---|---|---|
| looked back | lʊkt˺ bæk | look back | lʊk bæk |
| liked this | laɪkt˺ ðɪs | like this | laɪk ðɪs |
| gripped both | grɪpt˺ bəʊθ | grip both | grɪp bəʊθ |
| wiped clean | waɪpt˺ kliːn | wiped clean | waɪp kliːn |
| packed them | pækt˺ ðəm | pack them | pæk ðəm |

Sometimes the voiceless final plosive is replaced entirely by a **glottal stop** [ʔ]:

e.g. 'cut' [kʌʔ]
'kit' [kɪʔ]

A glottal stop is a plosive where the obstruction of the airflow is caused by closing the vocal cords. Glottal stops are found in many accents of English. This addition of a glottal stop is referred to as **glottalization**. In some accents, the glottal stop actually replaces the voiceless alveolar plosive [t] when it follows a stressed vowel:

e.g. witness ['wɪʔnəs]    sit down [sɪʔ daʊn]

Similarly, many accents of English replace [t] with [ʔ] when it precedes a weak syllable with a final [l] or [n].

e.g. bottle [bɒʔl] and kitten [kɪʔn]

Such glottal replacement also effects a small group of frequently used words, such as 'get, it, that, got, not, quite, right'. Again, this can confuse learners who are expecting to hear clear final consonants.

### Activity 4

◀ Underline the position of potential glottal stops in the following phrases. Then listen to the examples:

1. Got that?
2. Are you quite sure?
3. He's a fitness instructor.
4. Where's the kitten gone?

# Vowel shortening

In final position, the distinction between /p/ /t/ /k/ and /b/ /d/ /g/ is largely that vowels preceding the voiceless plosives /p/, /t/ and /k/ are much shorter than those preceding the voiced plosives /b/, /d/ and /g/.

| e.g. | shorter vowel | longer vowel |
|------|---------------|--------------|
|      | lap           | lab          |
|      | wrote         | road         |
|      | rack          | rag          |

Vowels traditionally labelled 'long' (e.g. /iː/ and 'short') (e.g. /ɪ/) can vary in length in this way. Vowels also have full length at the end of a word:

| shorter vowel | longer vowel | longer vowel |
|---------------|--------------|--------------|
| wrote         | road         | row          |
| wheat         | weed         | we           |

---

### Activity 5

◀ Listen and underline the longer vowels in these sets of words. Then practice saying them making a clear distinction in vowel length where necessary:

| shorter vowel | longer vowel | longer vowel |
|---------------|--------------|--------------|
| neat          | knee         | need         |
| wheat         | we           | weed         |
| light         | lie          | lied         |
| piece         | pea          | peas         |
| safe          | say          | save         |

---

Vowel shortening also occurs before mid word voiceless plosives /p/, /t/, /k/, as in:

| shorter vowel | longer vowel |
|---------------|--------------|
| whiter        | wider        |
| mucky         | muggy        |

It also occurs before voiceless fricatives /s/ /ʃ/ and affricates /tʃ/, as in:

| fussy | fuzzy |
|-------|-------|
| watch | wadge |
| lacy  | lazy  |

So, vowels tend to be shorter before voiceless final consonants and longer before voiced final consonants or at the end of words.

---

### Activity 6

Try to summarize how the following sets of plosives are distinguished in:

    (i)  p̱ig vs ḇig (initial position)
    (ii)  beṯṯing vs beḏḏing (intervocalic position)
    (iii)  bac̱k vs ba̱g (final position)

---

## Other context effects

Another common effect of context on consonants is **dentalization** of alveolar consonants, particularly /t/ /d/ and /n/ when they occur before interdental fricatives /θ/ and /ð/. The diacritic used to show dentalization is [ ̪ ]:

    e.g.  tenth      [ten̪θ]
          width     [wɪd̪θ] or [wɪd̪ð]

Similarly, /p/ /b/ are generally bilabial, but are labio-dental when they precede /f/ /v/ as in:

obverse
obvious
obviate
a cup full of coffee
on the top floor

Dentalization is an example of **fronting**, that is, place of articulation moving further forward or front in the oral cavity due to co-articulation. When sounds are co-articulated they become more like each other, that is, they become **assimilated**. It is common for a sound to become partially or fully assimilated to an adjacent sound, either in terms of place or manner of articulation. For instance, in 'sand' and 'sang' the vowel /æ/ becomes nasalized in anticipation of the following nasal consonants /n/ and /ŋ/. This is known as **anticipatory co-articulation** and is the commonest context effect in English.

Another example of co-articulation is the replacement of alveolar plosives /t/ and /d/ in medial position that is, within a word, preceding an unstressed syllable, for example, 'later'. Many, particularly American, speakers of English pronounce the /t/ or /d/ as a **flap** sound in which the tip of the tongue rapidly flaps against the alveolar ridge as it passes to the place of articulation of the next sound. A flap is transcribed as [ɾ]:

    e.g.  later      leɪɾə
          ladder    læɾə
          butter    bʌɾə

As we saw earlier, another example of allophonic variation is the production of /l/.

Dark and clear /l/ are in complementary distribution, that is, they are used in specific positional contexts and are not interchangeable. A clear /l/ is found before vowels while a dark 'l' shown by adding the diacritic [ ˟ ] to the /l/, producing [ɫ], is heard before consonants or before a pause;

e.g. *clear /l/*        *dark /l/*
    lea   [li:]       eels  [i:ɫ z]
    light  [lɑɪt]    bell  [beɫ]
    hello [heləʊ]   held  [heɫd]

---

### Activity 7

Underline the dark 'l's in this phrase. Then try saying it first with only 'light /l/s' and then only with 'dark /l/s'.

    'Bill heard the loud bell just as light fell.'

---

For some speakers, particularly speakers of East London or Cockney accents, /l/ loses its consonantal articulation completely and becomes a back vowel like /ʊ/ where velar /l/ would normally occur for other speakers:

e.g. help [help] becomes [heʊp]

/l/ can also, like /n/, become syllabic, that is, occur in weak syllables without a vowel:

e.g. table     [teɪbɫ]
     bottle    [bɒtɫ]  or  [bɒʔɫ]

The approximants /r/ /j/ and /w/ also have allophonic variants. As we have seen, the post-alveolar approximant /r/ has many variants depending on accent and distribution. In BBC English, the /r/ phoneme is only pronounced preceding a vowel:

e.g. red    arrive  hearing

and not after a vowel that is, there is no post-vocalic /r/. RP is a **non-rhotic** accent while many other accents, including General American, Canadian, Scottish, Irish and many accents of the west of England are **rhotic** accent:

### Activity 8

◀ Listen and practice saying these words in BBC English, taking note of whether the /r/ is pronounced or not:

| 1 | 2 | 3 |
|---|---|---|
| rare | rarely | rarer |
| ear | earplug | earring |
| tear | terror | terrorist |
| fear | fearful | fearing |
| snore | snored | snoring |

# Context effects on vowels

## Co-articulation

A sound, either a consonant or a vowel, said in isolation can be pronounced very differently in a stream of connected speech. We have already seen how some sounds can change because they **assimilate** some feature or features of a neighbouring sound. This blending of one sound with an adjacent one is called **co-articulation.**

e.g. sat   man

The phoneme /æ/ is the same in both words, but there is allophonic variation because the /æ/ in 'man' is slightly different from the /æ/ in 'sat'. /æ/ is normally pronounced with the soft palate raised to prevent air escaping through the nose. However in 'man' both the surrounding consonants are nasals, produced with the soft palate lowered. The soft palate cannot be raised very quickly, so it is likely that the vowel will be produced with the palate still partially lowered, giving it a nasal quality that is, **nasalized.** The diacritic used to show nasalization is [˜].

Vowels can also be influenced by surrounding sounds in other ways: they may be fronted, backed, raised or lowered. For instance, In BBC English, there would be little allophonic variation between the /e/ vowels in 'bet' and 'get', but in American English the /e/ in 'get' would be backed towards the hard palate (i.e. **palatalized**) because it follows a velar (back) plosive /g/.

## Vowel reduction

Vowels can also be subject to contextual effects when the vowel is **reduced** in some way. Vowel reduction occurs in unstressed or unaccented syllables.

In English, syllables can be **strong or weak** (we will come back to the distribution of strong and weak syllables later); vowels in strong syllables are **full** and vowels in weak syllables are **reduced.** Reduced vowels occur in unstressed, weak syllables.

Strong syllables will have any of the vowel phonemes except /ə/ as its nucleus. However, weak syllables can only have four types of nucleus or peak:

(i)   vowel /ə/ (schwa)
(ii)  a close front unrounded vowel between /iː/ and /ɪ/
(iii) a close back rounded vowel between /uː/ and /ʊ/
(iv)  a syllabic consonant

Generally, reduced vowels in weak syllables tend to be shorter, lower intensity and a different quality to full vowels:

e.g.  father      /fɑːðə/

The reduced vowel in the second syllable is shorter and softer than the first, full vowel. Similarly in:

e.g.  banana /bənɑːnə/

there are three 'a's, but only the second is a full vowel, the other two are reduced to schwa.

---

## Activity 9

◀ Listen and underline <u>schwa</u> in the following polysyllabic words:

| traitor | danger   | character | tomorrow |            |
|---------|----------|-----------|----------|------------|
| forget  | accurate | alone     | organize | appearance |

---

**Schwa** is the most frequently occurring vowel in English and its frequency increases in rapid casual speech. In quality, the schwa is **mid** (i.e. half way between close and open), **central** (i.e. half way between front and back) and **lax** (i.e. not articulated with much energy).

Two other vowels are commonly found in weak syllables: one close front and one close back. The close front vowel is somewhere between /iː/ and /ɪ/ and can be transcribed as [i] (i.e. like i: without the dots). This is the sound found in the weak syllable in words like:

happy        /hæpi̠/
easy         /iːzi̠/

The close back vowel is somewhere between /uː/ and /ʊ/ and can be transcribed as [u] (i.e. like u: without the dots) This is the sound found in the weak syllable in words like:

evacuation      /ivækju̠eɪʃən/
you     /ju̠/      - in an unstressed position

---

### Activity 10

Mark any occurrences of weak vowels other than schwa in these words:

many, funny, actually, misery, usual, poverty

---

In some cases, vowel reduction is taken to its extreme and the vowel actually disappears or is elided. This can be called **vowel elision**. There are two possible results. First, the vowel in a weak syllable disappears completely and is not replaced.

e.g. perhaps /præps/
usually /juːʒəli/

Elision of vowels usually happens when a short, unstressed vowel occurs between voiceless consonants, for example, bicycle, philosophy.

As we saw earlier in this chapter, sometimes, the vowel elision is replaced by a **syllabic consonant**:

e.g. sudden ˈsʌdn̩
awful ˈɔːf l̩

Elision often occurs with a vowel between one consonant and a final sonorant consonant (e.g. nasals and laterals).

## Phonemes and pronunciation change

As we know, languages are dynamic and constantly changing and evolving, whether we like the fact or not. This is true of pronunciation as much as grammar and vocabulary. Indeed, the pronunciation of Elizabethan or Chaucerian or Old English would have been far removed from modern English. For instance, London speech did not adopt the 'non-rhotic /r/' until the eighteenth century and this has since passed down into current RP. Also, many of RP's diphthongs were pure or 'steady state' vowels before what is known as the 'Great Vowel Shift' in the fourteenth century.

Currently, pronunciation change is still ongoing as evidenced by the spread of the post-vocalic glottal stop and the introduction of a dark 'l' following back vowels, both of which have been attributed to London influences.

Another ongoing phonemic change is the gradual loss of the centring diphthongs [ɪə] [eə] and [ʊə]. As we saw in Chapter 5, the [eə] diphthong traditionally in words like 'square' is now often realized as a long pure vowel [e:], as in 'there'. Similarly, the [ʊə] diphthong is increasingly pronounced as a single long vowel [ɔ:] in words such as 'sure' so there is no distinction in RP between 'sure' and 'shore'. Finally, the diphthong [ɪə] tends to be replaced by a long vowel [ɪ:] in words like 'really' [rɪ:li].

# Teaching implications

## Learner difficulties

Learners of English may have difficulties with:

(a) phonemes that do not exist in their L1 (e.g. /ɪ/ as in 'sit' does not exist in Italian) and

(b) with phonemes that are similar in the two languages but not exactly the same (e.g. the vowels in English 'two' /tu:/ and French 'tu' [ty] are similar but not the same) and

(c) with sounds that exist in the L1 but as variants of one phoneme rather than as separate phonemes (e.g. the consonants /s/ and /ʃ/ as in 'same' and 'shame' may not be distinguishable to a Greek L1 speaker).

## (a) Phonemes which do not occur in L1

If a sound does not exist in the L1, learners may substitute the 'nearest' phonemic equivalent from L1:

| e.g. /f/ or /w/ instead of /v/ | e.g. 'in<u>v</u>ite' |
| /t / or /f/ instead of /θ/ | e.g. '<u>th</u>ick' |
| /d/ or /v/ instead of /ð/ | e.g. '<u>th</u>is' |
| /s/ instead of /ʃ/ or /ʒ/ | e.g. 'televi<u>s</u>ion' |
| /l/ instead of /r/ | e.g. '<u>r</u>ide' ( in initial position) |
| /i:/ instead of /ɪ/ | e.g. 'sh<u>i</u>p' |

## (b) Phonemes which are similar in L1 and English

For instance, the plosives /p//t//k/ and /b//d//g/ may be similar in the L1 but learners may tend to lose the voice/voiceless contrast in English. Similarly the voicing distinction between affricates

/dʒ/ as in 'judge' and /tʃ/ as in 'church' may be lost

## (c) Sounds which are variants rather than distinct phonemes

In the L1 some phonemes which are distinct in English such as /r/ and /l/ or /l/ and /n/ may be in free variation, that is, they are interchangeable, so learners may substitute one for the other: for example, 'light' vs 'right'.

Native speakers are usually unaware of positional variants in phonemes in their own language. For instance, aspirated and unaspirated /t/ are positional variants in English while in Vietnamese they are contrasting sounds. Similarly /d/ and /ð/ are contrasting sounds in English but positional variants in Spanish. Therefore, teachers need to ensure that learners practise producing sounds in all positions.

The allophonic or regional variation in English consonant phonemes is relatively slight, therefore tolerance of mispronunciation (in stressed syllables) may be quite low. On the other hand, there is considerable allophonic variation in English vowels and consequently we could conclude that listeners would be more tolerant of such variation.

## Allophonic variants and the Lingua Franca Core

The allophonic variants of /l/, that is, its 'clear' (pre-consonantal) and 'dark' (post-consonantal or word final) variants are the second consonant pair (after /ð/ and /θ/) that are considered unnecessary in the Lingua Franca Core. The reasons being (a) that the lack of distinction does not cause intelligibility problems in the EIL research data and (b) that the dark /l/ is hard for L2 learners to acquire if it does not exist in their L1 and (c) that dark /l/ is in a process of change and is very variable across many British English varieties. In particular, it is becoming increasingly vocalic and lip-rounded, so that 'bill' is frequently pronounced as [bɪʊ] rather than [bɪɫ] I in many informal speech varieties.

For the sake of ease of learning, Jenkins (2000) advises the use of the rhotic rather than the non-rhotic variety where /r/ is omitted post-vocalically, for example, 'work' [wɜːrk] four [fɔːr]. In contrast, she suggests using the RP versions of /t/. Again, the argument is ease of teaching and learning as the RP /t/ is constant across contexts (apart from word initial aspiration) unlike in General American where, as we saw earlier, /t/ intervocalically is generally pronounced as a voiced flap (e.g. butter – bʌɾə).

The allophonic variants of /p/ /t/ and /k/ are considered important for L2 learners to master as the aspiration of the initial voiceless plosives is important to distinguish these sounds from the voiced counterparts /b/, /d/ and /g/. For instance, in 'bad vs pad', 'din vs tin' and 'got' vs 'cot'.

L2 learners cannot rely on the 'long vs short' distinction of vowels such as /ɪ/ and /iː/. For instance, in 'seat' /siːt/ and 'sieve' /sɪv/, the 'short' vowel /ɪ/ in 'sieve' may be phonetically as long as the 'long' vowel /iː/ in 'seat'. The contrast is more related to the greater effort or muscular activity in producing tense vowels like /iː/ rather than lax vowels like /ɪ/.

It is also important for L2 learners to understand that a final voiced consonant will lengthen the preceding vowel. For instance, 'eyes' /aɪz/ has a longer vowel than 'ice' /aɪs/ and 'seed' /siːd/ has a longer vowel than 'seat' /siːt/. Jenkins claims that lack of this distinction causes intelligibility problems in her EIL data (2000) and is not something that learners will pick up automatically.

As well as considering what sounds learners have difficulties with, there are other criteria for prioritizing which sounds to focus on, for instance '**functional load**' (i.e. how significant the sound is in the language in distinguishing meaning and 'return on investment') (i.e. how much effort is involved in teaching/learning the sound in relation to how much improvement will be gained in fluency and intelligibility (see Chapter 13 for more on this)).

## Functional load

We have seen that some phonemic distinctions carry a greater load in the language than others and that *Functional Load* can provide a theoretical framework for prioritizing segmental errors. It can be used to prioritize the teaching of phoneme contrasts according to their importance in English pronunciation. Furthermore, it appears that high functional load errors have the greatest impact on listeners' perceptions of accentedness and comprehensibility of L2 speech (Derwing and Munro 2005). Consequently, functional load could well be a useful tool to help select segmental teaching priorities (again see Chapter 13 for more on this).

For instance, the /p/, /b/ distinction is called upon much more than /θ/ and /ð/. As a result, teachers may focus more time on phonemes carrying higher phonemic burdens, for instance:

| | | |
|---|---|---|
| /p/ | vs | /b/ |
| /t/ | vs | /d/ |
| /s/ | vs | /z/ |
| /k/ | vs | /g/ |

However, it is difficult to determine which distinctions are most frequent in everyday English and as we have seen with the /θ/ /ð/ distinction, word counts are not necessarily representative.

---

### Activity 11

What does this mean for learners who do not have /θð/ in their first language (e.g. speakers of French, speakers of Italian)? How important is it that they achieve a reasonable approximation, given the frequency of the sound? Or, as Jenkins (2000) argues, are the /θ/ /ð/ phonemes unimportant particularly in EIL contexts? What are your views on this?

---

## Distinctive feature analysis

Distinctive feature analysis is an alternative approach to learning consonant (and vowel) phonemes based on the principle that phonemes should be seen, not as independent units but as combinations of different features. Distinctive feature analysis may be useful for language learning and teaching as pronunciation difficulties could be seen as due to the need to learn a specific feature (e.g. voicing or aspiration) or combination of features (e.g. voicing and vowel length) rather than the absence of a particular phoneme.

In a study of EFL pronunciation errors (Leahy 1980) it was found that the two main types of errors were based on voicing ('Sue', 'zoo') and continuant vs stop ('faith', 'fate'). In voicing errors, the problem with stop sounds was found mainly in final position ('cap', 'cab') and was directly related to the length of the preceding vowel. The voicing errors with continuants occurred in all positions, not just finally ('sink'/'zinc', 'bus'/'buzz', 'surface'/'service'). A distinctive feature approach has been used in some pronunciation textbooks (see Rogerson and Gilbert 1990).

## Key points

- Shorten vowels before a final voiceless plosive, fricative or affricate (e.g. /p/ /t/ /k/ /s/, /f/ /ʃ/ /tʃ/).
- Maintain vowel length before a voiced plosive, fricative or affricate (e.g. /b/ /d/ /g/ /v/ /z/ ʒ/ /dʒ/).
- /ð/ /θ/ may be non essential, at least in EIL contexts and could be replaced by /f/ /v/ or /t/ /d/.
- Dental allophones [t̪] [d̪] are acceptable.
- Aspiration of word initial voiceless plosives /p/ /t/ and /k/ is essential to distinguish them from /b/ /d/ and /g/.
- Acquisition of dark [ɫ] in post vocalic position is non essential and can be substituted for clear /l/ or /ʊ/ (as in some native UK accents).
- Dropping of post-vocalic /r/ (non-rhotic 'r') is non essential and can lead to sound/spelling confusions.
- Reducing vowel length in weak forms may be more important than use of schwa.

## Further reading

Brown, A. (1988) 'Functional load and the teaching of pronunciation', *TESOL Quarterly*, 22, 593–606.

Brown, A. (1995) 'Minimal pairs: minimal importance?', *ELT Journal*, 49 (2), 169–175.

Collins, B. and Meys, I. M. (2003) *Practical Phonetics and Phonology*. Sections A2 and B1. London: Routledge.

Garilanes, T. C. (1991) '"-ed": an extra syllable or not?', *Modern English Teacher*, 17 (3&4), 32–3.

Gill, S. (1997) 'Vite volves and wegetarian wampires', *Modern English Teacher*, 6 (3), 45–6.

James, P. (1991) 'Sounds useful: helping learners with pronunciation', in Brown, A. (ed.) *Teaching English Pronunciation: A Book of Readings*. Routledge, London, pp. 323–332.

Piechurska, E. (1996) 'Homophone dominoes', *English Teaching Forum*, 34 (1), 38–9.

Roach, P. (2000) *English Phonetics and Phonology*, 3rd edition. Chapters 5, 6, and 7. Cambridge: Cambridge University Press.

Rogerson, P. and Gilbert, G. (1990) *Speaking Clearly*. Chapters 23 and 24. Cambridge: Cambridge University Press.

Swan, M. and Smith, B. (1987) *Learner English: A Teacher's Guide to Interference and Other Problems*. Cambridge: Cambridge University Press.

Taylor, D. S. (1995) 'Vowels, consonants and syllables in English: An English teaching perspective', *IRAL*, 33 (1), 1–8.

Willis, K. (1993) 'A "new look" phonemic chart', *Professional English Teacher*, 13 (3) 35–6.

# Phoneme practice activities

## Activity 1

Try to read aloud the following and then write the words out:

| (a) biːn | (b) fɪl | (c) kæʃ | (d) ʃuːt |
|---|---|---|---|
| mes | puːl | θɪŋ | dʒæm |
| fʊl | bɜːd | ð en | hʌŋ |
| fæt | haːm | jɒt | ʃiːp |
| mʌtʃ | kɒt | tʃʌk | dʒuːn |

| (e) dʒəʊk | (f) maʊθ | (g) baɪk | (h) əraɪvd |
|---|---|---|---|
| weə | ʃeɪk | peɪs | əlaʊd |
| saɪz | fɪəs | feə | praɪvɪt |
| bɔɪl | ʃʊə | vɔɪs | kaːvɪŋz |
| wɪəd | tʃəʊk | ʃəʊldə | mɔːnɪŋ |

| (i) dʒəʊkɪŋ | (j) fɒrəst |
|---|---|
| ˈwɪʃʊl | ʃæləʊ |
| wʊlən | maʊntɪn |
| iːzi | finɪʃt |
| daːbi | fəgɒt |

## Activity 2

◀ Listen and underline the correct transcription for the following:

| | (i) | (ii) | (iii) |
|---|---|---|---|
| (a) fox | /fɒx/ | /fɒks/ | /fɔːks/ |
| (b) June | /ˈduːn/ | /ˈdʒuːn/ | /ˈdʒʌn/ |
| (c) double | /ˈdʌbl/ | /ˈdʊbel/ | /ˈduːbl/ |
| (d) idea | /ɪˈdɪə/ | /aɪˈdɪə/ | /aɪˈdɪɑ/ |
| (e) only | /ˈonliː/ | /ˈaʊnliː/ | /ˈəʊnli/ |
| (f) alarm | /əˈlaːm/ | /ɑˈ laːm/ | /æˈlaːm/ |
| (g) menu | /ˈmenuː/ | /ˈmenjuː/ | /ˈmenʊ/ |
| (h) message | /ˈmesædʒ/ | /ˈmesedʒ/ | /ˈmesɪdʒ/ |

## Activity 3

◀ Listen and transcribe the following into phonemic script (BCC English or your own variety if you prefer):

| | | | |
|---|---|---|---|
| (a) cab | (b) feel | (c) laugh | (d) catch |
| (e) voice | (f) fair | (g) harm | (h) chuck |
| (i) full | (j) then | (k) hung | (l) shoot |
| (m) bird | (n) news | (o) music | (p) dish |
| (q) queue | (r) join | | |

## Activity 4

◀ Listen and Identify the vowel sounds occurring in the following words and write the phonemic symbol, for example:

|    | sack | suck | sock | |
|----|------|------|------|---|
|    | /æ/  | /ʊ/  | /ɒ/  | |
| 1  | hot   | hate  | hit   | |
| 2  | cup   | cap   | cop   | |
| 3  | fill  | file  | full  | |
| 4  | dawn  | darn  | den   | |
| 5  | dirt  | dart  | debt  | |
| 6  | food  | fed   | fade  | |
| 7  | beer  | boy   | bow (tie a bow) | |
| 8  | tie   | toy   | tea   | |
| 9  | kite  | coat  | Kate  | |
| 10 | point | paint | pint  | |
| 11 | hat   | heart | hoot  | hut |
| 12 | rest  | roast | wrist | |
| 13 | horde | herd  | hard  | |
| 14 | sit   | seat  | sort  | |
| 15 | poor  | pear  | pier  | |

## Activity 5

◀ Listen and transcribe the following:

1. She ran to the station
2. What should she do now?
3. Can you give them a lift?
4. Please look straight ahead.
5. Tell me when you've finished.

# The Syllable  7

## The nature of the syllable

Many pronunciation problems result not only from differences in individual sounds between a leaner's L1 and the target language but also because of differences in how sounds are structured into syllables and words. Up to now our consideration of English phonology has looked at these individual sound segments or phonemes. However, there are units above the level of the phoneme which are phonologically significant. In this chapter we will look at a larger unit, the **syllable** which many would argue is of central importance to phonology and pronunciation. In particular, the syllable is an important bridge between individual sounds, word stress, rhythm and intonation, that is, between segmental and suprasegmental aspects of pronunciation. Many pronunciation problems can result from differences between a learner's own L1 syllable system and the wide variety of syllable types in English. An understanding of English syllable structure and how it compares with other languages can help teachers deal with some of these pronunciation difficulties.

Syllables are claimed to be the most basic unit in speech: every language has syllables, and babies learn to produce syllables before they can say a word of their native language. While native speakers often disagree about the number of syllables in a word or utterance (Roach, 1991:67), there is evidence from first language acquisition studies that infants perceive and segment syllable-length units of speech rather than individual phonemes (Garton 1992:60). Also, when a person has a speech disorder their speech will usually still show syllabic organization.

Even if people cannot define what a syllable is, they can usually count the number of syllables in a word, usually tapping or marking the syllables on their fingers at the same time, showing the importance of syllables to rhythm in speech. Syllables may be used to assist with the teaching of language and when teaching literature (particularly poetry) it is an important concept. Many learners will have been introduced to the concept at primary school level. In addition, if infants find the syllable useful as an aid to speech perception (Garton 1992) then it is possible that language learners rely on syllabic segmentation to assist their learning of a second language.

As with vowels and consonants, syllables can be described both phonetically and phonologically:

(a) *phonetically* – syllables are usually described as consisting of an alternation between vowel-like and consonant-like states, that is, moving from a centre which has little or no obstruction to the airflow and which sounds relatively loud to the beginning and end of syllables where there is greater obstruction to airflow and/or less loudness. So, from a speech production point of view, a syllable like 'ban' consists of a movement from a constricted or silent state to a vowel-like state and then back to a constricted or silent state again. Various theories have been proposed to account for syllables phonetically. 'Prominence Theory', for example, describes the centres of syllables are equivalent to prominence peaks, so the number of syllables are equal to the number of peaks. Syllable boundaries occur at points of weak prominence (valleys). The vast majority of words seem to be adequately explained by this theory, for example:

> visited (3)
> simplify (3)
> understand (3)

'Chest Pulse' theory relates the number of syllables to the number of chest pulses, accompanied by an increase of air pressure. However, this theory does not account for words with double vowels such as 'being' or 'saying' which would mistakenly be classed as single syllables. A third theory, 'Sonority theory', in a way combines both of the other two approaches, suggesting that the nucleus of a syllable corresponds to a peak in pulmonic activity which is represented by its '***sonority***' that is, 'the relative loudness of speech sound compared to other sounds' (Giegerich 1992:132). The idea is that sounds vary in their carrying power with open vowels being the most sonorous, as shown in Figure 7.1.

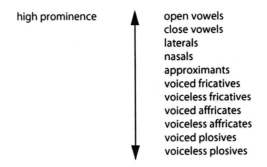

**Figure 7.1** Degrees of sonority (adapted from Cruttenden 1994:49)

In any utterance, it is believed that there are peaks of prominence that determine the number of syllables. In a word like sonority, the peaks occur in the following way:

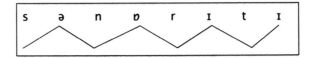

However, one of the difficulties with such phonetic descriptions, is deciding where to put the division between syllables and none of these theories help much in discussions of **syllable division**:

e.g. extra    /ekstrə/

Most people would feel the word has two syllables, but the syllable division could be:

e + kstrə   ek+strə   eks+trə   ekst+ r ə   or   ekstr +ə

Usually the second or third possibilities are chosen but there is no 'correct' choice.

---

### Activity 1

◀ Listen and transcribe the following words. How many syllables are there in each case?

(a) character       (b) library
(c) oasis           (d) sextant
(e) beautifully     (f) plain
(g) ordinary        (h) behaviour
(i) sudden          (j) little

---

(b) *phonologically* – looking at syllables phonologically involves considering their structure in linguistic terms that are language specific rather than universal (phonetic), which we will do below.

# The structure of the syllable

Most languages have syllables composed of a consonant plus a vowel (C + V). The words 'see' /siː/ and 'saw' /sɔː/ have a two phoneme (CV) syllable structure. This is commonly referred to as an **open syllable** because it ends in a vowel, while a syllable which is closed by a final consonant such as 'seen' /siːn/, which has three phonemes (CVC), is called a **closed syllable**. All languages have CV-type open syllables. Most European languages can have both open and closed syllables but some languages, like Japanese have only open syllables. For instance, 'ha' (CV) means 'tooth' and 'naka' (CVCV) means 'centre'. Other languages, such as Italian, rarely have consonants in syllable-final position, or only allow certain consonants in final position. English is marked in this respect with its common CVC syllable structure (e.g. 'set' /set/, 'sought' /sɔːt/, 'these' /ðiːz/) and in having many complex consonant clusters.

In some languages, the use of closed syllables is much more restricted. For example, in Cantonese and Vietnamese, only nasals (/n/ /m/ and /ŋ/) and voiceless plosives (/p/ /t/ and /k/) are possible in consonant final position. So a word like 'bad' with a voiced plosive in final position might be hard for such learners to pronounce and they might substitute a voiceless /t/ for the /d/, producing what sounds like 'bat'.

Many languages have fewer variations in syllable structure than English. For example, Japanese which has a much smaller range of possibilities at syllable level, with a maximum CVC structure compared to the English CCCVCCCC.

In English, the possibilities are great with the following very common:

| Word | Transcription | Syllable type |
|------|--------------|---------------|
| I, eye | /aɪ/ | V |
| sigh | /saɪ/ | CV |
| eyes | /aɪz/ | VC |
| size | /saɪz/ | CVC |
| spite | /spaɪt/ | CCVC |
| rights | /raɪts/ | CVCC |
| spliced | splaɪst | CCCVCC |

So, the word 'oasis' has three syllables o/a/sis with the structures V/V/CVC/. 'Ambassador' /æmˈbæsədə/ has four syllables along the pattern VC/CVC/V/CV. Of course, 'ambassador' could be analysed in a slightly different way: VC/CVC/VC/V depending on whether /ə/ or /əd/ is taken as the dividing point in the middle.

The study of sequences of phonemes is called **phonotactics**. Every language has phonotactic rules, that is, restrictions on which phonemes can go together at the beginning, middle or end of syllables and native speakers know these rules subconsciously. For instance, the combination:

mwankw

would not be considered acceptable as a syllable in English, because English syllables do not have mw or kw as consonant clusters (although phonologically /kw/ is possible, spelling rules would represent this as 'qu', as in queen. However, in the sentence:

'Their strengths triumphed frequently' if represented as a phonemic string, would be:

ðeəstreŋθstraɪjəmftfriːkwəntli

with some very 'unEnglish' looking sequences of consonants, such as /əmftfr/ and /ŋstraɪj/ but, knowing what we know of English phontactics, we can split these clusters into one part that belongs to the end of one syllable and one part that belongs to the beginning of another. So the first group can only be divided /streŋθs/, /streŋθ/ or /traɪjəmft/.

Syllables in English can vary considerably in length and the word 'strengths' is an example of one of the longest possible syllable combinations. Phonologically, the structure of a syllable can consist of three parts, the initial consonant in a syllable is called the **onset**, the middle is called the **peak** (normally a vowel) and final consonant is the **coda** (which is optional). The combination of peak and coda is called the **rhyme** (Figure 7.2). For example, in 'run':

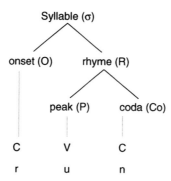

**Figure 7.2** Syllable structure

the rhyme is 'un', so in rhyming verse, the word could be rhymed with, for example, 'fun', 'bun'.

A minimum syllable can be as short as one vowel, that is, a peak:

e.g. I     /aɪ/
     oh    /əʊ/
     er    /ɜː/
     eye   /aɪ/

or, rarely, one consonant (although these are not really 'words'), that is, an onset:

e.g. sh    /ʃ/
     mm    /m/

It may consist of an onset and a peak, where there is **zero coda**:

e.g. me    /miː/
     go    /gəʊ/

or, a peak and and a coda, where there is **zero onset**:

e.g. at    /æt/
     eel   /iːl/

or, all three components, that is, onset, peak and coda:

gun      /gʌn/
ten      ten/

However, the onset and coda can consist of more than one phoneme, in which case there is a **consonant cluster**:

guns     /gʌnz/
snug     /snʌg/

# Consonant clusters

This refers to a sequence of consonants at the beginning or end of a syllable.

In English, as in all languages, there are restrictions as to which, how many and in what order phonemes can come at the margins of syllables. The example 'strengths' illustrates the longest combination of phonemes at onset and coda. English syllables can have a maximum of three consonants (e.g. /spr/ in 'spray') before the peak (i.e. **syllable-initial** consonants) and four consonants (e.g. /ksts/ in 'texts') after the peak (i.e. **syllable-final** consonants). The consonants that can occur in initial position are not necessarily the same as those that can occur in final position, so, for example we can have 'spray' but not 'haspr' and 'hold' but not 'ldon'.

In English, clusters of three consonants /str/ /spl/ /kts/ are common. Four consonants clusters, for example /ksts/ as in 'texts' or /mpts/ in 'attempts', are possible at the end of syllables but rare. Usually, they are reduced in connected speech to /ks/ and /mts/ respectively.

The maximum phonological structure of the English syllable is shown in Figure 7.3.

| Pre-initial | Initial | Post-initial | | Pre-final | Final | Post-final 1 | Post-final 2 |
|---|---|---|---|---|---|---|---|
| (C) | (C) | (C) | V | (C) | (C) | (C) | (C) |
| | onset | | peak (vowel) | | | Coda | |

**Figure 7.3** Maximum syllable structure in English

Looking first at syllable-initial consonants, there are very few possible combinations or consonant clusters (Figure 7.4).

| PRE-INITIAL | INITIAL | POST- INITIAL | | | |
|---|---|---|---|---|---|
| | | l | r | w | j |
| s | p | splay | spray | - | spew |
| | t | - | string | - | stew |
| | k | - | screen | squeak | skewer |

**Figure 7.4** Syllable-initial clusters

The combination of three initial consonants must have an initial /s/ and can be followed by either /p/, /pt/, or /k/ which in turn can be followed, in some cases, by /l/, /r/, /w/ or /j/. So a word like 'sdrew' or 'sklop' is not possible.

Looking at syllable-final consonants, any consonant can be a **final** consonant except /h/ /j/ /r/ or /w/. Only, /m/ /n/ /ŋ/ /l/ and /s/ can be in **pre-final** position and only / s/ /z/ /t/ /d/ and / θ / can be in **post-final** 1 position. A further consonant can be added in **post-final** 2 position if a plural ending /s/ or /z/ or past tense ending /t/ or /d/ is added, as in /'twelfths' and 'glimpsed' (Figure 7.5).

| | | Pre-final | Final | Post-final 1 | Post-final 2 |
|---|---|---|---|---|---|
| Bump | /bʌ | m | p | | |
| Prompts | /prɒ | m | p | t | s |
| Twelfths | /twe | l | f | θ | s |
| Bonds | /bɒ | n | d | z | |
| Banks | /bæ | ŋ | k | s | |
| glimpsed | /glɪ | m | p | s | t |

**Figure 7.5** Syllable-final clusters

## Activity 2

Which of the following non-sense words are possible syllables in English? Can you explain why?

a. /pti:d/          b. /gwɪnk/
c. /ŋosp/          d. /prɑ:h/
e. /slaɪp/          f. /skwel/
g. /pnɑ:m/         h. /li:mg/
i. /glæŋ/          j. /mrɔ:k/
k. /ʃrɒlts/         l. /vwæk/
m. /ʒʌms/         n. /knaɪf/

## Activity 3

◀ Listen and classify the following words according to their final cluster. Enter the phoneme in the appropriate column, under the example 'barged':

| | | Pre-final | Final | Post-final 1 | Post-final 2 |
|---|---|---|---|---|---|
| barged | bɑ: | | dʒ | d | |
| patch | | | | | |

### Activity 3—Cont'd

|  |  | Pre-final | Final | Post-final 1 | Post-final 2 |
|---|---|---|---|---|---|
| alps |  |  |  |  |  |
| pinched |  |  |  |  |  |
| seventh |  |  |  |  |  |
| rifts |  |  |  |  |  |
| against |  |  |  |  |  |
| judged |  |  |  |  |  |
| lapsed |  |  |  |  |  |

The syllable structure of English is relatively complex compared, for example, with Cantonese. The phonotactic rules for Cantonese are much more restrictive than for English, with the maximum syllable being (C) (C) V (C). So, the only possible consonant clusters consist of two, syllable-initial consonants and here the only possibilities are /gw/ or /kw/.

### Activity 4

◀ Listen and transcribe the following words into phonemic script:

| | |
|---|---|
| helps | sixth |
| squash | next |
| spray | boxes |
| twelfths | reached |

Now write out the following words in normal script:

| | |
|---|---|
| /plʌndʒd/ | /klaʊdz/ |
| /skrɪpts/ | /krʌnʃt/ |
| /græbd/ | /θænkt/ |
| /spreɪd/ | /riːtʃt/ |

## Dealing with consonant clusters

The complexity of English consonant clusters can pose considerable pronunciation problems for some learners and typically they deal with them in one of two ways: **vowel insertion** or **consonant deletion**.

*Vowel insertion*

Vowel insertion involves adding an additional vowel to ease a difficult articulation. It can either be between two consonants (known as '**epenthesis**' /eˈpenθəsɪs') or after a final consonant (known as '**paragoge**' /pærəˈɡəʊdʒi/).

For instance, Japanese has few consonant clusters and the normal syllable structure is CVCC or CVV (where VV is a double vowel), so the dominant learner strategy is vowel insertion between consonants to break the syllable up:

> e.g. syllable-initial cluster (epenthesis):
> screw /skru:/ becomes /sukuru/
>
> syllable-initial cluster (epenthesis) and syllable-final consonant (paragoge):
> steak /steɪk/ becomes /suteki/

Similarly, Spanish L1 learners may have difficulties with initial /s/ cluster, for example, 'scream', 'slow', as this combination does not occur in Spanish. So, learners tend to insert a vowel before the initial /s/:

> e.g. scream /skri:m/ becomes /əskri:m/

## Consonant deletion

Chinese learners tend to use the consonant deletion strategy rather than vowel insertion for final consonant clusters. In final clusters, the consonants most frequently deleted are /r/ /l/ /t/ and /d/:

> e.g. hold /həʊld/ becomes /həʊl/
> past /pæst/ becomes /pæ/

In initial clusters, /r/ following /p/ or /b/ is frequently deleted:

> e.g. brothers /brʌðəz/ becomes /bʌðəz /

With word medial clusters, such as 'simpler', the most frequently deleted consonants are /r//l//t//d//f/ and /v/:

> e.g. older /əʊldə/ becomes /əʊdə/

Consonant clusters also frequently occur at word boundaries in English.

> e.g. around three /əraʊnd̲θri:/
> six thirty /sɪks̲θɜ:ti/

Research shows that when three consonants occur together, learners deleted one of them 95 per cent of the time. (Anderson 1983). Also, Chinese L1 learners tend to insert a glottal stop [ʔ] (as described in Chapter 6) in words beginning with a vowel. Such strategies show that word boundaries are often poorly negotiated.

It should be realized however, that native English speakers also frequently use strategies of consonant deletion to simplify rapid, natural speech:

e.g.   hand made   /hænmeɪd/
       textbook   /teksbʊk/
       last one   /læswʌn/

Nevertheless, such deletions are not random but based on the phonotactic rule that the central consonant in a three consonant cluster can be deleted. L2 learners need to be aware of such rules so that they know when it is and is not appropriate to make such deletions.

# Syllabic consonants

Although typically a syllable in English contains a central vowel, there are cases where a vowel is elided in natural rapid speech (as described in Chapter 6) and is replaced by a **syllabic consonant**. For instance, 'kitten' is often heard as /kɪtn̩/ and 'student' as /stjuːdn̩t/ A syllabic consonant is one which stands at the centre of the syllable in the absence of a 'V' element (vowel). /l, n, m, ŋ, r/ all occur as syllabic consonants. In transcription, a syllabic consonant is marked by placing the diacritic [ ˌ ] a small vertical line, beneath the symbol, e.g. /l̩/

(a) /l̩/ occurs:
 – after alveolars /t/ /d/, and /s/, /n/, /z/ as in 'settle' /setl̩/ (e.g. 'muddle', 'sizzle', 'castle', 'pedal', 'kettle')

 The alveolar articulation is maintained; the sides of the tongue are lowered and there is lateral release of air.

 – after plosives: /p/ /b/ /g/ /k/, as in 'tackle' /tækl̩/ (also 'gabble', 'people', 'suckle', 'boggle')

(b) /n̩/ occurs in final position
 – after plosives and fricatives in weak syllables, such as 'cotton', 'mission', 'trodden', 'vision', but not in weak syllables occurring in word initial position as in 'contain' /kənˈteɪn/.

In short, then, syllabic /l/ and /n/ may operate as syllables on their own, for example, in 'sudden', 'little', 'bottle':

/sʌdn̩/
/lɪtl̩/
/bɒtl̩/

## Activity 5

◄ Listen and decide how many syllables you hear in the following words and then transcribe them:

(a) bottling     (b) capital
(c) kitten       (d) carnation
(e) threatening  (f) puzzle
(g) gardener     (h) sudden

Nasals and laterals are phonetically and phonologically consonants but they occasionally appear to function like vowels and this is when they are syllabic. As a result, they may be referred to as syllabic consonants. They can result in clusters which some learners may find difficult.

# Syllables and grammatical endings

Some learners may have a first language where open syllables are the norm, that is, that does not normally have consonants at the end of words. They may therefore not pay enough attention to word-final consonants in English. One way of reinforcing the importance of these closing consonants is by explaining the grammatical significance of their presence or absence.

There are two main areas where a closing consonant identifies a grammatical suffix, these are for the regular past tense and the plural and possessive endings.

## Past tense rule

## Activity 6

Revise the rule for pronunciation of the simple past tense morpheme based on the evidence of the following examples. To help you formulate the rule tabulate them according the pronunciation of the word-final consonant. Decide how many syllables there are in each example. Consider learners' pronunciation difficulties with respect to this form of the verb.

| | | |
|---|---|---|
| helped | robbed | abated |
| potted | herded | lasted |
| picked | begged | wanted |
| laughed | loved | founded |
| roasted | loathed | ended |
| passed | buzzed | poured |

## Activity 6—Cont'd

| washed   | massaged | boosted |
|----------|----------|---------|
| belched  | wedged   | pulled  |
| rimmed   | pinned   | banged  |

| /d/ | /t/ | /ɪd/ |
|-----|-----|------|
|     |     |      |

## Plural endings

A similar rule applies with plural noun forms which can end in /s/ /z/ or /ɪz/.

## Activity 7

Classify the following words into three groups, depending on their ending:

| taps    | caps    |
|---------|---------|
| bits    | bids    |
| sacks   | locks   |
| batches | badges  |
| cars    | doves   |
| plinths | reefs   |
| pulses  | houses  |
| dishes  | garages |
| plums   | pans    |
| tools   | pears   |
| ways    | oars    |
| peas    | rings   |
| prawns  |         |

Again, a table may help

| /s/ | /z/ | /ɪz/ |
|-----|-----|------|
|     |     |      |

The same rule applies to third person singular present tense endings and possessive endings. So, for example, in 'he holds' the final sound is pronounced /z/ following the voiced /d/ while for the possessive 'Jack's' the final sound is pronounced /s/ after the voiceless /k/. To summarize:

| 3rd person singular present tense | | | Possessive nouns | | |
|---|---|---|---|---|---|
| /s/ | /z/ | /ɪz/ | /s/ | /z/ | /ɪz/ |
| hits | holds | reaches | Jack's | Dave's | Liz's |

---

**Activity 8**

What is the longest and shortest syllable structure in another language that you know? Find an example of each and then transcribe the word phonetically.

Take another language with which you are familiar and identify possible problem areas for speakers of that language, with regard to English syllable structure and consonant clusters.

---

# Teaching implications

Syllable sensitivity is important because the syllable is the basic unit of English pronunciation and an awareness of syllables is fundamental for an awareness of other aspects of pronunciation. Although the notion of the syllable may be universal, its structure seems to vary considerably from language to language.

The syllable has been the subject of an increasing amount of research in both L1 and L2 studies. It is suggested that the syllable might be central to lexical recall (Mehler and Christophe 1992) and more central to L2 learner processing than either the phoneme or distinctive features (Eckman and Iverson 1994). In particular, it is suggested that L2 learners commonly adjust words in the L2 towards the syllable structure of the L1.

It is important to remember that some learners will have an L1 like English which is based on an alphabetic writing system, like Spanish or German, while others, like speakers of Chinese or Japanese, are used to a writing system which represents larger units like syllables. As Dalton and Seidlhofer say:

> For those of us who are familiar only with an alphabetic writing system, the existence of single letters suggests that speech is segmented into individual sounds. However, people who have not been taught an alphabetic writing system find it easy to syllabify words but difficult to segment them into sounds. This also holds true for pre-school children, who have not yet been taught an alphabetic writing system. (Dalton and Seidlhofer 1994:35)

Differences in syllable structure across languages can cause difficulties for language learners who may transfer phonotactic restrictions from the L1 to the L2. One obvious area of potential difficulty is consonant clusters, where a learner with a L1 like Cantonese which has very few consonant clusters may have difficulties producing some English clusters. Generally, learners cope with such difficulties by using one of two strategies, either consonant *deletion* or vowel *insertion*.

Most languages have syllables composed of a consonant plus a vowel (C + V) and rarely have consonants in syllable final position. English is marked in this respect with its CVC syllable structure and in having many complex consonant clusters.

Most native speakers are unaware of phonotactic rules such as those governing the pronunciation of past tense and plural endings but they are easily predictable based on the phonetic context.

Again, in relation to phonological universals, voiced consonants are more distinctive or marked than voiceless consonants, especially in final position. In English, syllable-final voiced consonants are common. Similarly, fricatives and affricates are marked, in that they are relatively rare across languages, especially in final position and are likely to cause difficulties for pronunciation learning. However, while such knowledge of phonological universals can help predict likely areas of difficulty, it is not automatically the case, nor does it suggest such features are unteachable. In fact, it appears that sometimes the most 'foreign' or exotic sounds can be readily teachable.

## Key points

- There is a universal preference for a CV syllable structure, so English is 'marked'.
- English syllable structure is more complex than that of most languages.
- Syllable simplification is potentially more damaging to intelligibility than phoneme substitution or reduction.
- The complexity of syllable structure results in two common learner strategies (a) sound deletion and (b) sound insertion.
- Sound deletion tends to be an earlier learning strategy than sound insertion (Jenkins 2000).
- Sound insertion (epenthesis and paragoge) tends to aid intelligibility by reducing ambiguity and facilitating the recovery of the original word (Suenobo et al. 1992).

## Further reading

Anderson, J. (1983) 'The difficulties of English syllable structure for Chinese ESL learners', *Language Learning and Communication*, 2 (1), 53–61.

Chang, J. (1987) 'Chinese Speakers', in Swan, M. and Smith, B (eds) (1987) *Learner English*. Cambridge: Cambridge University Press, pp. 224–237.

Garilanes, T. C. (1991) '"-*ed*": An extra syllable or not?', *Modern English Teacher,* 17 (3 & 4), 32–3.

Hancin-Bhatt, B. and Bhatt, R. M. (1997) 'Optimal L2 syllables: Interactions of transfer and developmental effects', *Studies in Second Language Acquisition,* 19, 331–78.

Major, R. C. (1994) 'Chronological and stylistic aspects of second language acquisition of consonant clusters', *Language Learning,* 44 (4), 655–80.

Odisho, E. Y. (1979) 'Consonant clusters and abutting consonants in English and Arabic: Implications and applications', *System,* 7, 205–10.

Osburne, A. G. (1996) 'Final cluster reduction in English L2 speech: A case study of a Vietnamese speaker', *Applied Linguistics,* 17 (2), 164–81.

Roach, P. (2002) *A little encyclopedia of phonetics.* Available online at http://www.cambridge.org/elt/peterroach/resources/Glossary.pdf.

Taylor, D. S. (1995) 'Vowels, consonants and syllables in English: An English teaching perspective', *IRAL,* 33 (1), 1–8.

# 8 Phonology Review 1

This review is to give you an idea of how well you are keeping up with the areas covered so far. Complete the following activities which relate to the topics in previous chapters.

## A: Phonology review

### Activity 1

1. What is the difference between phonology and phonetics?
2. What is a phoneme?
3. Where is the hard palate?
4. What role does the nasal cavity play?
5. What distinguishes a consonant from a vowel?
6. What is the role of the larynx?
7. Why are consonants generally more easily described than vowels?
8. Name any key characteristics of English articulatory settings.
9. What are the three sections of the speech mechanism called?
10. What is the difference between a pronunciation model and goal?

### Activity 2

*Fill in the blanks with an appropriate word or symbol:*

1. The ............................... is the hard gum ridge just behind the upper teeth.
2. English sounds are produced with an outward airflow from the lungs: they are described as ......... .........................
3. For oral sounds, the velum is ................................
4. In the symbol [ æ̆ ], the diacritic shows the phoneme is ...............................
5. The most common English vowel phoneme is called ...............................
6. Vibration of the vocal cords gives rise to ............................... sounds.

7. Add diacritics to mark the following symbol as aspirated [p ]; and the following as unreleased [t]:
8. When the vocal cords ................................, the pitch of the voice goes up.
9. The overlapping of the articulations of adjacent sounds is called ...............................
10. A syllable can consist of a single ................................, without preceding or following consonants.

## Activity 3

*Circle the following statements as either 'True' or 'False':*

| | | |
|---|---|---|
| 1. In English there are four affricates, two voiced and two voiceless. | T | F |
| 2. More English consonant phonemes occur at alveolar position than at any other place of articulation. | T | F |
| 3. The vowel in 'man' is often nasalized. | T | F |
| 4. Plosives form the largest group of consonants in English. | T | F |
| 5. A vowel is a voiceless sound. | T | F |
| 6. There are two nasal consonants in English. | T | F |
| 7. The structure of the longest possible English syllable is CCVCCC | T | F |
| 8. In English, syllable-final voiceless plosives are aspirated. | T | F |
| 9. Unstressed syllables never have full vowels. | T | F |
| 10. /j/ and /w/ are semivowels. | T | F |

## Activity 4

*Now write the phonemic symbols for the following:*

1. The most front close spread vowel in English.     /iː/
2. The most back close rounded vowel.                 /oː/
3. The four English front vowels.                     ------------
4. The two English front diphthongs.                  /eɪ/ /aɪ/
5. The central lax vowel used in unstressed syllables. ------------
6. A voiced palato-alveolar affricate.                ------------
7. A bilabial nasal consonant.                        ------------
8. A voiced alveolar fricative.                       ------------
9. A voiceless bilabial plosive.                      ------------
10. A voiceless glottal fricative.                    ------------

## Activity 5

*Describe the underlined consonant sounds*

     e.g.     ba<u>d</u> = a voiced alveolar plosive

1. televi<u>s</u>ion  ..................................................................
2. sha<u>k</u>ing  ..................................................................
3. ba<u>dg</u>er  ..................................................................
4. fa<u>th</u>er  ..................................................................
5. du<u>ng</u>  ..................................................................
6. pu<u>sh</u>ing  ..................................................................
7. so<u>l</u>id  ..................................................................
8. re<u>g</u>ard  ..................................................................
9. pa<u>tch</u>y  ..................................................................
10. re<u>v</u>eal  ..................................................................

## Activity 6

*Try and complete the tables with all the English consonants and vowels:*

| CONSONANTS | |
| --- | --- |
| PLOSIVES | |
| FRICATIVES | |
| AFFRICATES | |
| NASALS | |
| LATERALS | |
| APPROXIMANTS | |

| VOWELS | |
| --- | --- |
| SHORT VOWELS | |
| LONG VOWELS | |
| DIPHTHONGS | |

## Activity 7

Complete the following statements:

1. Different phonetic variations of a sound which are recognized as a single phoneme, are called ....
   ..................................................................................................... .

2. When two variants of one phoneme are freely interchangeable and both are represented by the same phoneme, it is called ........................................................... .

3. Write the two phonetic symbols, other than schwa, which can be used to represent reduced vowels .......................................................................... .

4. Accents which do not pronounce a post-vocalic /r/ are called ..........................................
   .......................................................... .

5. Write the diacritic which is used to show aspiration ..................................................
   .......................................................... .

6. Give an example of a word with a syllabic consonant and transcribe the word phonemically ........
   .......................................................... .

7. Mark any co-articulation in the words 'sang' and 'tenth' and describe what kind of co-articulation it is ................................................................................ .

8. What is the minimum structure of a syllable in English? Give an example ...................................
   .......................................................... .

9. What is the maximum structure of a syllable in English? ..................................................
   .......................................................... .

10. Is the word "fngudr" possible in English? If not, why not? ..................................................
    .......................................................... .

# B. Transcription practice

## Activity 1

◄ Listen and pick out the sound that is different from the rest. Choose A, B, C or D.
   Example    bean    bean    bun (c)    bean
   *Then listen again and transcribe the word you picked, for example, /bʌn/*

1. .................................................................................................
2. .................................................................................................
3. .................................................................................................
4. .................................................................................................
5. .................................................................................................
6. .................................................................................................
7. .................................................................................................
8. .................................................................................................
9. .................................................................................................
10. .................................................................................................

## Activity 2

   a. Which of these is the phonemic script for 'car'?
      i. /kɑ:r/
      ii. /kæ/
      iii. /kɑ:/
      iv. /ka/

   b. Which if these is the phonemic script for 'witch'?
      i. /wɪs/
      ii. /wɪʃ/
      iii. /wɪtʃ/
      iv. /wɪʒ/

   c. Which of these is the phonemic script for rude?
      i. /ru:d/
      ii. /ri:d/
      iii. /rud/
      iv. /rɑd/

   d. Which of these is the phonemic script for 'judge'?
      i. /jʌdʒ/
      ii. /jʌj/
      iii. /juj/
      iv. /dʒʌdʒ/

   e. Which of these is the phonemic script for women?
      i. /wɪmɪn/
      ii. /wɪmen/
      iii. /wʊmən/
      iv. /wʊmɪn/

## Activity 3

◀ Listen and transcribe the one syllable words you hear, using phonemic symbols. Each word is said twice.

   1. ............................................................................................................

   2. ............................................................................................................

⇨

| 3. | ..................................................................................................... |
|---|---|
| 4. | ..................................................................................................... |
| 5. | ..................................................................................................... |
| 6. | ..................................................................................................... |
| 7. | ..................................................................................................... |
| 8. | ..................................................................................................... |
| 9. | ..................................................................................................... |
| 10. | ..................................................................................................... |
| 11. | ..................................................................................................... |
| 12. | ..................................................................................................... |
| 13. | ..................................................................................................... |
| 14. | ..................................................................................................... |
| 15. | ..................................................................................................... |
| 16. | ..................................................................................................... |
| 17. | ..................................................................................................... |
| 18. | ..................................................................................................... |
| 19. | ..................................................................................................... |
| 20. | ..................................................................................................... |

## Activity 4

Now write out the following words in normal script:

1. /bred/
2. /ʃi:p/
3. /laɪt/
4. /'leɪzi/
5. /'bʌtn̩/
6. /'bri:ðɪŋ/
7. /'leʒə/
8. /'taɪəd/
9. /'meni/
10. /'flaʊəd/
11. /'prɪti/
12. /'mɪʃn̩/
13. /'fɪŋgə/
14. /mə'tjʊə/
15. /'bɒtl̩/
16. /'lesən/
17. /'ri:tʃəs/
18. /fɪfθ/
19. /'bɒksɪz/
20. /ʃræŋk/

## Activity 5

◀ Listen and transcribe the following words using phonemic script:

1. thanked
2. texts
3. helped
4. sixths
5. scripts

6. squashed
7. risks
8. sprayed
9. reached
10. clouds

## Activity 6

Now write out the following words in normal script:

1. /ˈtʌnl̩/
2. /ˈfraɪtn̩d/
3. /ˈnekləs/
4. /ˈwɪmɪn/
5. /ˈmɪrə/

6. /fjuː/
7. /feɪld/
8. /lɑːʤ/
9. /ˈsɪti/
10. /luːz/

## Activity 7

◀ Listen and transcribe these words. Mark any weak syllables you hear in each word. Write the phonetic symbol for each weak syllable (e.g. [ə] or [i])

about      again      surprise
forget     suggest    standard
easy       nature     colour
only       hundred    thorough

# Word Stress 9

## Introduction

Cruttenden (2008:249) claims that 'differing accentual patterns of words are as important to their recognition as the sequence of phonemes'. The importance of word stress patterns is further illustrated by the fact that native English speaking children frequently omit unstressed syllables when learning words, such as 'banana' /nɑːnə/ and 'guitar' /tɑː/. While the significance of word stress might be greater for native speaker comprehension than NNS (Jenkins 2000), there is little doubt that the complexity of English word stress can be challenging to many L2 learners.

Many learners have first languages where word stress or accent is regular or fixed, such as French or Turkish where stress falls on the final syllable, or Polish or Spanish where stress falls on the penultimate syllable. In English, however, word stress is variable across words which can problematic for such learners. Nevertheless, there are patterns and tendencies which are relatively easily taught and can be of considerable help to L2 learners.

---

**Activity 1**

Think of languages with which you are familiar. Does word stress fall regularly on a certain syllable? Does it vary? Are there any 'rules' that you are aware of?

---

## The concept of stress

This is not an easy concept to define but it is possible to illustrate. In addition, most people are able to accept that some syllables are perceived as having greater stress than others. Stress can also be referred to as 'prominence', 'emphasis', or 'accent'. Cruttenden (2008) calls stress **'accent'** and he illustrates the concept in the following way:

> 'The syllable or syllables of a word which stand out from the remainder are said to be accented, to receive the *accent*.'

(Cruttenden 2008:235)

The hearer perceives an accented or stressed syllable as more **prominent** than an unstressed syllable. Prominence relates to the amount of muscular energy used to produce a syllable. The main acoustic signals of prominence are:

**(a) pitch change or a change in the frequency or speed of vibration of the vocal cords**
If a syllable is said with a change in pitch, either higher or lower, it will be heard as more prominent. Adding pitch movement on the syllable will make it even more prominent.

e.g.       ba
        ba     ba  ba

**(b) Syllable length or duration**
The length of syllables is an important factor in perceptions of prominence. If one syllable in a word is longer than the others there is a tendency to hear it as stressed.

e.g. ba baa ba ba

Long vowels (/iː/ /ɔː/ /ɑː/ /ɜː/ /uː/) and diphthongs generally appear more prominent than shorter vowels. However, long vowels and diphthongs also appear in unaccented syllables. In the examples below, they are not stressed but they still give an impression of prominence (in these and further examples, the stressed syllable is marked with a ' ).

| | |
|---|---|
| 'phon<u>eme</u> | /'fəʊniːm/ |
| 'pla<u>card</u> | /'plækɑːd/ |
| 'rail<u>way</u> | /'reɪlweɪ/ |
| 'pill<u>ow</u> | /'pɪləʊ/ |

**(c) Syllable loudness or amplitude** (although it is important to realize that it is difficult to increase loudness without altering other qualities such as pitch level,

ba BA ba ba

**(d) Vowel quality**

e.g.      bi
       ba     ba ba

The most important aspect of differences in vowel quality is that unstressed syllables typically have a reduced vowel (either /ə/ or /i/ or /u/) and therefore stressed syllables tend to stand out by having a full vowel.

The quality of the sound also contributes to the listener's impression of stress with relative degrees of prominence (and sonority, as explained in Chapter 7) on a scale high to low:

- vowels are more prominent than consonants open vowels are more prominent than close vowels;
- syllabic consonants (m̩ n̩ l̩ r̩) have greater prominence than all other consonants;
- fricatives are more prominent than plosives;

To recap, syllable prominence or stress is achieved through:

a. loudness
b. pitch change
c. quality of sound
d. length of sound.

By far, the most important characteristic is pitch change. Loudness is the least important, especially as some sounds are intrinsically louder than others.

Most languages use a combination of these signals, but to different degrees. The most significant qualities in English are length and pitch. What is particularly important in English is the *contrast* between *stressed* and *unstressed* syllables. Stress in English relies more heavily on the weakening or reduction of unstressed syllables than most other languages.

# Levels of stress

Unfortunately stress is not as simple as a binary distinction between stressed and unstressed syllables. There are different levels or degrees of stress, both within words and within phrases or utterances. For instance, there can be more than one stressed syllable in a word, leading to a **primary** and a **secondary** stress.

Primary stress is indicated by a high mark [ ' ],

re'turn     /rɪ'tɜːn/

while secondary stress may be indicated by a low mark [ˌ] , as in

ˌreve'lation          /ˌrevə'leɪʃn̩/
conˌtami'nation      /kənˌtæmɪn'eɪʃn̩/

(The stress marks are placed at the beginning of the stressed syllable.) So, we have three 'levels' of stress:

1. Primary stress          e.g. 'around'          /ə'raʊnd/
2. Secondary stress      e.g. 'photographic'    ˌfəʊtə'græfɪk/
                                     e.g. 'mountaineer'     /ˌmaʊntɪ'nɪə/
3. Unstressed/destressed  e.g. 'banana'          /bə'nɑːnə/

Although it is possible to add a fourth level of stress, it seems unnecessarily complex to do so. It can be seen that there is a general tendency in English to alternate stressed/unstressed syllables or to avoid having successive stressed syllables.

# Word stress

The stress pattern of a word is an important part of its identity for the native speaker and incorrect stress placement is a common cause of intelligibility problems. There is evidence to suggest that listeners pay at least as much attention to word stress as to individual sounds and that native speakers store words according to stress patterns (Grosjean and Gee 1987). So, if a listener expects a certain stress pattern and hears a different one, he/she may not recognize the word. In other words, what is heard does not match the listener's mental dictionary. For example if the word 'alibi' /ˈælə͵baɪ/ is pronounced as /əˈliːbi/.

The system of stress in English is not random and there is a pattern that native speakers internalize, otherwise we would not be able to cope with the pronunciation of unknown words as they arise in texts. However, we know little about the acquisition of first language stress patterns. Awareness of stress patterns allows native speakers (and gradually, NNS) to cope as they meet words like:

men'dacious, cu'pidity, prevari'cation, medi'ocrity

This awareness allows people to render quite faithfully even non-sense words:

fragi'listic, 'pordock, pun'dacious, drostifi'cation, expiali'docious

However, L2 learners should ideally learn both stress placement patterns as well as the stress for each new word as it is presented to them. It is important that the teacher gives adequate attention to the issue as problems of comprehension and production can arise as a result of poor acquisition of word stress.

# Stress placement

Stress placement in English is variable, that is, the syllable or syllables that are stressed can vary depending on, for instance, the structure and function of a word. Some languages do not have variable stress and it is therefore easy to predict stress placement. For instance, French (where the last syllable is usually stressed, for example, bon'soir) or Polish (where the first syllable is usually stressed, for example, 'jen dobry'), or Spanish (where the penultimate syllable is stressed, for example, zapate'ria) and Finnish (with regular initial syllable stress, for example, 'hyvää 'päivää , which sounds like *HUU-vaa PIGH-vaa*). English word stress varies considerably and its complexity can mean that it is at times distinctive as in:

| | |
|---|---|
| 'billow | be'low |
| 'convict (noun) | con'vict (verb) |
| 'insight (noun) | in'cite (verb) |

although the number of minimal pairs is fairly limited.

Stress placement rules exist for English but they are rather complex. This means that although native speakers can usually predict accurately where to put the stress on an unknown word it can be very difficult for non-native learners.

Stress placement depends on:

1. whether a word is morphologically simple or complex or a compound
2. the grammatical category of a word
3. the number of syllables in a word
4. the phonological stucture of the syllables (e.g. final syllables with short vowels, one final consonant, or /ə/ are not stressed).

## Stress in simple words

For words of one syllable we can state the stress patterns fairly comfortably. Words of one syllable are generally unstressed if they are **function** words like 'to', pronouns like 'me', articles like 'the' or 'some' or 'a'. One syllable words have primary stress if they are nouns, verbs or adjectives. Prepositions, pronouns and articles of one syllable tend to remain unstressed. Unstressed syllables, such as the indefinite article 'a' (e.g. a book) tend to contain the vowel /ə/ which can never occur in a stressed syllable.

Here are some general tendencies for stress placement in simple lexical words.

### Two syllable words

### a. Nouns

The majority of two syllable nouns (especially proper nouns) have stress on the first syllable.

| e.g. 'Peter | 'Christmas |
|---|---|
| 'Richards | 'Miller |
| 'coffee | 'basket |

However, if the second syllable is **strong** (i.e. either has a long vowel or a diphthong or ends in two consonants), the stress will go on the second syllable.

e.g. de'sign     e'state

Final syllable stress on two syllable nouns is quite rare in English and it is often related to borrowed words:

la'goon     sa'loon

### b. Verbs

The majority of two syllable verbs have stress on the second syllable, if that syllable is strong.

> e.g. ap'ply     al'low
>      di'vide    re'strict

If the final syllable is **weak** (i.e. with either a short vowel or schwa and has no, or a single, final consonant), then the first syllable is stressed. A final syllable is also unstressed if it contains /əʊ/ as in 'borrow' /'bɒrəʊ/. Two syllable adjectives tend to follow the same pattern as verbs. So we have:

> e.g. 'hollow    /'hɒləʊ/
>      'pretty    /'prɪti/
>      'open      /'əʊpən/
>      'normal    /'nɔ:məl/
>      co'rrect   /kə'rekt/

There are of course exceptions, such as the adjective 'honest' /'ɒnəst/ which ends in a strong syllable.

---

## Activity 2

a. Look at the following verbs and divide them into two columns according to their stress pattern:

apply, arouse, assist, attempt, adjoin, borrow, collect, insist, open, detract, declare, equal, enter, follow, marry, extend, surmise, practice, resist, deepen, happen, design, rummage, depend, invest, intend, refuse

b. Now, do the same for the following adjectives:

merry, valid, eager, open, common, immune, able, adept, pretty, hollow, jolly, correct, malign, fallow, , final, second, careless, mundane, afraid

c. Classify the following two syllable nouns into those with initial and those with final stress:

hamster, limit, pocket, pencil, paper, mutton, table, mirror, saloon, canteen, police, panel, penny, honey, giraffe, danger, cotton, money, carrot, booklet, shower, report, repose, furrow, spittoon

---

### Word-class pairs

There are a group of words, known as **word-class pairs**, which can operate as nouns or verbs. They can be distinguished by the stress placement:

| Noun | Verb |
|------|------|
| 'record | re'cord |
| 'present | pre'sent |
| 'object | ob'ject |

---

## Activity 3

Mark with ' the primary stress in the underlined word-class pairs.

1. This food is very difficult to <u>digest</u>.
2. The director asked his colleague to provide him with a <u>digest</u> of the report.
3. The children's <u>conduct</u> leaves a lot to be desired.
4. I couldn't <u>conduct</u> business with a man like that.
5. I am happy with your <u>progress</u>.
6. All students <u>progress</u> at different rates.

---

There is a small number of words that exhibit such stress pattern distinctions which have a distinguishing grammatical function. Vowel quality may be affected by the change as in:

|  | Nouns/Adjectives | Verb |
|------|------|------|
| conduct | 'kɒndʌkt | kən'dʌkt |
| progress | 'prəʊgres | prə'gres |
| convict | 'kɒnvɪkt | kən'vɪkt |
| contract | 'kɒntrækt | kən'trækt |
| frequent | 'friːkwənt | frɪ'kwent |
| present | 'prezənt | prə'zent |
| project | 'prəʊdʒekt | prə'dʒekt |
| protest | 'prəʊtest | prə'test |
| record | 'rekɔːd | rə'kɔːd |
| subject | 'sʌbdʒekt | səb'dʒekt |
| digest | 'daɪdʒest | dɪ'dʒest |

## Three syllable words

Here there is a tendency to put the stress towards the end of the word on verbs and the front of the word for nouns.

So, in verbs, if the final syllable is strong, it will be stressed, as in:

enter'tain      under'stand

If the last syllable is weak, it will be unstressed and the stress will move forward to the preceding (penultimate) syllable, if that syllable is strong, as in:

de'velop      di'rection
su'rrender    e'xamine

Again there is a tendency to front stress three syllable nouns, for example:

'customer                    'cinema
'quantity                    'emperor

However, stress tends to go on strong syllables, so we have:

di'saster                    enter'tain
de'termine                   en'counter

Also, with words of more than two syllables, a general rhythmical pattern often emerges reflecting the tendency to alternate between stressed and unstressed syllables. If there are two syllables before the primary stress, a secondary stress is often placed on the first syllable, with a full vowel in that syllable:

**e.g.**  ˌenter'tain      ˌrepre'sent      ˌmaga'zine      ˌmedi'eval

Again, these are tendencies rather than hard and fast rules and there are many exceptions but they do provide useful guidelines.

## Stress in complex words

So far, we have looked at 'simple' words, that is words composed of a single grammatical unit but there are many words which consist of more than one grammatical part, such as 'fool' + 'ish' = 'foolish' and 'care' + 'less' = 'careless'. Such complex words are of two types:

(a) words made from a basic stem plus an affix (i.e. a prefix such as 'un' + pleasant = unpleasant, or a suffix such as 'able' + comfort = comfortable)
(b) compound words (e.g. armchair, ice-cream)

While it is impossible and unnecessary for learners to know all the patterns governing word stress placement in complex words, an awareness of the most common and useful ones can be very helpful.

### (a) Words with affixes (prefixes and suffixes)

Affixes can have one of three possible effects on word stress:

(i)   the affix is stressed – e.g. 'ciga'rette
(ii)  the affix has no effect – e.g. 'market-'marketing, 'pleasant-un'pleasant, co'rrect-inco'rrect
(iii) the affix is not stressed but the stress on the stem moves – e.g. 'magnet-mag'netic

#### (i) the affix is stressed

In some cases, the primary stress is either on the suffix (e.g. ciga'rette) or moves onto a suffix, as in:

Ja'pan – ‚Japa'nese
'mountain    – ‚mountain'eer

If the word has more than two syllables, the root may have a secondary stress, as in the examples above.

Single-syllable prefixes do not usually carry stress (e.g. mis'place, disa'gree) but longer prefixes can carry secondary stress (e.g. ‚semi'circle, ‚anti'clockwise).

### (ii) the affix has no effect

In these cases, the suffix (or prefix as explained above) does not affect the stress placement. For instance,

-able – under'stand, under'standable; 'comfort, 'comfortable
-age – 'cover, 'coverage, 'bag, 'baggage
-al – eco'nomic, eco'nomical; geo'graphic, geo'graphical
-ful – 'care, 'careful; 'wonder, 'wonderful

### (iii) the affix is not stressed but the stress on the stem moves

Here the suffix cause the stress on the word stem to move. For instance,

-eous –ad'vantage; advan'tageous
-ic – e'conomy, eco'nomic; 'strategy, stra'tegic

It can be useful for L2 learners to learn the most common suffix patterns.

---

## Activity 4

a. ◀ Listen and mark the stress placement on these words. What is the pattern:

| | | |
|---|---|---|
| calculation | decision | reaction |
| relation | association | operation |
| solution | distribution | television |

b. ◀ Listen and mark the stress placement on these words. What is the pattern:

| | | |
|---|---|---|
| economic | terrific | strategic |
| logic | pathogenic | domestic |
| metabolic | statistic | melodic |

c. ◀ Listen and mark the primary stress placement on these words. What is the pattern:

| | | | |
|---|---|---|---|
| biology | biological | policy | political |
| photography | photographical | society | sociological |
| technology | technological | electricity | electrical |
| geography | geographical | university | managerial |

⇨

---

### Activity 4—Cont'd

d. Now mark the primary stress in these words and then transcribe them:

| | |
|---|---|
| personality | antibiotic |
| computerization | surgical |
| agricultural | transmission |
| pharmacology | digital |
| analytical | microscopic |

---

Words often have a different stress pattern when they have a different grammatical function. For instance:

| *verb* | *noun* |
|---|---|
| in'form | infor'mation |
| 'specialize | speciali'zation |
| ex'port | 'export |

## (b) Compound words

---

### Activity 5

Complete the columns below marking the primary stress in each word:

| Verb | Noun |
|---|---|
| present | ............................................ |
| examine | ............................................ |
| ............................................ | production |
| insult | ............................................ |
| ............................................ | record |
| reduce | ............................................ |

| Noun | Adjective |
|---|---|
| history | ............................................ |
| ............................................ | secretarial |
| analysis | ............................................ |
| ............................................ | political |

---

These are words that are made up of two separate words but when put together have a single meaning.

**Activity 6**

Read the following words and write them in Roman script:

/ˌlaʊd 'spiːkə/
/ˌbæd-'mænəd/
/ˌkɒtən 'wʊl/

Now transcribe the following words phonemically and mark the primary stress:

| armchair | keyboard | microwave |
|----------|----------|-----------|
| doorbell | first-class | north-east |

(i) compounds made up of two nouns and functioning as nouns, generally put the stress on the first noun:

e.g.  'typewriter       'sunrise
        'suitcase          'car-ferry
        'whiteboard      'greenhouse

(ii) compounds which function as adjectives, adverbs or verbs, typically put the stress on the second element:

e.g. bad-'tempered     ill-'fitting
       second-'class       three-'wheeler
       head-'first            heavy-'handed
       ill-'treat              down-'grade

Sometimes word stress can be used to differentiate the meaning of compound words. For example, green'house (a house that is green) and 'greenhouse (a glass house used for gardening); white 'house (a house that is white) and 'White House (the house where the president of the United States resides).

## Shifting stress placement

Finally, the stress patterns of words are liable to change and shifting stress patterns have occurred across the centuries. The writer Samuel Rogers noted in 1855, 'The new fashionable pronunciation of several words is to me at least offensive. CONtemplate is bad enough but BALcony makes me sick' (quoted in Crystal 1988:64). While both of these stress patterns are firmly established now there are inevitably present changes afoot which invoke similar reactions, for instance, con'tribute is tending to have the primary stress moved to the first syllable ('contribute) and the stress on 'mischievous is tending to move to the second syllable (mis'chievous). These and similar changes are documented by John Wells in his latest edition of the *Longman Pronunciation Dictionary* (2000).

---

**Activity 7**

a. Read the following sentences and write them in normal script:

ɪn'tɒlərəns ɪz ən ʌn'riːznəbl̩ ʌnə'kseptəbl̩ 'ætitjuːd
haɪpər'æktɪv 'ʧɪldrən kæn ʌn'duː: ðə məʊst 'keəfəl 'plænz

b. Transcribe the following into phonemic script marking primary and *secondary stress:*

(i) The unseasonal weather seemed to bring about a personality disorder in some people.
(ii) The accident left the man feeling helpless.

---

# Weak forms

So far in this chapter we have been looking at stress placement in words and how this relates to stressed and unstressed syllables. Although word stress placement is very variable between words, it is fixed in the sense that each word has a specific stress pattern which needs to be learned as part of the pronunciation of that word. However, there is also a group of words in English which have two stress patterns, that is, what is termed a 'strong' and 'weak' form.

There are about 40 such words in English and almost all of them belong to a category of words that can be called **function words**. Function words (also known as 'grammar words' or 'structure words') include words such as pronouns (e.g. 'she', 'their'), determiners (e.g. 'a' 'the'), auxilliary verbs ('be', 'do'), conjunctions ('and', 'but') and prepositions ('on', 'in'). Function words typically carry relatively little information, compared with **content words** (also known as 'lexical words') which include main verbs, adjectives and adverbs which contain more information.

When function words are unaccented, they tend to have vowels which are reduced or weakened in length and quality. So for instance, 'for' becomes /fə/ and 'could' becomes /kəd/. In fact, many function words (i.e. auxiliaries, determiners, pronouns, prepositions and conjunctions) can often be pronounced in two different ways: in their '**strong**' form and their '**weak**' form. For instance,

Where are you from? I'm from Leicester
/'weə ə jə 'frɒm/ /'aɪm frəm 'lestə/

In total, there are approximately 50 words having weak and strong forms. The vast majority of the weak forms are characterized by the reduced vowel /ə/ for example, a /ə/ book, while the rest tend to contain unstressed /i/, and occasionally unstressed /u/. One such group of function words is conjunctions:

| Written form | Strong form | Weak form |
|---|---|---|
| and | /ænd/ | /ən/ |
| as | /æz/ | /əz/ |
| but | /bʌt/ | /bət/ |
| than | /ðæn/ | /ðən/ |
| that | /ðæt/ | /ðət/ |

Strong forms are much less frequent than weak forms in L1 English speech. Consequently, it is important that learners recognize unstressed, weak forms in English for reasons of listening comprehension. For instance, the conjunction 'and' can be pronounced as /ænd/ in its strong form or citation form, as /ənd/ or more commonly /ən/ before vowels and/or other consonants and as a syllabic consonant /n̩ / as in:

fish and chips      'fɪʃ n̩ 'tʃɪps.

Strong and weak forms are discussed further in Chapter 10.

# Teaching implications

## Weak forms

The rules governing weak forms are relatively easy and consistent which is probably why they are frequently taught, however Jenkins claims (2000:149) that it is not evident that they are learned or used outside the classroom. A compromise solution suggested by Jenkins is to teach learners to shorten the vowel in weak forms but maintain vowel quality, in other words not insist on the use of reduced vowels such as schwa. Her rationale for this is that it makes the word easier for the L2 listener to understand as most languages distinguish between stressed and unstressed syllables but most do so by reducing vowel length rather than quality.

## Word stress

There is also some debate regarding the importance of correct word stress placement for L2 learners. Roach (2000:100) suggests that 'incorrect word placement is a major cause of intelligibility problems for foreign learners'. Similarly, Cruttenden sees accenting the correct syllable of words as a high priority for learners of RP (2008:322). However, Jenkins (2000:14) claims that word stress alone rarely causes intelligibility problems in lingua franca contexts. Nevertheless, many phonologists and pronunciation teachers agree that learners can be helped by encouraging them to mark word stress when they learn new words and by learning the key patterns of English word stress.

Learners need to be aware that:

(i)   stressed syllables have full vowels
(ii)  unstressed syllables usually have reduced vowels (but can have full vowels)
(iii) word stress is systematic but quite complex and only the most frequent and useful patterns need to be learnt.

It is important for learners to understand that word stress in English helps L1 listeners to recognize words. It appears that native speakers store vocabulary according to stress patterns and when the wrong pattern is heard, the listener may spend time searching for stored words in the wrong category. Brown (1991) explains for instance:

> The stress pattern of a polysyllabic word is a very important identifying feature of the word . . . We store words under stress patterns . . . and we find it difficult to interpret an utterance in which a word is pronounced with the wrong stress pattern – we begin to 'look up' possible words under this wrong stress pattern. (1991:51)

For instance, 'also' with the stress misplaced on the second syllable, mistaken for 'although', similarly 'foreign' could be confused with 'for rain' and 'his story' for 'history' (examples from Gilbert 2008:5).

## Word stress and EIL

Regarding teaching priorities, Jenkins describes word stress as 'a grey area' claiming that whereas word stress seems to be important for NS listeners, it rarely causes intelligibility problems on its own for NNS-NNS interactions and that 'word stress rules are so complex as to be unteachable' (Jenkins 2000:150). Although she considers the full scale teaching of word stress as 'not feasible' and 'not crucial' to the intelligibility of individual words in EIL (2000:151), she acknowledges the importance of the link between word stress placement and nuclear stress, which she does see as important.

In contrast, Dauer (2005) claims that word stress is readily teachable with a handful of basic rules accounting for 85 per cent of polysyllabic words. She also suggests that it is hard to understand how to teach aspiration, vowel length or nuclear stress (all of which are part of the LFC and are associated with word stress) without students having been taught which syllable to stress in a word. She also claims that students need to be taught word stress because it does not appear in the writing system and many are not aware of its importance.

Indeed, many pronunciation specialists, such as (Kenworthy 1987, Vaughan-Rees 1997, Gilbert 2005) conclude that it is important to teach learners general guidelines about word stress placement, particularly regarding stress in single and two syllable nouns and verbs and the effect certain suffixes (such as 'ion' and 'ic') can have on word stress.

# Key points

- The majority of two syllable *nouns* and *adjectives* have stress on the first syllable: for example, 'butter, 'pretty
- The majority of two syllable *verbs* have stress on the second syllable: for example, be'gin, pro'duce
- Stress goes on the penultimate syllable for words ending in '*ic*' and '*ion*': for example, tele'vision, so'lution, 'static, rea'listic.
- Stress goes on the anti-penultimate syllables for words ending in '*cy*', '*ty*', '*phy*', '*gy*': for example, de'mocracy, 'relia'bility, and '*al*': for example, 'critical, eco'nomical.
- *Multisyllablic* words usually have more than one stress, that is, a 'primary' and a 'secondary' stress: for example, ˌinter'national, ˌantibi'otic. Often such words contain a prefix (such as 'inter' and 'anti' above) and this prefix has secondary stress (this is common with many long technical words).
- *If a compound* word is a noun, the stress usually goes on the first part: for example, 'greenhouse, 'blackbird. If the compound is an adjective, the stress usually goes on the second part: for example, down'grade, ill-'treat.
- English word stress is 'marked' in that it is more complex and more dynamic than many other languages (e.g. Finnish, French, Polish, Spanish have relatively fixed word stress patterns).
- Word stress in English relies on a greater use of vowel duration than many languages.
- Reduction of unstressed vowels is also much more significant in English than many other languages.
- Misplaced word stress, together with phoneme deletion can cause significant intelligibility problems for both native and non-native speakers, for example, a Taiwanese speaker's production of [epeʔ'dɪʃə] for ex'penditure /ek'spendɪtʃə/ (Jenkins 2000:42).

# Potential problems

Learners frequently have difficulty with word stress for several reasons:

(a) Although there are some rules for word stress these rules are subject to a great many exceptions.
(b) It is generally true to say that stress patterns in English vary more than in many other languages.
(c) There may be interference from the learner's L1.
   i. This is particularly true of 'international' words that is, cognates such as 'television' which typically does not have penultimate stress and has five rather than four syllables in many languages.
   ii. All syllables may have full vowels.
   iii. There may be a tendency to give both stressed and unstressed syllables full vowels (i.e. vowels in unstressed syllables are not weakened), as for example in French and Italian.

iv. Word stress may be fixed in the L1 (i.e. stress falls regularly on a particular syllable. For example, the final syllable in French and Thai and the penultimate syllable in Swahili.

v. The L1 may have variable rather than fixed stress placement (as in English) but different rules, as in Turkish, Italian and Arabic. This may cause particular problems with cognates.

vi. The L1 may only have primary stress, as in Russian, Greek and this may cause problems with multisyllabic words.

vii. In many languages there is no compound word stress distinction, for example, white 'house' vs 'White House' and the difference is signalled by word order rather than word stress.

viii. Compound word stress may always be on the first syllable (e.g. 'prime minister', 'front door') as in Scandinavian languages and German.

# Further reading

Adams, C. and Munro, R. R. (1978) 'In search of the acoustic correlates of stress: Fundamental frequency, amplitude and duration in the connected utterance of some native and non-native speakers of English', *Phonetica*, 35, 125–56.

Alexander, J. D. (1986) 'The stress factor in spoken English', *English Today*, 5, 31–34.

Benrabah, M. (1997) 'Word-stress: A source of unintelligibility in English', *IRAL*, 35 (3), 157–65.

Haycraft, B. (1985) 'Put life into drills – with the right stress', *Professional English Teacher*, 5 (4), 39–41.

Haycraft, B. (1986) 'The shape of English words', *Professional English Teacher*, 6 (2), 29–31.

Haycraft, B. (1992) 'Sentence stress – for more meaningful speech', in Brown A. (ed.) *Approaches to Pronunciation Teaching*. London: Macmillan & The British Council, pp. 57–72.

Taylor, D. (1991) 'Compound word stress', *ELT Journal*, 45, 67–73.

Vaughan-Rees, M. (1999) 'Word-stress rules', *Speak Out!*, 23, 38–9.

Woodward, T. (1991) 'Making stress physical, visible & audible', *Modern English Teacher*, 17 (3 & 4), 38–9.

# Features of Connected Speech

## Introduction

There is more to producing speech than putting individual words together, as anyone who has listened to synthetic speech for instance on a satellite navigation system or an automated telephone message will know. Indeed, it has taken a combination of phoneticians, artificial intelligence and computer experts many decades to reach the level of relative sophistication that artificial speech has reached today but there is still a way to go.

There are several factors that combine to create the perception of natural fluent speech. One is the *process of modification* of speech sounds. This 'simplification' of articulations occurs in all language but in different ways and to different degrees.

The way we say a word on its own, that is, its **citation form**, can be quite different to the way the word appears in connected speech.

---

### Activity 1

◀ Listen and then say these words and phrases, first in their citation form and then as they appear in connected speech:

| | |
|---|---|
| perhaps | /ˈpræps/ |
| headquarters | /ˈhegkwɔːtəz/ |
| excuse me | /ˈskjuːzmi/ |
| give him it | /ˈgɪvɪmɪt/ |

---

Most native speakers are unaware of such modifications and may even deny making them or consider them 'sloppy' or 'careless' speech. However, differences between citation forms and connected speech are not random but systematic and based on clear patterns.

A second and related factor, which heavily influences connected speech, is the *process of accentuation* whereby meaning is signalled in English through stress and intonation. This process results in the characteristic rhythmic, stress and intonation patterns of English utterances and some of the modifications of sounds that occur in natural fluent speech. Together, these processes of accentuation and modification contribute to various features that characterize connected speech. These include:

rhythm
weak forms (reductions)
assimilation
elision (contractions)
linking

We will look at these features of connected features in this chapter and consider their relation to pronunciation teaching and learning. In terms of teaching, some of these features are more important than others; in terms of learning some of them are more important for recognition than production.

# The process of accentuation

Just as one or more syllables is stressed or accentuated in a multisyllabic word, so some parts of an utterance are accentuated in connected speech. However, unlike in word stress, the purpose of accentuation in speech is to make some parts of the message stand out and is largely determined by the meaning that the utterance is intended to convey. Although there is therefore considerable freedom in where to place accent or stress in an utterance, some words are more likely than others to be stressed, because of their function in the language. As explained in Chapter 9, these **lexical** or **content** words are typically main verbs, adverbs, nouns, adjectives and demonstratives which generally convey more information. Other categories of words, such as pronouns, auxiliary verbs, conjunctions, articles and prepositions, known as **function** or **grammatical** words, typically convey grammatical relationships but little or no meaning in themselves. These words tend to be unaccented, although they can be stressed to convey a particular meaning.

---

**Activity 2**

*Content Words*

Can you come to the office at six this evening.

*Function Words*

Mark each word in the sentence above as either a 'function' or 'content' word.

---

## Basic stress pattern

A clear distinction between words which are accentuated or stressed and words which are not is essential to intelligibility, both for speech production and listening comprehension. Accentuation has both a grammatical and pragmatic function in English, showing which information is in the foreground and which is in the background. L1 speakers of English typically use a basic stress pattern in speech whereby content words are stressed and function words are unstressed. So, for instance, in the examples below the content words are underlined:

> I <u>find</u> it <u>difficult</u> to <u>understand</u>
> <u>thanks</u> for a <u>lovely meal</u>
> I <u>usually visit</u> my <u>parents</u> on <u>Tuesdays</u>

The basic stress pattern of an utterance can be altered to focus the listener's attention on what the speaker wants to highlight. While all content words are stressed, one content word within an utterance will typically receive greater stress than the others. We will refer to this as the **nucleus**, although other terms are also used, such as 'sentence stress', 'focus' or 'tonic syllable'. Regardless of terminology, the aim of this process of accentuation is to focus the listener's attention on the information contained in that particular part of the message. The term 'sentence' is deliberately avoided as it refers to a unit of grammar, typically relating to written language while our concern here is with phonology and the spoken language.

Focus helps to contextualize messages, that is, it helps the listener relate something to what has been said before and to predict what is likely to be said next. When a conversation begins, the nucleus is usually on the last content word. The nucleus is in bold in each of the examples below:

> e.g. 'What's the '**matter**?
> 'Where are you '**going**?
> 'Put the '**coffee** in it.

However, focus is rarely repeated on the same lexical item in an utterance or exchange. So, in the dialogue below, the nucleus shifts from 'live' in A's first utterance, to 'you' in B's response:

> e.g. A: Where do you **live**?
> B: In **Leicester**. Where do **you** live?
> A: I live in Leicester **too**.

The focus can be **broad** [1] (i.e. stress is on more than one word, or a phrase – but the nucleus of the focus is on the last content word). This is typical of an opening statement or remark in a conversation where more than one piece of information is said to be 'new'.

> e.g. I've '**lost** my '**keys**.
> My 'flight 'leaves at **e'leven** '**thirty** on 'Tuesday the '**sixth**.

The focus can be **narrow** (i.e. on one word), which is more likely in response to an earlier remark or question.

e.g. **'Here** they 'are?
I'm 'not **'ready**
**'Who's** 'stolen your 'bag?

The speaker can choose to focus on **new** information (something mentioned for the first time) or **old** or **given** information (something referred to or mentioned before). All languages have ways of doing this, but English relies heavily on stress to relay specific meaning. In particular, in English we typically use stress to contrast or correct information, whereas many languages use word order or vocabulary to signal such intentions.

e.g. A: I'm 'glad you're 'coming on **'Friday**.
B: But I **'can't** 'come.
A: 'Have you 'ever 'visited **'Bangkok**?
B: 'No,' **I** 'haven't but 'my **'sister** 'has.

This accentual function of stress is considered further in Chapter 11 on intonation.

## Rhythm

### Activity 3

*a. Basic accentuation patterns*

◀ Listen to these utterances and underline the content words:

1. The Queen is visiting Cairo this morning.
2. Do you want a cup of coffee?
3. Can you tell her I called?
4. I'm sorry to trouble you but it's rather urgent.

*b. Focus*

◀ Listen to these utterances and highlight the nucleus in each:

1. The film was brilliant!
2. Are you coming on Saturday?
3. Can you give it to him?
4. I think I left it in the kitchen.

*c. New focus*

◀ Listen to the following conversation and highlight the nucleus in each utterance. Notice the changes in focus:

A: What are you doing?
B: I came to see Barbara.

A: Well, Barbara's not here.
B: I can see she's not here. Where is she?
A: I don't know where she is.
B: Not very friendly, are you?
A: Neither are you!

*d. Contrastive focus*

◄ Listen to the dialogues and highlight the nucleus in each utterance:

A: David's funny.
B: He isn't funny. He's strange.
A: So the number is 493656.
B: No, it's 492656.
A: That's £10.30 altogether.
B: £10.13?
A: No, £10.30.

English has a characteristic rhythm and L1 listeners expect to hear this rhythm, that is it is an essential ingredient for intelligibility. According to Brown (1977) and Cutler (1993), rhythm is a guide to the structure of information in the spoken language, not something added to the basic sequence of consonants and vowels.

Accentuation and word stress together contribute to the rhythmic patterning of English. Each language has its own, distinctive rhythm. In English, it is closely related to the distribution of strong and weak syllables (i.e. stressed and unstressed syllables). The most important feature of English rhythm is that the syllables are not equal in duration (Klatt 1975, Taylor 1981, Roach 1991). Just as we tend to get an alternation of stressed and unstressed syllables in multisyllabic words, when words are combined together in connected speech we perceive a similar rhythmic effect.

e.g. · ● ·    · ● ·
     baNAna   in LONdon

● · ·    ● · ·
ABsolute   HAVE some FRUIT

There is an alternation of strong and weak syllables with strong syllables coming at intervals and weak syllables 'borrowing time'[2] between them.

e.g. · · ● · · ● · · ●
     do you KNOW if he's BUsy this MORning?

The difference is syllable length is largely related to differences in the length of vowels (as explained in Chapter 6). There are three main lengths:

(a) reduced (e.g. <u>a</u>GAIN)
(b) full vowel, unstressed (e.g. WIN<u>dow</u>)
(c) full vowel, stressed (ba<u>NA</u>na)

When two full vowels follow each other, they tend to be lengthened even more.

e.g.
GET OUT

FIRST CLASS

English rhythm is based not only on variation of syllable length, but also accentuation processes. These are very different: for example, English and Spanish use similar accentuation patterns but their syllable timing is very different so the rhythmic impression is different.

Traditionally, it has been common to refer to languages as falling into one of two distinct rhythmic groups, that is, **stress-timed** or **syllable-timed** (Abercrombie 1965, Halliday 1967). According to this theory, languages such as Russian and English are said to be a stress-timed (as opposed to syllable-timed) languages, with stressed syllables occurring at regular intervals, regardless of the number of unstressed syllables between them. The theory claims that the time between stressed syllables will tend to be the same and the more unstressed syllables there are between stressed syllables, the more they will need to be compressed or squeezed in, to fit into the regular pattern. So, for example, the message:

●      ●      ●
kids    like    sweets
1      2      3

Has three stressed syllables (which are all content words) occurring at regular intervals. If unstressed syllables are added:

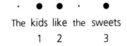

The kids like the sweets
1   2     3

There are still three stressed syllables and the additional unstressed syllables are shortened to fit into the regular rhythm. The same process occurs if further unstressed syllables are added:

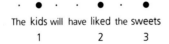

The kids will have liked the sweets
1      2     3

Based on this approach, the following sentence illustrates a typical, alternating stress pattern in English:

● · ● · ● · · ● ·

Peter said he'd sent you an email

● · · ● · ● · · ● ·

Jonathan's coming to see me on Monday

If you say the above examples carefully it is possible to tap out the rhythm with a pencil while you do so.

---

### Activity 4

◀ Listen and mark stress in the same way, in the following word groups:

    (a) Let her take it.
    (b) Show me the way to go home.
    (c) What's happened to the doctor?
    (d) Meet me at the entrance to the station.

---

According to stress-timed rhythm theory, other languages, such as French, Spanish, Greek, Polish or Yoruba, are syllable-timed. It is claimed that they do not have such a clear alternation of strong and weak syllables but give the impression of roughly equal length to each syllable regardless of stress. For instance, in French, all syllables appear to have approximately equal value in terms of time, except for the final syllable in the word group which tends to be extended:

Je vais à Pa ris (I'm going to Paris)
1  2   3 4 5

C'est gé ńe rale ment fa cile (Normally, it's easy)
  1  2  3  4   5  6  7

However, the theory of stress-timed and syllable-timed languages seems to be hard to confirm empirically and this neat distinction has been called into question by some researchers. Dauer (1983), for instance, proposes an avoidance of the word 'timing', favouring the term 'stress-based' (following O'Connor 1973, Allen 1975). For Dauer, a stress-based language is one in which stress plays a large role in word-stress, syllable structure and vowel reduction. Ladefoged refers to stress timing as a 'tendency' (1983:224), while Caudwell argues it is a 'myth' (1996:33). Similarly, Roach states that in research studies, 'it has not been possible to show a real difference between "stress-timed" and "syllable-timed" languages' and suggests that stress-timed rhythm may only operate in certain styles of speaking, such as in formal, public speaking, rather than across English speech as a whole (2000:136). Roach goes on to conclude that rather than seeing 'stress-timed' and 'syllable-timed' languages as polar opposites, they should be seen as occupying a point along a continuum and that 'different types of timing will be exhibited by the same speakers on different occasions and in different contexts' (2000:136).

Despite the uncertainty regarding the nature or indeed reality of 'stress-timing', what is clear is that English is not 'syllable-timed' in the sense that some languages are, like French, Hindi, Cantonese or Spanish, which do not make notable use of reduced syllables. Regardless of the uncertainty of how regular English speech rhythm is, the contrast between stressed and unstressed syllables is a distinctive feature of the language. Furthermore, rhythm obviously has a role in some types of speech, such as oratory, advertising, drama or rapping, or even in everyday speech where rhythm is used to add extra emphasis.

## Weak and strong forms

Another outcome of the accentuation process in connected speech is that changes occur in unstressed words. We saw in Chapter 9 that there is a group of function words that are typically unstressed, that is, which normally appear in their weak form. In total, there are approximately 50 such words with weak and strong forms.

There are certain contexts where only the strong form of these words is acceptable and others where the weak form is normal but the weak forms of most function words are much more common than the strong form and should be considered the normal pronunciation. It is possible to use strong forms all the time, but L2 learners who do this sound very unnatural. Compare, for instance:

> . . . and there was a man at the door.
> ən ðə wəz ə mæn ət ðə dɔː

with:

> ænd ðeə wɒz æ mæn æt ði: dɒ

These structural or function words account, on average, for every seventh word of English discourse. Typically, they appear in their weak form, that is the strong form is 'marked'. There are some simple rules to help remember when the strong forms are used.

They are used in their strong form:

> *(i) at the end of a sentence:*
> He's older than I <u>am</u> (æm)
> Why <u>am</u> (əm) I so tired?

Many words, however, that have a weak and strong form never occur at the end of a sentence, for example, 'your', 'the'

    *(ii) to mark contrast:*
        A: I'm surprised you (ju) find it so difficult to stop smoking!
        B: Well how did <u>you</u> (ju:) stop?

    *(iii) to mark emphasis:*
        A: You can (kən) stay <u>here.</u>
        B: <u>Can</u> (kæn) I? That's so kind of you.

However, the above examples are only guidelines. Any speaker has the option to choose which words to emphasize or highlight, depending on his/her intended meaning.

---

### Activity 5

    (a) What are the weak and strong forms of the words below?

        *a    and    but    that    the    as    than*

    (b) Read the following, find and underline all the weak forms of the above and note a transcription for each:
        (i) Stephen is younger than Matthew.
        (ii) He left as soon as he could.
        (iii) The director said that Tom and Alan would do it.
        (iv) That is not what the rest said that they wanted.
        (v) Star Wars is good, but it's not as good a film as people say.

    (c) Now, read the following idioms:

        'hiːz əz 'fɪt əz ə 'fɪdl
        ɪts 'reɪnɪŋ 'kæts ən 'dɒgz
        'betə 'leɪt ðən 'nevə

---

When function words begin with /h/, such as the pronouns 'her', 'him', 'he', the initial /h/ often disappears when the word is in its weak form (i.e. in medial or final position).

    e.g. A: did you see (h)im?
        B: yes, I saw (h)im earlier

However, when such words are in their strong form, that is for emphasis or at the beginning of utterances the /h/ is not omitted.

e.g.  A: <u>her</u> paintings are wonderful

B: she's good but <u>he's</u> better

---

### Activity 6

Write out the following phrases in normal script:

'hæv səm 'mɔː 'tiː

'pɑːs ər ə 'bɪskɪt

'liːv ɪm ə'ləʊn

'hə 'sɪstəz ət ðə 'dɔː

---

# Modifications of sounds in connected speech

The process of accentuation, through stress placement and rhythm, has a profound effect on the pronunciation of sounds in connected speech. Furthermore, the speed of natural fluent L1 speech can reach 350 syllables per minute. At such speeds, certain modifications are essential to facilitate the articulation and production of connected speech. Some people may consider such modifications as features of careless speech. However, they are an obligatory feature of the phonology of English.

In this section we look at the various ways that sounds are modified in connected speech, through the processes of elision, assimilation and linking. An awareness of these modifications is essential to help learners understand L1 speech and also to enable those who want to aim towards fluent, near-native production of English.

## Assimilation

In natural fluent speech, it is quite common for phonemes at word boundaries to be influenced by each other, that is, a sound belonging to one word can cause changes in sounds belonging to neighbouring words. This change or difference in pronunciation is called **assimilation**. In general, it is consonants that are subject to assimilation. For instance,

| | |
|---|---|
| broadcast | /brɔːdkɑːst/ becomes /brɔːgkɑːst/ |
| light blue | /laɪt bluː/ becomes /laɪp̚ bluː/ |

Assimilation can be **regressive**, that is the final consonant of the first word (e.g. the /t/ in 'light' /laɪt/) assumes the phonetic characteristics of the first consonant of the following word (e.g. the /b/ in 'blue' /bluː/). So, /laɪt/ sounds like /laɪp/. We refer to the final consonant as 'consonant final' (abbreviated to 'Cf') and the initial consonant as 'consonant initial' (or 'Ci'). In English, regressive assimilation of this type is the most common.

The most common type of regressive assimilation is called **assimilation of place.** Typically this involves the alveolar consonants /t, d, n, s, z/ assimilating to the **place** of articulation of the following initial consonant. In the example below, /s/, the Cf of the first word 'this', assimilates to the place of articulation of /ʃ/, the Ci of the following word 'shop', so it sounds like /ðɪʃ/:

this shop  / ðɪs ʃɒp/ ⟶ / ðɪʃ ʃɒp/

Here are some further examples:

| | |
|---|---|
| that person | /ðæp pɜːsən/ |
| good boy | /ɡʊb bɔɪ/ |
| is she ready | /ɪʃ ʃɪ redɪ/ |
| in case | /ɪŋ keɪs/ |
| in public | /ɪm pʌblɪk/ |
| that class | /ðæk klɑːs/ |
| this year | /ðɪʃ jɪə/ |

So, for example, /t/ can become /p/ (bilabial) before /m/, /b/ and /p/ (as in 'that person') and it can become /k/ (velar) before /g/ and /k/ /d/ (as in 'that class'). /n/ can become /m/ before bilabial consonants (as in 'in public') and /ŋ/ before velar consonants (as in 'in case').

In addition, /s/ can become /ʃ/ (palato-alveolar) before /ʃ/ /tʃ/ /dʒ/ or /j/, as in:

| | |
|---|---|
| this sheep | /ðɪʃ ʃiːp/ |
| pass your cup | /pɑːʃ jə kʌp/ |

/z/ can become /ʒ/ before /ʃ/ /tʃ/ /dʒ/ / j/, as in:

| | |
|---|---|
| has she? | /hæʒ ʃi/ |
| is she ready | /ɪʃ ʃɪ redɪ/ |

**Activity 7**

Can you explain why 'good morning' /ɡʊd mɔːnɪŋ/ becomes /ɡʊb mɔːnɪŋ/ and why 'what side' /wɒt saɪd/ becomes /wɒs saɪd/?

A notable example of assimilation of place in English involves regressive **assimilation of nasals.** In these examples, the Cf nasal of the first word assimilates to the place of assimilation of the Ci of the second word but remains nasal in manner:

e.g. handbag /ˈhæm̱bæg/
rainbow /ˈreɪm̱bəʊ/
sandwiches /ˈsæm̱wɪd̠ʒɪz/

---

## Activity 8

Can you transcribe the following and mark the assimilations:

I've got a sandwich in my handbag

---

It is also possible, if less common, for assimilation to involve a change in the **manner** of articulation rather than place. For instance,

'good night' /gʊd naɪt/ becomes gʊṉ naɪt/

Here the final consonant of the first word (/d/) and the initial consonant of the second word /n/ are both alveolar but the Cf /d/ assimilates the manner of articulation of the Ci /n/ and becomes a nasal /n/ rather than plosive.

Assimilation can be **progressive** – that is the initial consonant (Ci) of the second word is affected by the final consonant of the preceding word (Cf). This is relatively rare in English but there are some fairly common examples in rapid, informal speech, such as:

| | | | |
|---|---|---|---|
| will there | /wɪl ðeə/ | ⟶ | /wɪl leə/ |
| although | /ɔːl ðəʊ/ | ⟶ | /ɔːḻ ləʊ/ |
| all their | /ɔːl ðeə/ | ⟶ | /ɔːḻ leə/ |
| read these | /riːd ðiːz/ | ⟶ | /riːḏ diːz/ |

Another type of progressive assimilation which has become a fixed phonological rule in English is progressive **assimilation of voice** within words, with the suffixes /s/ and /z/. The rule is that when a third person singular verb or a noun ends in the sibilant 's' and the preceding consonant is voiceless (e.g. /t/), the 's' will also be pronounced as a voiceless /s/. If the preceding consonant is voiced (e.g. /g/) then the 's' will also be pronounced as a voiced /z/.

| | | |
|---|---|---|
| cats | /s/ | /kæts̱/ |
| dogs | /z/ | /dɒgẕ/ |
| jumps | /s/ | /dʒʌmps̱/ |

The same modification can occur across word boundaries like 'I have to' where the final consonant in 'have', /v/, changes to /f/ before the initial /t/ of 'to'. Such assimilations of voice across words are always from voiced to voiceless. The reverse voiceless to voice assimilations (e.g. 'black dog' /blæg dɒg/ or 'nice voice' /naɪz vɔɪs/ is not possible in English, although they are common in some languages, such as German, French and Dutch.

Another common type of assimilation of place involves words beginning with **palatals** such as the semi-vowel /j/, such as 'you' and 'yet' which can merge with preceding words ending in alveolars, such as /t/, /d/ . So, for example, /d/ + /j/ becomes /ʤ/ (as in 'did you' /dɪʤə/) and /t/ + /j/ becomes /ʧ/ (as in 'what you' /wɒʧə/:

> Did you see him /dɪd jə/ becomes /dɪʤə/
> Would you /wʊd jə/ becomes /wʊʤə/
> Did you tell her what you saw /'dɪʤə 'tel ə 'wɒʧə 'sɔ:/

These assimilations are very common in L1 connected speech and are therefore important for learners to be aware of if they want to understand such speech.

In sum, assimilation can be of three types:

> i. place of articulation
> ii. manner of articulation
> iii. voicing

Assimilation is a natural phenomenon and in terms of teaching pronunciation, recognition is generally more important than production, particularly for common or frequent assimilations which create modifications to common words or phrases which are significantly different from what a learner may expect, such as 'handbag', 'sandwiches', 'did you'.

Other **high frequency modifications** in L1 speech include the forms 'wanna' /'wʌnə/ for 'want to' and 'dunno' /də'nəʊ/ for 'don't know' 'in informal fluent speech'.

> e.g.  Do you want a cup of coffee        /ʤə 'wʌnə 'kʌp ə 'kɒfi/
>       I don't know where she went        /aɪ də 'nəʊ 'weə ʃi 'went/

In American English, the modification of 'going to' to 'gonna' /'gʌnə/ is also common in connected speech.

---

## Activity 9

◂ Listen and transcribe the following dialogue. Note any assimilation.

> A: What would you like?
> B: A coffee please
> A: Do you want a cake or something?
> B: I don't know really . . . . er..
> A: Will that be all then?
> B: Yes thanks

## Elision (contractions)

In natural fluent L1 English speech, quite a lot of sounds not only change or are assimilated but are not actually pronounced. This process, which is called **elision**, involves the loss of a phoneme in connected speech which would be pronounced if the word occurred in isolation, as in the examples above.

/ˈwʌnə/ for 'want to' and /dəˈnəʊ/ for 'don't know'.

Phonemes have a tendency to disappear in unstressed syllables in connected speech. In a sense, elision is a simplification, an economy made in rapid colloquial speech. The omission of a sound is most likely to occur as follows.

### (i) loss of weak vowels (in unstressed syllables)

It is common for a vowel in a weak syllable to be reduced to schwa and sometimes this weak vowel disappears altogether, as in the following examples:

| potato | /pˈteɪtəʊ/ | perhaps | /pˈræps/ |
| I'm afraid so | /ˈfreɪd səʊ/ | because | /bˈkɒz/ or /ˈkɒz/ |
| secretary | /ˈsekrətri/ | excuse me | /ˈskjuːz mi/ |

When /n/ or /l/ follow a weak vowel often become syllable, as in:

| tonight | /tˈn̩aɪt/ |
| police | /pˈl̩iːs/ |

---

### Activity 10

◀ Listen and then mark any elided vowels in these words and then transcribe the words:

'rectory
'preferable
'library
coˈrrect
baˈlloon

---

### (ii) loss of medial consonant in clusters of three consonants

Native speakers typically simplify complex consonant clusters, generally by eliding the middle consonant (typically /t/ or /d/) in a cluster of three (as we saw in Chapter 7). For example

| acts | /æk(t)s/ | he looked back | /hiː lʊk(t) bæk/ |
| scripts | /skrɪp(t)s/ | three fifths | /θriː fɪf(θ)s/ |

| | | | |
|---|---|---|---|
| ne<u>x</u>t week | /neks(t)wi:k/ | ju<u>st</u> <u>stand</u> <u>there</u> | /dʒəs(t)stæn(d)ðeə/ |
| I do<u>n't</u> <u>know</u> | /aɪ dən(t)nəʊ/ | le<u>ft</u> luggage | /lef(t)lʌgɪdʒ/ |

It can be seen that the avoidance of such consonant clusters can result in the loss of past tense endings, as in the example above, 'he loo<u>ked</u> <u>back</u>' /hi: lʊk(t) bæk/ (as we saw in Chapter 6). This can result in confusion between past and present tense which has to be deduced for the context of the utterance. For example:

| | |
|---|---|
| They seemed glad | /ðeɪ si:m(d)glæd/ |
| They seem glad | /ðeɪ si:m glæd/ |

---

## Activity 11

◀ Listen and then mark any elided consonants in these words and then transcribe the words:

'conscripts
facts
'dustmen
cold 'coffee
last 'month
the 'fact that

---

### (iii) Elision of /h/ in weak forms of pronouns

/h/ is regularly elided from the weak forms of function words such as (h)is, (h)er, (h)im (see section on 'weak forms' earlier). This is heard even in formal registers of all varieties of L1 English speech. Silent letters in words like 'comb', 'knee', 'talk', provide evidence of elisions that have occurred in the past and are now 'fixed' in present day pronunciations.

| | | |
|---|---|---|
| e.g. | 'leave (h)im a'lone | /'li:v (h)ɪm ə'ləʊn/ |
| | is (h)e 'here 'yet | /ɪz (h)i 'hɪə 'jet/ |
| | 'give (h)im a 'ring | /'gɪv (h)ɪm ə 'rɪŋ/ |

### (iv) contraction of verb forms (auxiliaries and modal auxiliaries)

Elisions frequently occur between weak forms, producing contracted forms or **contractions**, for example, 'he + will' → 'he'll', 'do + not' → 'don't'. Such contracted forms can be stressed, unlike weak forms, for example:

'Well, <u>'I'll</u> 'do it then

All such contractions are marked in writing with an apostrophe ('he'll)

Typically, main verbs and modals are not contracted, while auxiliaries are:

e.g. 'to have'

| | |
|---|---|
| main verb – | I 'have a 'watch |
| auxilliary – | I've 'bought a 'watch |
| | I've 'got a 'watch |
| | I've 'got* to 'buy a 'watch |
| modal – | I 'have to 'buy a 'watch |

*with the verb 'have got', 'have' is an auxiliary and therefore can be contracted.

---

**Activity 12**

In the examples below, draw a line through the letters that can be omitted in the verb 'have':

1. He has got a cold.
2. Do you think she has finished?
3. Where have they been?
4. I have to go to work.
5. We have got to work hard.
6. She has four children.
7. Have you seen David?
8. I have never been to India.

---

Other auxiliary verbs (e.g. 'will', 'can', 'is') are also regularly contracted in connected speech and in informal writing (but not in formal writing). Contractions are used to de-emphasize the less important words which helps to highlight more important information.

Some examples:

| Full form | Contracted form | Full form | Contracted form |
|---|---|---|---|
| I am | I'm | I would/should | I'd |
| we are | we're | I will not | I won't |
| that is | that's | he does not | he doesn't |
| there are | there're | we cannot | we can't |

Negative auxiliaries are also regularly contracted but they are stressed to emphasize 'negation', for example:

| | |
|---|---|
| They are not coming | they 'aren't 'coming |
| | they're 'not 'coming |
| She did not go | she 'didn't 'go |
| We will not be there | we'll 'not be 'there |
| | we 'won't be 'there |

However, when an auxiliary comes at the end of an utterance, it is not contracted (following the weak form rules explained earlier in this chapter).

**Activity 13**

◀ Mark the stressed words and possible contractions in these examples and then listen and practice saying them.

1. No, I do not think she has.
2. They would help you if they could.
3. No, I should not imagine he is.
4. I am sure you are.

# Linking

It can be seen that in fluent speech a lot of changes and deletions occur in weak syllables and at word boundaries, in order to make articulations more efficient and enhance the 'flow' of speech. In connected speech, words often blend together: this process is called **linking**. So, for example, the following phase can be said with no discernable break between words:

First ͜ of ͜ all ͜ I ͜ ought ͜ to ͜ ask ͜ him

This results from a combination of processes, including assimilation (e.g. ought to), elision (e.g. ask (h)im) and liaison (e.g. first ͜ of ͜ all).

There are different types of linking.

## (i) consonant-to-vowel

When a word ends in a consonant and the following word starts with a vowel, the consonant is 'attracted' to the beginning of the next word (e.g. 'turn it on' – 'tur ni ton'). For instance:

| | | | |
|---|---|---|---|
| where ͜ is | /weərɪz/ | laugh ͜ at | /lɑːfət/ |
| miss ͜ *(h)im | /mɪsɪm/ | with ͜ us | /wɪθəs/ |

*function words beginning with an elided /h/ are treated as if they begin with a vowel ('give (h)er it' – 'giverit').*

## (ii) vowel-to-vowel

When a word ends in a vowel and the following word also starts with a vowel, an additional semivowel (/w/ or /j/) may be inserted to link the two words together. Linking from a rounded vowel tends to create an intrusive [w] sound whereas linking from a spread vowel creates an intrusive [j].

For instance:

| Linking with intrusive [w] | | Linking with intrusive [j] | |
|---|---|---|---|
| who are | /huːwɑː/ | she is | /ʃiːjɪz/ |
| how often | /haʊwɒftən/ | high up | /haɪjʌp/ |
| you ought | /juːwɔːt/ | we ought | /wiːjɔːt/ |

### (iii) linking /r/

We have seen that English accents can be divided into 'rhotic' and 'non-rhotic' varieties, with the latter only pronouncing /r/ before a vowel (e.g. in 'tree' but not in 'tear'). However, in connected speech, this pattern is extended across word boundaries, so that in non-rhotic accents, the /r/ is often reinstated to form a link to a word starting with a vowel:

| e.g. | here is | /hɪərɪz/ | four eggs | /fɔːregz/ |
|---|---|---|---|---|
| | are in | /ɑːrɪn/ | fire exit | /faɪəreksɪt/ |

With many speakers with non-rhotic accents, it is also possible to hear linking /r/ when there is no 'r' in the spelling of the word. This is termed **intrusive 'r'**. It occurs quite commonly in /ə/ endings and before the conjunction 'and'. For example:

| Australia all out | /ɔːstreɪlɪərɔːlaʊt/ | media event | /miːdɪəriːvent/ |
|---|---|---|---|

It is also heard, though less frequently, after /ɑː/ and /ɔː/ endings, such as:

| law and order | /lɔːrənɔːdə/ | awe-inspiring | /ɔːrɪnspaɪrɪŋ/ |
|---|---|---|---|

There is a strong tendency to use intrusive /r/ of the type noted above, even by those who protest that it is wrong. Occurrences of the second type (i.e. non-schwa endings) are less frequent and perhaps because of their rarity of occurrence they cause disapproval from some people.

Linking and intrusive 'r' are examples of **'juncture'** which refers to the way listeners perceive word boundaries so that they do not confuse similar utterances. For example:

All that I'm after today
All the time after today (Roach 2000:145)

In rapid natural speech, the only perceptual difference between the two phrases is one of juncture, in (a) the /t/ at the end of 'that' is unaspirated whereas it is in (b) Although such distinctions are unlikely to be helpful to most learners, they do show how complex the process of word boundary identification is and the range of cues and information that we employ to extract meaning from speech.

---

### Activity 14

◀ Listen to the following utterances and then transcribe them, showing stress, focus and any sound modifications you can hear:

1. Do you know if he is busy this afternoon
2. If I had known about the party I would have come
3. I will ask him to come over as soon as possible
4. Do you want a sandwich or an apple?
5. I do not know where he is actually
6. Will there be a message in case he is late?

---

### Activity 15

Read and then write out the following in normal script:

/'helənz mə'ʃiːn 'stɒp 'prɪntɪŋ/
/'tɒm 'krep 'kwaɪətlɪ ə'weɪ/
/'ɪz 'smaɪl 'dʒentlɪ/
/hɪ 'pɑːst ɪz ɪg'zæm/
/gɪ mɪ ə breɪk/
/aɪ wʌnə həʊld jɔː hænd/

---

# Teaching implications

We have seen from the processes and features that have been described in this chapter that there is a considerable difference between the way words are pronounced in isolation and in connected speech. Perhaps the most important conclusion that can be drawn from this is that learners need to be aware of some of the difficulties they may face when listening to fluent, colloquial speech.

The processes of accentuation and modification of sounds have a profound effect in fluent speech enabling sounds to be articulated as efficiently as possible while highlighting important information. However, if learners are unaware of these processes in connected speech and rely solely on having learned the pronunciation of citation forms of words, they are likely to be very ill-equipped to deal with understanding normal, fluent L1 speech.

For instance, simple vocabulary items may be totally misunderstood if a learner is expecting to hear citation forms, rather than the modifications and accentuation that typically occur in fluent speech to phrases such as:

| | | | |
|---|---|---|---|
| 'Is he busy' | → | 'izzybizzy' | /ˈɪziˈbɪzi/ |
| 'What is his name' | → | 'watsiz name' | /ˈwɒtsɪzˈneɪm/ |

However, there is considerable disagreement about the importance of the various features in this chapter with regard to pronunciation teaching.

Regarding the process of accentuation, most phonologists and pronunciation teachers would agree that an understanding of accentuation and an ability to produce basic stress patterns in English is essential to understand and be understood by L1 speakers. Many would also feel that the same targets should be expected of learners who plan to use English largely as an international language. However, both Cruttenden (2008) and Jenkins (2000) suggest that the use of weak forms and the reduction of vowels to /ə/ in unstressed syllables is unnecessary in such contexts of use, although admitting that this will likely result in a sort of 'syllable-timed' rhythm (Cruttenden 2008:332).

Regarding the modifications that occur in connected speech, Jenkins (2000:148) argues that most L2 speakers do not reach anything like the speed of speaking that fluent native speakers achieve and claims that the use of such features at slower speeds would sound very unnatural and actually reduce intelligibility. Many phonologists and pronunciation teachers agree that it seems advisable to help learners *recognize* native speakers' production of such features in fluent connected speech but not encourage learners to *produce* all of them themselves. Priority should probably be given to practice with accentuation and rhythm, while linking and elisions should be given greater emphasis than assimilations. There is some suggestion that, similarly to intonation patterns, as learners gain fluency they are likely to acquire such features naturally outside the classroom.

## Accentuation

Many L2 learners do not distinguish clearly enough between words that are emphasized and words that are not. Ignorance of the basic patterns of accentuation not only adds an element of confusion to the learner's speech but also means he/she is missing important signals in listening comprehension.

| *To recap the main accentuation patterns* | |
|---|---|
| Basic stress pattern | Content words are usually stressed Function words are usually unstressed, for example she 'WANTS a 'COFFEE |
| Focus | The final content word in an utterance is usually the focus.<br>for example he 'rang the <u>'doctor</u> |

⇨

| New focus | We don't repeat emphasis on a piece of information that is repeated – so we move the focus to a word or words that give new information in a conversation. <br> For example  A:  He's 'bought a '<u>car</u> <br> B:  what '<u>kind</u> of 'car |
|---|---|
| Contrastive focus | We can accentuate words to contrast an idea with a previous idea, for example when correcting or contrasting information, for example   A: So, the appointment is the fifteenth of '<u>October</u> <br> B:  No, it's the <u>sixteenth</u> of October |

*Learners need to be aware of:*

- content and structure words
- basic accentuation patterns
- the functions of focus and how to manipulate it.

# Weak and strong forms

English is unusual in the number and frequency of its weak and contracted forms and the use of such forms does not come easily to L2 learners. Even learners whose first language does contain weak forms, such as Dutch, are unlikely to have such a complex and extensive system as English. It is commonly assumed that the use of such forms is an important goal for those wishing to achieve fluent near native English speech and while these forms are not essential for intelligibility, they do make speech sound more fluent and effective. However, there is some debate regarding their importance for learners with more modest goals, particularly if the main use will be for lingua franca communication. Here the argument put for instance by Jenkins (2000) and Cruttenden (2008) is that the production of such forms is not necessary.

Cruttenden for instance, acknowledges that different targets are appropriate for different types of learners. He suggests that the use of correct word stress patterns and weak forms are equally important for those aiming at a near native speaker accent and for those aiming at 'Amalgum English', who will at times need to communicate with native English speakers. Cruttenden (2008:323) claims that the 'foreign learner must regard the strong forms as being "marked", that is having a special meaning compared with the "unmarked" sense of the usual weak forms'. He also suggests that using strong forms with full vowels rather than weak forms with reduced vowels 'will produce a rhythm which is seriously different from that of native-speaker RP (and almost all other varieties of English in the UK, Ireland, North America, Australia and New Zealand)'. He further predicts that for learners whose L1 does not make this distinction between strong and weak forms (such as French, Italian, Spanish, Japanese and some African tone languages) 'this problem is especially great and will require prolonged attention' (2008:323).

However, his advice is surprisingly different for those who intend to use English primarily in an international context, that is as a lingua franca. Here he claims that, as there will be no need for /ə/, weak forms will be replaced by strong forms, which he predicts will give rise to a sort of 'syllable-timed rhythm'.

*To summarize the weak and strong form patterns:*
In weak forms:

   i. Vowels usually reduce to schwa
  ii. Initial consonants can be lost, as with pronouns (h)im, (h)er, (th)em
 iii. Some final consonants can be lost, especially in 'o(f) and an(d).

Strong form rules:
i.e. weak form words usually have full vowels when they are:

   i. at the end of a sentence
  ii. used for emphasis
 iii. used for contrast.

*Learners need to be aware of:*

- Strong and weak form uses
- Frequency of weak forms in fluent L1 speech
- The connection between the use of weak and strong forms and speech rhythm and accentuation patterns.

# Rhythm

We have seen that differentiation between stressed and unstressed syllables, the reduction of function words, the linking of words and phrases etc. all combine to create the characteristic rhythm of English. Many feel that developing learners' awareness of, and some proficiency in, speech rhythm is essential to gaining fluency in spoken English (Adams 1979, Taylor 1981, Gilbert 2008).

It should be remembered, however, that despite being a popular focus in many pronunciation courses, the stress-timed rhythm theory seems to be hard to confirm empirically. Nevertheless, it is clear that some languages do not make such an important distinction between stressed and unstressed syllables as English does. Some varieties of English used as a second language, such as many Indian or African varieties, tend to be influenced by the syllable-timing of the mother tongue which can make them very difficult for L1 English speakers to understand. English rhythm can cause difficulty for learners whose first language is syllable-timed. Speakers of such languages (such as Japanese, Spanish or Hungarian) may find it helpful to practice repeating strongly rhythmical utterances, such as limericks and poems, as this forces them to concentrate on making a clear contrast between strong and weak syllables. However, it must be made clear that such exercises do not represent the way most people normally speak.

Pedagogically the danger is that learners conclude that English should be spoken with a consistent rhythm which they have been taught through limericks and poems. Nevertheless, the notion of alternating strong and weak syllables can be very useful to convey the importance of accentuation and the lengthening of stressed syllables should be seen as 'crucial to intelligible English pronunciation' (Jenkins 2000:150).

*Learners need to be aware:*

- of the relationship between syllables, stress/ accent and rhythm
- that stressed syllables tend to occur at fairly regular intervals
- that there is a tendency to alternate between stressed and unstressed syllables
- that consecutive stressed syllables add length.

## Assimilation

Assimilation is a natural but complex phonological process which has limited value for pronunciation learners. Recognition is more important than production for most L2 learners. However, an awareness of high frequency assimilations in colloquial fluent speech is useful (e.g. 'handbag /hæmbæg/, sandwiches /sæmwɪdʒɪz/).

*To summarize the main assimilation patterns:*

i. Plural 's' assimilates voicing of preceding final consonant (Cf) for example, 's' is pronounced /s/ in 'cats' /kæts/ and /z/ in 'dogs' /dɒgz/
ii. Regressive assimilation is common, for example with Ci plosives, so for example /n/ often sounds like /m/ before /p/ or /b/ (e.g. he can pay – /hi: kæm peɪ/, on purpose – /ɒm pɜːpəs/)
iii. Progressive assimilation is less common but frequent examples include /ð/ sounding like /l/ (e.g. will there /wɪl leə/).

*Learners should be aware:*

- of common assimilation patterns
- of high frequency assimilations in words and phrases
- that assimilations are more common in unstressed rather than stressed syllables and in informal rather than formal speech.

## Elision

It is important for learners to know that when L1 speakers talk naturally, quite a lot of sounds that they might expect to hear are not actually pronounced.

It is worth remembering that elision relates to fluency. As learners develop fluency they may acquire the confidence to elide the forms listed above, but this is by no means obligatory. They need to know of the existence of patterns of elision and receive appropriate listening practice.

*To summarize the main elision patterns:*

i. A weak vowel (i.e. in an unstressed syllable) is often elided (e.g. 'perhaps' – /præps/, 'vegetable' – /'vedʒtəbl,/)
ii. When weak forms begin with /h/, the /h/ often disappears (e.g. give (h)er in)
iii. Consonants can disappear in complex consonant clusters. In particular /t/ and /d/ are often elided in medial position in clusters (e.g. 'ac(t)s', 'soun(d)s').

*Learners should be aware:*

- of common elision patterns
- of high frequency elisions in words and phrases
- that elisions can lead to loss of past tense endings.
  (e.g. 'they seemed glad' v 'they seem glad'   /ðeɪ siːm glæd/

## Contractions

Weak forms and contractions are common in fluent speech and in informal writing and learners should to be able to recognize both these features. The production of weak forms and contractions is a characteristic of fluent speech and an overuse of full vowels and stressed syllables can be very confusing to the L1 listener. L2 learners often avoid the use of contractions, either because they associate their use with careless speech or because the consonant clusters that may result can seem difficult to pronounce.

*To summarize the main contraction patterns:*

i. Elisions frequently occur between weak forms, producing contracted forms (e.g. 'he will' – he'll')
ii. Typically, main verbs and modals are not contracted, while auxiliary verbs are
iii. Negative auxiliaries are also regularly contracted but they are stressed to emphasize 'negation' (e.g. 'I 'won't do it')
iv. When an auxiliary comes at the end of an utterance, it is not contracted
v. All such contractions are marked in writing with an apostrophe (he'll).

*Learners need to be aware:*

- that auxiliary verbs are regularly contracted in fluent speech, if unstressed
- of the connection between function words, weak forms and contractions.

## Linking

The most valuable aspect of linking for L2 learners is that it can increase perceptions of fluency as it enables the production of connected speech without breaks between words. Linking is a common feature of native speaker English, although there is considerable variation in the use of linking between speakers and it can also be perceived (as have other features of connected speech) as a sign of 'lazy' or 'uneducated' speech. There is some research evidence to suggest that NNS of English do significantly less linking than native speakers (Hieke 1984).

*To summarize the main linking patterns:*

i. Consonant to vowel, that is the word final consonant links to the word initial vowel (e.g. this ‿ afternoon)
ii. Vowel to vowel, that is the words are linked by inserting a semi-vowel. If the final vowel of the first word is lip rounded, a rounded semi-vowel /w/ is used for linking (e.g. 'so ‿ am ‿ I' /səʊwəmaɪ/). If the final vowel of the first word is spread, a spread semi-vowel is used (e.g. 'yes ‿I ‿am') /jesaɪjæm/
iii. Intrusive /r/ – words ending in /r/ followed by a word beginning with a vowel are linked by the /r/, which would not normally be pronounced in a BBC or other non-rhotic accents (e.g. 'where are' /weərɑː/, 'here is' /hɪərɪz/.

*Learners need to be aware:*

- of consonant attraction (i.e. the tendency to link consonants to following syllable if it starts with a vowel – to avoid VC syllable structure)
- that negotiation of word boundaries in English may be quite different from that of the L1.

## Key points

An ability to recognize and produce the main accentuation patterns in English is important in order to understand others and to be understood clearly. What is significant about English is the alternation of strong and weak syllables and the degree of contrast between highlighted, or stressed syllables and reduced or weakened ones. Therefore, teaching learners to lengthen stressed syllables and shorten unstressed one is important to intelligibility.

It is also important for learners to be aware of the differences between citation forms and modifications in connected speech so that they know what to expect when listening to fluent, native speaker English.

It is probably not practical or useful to teach all learners to produce assimilations. However, an awareness of some of the most common cases can be very useful for listener comprehension. Occasionally, L2 learners of English bring their first language habits of assimilation to their pronunciation of English.

Speech rhythm is a distinguishing factor between languages, and is considered by many as a key factor in pronunciation learning. However, the stress-timed rhythm theory of English is largely unproven. It has been suggested that it is not easy to eradicate L1 rhythmic patterns which can still influence L2 pronunciation at advanced levels of proficiency (Wenk 1985).

English has an unusually high number of weak forms and contracted forms and these are much more common than strong forms in L1 fluent speech. They are not signs of 'careless' speech but normal phonological processes and they are not restricted to very informal speech. Avoidance of the use of contracted forms will not usually result in misunderstandings but will make speech sound less fluent and more unnatural to native speakers of English.

# Notes

1   The terms 'broad' and 'narrow' focus are used by Cruttenden (1997), among others.
2   The 'borrowing rule' explained by Gimson (1994) and first introduced by Bolinger (1981) states that a syllable with a reduced vowel borrows time from any immediately preceding syllable with a full vowel.

# Further reading

Adams, C. (1979) *English Speech Rhythm and the Foreign Learner.* Mouton, The Hague.

Alexander, J. D. (1986) 'The stress factor in spoken English', *English Today*, 5, 31–4.

Benrabah, M. (1997) 'Word-stress: A source of unintelligibility in English', *IRAL*, 35 (3), 157–65.

Chela de Rodriguez, B. (1983) 'Recognizing and producing English rhythmic patterns', *English Teaching Forum*, 21 (3), 27–9. Also in Brown, A. (ed., 1991) *Teaching English Pronunciation: A Book of Readings.* Routledge, London, pp. 350–6.

Chela-Flores, B. (1994) 'On the acquisition of English rhythm: Theoretical and practical issues', *IRAL*, 32 (2), 232–42.

Faber, D. (1986) 'Teaching the rhythms of English: A new theoretical base', *IRAL*, 24, 207–16. Also in Brown, A. (ed., 1991) *Teaching English Pronunciation: A Book of Readings.* London: Routledge.

Haycraft, B. (1985) 'Put life into drills with the right stress', *Professional English Teacher*, 5 (4), 39–41.

Haycraft, B. (1992) 'Sentence stress – for more meaningful speech', in Brown, A. (ed.) *Approaches to Pronunciation Teaching.* London: Macmillan & The British Council, pp. 57–72.

Marks, J. (1999) 'Is stress-timing real?', *ELT Journal*, 53 (3), 191–9.

Taylor, D. (1981) 'Non-native speakers and the rhythm of English', *IRAL*, 14 (3), 219–26.

Taylor, D. (1991) 'Compound word stress', *ELT Journal*, 45, 67–73.

Vaughan-Rees, M. (1995) 'Rhymes and rhythm', in Brown, A. (ed.) *Approaches to Pronunciation Teaching.* Singapore: The British Council, pp. 47–56.

Wenk, B. J. (1985) 'Speech rhythms in second language acquisition', *Language & Speech*, 28, 157–75.

Woodward, T. (1991) 'Making stress physical, visible & audible', *Modern English Teacher*, 17 (3 & 4), 38–9.

# Intonation 11

## Introduction

Many of the earlier chapters in this book are concerned with describing individual phonemes or sound segments, which is often termed **segmental phonology**. However, later chapters move on to look at larger parts of speech, such as syllables, words and then connected speech: the study of these broader aspects of the sound system is known as **suprasegmental phonology**. This chapter aims to introduce the key element of suprasegmental phonology, that is, intonation. We will consider what form intonation takes, how it functions in English and what that implies for pronunciation teaching and learning.

There can be considerable difference in the way intonation is defined, sometimes meaning is restricted narrowly to tone choice while at others it includes broader aspects of stress, rhythm and prominence. This broader perspective is also sometimes referred to as **prosody**. However, definitions generally include linguistically significant variations in pitch level, or **speech melody**, across an utterance or part of an utterance. Pitch refers to our perception of how 'high' or 'low' the voice sounds based on the 'fundamental frequency' (speed of vibration) of the vocal folds: the higher the frequency the higher the perceived pitch and vice versa. To be linguistically significant, pitch variations have to be under a speaker's control and not based for instance on physiological difference, for instance differences in physical size (e.g. height) or activity (e.g. running or riding) can result in differences in a speaker's pitch.

Intonation in English is an important vehicle for meaning. It helps the listener to get a clearer picture of what the speaker intends to mean and fulfills many, overlapping functions including attitudinal, grammatical, discursive and pragmatic. However, there is still much to be learned about how we acquire and use intonation systematically and how, or if, it can be taught to second language learners.

Research suggests that intonation is acquired very early in English and many babies can mimic intonation patterns (Peters 1977). Similarly, most children will make a distinction in meaning between the use of falling and rising pitch by the age of two, if not earlier. Jenkins (2000) concludes that this suggests that the L1 intonation system is deeply ingrained at a subconscious level which makes it particularly difficult to modify in terms of learning L2 intonation patterns.

## Tone vs intonation languages

Pitch variation plays an important role in language by adding meaning in addition to that conveyed by the speech segments or phonemes. The type of meaning that pitch movement conveys varies among languages.

In some languages, changing the pitch level (e.g. high, mid, low) or contour (falling or rising) on a particular word can change the lexical meaning. Each word or morpheme has its tone and in suprasegmental analysis the main phonological unit would be the syllable. So, in Mandarin Chinese, for example, '¯ma' with a high level tone means 'mother' while ˏma' with a low rising tone is 'hemp' and ˎma' with a low falling tone is 'scold'. Such languages are known as **tone languages** and many of the world's languages, especially in South East Asia (e.g. Chinese, Thai and Vietnamese) and Africa (e.g. Bantu) are tonal. Most European languages are not tonal although languages such as Serbian, Croatian, Swedish and Norwegian do have a tonal element.

In intonation languages like English, tones are only found on a small number of prominent syllables in connected speech. They do not, generally, change the lexical meaning of a word, but can affect the interpretation of an utterance in terms of the speaker's intended meaning. It is common in such languages to hear people make statements like 'it's not what he said, it's the way that he said it!'.

The general effect is a different perception of the 'melody' of tone and intonation languages; tone languages can be perceived as a series of changing levels or pitch (i.e. from syllable to syllable); intonation languages can be perceived as dynamic pitch glides (i.e. from one prominent syllable/s to the next).

## The structure of intonation (form)

We will now look at the structure or form of intonation in English before we move on to consider how it functions in the language.

Writers on English intonation have found it difficult to arrive at a completely satisfactory description of the system and there is some discrepancy in the use of terminology between authors. However certain key components of English intonation are agreed:

- Connected speech is divided into units known as **thought groups** or tone units. This is a melodic unit made up of a specific pitch contour segmenting the stretch of discourse into thought groups or message blocks.
- Within the thought group some syllables are more **prominent** than the rest.
- The most prominent syllable in the thought group is the **tonic** (also known as the nuclear or tonic syllable or focus). This marks the most important information in the thought group.
- **Tonicity**: this is the placement of the nuclear syllable. It is unpredictable and can vary according to context and speaker intention.

- The pitch pattern that begins on this nuclear syllable and continues through the rest of the thought group is called the nuclear **tone**.
- Prominent syllables before the nuclear syllable tend to derive their meaning from the tone starting on the nuclear syllable.
- **Pitch range** refers to the upper and lower limits of a speaker's vocal pitch.

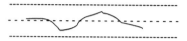

Most of the time speakers stay within the lower half of their pitch range, extension into the upper half usually signifies added involvement of some sort. Some phonologists have divided pitch range into three sectors, that is, 'low', 'mid', 'high' (e.g. Sweet 1906, Brazil 1994), which is sometimes referred to as **key**.

There are basically three main areas of interest: (a) tone choice – the shape of tones created by pitch movement can carry various types of meaning but primarily discoursal and attitudinal, (b) nuclear stress placement, which relates to the accentual function of intonation and (c) thought groups which refers to the division of utterances into smaller chunks or meaningful units. In fact, there is little disagreement regarding the components of intonation, differences emerge rather in how significance is ascribed to them.

# The structure of intonation in English

## Thought groups (tone units)

While we speak we organize our thoughts by chunking speech into small units, or groups of words, called 'thought groups' or sometimes referred to as 'tone units'. The division of speech into thought groups is important for the speaker as well as the listener, allowing time for speech planning and decoding. In written English we commonly use punctuation to demarcate meaning and show which bits of language 'go together': we can also re-read text if we are unsure of the meaning of a sentence or phrase. In speech however we rely only on prosodic cues to know which words are grouped together.

We regularly use several cues to signal thought group boundaries, including:

(a) a pause
(b) a fall in pitch
(c) lengthening of the last stressed syllable (the most subtle signal)
(d) key change.

Thought group boundaries are often marked by pauses as well as pitch movement or key change and often coincide with syntactic boundaries.

In slow, careful speech it is easier to hear the use of pauses to signal the end of a thought group.

/When you're ready to **pay** / /(pause) //please go to the **cash** desk //(pause)

However, if more rapid speech, there is less time to produce or hear pauses so the use of pitch fall is important. The fall in pitch signals finality and the bigger the fall, the greater the degree of finality signalled. So, a slight fall would typically signal the end of an idea or thought group;

//This is the ten o'clock **news**//

a bigger fall might indicate the end of a comment:

//It will be wet and windy **tomorrow**//

while an even bigger fall could signal the end of a speaker's turn and an invitation to others to speak:

//and that's the end of the **news**//

The final stressed syllable is often lengthened as well to help signal the end of the thought group. The end of a thought group is demarcated by the slanting lines //.

Early models of intonation, frequently associated thought groups with grammatical clauses but anyone who listens to authentic speech soon realizes that this does not automatically happen. In connected speech, it is not always very easy to divide up utterances in such a syntactically neat way as there is a lot of interference from performance features such as hesitation, trailing off, failures to complete utterances. So, a thought group can minimally consist of a single word, as in:

// **Jane**//

or several words:

// has anyone seen **Jane**//

Sometimes, as in the examples above, it is relatively easy to decide where thought group boundaries go but it can also be difficult to know where to mark the division between thought groups. In the example:

(a) //Is that you **Jane**//
(b) // **Jane**// is that **you** //

In (a) the phrase could be said as a single thought group, or it could be said as two thought groups with a division between 'you' and 'Jane'. In (b) it seems more obvious that there are two separate thought groups even if a clear pause is not distinguishable between 'Jane' and 'is'.

## Structure of the thought group

We have seen that a thought group can be difficult to demarcate but we can say that is consists of at least one prominent syllable, known as the **nuclear** or **tonic syllable**, and any number of non-prominent syllables. Thus,

// **news** //

is one thought group, with one tonic syllable:

// here is the **news** //

is one tone group with two prominent syllables, 'here' and 'news'. The tonic is again 'news'. Before the tonic is the **head**, that is, the part of the tone unit starting at the first stressed syllables and extending up to the tonic syllable. In this case, the head is 'here is the', consisting of the **onset** syllable 'here' and the unstressed syllables 'is, the'. In the next example,

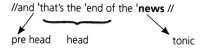

//and 'that's the 'end of the '**news** //

pre head    head                tonic

the initial unstressed 'and' is described as the **pre-head.** The head is 'that's the end of the', starting with the prominent onset syllable 'that's' and containing an additional prominent syllable 'end', with unstressed syllables 'the, of, the', which are weak forms. In the following example:

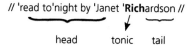

// 'read to'night by 'Janet '**Rich**ardson //

head    tonic    tail

there are three prominent syllables in the head including the onset syllable 'read', and after the tonic syllable '*Rich*' – there are two unstressed syllables -*ard*, -*son* in what is known as the **tail**.

## Activity 1

◀ Listen and then divide the following into thought groups and mark the nucleus in each thought group. Then practise reading it in the same way.

that's all from the ten o'clock news team have a good week-end

## *Analyzing simple thought groups*
Consider the utterance:

The students enrolled at the beginning of the year

The first tone unit is:

//the students **enrolled**//

The structure is:

| Pre-Head | Head | Tonic | Tail |
|----------|------|-------|------|
| the | students en | rolled | ø |

The second thought group is:

//at the beginning of the **year**//

In this case the structure is:

| Pre-Head | Head | Tonic | Tail |
|----------|------|-------|------|
| at the be | ginning of the | year | ø |

The pre-head has no stressed syllables. The head begins at a stressed syllable and continues up to the tonic. In this case, there is no tail.

So, to recap:

prehead – all unstressed syllables preceding first stressed syllable

## Activity 2

◀ Listen and analyze the utterance below in the same way, marking the various components of the thought group:

The car was where I left it

head — from first stressed syllable (onset) up to tonic syllable
tail — syllables between tonic and end of tone unit (tone can be spread over tail).

# Nuclear stress placement (tonicity)

Tonicity is the marking of the tonic syllable (or nucleus, or focus) in a tone unit. The nucleus marks the most significant part of the tone unit. Normally, this will mark the end of the new information. Within a thought group there can be a number (although usually not more than two or three) of prominent syllables. As in the examples above, the last of these prominent syllables is usually the nuclear syllable or tonic, and it is on this syllable that we normally hear a marked change in pitch direction of the speaker's voice. This change in pitch direction is referred to as **tone**.

As we saw in Chapter 10, the tonic is commonly on the last **lexical** item (the last content word) in the thought group, that is, a verb, noun, adjective or adverb, for example:

// What was he **talking** about //
// His performance was very **impressive** //

where there is a choice between a noun and other parts of speech, the tendency is generally to put the tonic on the noun, as in:

// The **kettle's** boiling//
// They've all got **jobs** to do //

We also saw in Chapter 10, that this last-lexical-item tendency can vary if we want to use contrastive focus to contrast, correct or emphasize some information, for example:

// Can I have a **hot** plate please //(when you have been given a cold one)

And similarly in the exchange below:

## Activity 3

◀ Identify what would be the most likely tonic in the following dialogues between speakers A and B. Then listen to the dialogues.

| | |
|---|---|
| A: Where does she work? | B: At the hospital. |
| A: Are you OK? | B. My leg hurts. |
| A: Would you like something to drink? | B: A cup of coffee, please. |
| A: Do you come here often? | B: Not very often. |
| A: Does she work in a school? | B: Yes, it's the British School. |
| A: Does this bus go to the station? | B: Only on weekdays, I'm afraid. |

A: //did you have a good **day**//
B: //I had a bloody **horrible** day//
(From Cruttenden 1986)

## Tone choice

The study of intonation throughout the twentieth century in both Britain and the United States, led to many detailed and complex descriptions, particularly of tones. English tones are defined phonetically as changes in pitch direction. This includes both pitch movements (i.e. rise, fall and combinations of these, fall-rise, rise-fall, rise-fall-rise) and level tones. All of these can be at a variety of heights. Tones at low, mid, high and extra high have all been identified by different writers on intonation. In theory there are some 20 different possibilities of tone type.

In Britain, there have been several influential descriptions during the twentieth century, starting as long ago as Palmer (1922) and followed for instance by Crystal (1969), O'Connor and Arnold (1973), Ladd (1996) and Cruttenden (1997). Such studies have attempted to simplify the description of the system to capture its essence. Yet these attempts have been surprisingly unsuccessful, which is frustrating given that most 5-year olds are proficient users of the system. One of the reasons may be that it is not always easy to hear the way that pitch movements go in casual colloquial speech. Even today, with the benefit of instrumental techniques, trained linguists can find it difficult to agree among themselves on the analysis of recorded samples of colloquial speech.

## English tones

Although more tones have been described, the outline here will be limited to the five basic tones which are common to most studies. These include, fall, rise, fall-rise, rise-fall and level tones. We will consider these tones below.

### Fall

Falling and rising tones in English clearly involve movement of the pitch of the voice. The movement is more pronounced in animated conversation, and in the prepared speech of actors or professional readers.

Falls have been found to be by far the most common type of nuclear tone, accounting for around 50–60 per cent of tones in all styles of English speech and slightly more in conversation (Crystal and Quirk 1964:681, Crystal 1969:225). The amount of pitch movement on the fall can vary: a high fall is a swoop down from a high to a low pitch while a low-fall has much less pitch movement.

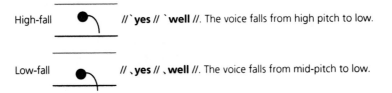

High-fall    // `**yes** // `**well** //. The voice falls from high pitch to low.

Low-fall    // ˎ**yes** // ˎ**well** //. The voice falls from mid-pitch to low.

As we saw earlier, we usually speak within the lower half of our pitch range but can use extra pitch height to show more emotional involvement, whether positive (e.g. 'great') or negative ('leave').

---

### Activity 4

◀ Listen and repeat these examples of falling tones:

Say the following words on a low fall:
ˌyes,   ˌno,   ˌthanks,   ˌgreat

Now, say them on a high fall
ˋyes,   ˋno,   ˋthanks,   ˋgreat

---

### Rise

Rising patterns are less common than falling ones but are estimated to account for a further 30–40 per cent of tones. The most frequent rise has a pitch movement from low to mid (i.e. \a 'low rise). Typically, a rise is seen as signalling incompleteness in some sense. Cruttenden (2008:282) claims that rises and fall-rises are frequently used as a cohesive marker, signalling more to follow, so it is not surprising they are more commonly used in contexts like reading aloud.

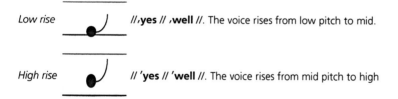

Low rise · //ˌ**yes** // ˌ**well** //. The voice rises from low pitch to mid.

High rise · // ʹ**yes** // ʹ**well** //. The voice rises from mid pitch to high

---

### Activity 5

◀ Listen and repeat the following, noting the rising tones:

A: // ˌ**Peter**//
B: // ˌ**yes**//
A: //you turn right at the ˌ**cross** roads//
B: // ˌ**yes**//
A: //then go ˌstraight **on** //
B: // ˌ**yes**//

⇨

---

### Activity 5—Cont'd

◄ Listen and repeat these examples, noting B's rising tones:

> A: guess what's for **dinner**.
> B: chicken ⸍**casserole?**
> A: **no**
> B: spaghetti ⸍**bolognese**?

---

It has frequently been observed that items in open, or incomplete lists, typically have a rising intonation, as in:

> //⸍**Monday** // ⸍**Tuesday** // ⸍**Wednesday** // ⸍**Thursday** //

and when the list comes to an end, falling intonation is used to indicate completion or closing of the list.

> // ˏ**January** // ˏ**February** // ˎ**March**//

This association of rising tones with incompleteness and falling tones with completion is one of the few reliable observations that can be made about tone choice.

### Level

Rather less frequent in English as a nuclear tone is the level tone, though it may occur frequently in certain registers of stylized speech (Brazil 1997, Wells 2006). On the words 'yes' or 'no' it might give the impression of being 'flat' or 'routine'.

This tone is generally produced in the middle of the pitch range, though high level tones can also be heard in certain styles of speech.

> *Level*  ●———  // _**yes**   // _**well**//.

It is used in a fairly restricted context: typically to convey lack of interest or boredom at routine events.

---

### Activity 6

◄ Listen and repeat these examples of level tones:

> A: //**OK**// let's do the **register** / /ˏ**Peter**//     A: //ˏ**Jane**//
> B: //_**yes**//                                              C: //_**yes**//

---

## *Fall-rise*

In the fall-rise tone the voice falls from mid to low, followed by a rise back to mid. A fall-rise tone on 'yes' often indicates partial agreement with a preceding statement, or some kind of reservation.

Fall-rise     //ˇyes // ˇwell //

---

### Activity 7

Listen and repeat the following, noting B's fall-rise tone:

    A: //Brian's **nice**// **isn't** he//
    B: //ˇ**yes**//
    A: //well **I** like him//

---

## *Rise-fall*

The rise-fall starts with a rise from mid to high and a fall back to mid. The rise-fall is often associated with emphatic statements.

Rise-fall     // ^**yes** // ^**well** //

    The rise-fall is regarded by Gimson (1994:275) as an emphatic or 'reinforced' version of the high fall. It is more frequent in regional varieties than in BBC English.

---

### Activity 8

◀ Listen and repeat the following, noting B's rise-fall tones:

    A: //did you meet her ˏ**brother**//
    B: // ^**yes**//
    A: //isn't this view ^**lovely**//
    B: // ^**marvellous**//

---

## *The tonic and the tail*

The tone on the tonic conveys a meaning for the whole thought group. The tonic is the point at which the tone begins, and if there are unstressed syllables after the nuclear syllable, the pitch direction of the nuclear tone continues through these tail syllables.

If the tone is falling, then the syllables in the tail will continue to fall. For example:

(1) // That's `ridiculous //

(2) (What does she do?) // She's an `English teacher //

If the tone is rising the rise in pitch continues through the tail. For example:

(3) // Are you 'going 'swimming now //

In the fall-rise the overall movement of the tone can extend over a number of unstressed syllables, as in:

(4) // I 'said she'd be 'coming // (and she did)

## Symbols for tones

In order to transcribe speech easily, we use the following notation to indicate tones at the point where they begin in the utterance. This system of on-the-line notation is in the British tradition as exemplified by O'Connor and Arnold (1973), Wells (2006). The symbols are available within Unicode fonts, such as Arial or Lucida:

| | |
|---|---|
| Low Fall | ˏyes |
| High Fall | `yes |
| Low Rise | ˏno |
| High Rise | ′no |
| Fall-rise | ˇno |
| Rise-fall | ^no |
| Level | _yes |

We can only broadly connect meaning to the nuclear tones, as so much depends on the context in which they are used. However some general interpretations have been given:

| | |
|---|---|
| Falls (high fall, low fall, rise-fall) | finality, giving information |
| rises (low rise, high rise, fall-rise) | non-finality, incompleteness, sharing or seeking information |
| fall-rise | reservation, doubt, correction |
| rise-fall | confidence, being impressed, arrogance |
| level | boredom, lack of interest |

**Activity 9**

◄ Review the tones by listening and marking 'B's tone choices and then repeating the following:

A: // it's five o'**clock**//
B: // **mm**//
A: // ˌ**John**//
B: // **mm**//
A: // are you ˌ**hungry**//
B // **mm**//
A: // piece of ˌ**chocolate** cake//
B: // **mm**//

The descriptions of tone choice outlined here are based on BBC English. While there is little variation between General American and BBC English, there is considerable variation between BBC and some northern English accents. In particular, there is much greater use of rising tones in some urban northern accents, such as those of Newcastle, Belfast, Glasgow, Birmingham and Liverpool (Cruttenden 1997).

Another area of variation in tone patterns is the use of rising tones on declaratives, used apparently to check or reinforce the involvement of the listener. This variation is stylistic rather than regional and, although it seems to have originated in Australia and New Zealand, it is now a common pattern particularly with young people in England. These stylistic intonation patterns are sometimes referred to as 'upspeak' (Bradford 1997).

## Key

A final component of intonation which has received relatively little attention, is the concept of key, which we introduced earlier in this chapter. Key operates between successive thought groups and involves the variation in pitch level at the head, compared with preceding and following thought groups. Low key involves an abrupt downward shift in pitch range while high key involves an abrupt upward shift. Key shifts can be illustrated by using an upward[↑] arrow for high key and a downward [↓] arrow for low key.

One use of key is to signal the structure of spoken discourse, for example, a newsreader or lecturer might use high key draw listeners' attention to particular information, such as the beginning and end of a new topic. For example:

// ↑ my ˇ '**first** point concerns . . .
// ↑ 'let's look ˌ **now** // at the question of . . .
// ↑ the prime ˇ **minister** // is visiting ˌ**Thailand** today//
// ↑ ˌ**so** // that's ˌ**it** // for ˌ**today**//

Similarly, high key can be used to emphasize a stretch of speech as especially important. For instance:

// it isn't ˅ **clever** to drive dangerously// ↑ it's ˎ**irresponsible**//

In contrast, low key can be used to signal something is not central to the speaker's main topic. In this case, both pitch and volume may drop. For example:

// his ˅ **'father** // ↓ so I've ˅ **heard** // is chairman of the ˎ**bank** //
// the winning ˅ **goal**// was scored by ˎ**Marcos**//↓the Spanish ˎ**captain**//

# Functions of intonation

Intonation in English is obviously an important vehicle for meaning: helping the listener to get a clearer picture of what the speaker intends to convey. It has been claimed, that inappropriate use of intonation can mislead people, disrupt communication and cause annoyance. Moreover, monotonous speech patterns are also marked (for boredom, contempt or disinterest). However, the ways that intonation conveys meaning are very complex and it appears that in English intonation fulfills many, overlapping functions. The main ones appear to be:

| | |
|---|---|
| *attitudinal function* | – facilitating the expression of emotions and attitudes |
| *accentual function* | – helping the speaker to accentuate some bits of information and de-emphasis others |
| *grammatical function* | – enabling the listener to recognize the grammatical structure of spoken language |
| *discourse function* | – showing how one piece of information relates to another in speech; which pieces of information are 'new' or 'old' and signalling the beginning and end of speaker turns in conversation. |

Traditionally, the functions of pitch movement has been associated with attitude, grammar and information signalling. Earlier descriptions of pitch movement associated specific tone choice to attitudinal meaning (e.g. O'Connor and Arnold 1973). Many researchers now indicate that such correlations are largely subjective and not open to generalization. It has also been suggested (Taylor 1993, Jenkins 2000) that such nuances are impossible to teach. We will now consider each of the four functions outlined above.

## (a) Attitudinal function

In its narrowest sense, the attitudinal function of intonation relates the use of a particular tone to the expression of a particular attitude:

e.g. //I like the ˅ **sitting** room // (reservation)
// I can't accept ˎ**this** // (grumbling)

However:

(i) conveying attitude through intonation involves a lot more than tone choice, for example, voice quality, speed, loudness, pitch range, non-verbal features,

(ii) it is difficult to make generalizations about implied meanings or attitudes, as in the example above, 'I can't accept ˏ**this**', the implication could be reluctance to accept a gift rather than 'grumbling', depending on the context and other non-verbal cues.

While it is obvious that intonation conveys the attitude of a speaker, it is not straight-forward describing the attitudinal functions of tone. An extensive and systematic study of intonation attitudes was made by O'Connor and Arnold (1973) who proposed a set of attitudes relating to each of ten intonation patterns. They used some 150 labels, making such subtle distinctions as *self-satisfied; disclaiming responsibility; censorious; mildly puzzled; tentatively suggesting*. Subsequently, some generalizations have been identified, for example:

Falling tones:
>    // ˏ**thank** you // `**thank** you // (gratitude)
>    // get `**lost** // (brusqueness)

Fall-rise tone:
>    //ˇ never **mind** // (consoling)
>    // I wouldn't say ˇ**that** // (reservation)

However, the main problem with the attitudinal approach is that it is basically a labelling approach from which it is difficult to make any systematic generalizations about the functions of the tones. As a result, some phonologists, in particular, Brazil et al. (1980), reject the attitudinal approach in favour of one that identifies the basic underlying meanings of the tones in terms of the relation between speaker and listener. We will look at this approach in a later section.

Nevertheless, an approach that shows how attitudes are expressed with 'tone of voice' may encourage learners to listen to and notice the way the voice expresses the emotional content of a message in English. One example is the use of the fall-rise tone which is often seen as a very 'English' intonation pattern, that is 'rare or absent from most other languages' (Wells 2006:70). It is often associated with hesitant, undecided or partial responses.

---

## Activity 10

◄ Listen and try saying the following using a fall-rise tone in the same way (see Wells 2006:30–5):

(1) Did you like it? // It was ˇ**quite** good //
(2) What did you think of my poem? // ˇ**Interesting** //
(3) Are you sure? // I'm ˇ**fairly** certain //

Remember that the falling-then-rising pattern continues through the tail syllables following the tonic.

---

### Activity 11

◀ Listen and then practise reading the following dialogue aloud, trying to use the same tones on the focus words (nucleus):

A: // ˌOK.// ˌbye then Paul// . . . that was ˌ**Paul** on the phone//
B: //ˌ**right**// (watching football on television)
A: // he's getting ΄**married**// on ΄**Saturday**// in ˋ**Barbados** // and he's invited us to the ˌ**wedding**//
B: // **mm**//ˌ**sorry** dear// ˌ**what's** Paul doing//
A: // he's getting ˋ**married**//
B: // that's ˌ**nice**//
A: // on ˋ**Saturday**//
B: // ˌ**sorry**//ˌ**what's** he doing on Saturday//
A: // he's getting ˋ**married**//
B: //getting ˇ**married**?
A: //ˋ **yes**// he'sˋ **invited** us//.
B: // ˌ**where's** the wedding again//
A: // in ^**Barbados**//
B: // in ^**Barbados**// on ^**Friday**// we'd better get a ^**move** on then//

---

### (b) Grammatical function

Another explanation of intonation focuses on the links between grammatical structure and intonational components, such as thought group boundaries and clause/sentence boundaries, tone choice and sentence type. In a few specific respects, intonation can be said to have a grammatical function. The example of adverbial modification or defining vs non-defining relative clauses shows the relationship between intonation and syntax. In writing, the distinctions may be made with commas:

> e.g. (a) The passengers who had children, were told to board the plane.
> (b) The passengers, who had children, were told to board the plane.

In example (a), the relative clause is defining. The sentence refers to just those passengers who have children. In the second case, the subordinate clause describes, rather than defines, the passengers. In speech, thought group boundaries perform this function and are marked by pauses, or by a different placement of nuclear tones.

> (a) //The passengers who had ˌ**children**// were told to board the ˌ**plane**//
> (b) //The ˌ**passengers** //who had ˇ**children**// were told to board the ˌ**plane**//

For the language teacher, the example of defining vs non-defining relative clauses may serve to illustrate the importance of thought group boundaries.

**Activity 12**

◀ Divide the following utterances into thought groups to signal the syntactic meaning. Also mark focus words and tone choice. Then listen and practise the examples.

    (a) Alfred said 'the boss is stupid'
    (b) I quite like rice but I prefer potatoes
    (c) His phone number is 0116 2527485
    (d) 5 + (7−3) = 9
    (e) Alison is leaving work so I've been told

This relationship of intonational phrases to syntax is a helpful feature that the language teacher can usefully exploit. Particularly the fact that boundaries between thought groups often correspond syntactically with clause and major syntactic phrase boundaries. However the relationship between grammar and tone choice is far from clear and there are obvious limitations of trying to match intonational patterns to decontextualized syntactic phrases. For instance, traditionally, tone choice has been seen as an indicator of sentence type with falling tones associated with Wh-questions and rising tones associated with 'yes/no' questions:

    e.g. (a) //where did you see ˏ **Brian**//
        (b) //did you see ˏ **Brian**//

Similarly, with question tags ('isn't it', 'can't she'), a falling tone is claimed to expect the listener to confirm what has been said while a rising tone indicates less certainty functioning more like a genuine request for information:

    e.g. // there are ˏ **five** of them// ˎ **aren't** there//
        // there are ˏ **five** of them// ˏ **aren't** there//

Similar claims about links between tone choice and grammatical function have been called into question. For instance, Kriedler claims that 'contrary to popular belief, all analysts of English intonation have insisted that there is no melody which is exclusively associated with one type of sentence: statements do not necessarily have a falling tone, questions do not necessarily rise. The tones do not necessarily correlate with any specific kinds of grammatical structure' (1989:182–3). Similar views are taken by McCarthy (1991:106) who claims 'the more we look at intonation and grammar, the more we are forced to conclude that they are separate systems which work independently, but in harmony, to contribute to discourse meaning'. Levis (1999) also claims that the relative insignificance of tone choice in yes/no questions suggests that it 'should thus be de-emphasised in pedagogy' (1999:378–9).

## (c) information structuring (accentual)

A third focus concentrates less on intonation and grammar and more on intonation and information flow or structuring. This approach, which developed through the work of Chafe (1979) and others such as Du Bois (1991), is unlike the earlier two, in that it tends to take examples from authentic discourse rather than introspection. The emphasis is on how intonation helps foreground new or salient information and background old or given information.

In English, pitch changes are the most important signal of information value.

We have seen (in Chapter 10) that commonly, the tonic is on the last lexical item (the last content word) in the thought group hence a verb, noun, adjective or adverb. Where the thought group consists of entirely new information the tonic falls on the stressed syllable of the final lexical word, for example:

'Debbie's 'had a 'baby '**girl**

The tonic is the minimum element of a thought group, it is where major pitch movement begins and marks the focal point of a message. The placement of nuclear stress relates to the communicative value of a word, it marks what we see as significant in the developing discourse:

e.g. A: // any 'news of **Peter**//
     B: // I 'saw him on **Tues**day //

     A: // any 'news of **Peter**//
     B: // I **saw** him // on **Tuesday**//

Of course, there may be many reasons why the last item should not have the nuclear stress. The location of the tonic in the thought group is said to determine the *focus* of information.

e.g. Sarah went on **holiday** yesterday   (focus on what Sarah did yesterday)
     **Sarah** went on holiday yesterday   (focus on who went on holiday yesterday)
     Sarah went on holiday **yesterday**   (focus on when Sarah went on holiday)

---

### Activity 13

Mark the nucleus in the sentences below, implying the meaning in brackets:

(a) // Wheel your bike into the shed // (not the garage)
(b) // Wheel your bike into the shed // (not that scooter)
(c) // Wheel your bike into the shed // (don't try to carry it)
(d) // Wheel your bike into the shed // (not my bike)

Unlike tone choice, nuclear stress placement, and in particular, contrastive stress, is one aspect of English phonology which is quite distinctive or marked. Unlike many other languages, where grammatical inflection, word order or lexis is used to signal contrast or important information, English does this largely through phonology. Even where contrastive stress is used similarly in the L1 (as in Spanish) this does not necessarily mean it is automatically transferred to the L2 (Kellerman 1979), so it can be a useful aspect of intonation to teach language learners.

---

### Activity 14

◀ Mark the focus words in the following dialogue and then listen and practise reading it with a partner:

Customer: Can I have one chicken sandwich and two cheese rolls, please?
Waiter: That's one cheese sandwich.
Customer: No, one chicken sandwich.
Waiter: Sorry that's one chicken sandwich and two cheese sandwiches.
Customer: No, two cheese rolls.
Waiter: Right. You did want two chicken sandwiches, didn't you?
Customer: No I didn't. Just one.
Waiter: I think I'd better write this down.

---

## (d) discourse function

The most recent approach to studies of intonation takes the notion of accentuation or information structuring one step further, by linking it to the interactional nature of discourse. Rather than looking at decontextualized samples, this approach is firmly based on the analysis of authentic, interactive speech. Intonation is seen as important not only in focusing the listener's attention on significant information (i.e. accentuation) but also in regulating interactive behaviour, (for instance by signalling when someone has finished speaking or showing the relevance of one utterance to preceding and following utterances).

As mentioned earlier, this approach is founded in Halliday's work on intonation and information structure in conversation (1970) and then Brazil et al.'s research on the analysis of classroom discourse (1980). This led to a detailed description of intonation in discourse which has since been modified and extended by others such as Couper Kuhlen (1986) and Cruttenden (1986). The main points of Brazil et al.'s approach to the discourse functions of intonation are outlined here.

## 1. Tone choice and relevance

The discourse intonation approach summarizes the significance of tones as two basic tones, that is, falling and rising, which can be subdivided as follows:

(a) proclaiming (labelled 'p') – fall [ ˎ ]and [ ˆ ] rise-fall
(b) referring (labelled 'r') – rise [ ˌ ] and [ ˇ ]fall-rise

So, a falling tone is 'proclaiming' while a rising tone is 'referring'. Proclaiming tones (*p*) carry unshared or new information. Given or shared information is signalled by referring tones (*r*), that is to say, what the speaker considers to be known or already negotiated knowledge. Following Brazil's framework, Bradford (1988) suggests that the two most common tones are the fall and fall-rise. To illustrate:

---

### Activity 15

◄ Listen to these examples of proclaiming tones ('p' – falling or rise-fall tone):

(i) telling – giving new information:

> e.g.  p // this is **Jane**//

(ii) asking – finding out new information:

> e.g.  p // where's **Peter**//
> p // are you the new **secretary**//

(iii) responding:
(a) telling/confirming new information:

> e.g.  A: // p will that be from the same **platform**//
> B: // p **yes** // p platform **three** //

(b) telling us if we are right or wrong:

> e.g.  A: // p is this what you're **looking** for//
> B: // p **no** // p it's **not** //

---

### Activity 16

◄ Listen to these examples of referring tones ('r' – rising or fall-rising):

(i) telling – giving information that is 'shared' in some way:

> e.g.  // r 'this is '**Peter**// (remember, I told you about him before)
> // r 'this is the '**bathroom**// (obviously)

(ii) asking – making sure of information ( often used for 'social' enquiries )

> e.g.  // r 'did you 'have a 'good '**trip**//
> // r 'will you 'have some 'more '**coffee**//
> // r are 'you the 'new '**secretary** //

(iii) responding – when you cannot give the information the enquirer expects:

> e.g.  A: //r 'is it a '**recent** 'publication //
> B: // r well it '**could** be //

Brazil et al. (1980) claim that tone choice is not only linked to the information structure of discourse but also to the social relationship between speakers, particularly their status. For instance, they suggest that in situations where one speaker has higher status than another (e.g. the chair of a meeting) that speaker is likely to mark their status phonologically by using rising rather than fall-rising tones, as rising tones are said to signify dominance in such contexts. To give an example from Brazil (1994:54) where the chairperson is opening a meeting:

// ER // ↗ GOOd Evening // ER // ↗ good Evening to one and ALL// WELcome// TO// OUR// ↗FEBruaruy MEEting// ERM// and WELcome// of COURSE to our// ↗ to our REGular// members

In Brazil's system, prominent syllables are indicated in capital letters. Where there are two prominent syllables in a thought group, the nuclear syllable is underlined and the non-nuclear appears in capitals.

## 2. Key choice and relevance

The concept of key was introduced earlier in this chapter to refer to the overall pitch height of a thought group, in relation to surrounding thought groups. Brazil et al.'s (1980) description of intonation is unusual in that it pays significant attention to the feature. They divide key into three levels, 'high', 'mid' and 'low'. They see mid key as a sort of neutral reference point while high key is used to add emphasis or contrast to information. A related concept is 'termination'. The function of termination is essentially to predict or signal the key expected when the hearer responds. According to Brazil (1994:246):

high termination expects high key response (evaluation or adjudication)
mid termination expects mid key response (agreement or concurrence)
low termination has no particular expectations.

A first speaker's choice of termination influences the second as in the following snippet of doctor-patient conversation (about dry skin):

**high**                        IRRitating you say
**mid** // Doctor:    p VERy
**low**

**high**              p VERy  irritating
**mid** // Patient
**low**                                              (Brazil et al. 1980:75)

As we saw earlier, key can be used to draw attention towards a particular stretch of speech while low key can draw attention away from parts of an utterance. In terms of teaching, it can be useful to show how speakers can signal that one thought group is less important than another by using low key.

---

### Activity 17

◀ Listen and read these examples, practising lowering pitch and speaking more quietly on the low key thought groups:

A:  // Peter's leaving`**work**// ↓so I've been ˌ**told**//
B:  //^**really**//
A:  //↓don't ˌ**tell** anyone// but . . . he's been`**sacked**//
B:  //`**no** //
A:  // his ˌ**wife**// ↓who's over there talking toˌ**Mary**// is very`**upset** //
B:  // oh ˌdear //
A:  // they're ˌ**moving** // ↓so I'veˌ**heard** // to the`**south**//

---

Brazil's framework of discourse intonation is undoubtedly well grounded in his observations, although there are criticisms that the concept of 'shared' or 'new' information does not always explain choice of tones and that some of the descriptions of tone choice are not generalizable to all speech contexts. Nevertheless, the approach does show the inadequacy of trying to analyse the functions of intonation based on isolated sentences rather than within a broader interactive context. It also suggests that the separate functions of intonation, such as attitudinal, grammatical, accentual might all come under one umbrella, that is, discourse, and that intonation might best be looked at in terms of how it influences communication between individuals that is, interaction.

Despite the attraction of the discourse intonation approach as an explanation of how intonation functions in L1 interactions, it is not easy to transfer it to L2 teaching contexts, although both Brazil (1994) and Bradford (1988) have attempted to do so. This is partly because Brazil's description, although inherently sound on a theoretical level, is also complex and what counts as 'old' or 'new' information can be difficult to explain, even for native speakers. On a practical level, it is also notoriously difficult for teachers (both native and non-native speakers) to detect, analyse and reproduce pitch movements. Jenkins suggests this may be because pitch distinctions are acquired so early in life and may therefore be very hard to bring to a level of consciousness (2000:152). She also claims that tone choice rarely gives rise to intelligibility problems in her EIL data.

---

### Activity 18

◀ To put into practice what we have covered regarding intonation in this unit, listen to the recordings of various speakers talking about themselves and:

1. Mark the thought group boundaries (//)
2. Mark the stressed syllables ( ' )
3. Mark pauses ( - )
4. Mark the tonic in each thought group (**bold**)
5. Mark pitch movement on the tonic syllable [as falling (¥) or rising (/)].

# Teaching implications

It is perhaps in the area of intonation that there is the biggest divide among teachers regarding its importance in pronunciation learning. On the one hand, some teachers and researchers hold the view that it is impossible to teach while others feel it is the key to 'sounding English'. Such opposing views reflect to some extent the changing focus on prosody and the importance of suprasegmentals in pronunciation teaching in recent decades. Following the general emphasis on segmental aspects of phonology until the last quarter of the twentieth century, the focus then shifted to promoting the role of suprasegmentals in pronunciation acquisition (e.g. Morley 1991, Avery and Ehrlich 1992, Gilbert 1993). There is currently some evidence of a further shift back towards the importance of segmentals, particularly in lingua franca communication (Levis 1999, Jenkins 2000, Cruttenden 2008). Even for those who advocate the centrality of suprasegmentals, it is by no means clear that all aspects, especially of intonation, are equally learnable.

It is clear that intonation is a rather complex, multi functional aspect of phonology and there is still much to be researched and learned about how intonation relates to other areas of language and communication. In terms of teaching pronunciation, in the second half of the twentieth century there was much hope that the scientific study of intonation would lead to the full and clear description of the function of each aspect of intonation which could then be taught effectively to learners through a set of straight forward rules. However, more recently, many experts (e.g. Jenkins 2000, Roach 2000, Gilbert 2008, Cruttenden 2008) have concluded that it is impossible to teach some aspects of intonation formally. For instance, Roach states that:

> 'It is perhaps a discouraging thing to say, but learners of English who are not able to talk regularly with native speakers of English, or who are not able at least to listen regularly to colloquial English, are not likely to learn English intonation.' (2000:153)

Brazil et al. (1980:113–44) also raise issues about intonation and language teaching, claiming the inadequacy and inaccessibility of most descriptions for practical pedagogic purposes. They argue that 'the incursion of intonation into the general language syllabus has been minimal' (1980:113). The view of Brazil et al. is that 'the meaning of intonation is inseparable from context' (1980:126). This means that phonetic exercises in intonation (quite common in textbooks) may lead the learner to make unhelpful generalizations. Others, particularly Jenkins (2000) and Cruttenden (2008) see teaching of tones as unnecessary in EIL contexts, while accepting the importance of awareness of prominence and nuclear stress placement.

In this chapter we have covered three key areas of intonation in some detail. These are:

- thought groups
- Tonicity/nuclear stress placement
- tone choice

We will consider the importance of each for pronunciation teaching and learning.

## Thought groups

Cruttenden suggests that there is considerable similarity across languages regarding the placement of thought group boundaries and therefore this is unlikely to be an issue for intelligibility (Cruttenden 2008:329). However, he does add that chunking speech into appropriate thought groups will make pronunciation sound both more natural and more lively (2008:324). It helps the listener process speech into meaningful units and it gives the speaker time to plan what is coming next. It can also be helpful that learners are aware that adverbials such as 'actually', 'finally', are often assigned individual thought groups in English. Being able to produce this pattern, particularly in longer sentences, can be a considerable aid to comprehension and fluency. Finally, and perhaps most importantly, it is also essential that learners are aware of the concept of thought groups in order to be able to understand and assign nuclear stress properly.

As with nuclear stress placement, dividing speech into thought groups is relatively easy to teach and can be integrated into other aspects of language learning. It has been suggested (Dalton and Seidlhofer 1994), that many such thought groups consist of prefabricated lexical phrases, for instance, 'you must be joking'. Kaltenboeck (2002) further suggests that such lexical phrases could be a good way of approaching the teaching of intonation.

## Tonicity/nuclear stress placement

Many researchers (e.g. Brazil 1994, Roach 2000, Cruttenden 2008, Gilbert 2008) and teachers would agree that receptive and productive skills in nuclear stress placement are important in achieving near-native pronunciation proficiency.

Jenkins claims that, unlike pitch movement, correct nuclear stress placement is also essential for intelligibility and frequently the source of misunderstandings in her EIL data, especially if linked to segmental errors.

While many languages tend to accentuate the last lexical item in an utterance, by giving it pitch prominence, not all languages de-accentuate old information at the end of a thought group. So learners whose L1 is, for example French, Spanish or Italian need to be careful to de-accent appropriately. Also, some languages use other signals, such as word order, to focus attention to the key idea in an utterance, so L2 learners of English often do not notice this specifically English system for signalling emphasis. As this use of emphatic stress may be quite foreign to many learners, it can help to present a set of basic rules about how this works, as presented in the pronunciation textbook 'Speaking Clearly' (Rogerson and Gilbert 1990). Nuclear stress placement is not only important for production, that is, to be easily intelligible but also to enhance listening skills. Listening for the additional emphasis given to prominent words helps students to learn to listen selectively, rather than giving equal attention to every word they hear. Listening for emphasis guides listeners to the essence of the message (Bradford 1988, Brazil 1997, Gilbert 2008).

Pedagogically, the rules for nuclear stress placement are relatively easy to teach and can be linked to other aspects of language learning, such as listening, speaking and grammar. However, developing productive competence is much slower than receptive competence. Many experts agree that because of the link between nuclear stress placement and speech clarity at both segmental (e.g. vowel quality and length) and suprasegmental levels (e.g. stress, rhythm and phrasing), this is one area of intonation which is important for L2 pronunciation learning, regardless of the level of proficiency aimed at.

## Tone choice

This is perhaps the area of biggest debate regarding intonation and pronunciation teaching.

As mentioned earlier, Jenkins (2000:153) claims that there is no evidence of tone choice causing intelligibility problems in her EIL research study and that it is therefore both unnecessary and infeasible to teach in such contexts. She supports her argument with the explanation that pitch movement is acquired in the L1 at a very early stage suggesting that it is deeply rooted and difficult to access at a conscious level. She illustrates by saying that even experienced teachers find it hard to identify and model tones and if they have such difficulties it would seem to be a hopeless task for learners.

Gilbert similarly concludes that in intonation languages such as English (as opposed to tone languages), where pitch does not distinguish lexical meaning, the direction of the pitch change is rarely crucial to understanding. She states 'if a pitch movement is used to signal focus on a word, it may matter little to a listener if the movement is upward or downward, as long as it is salient and detectable' (2008:234).

Cruttenden (2008) suggests that teaching English tones should be restricted to those learners who are aiming at a near-native pronunciation target. For this group he states 'The most difficult area of intonation for foreign learners concerns its attitudinal uses. But some effort should be made to master some of the uses of fall-rise, for example, for warnings, reservations and contradictions' (2008:325). He also suggests that the high level learner should pay particular attention to the use of the fall-rise with interrogatives, which (unlike in many other languages) he claims is used much more commonly than the high-rise. Cruttenden further claims a learner wishing to acquire a native-like accent should be aware of pre-nuclear intonation patterns. He advises the avoidance of a series of low-pitch syllables, as this can give the impression of boredom and suggests the learner aims for the common BBC English pattern of a series of descending pitch plateaux (Cruttenden 2008:325).

Despite what is said in many English language teaching materials, there does not appear to be a simple correspondence between tone choice and attitudinal or grammatical function. For instance, Brazil et al. are particularly critical of approaches to the teaching of intonation in terms of attitudinal meanings, stating:

'There are no arguments for teaching intonation in terms of attitude, because the rules for use are too obscure, too amorphous, and too easily refutable.' (1980:120)

Given the lack of a convincing framework, the teaching of the attitudinal function may appear daunting. Nevertheless, some generalizations may be helpful provided that we always remain conscious of their limited range of application. It should also be remembered that almost any tone can be applied to any stretch of language depending on circumstances and intention. The system of intonation is very elastic. For the language teacher, the most useful activity is likely to involve the students in listening to authentic connected speech and identifying the likely attitudes of the interlocutors.

Similarly, various researchers have questioned the 'rule' that falling tones are used on 'wh-questions' and rising tones on 'yes/no questions', claiming that both falling and rising tones occur frequently on yes/no-interrogatives and on wh-interrogatives (Rogerson and Gilbert 1990, Caudwell and Hewings 1996, Cruttenden 2008). Cruttenden further suggests that 'Learners can sound completely natural making use of only two tones, low rise and high fall, on all types of interrogatives' (Cruttenden 2008:325).

Given the difficulty of distinguishing pitch movement in colloquial speech, the teacher who wishes to help learners acquire some mastery of English tones may find it more productive initially to concentrate on fairly stylized, well defined registers of speech such as news readings, narratives or simple announcements for the recognition of tones.

# Key points

- The gap between receptive and productive competence is bigger with regard to intonation than other aspects of pronunciation (Jenkins 2000:47).
- The appropriate division of speech into thought groups is very important both for comprehension and fluency.
- Thought group boundaries often (but don't always) correspond to grammatical boundaries but the thought group is typically shorter than the grammatical phrase.
- Nuclear stress placement needs to be learned productively as well as receptively.
- It is essential to put the nuclear stress on the focal point of a thought group or utterance. The default position for the tonic is the last lexical item in a thought group but it can go on anywhere. Some languages regularly have the primary accent on the last word in the intonational phrase (e.g. French, Italian, Spanish).
- 'Old' information should be de-accented, especially at the end of a thought group:

    For example, A: Do you want to come *shopping* with me?
    B: /I *told* you/ /I don't *like* shopping/

- Tone choice seems to operate largely at a subconscious level and may therefore be hard to teach.
- It is hard for both native and non-native speakers to recognize and model pitch movement.

- It is hard to formulate clear guidelines for attitudinal and grammatical functions of tone choice.
- There is considerable regional variation in the realization of pitch movement and tone choice, unlike other components of intonation such as nuclear stress placement and thought group division where there is little variation.
- The fall-rise tone is common in English, unlike many languages. It is commonly used on phrase-initial adverbials (e.g. /˰actually/) and to signal warning, reservation or contradiction (e.g. /˰careful/).
- Perhaps the most useful generalization to make regarding tone choice is that falling tones typically signal some sort of 'completeness' while rising tones tend to signal 'incompleteness'. This point can be demonstrated in the reading of open and closed lists.

# Further reading

Bradford, B. (1997) 'Upspeak in British English', *English Today,* 51, 13.3, 33–6.

Brazil, D. (1997) *The Communicative Value of Intonation in English.* Cambridge: Cambridge University Press.

Brazil, D., Coulthard, M. and Johns, C. (1980) *Discourse Intonation and Language Teaching.* London: Longman.

Caudwell, R. and Hewings, M. (1996) 'Intonation rules in ELT textbooks', *ELT Journal,* 50 (4), 327–34.

Clennell, C. (1997) 'Raising the pedagogical status of discourse intonation teaching', *ELT Journal,* 51 (2), 117–25.

Cruttenden, A. (1986) *Intonation.* Cambridge: Cambridge University Press.

Crystal, D. (1969) *Prosodic Systems and Intonation.* Cambridge: Cambridge University Press.

Currie, K. and Yule, G. (1982) 'A return to fundamentals in the teaching of intonation', *IRAL,* 20, 228–32. Also in Brown, A. (ed., 1991) *Teaching English Pronunciation: A Book of Readings.* London: Routledge, pp. 270–5.

Cutler, A., Dahan, D. and van Donselaar, W. (1997) 'Prosody in the comprehension of spoken language: A literature review', *Language and Speech,* 40 (2), 141–201.

De Bot, K. and Mailfert, K. (1982) 'The teaching of intonation: Fundamental research and classroom applications', *TESOL Quarterly,* 16, 71–7.

Hewings, M. (1986) 'Problems of intonation in classroom interaction', *Guidelines* (RELC, Singapore), 8 (2), 45–51.

Hewings, M. (1995) 'Tone choice in the English intonation of non-native speakers', *IRAL,* 33 (3), 251–65.

Kenworthy, J. (1992) 'Interactive intonation', in Brown, A. (ed.) *Approaches to Pronunciation Teaching.* Macmillan & The British Council, London.

McCarthy, M. (1991), *Discourse Analysis for Language Teachers.* Cambridge: Cambridge University Press. (Chapter 4 pp. 88–114 on discourse intonation).

O'Connor, J. D. and Arnold, G. F. (1973) *Intonation of Colloquial English,* 2nd edition. London: Longman.

Pickering, L. (2004) 'Structure and function of intonational paragraphs in native and nonnative speakers' instrumental discourse', *English for Specific Purposes,* 23, 19–43.

Thompson, S. (1995) 'Teaching intonation on questions', *ELT Journal,* 49 (3), 235–43.

Wennerstrom, A. (1994) 'Intonational meaning in English discourse: A study of non-native speakers', *Applied Linguistics,* 15 (4), 399–420.

Woolard, G. (1990) 'Discourse intonation: Tone (pitch movement)', *Modern English Teacher,* 17 (1 & 2), 7–11.

Woolard, G. (1993) 'A question of intonation', *Professional English Teacher,* 13 (3), 33–4.

# 12 Phonology Review 2

This unit provides you with further opportunities to review and practice your skills in phonemic transcription.

ɪf jə kən ˈriːd ðɪs wɪðˈaʊt ænˈzaɪətɪ ən hezɪˈteɪʃn̩ ðen jʊə ˈduːɪŋ ˈverɪ ˈwel ɪnˈdiːd

and if you can transcribe such words without hesitation you are doing even better!

## Phonological variation and transcription

Apart from regional and national variations, remember that there will always be a degree of variation tolerable in transcriptions from the written word, because

Some say       /ˈiːðə/       and others say       /ˈaɪð ə/
Some say       /ˈnˈiː ðə)/   and others say       /ˈna ɪðə)/
Some send 'letters' in /ˈenvələʊps/ while others send them in /ˈɒnvələʊps/
Cars go in the /ˈɡærɑːʒ/, /ˈɡærɑːdʒ/, or /ˈɡærɪdʒ/ depending on your preference;
It /ˈɒfn̩/ rains in England, or /ˈɒftən/ but in parts of the US it /ˈɔːfn̩/ rains.

'Direct' can be /də/, /dɪ/ or /daɪ/ in the first syllable.
'Dimension' can be /dɪ/, /daɪ/ or /də/ in its first syllable.
'Dissect' can be /dɪ/ or /daɪ/ but not /də/.

---

### Activity 1

Transcribe the following words and then consult a pronunciation dictionary (e.g. Wells 2000) or a learner's dictionary (e.g. Oxford University Press 1995) to check the variations possible:

(a) forehead
(b) forensic
(c) honour
(d) hegemony
(e) interest
(f) intrinsic
(g) invalid (noun)
(h) lawsuit
(i) mosquito
(j) quagmire
(k) recall (noun)
(l) supervise
(m) superb
(n) version

# Features of connected speech

Before you practise transcribing longer stretches of connected speech, try these exercises revising some of the key features of normal fluent speech.

---

### Activity 2

(1) Elision

◀ Listen and transcribe phonemically what you hear then mark any cases of elision:

    (a) camera
    (b) excuse me
    (c) tomato
    (d) secretary
    (e) memory

(2) Assimilation

◀ Listen and transcribe phonemically what you hear then mark any cases of assimilation:

    (a) Have the last cake . . .
    (b) Hold the door
    (c) It's lunchtime
    (d) That was last year
    (e) A good place to go

(3) Vowel reduction

◀ Listen and transcribe what you hear then mark any cases of vowels reductions.

    (a) He ran to the top of the hill as fast as his legs would carry him.
    (b) I went to the hotel and booked a room for two nights for my father and his best friend.
    (c) He'll be arriving here on the evening of the tenth.
    (d) She ran to the station.
    (e) One boy ran to his mum to tell her about the accident.

---

# Punctuation and transcription

When transcribing, it is important to remember that standard English punctuation does not apply. Question and exclamation marks do not occur and nor to capital letters and full stops. Remember that divisions between thought groups or tone groups are marked by '//'.

## Activity 3

Translate the phonemic script below into ordinary written English, adding punctuation where necessary:

1. // aɪ 'dʌnəʊ 'weərɪz 'gɒn 'ækʃli // aɪm 'ʃɔː ɪ wəz ɪn ðə 'lekʃə 'ɜːlɪə //
2. // 'skjuːz miː// djə 'nəʊ wɪf ðɪs 'kəʊtʃ 'gəʊz tə 'ʃefiːld //
3. //aɪ 'spəʊz ðə 'bes 'θɪŋz tə 'aːsk ɜː jə'self //
4. // 'əʊ 'dɪə ‖ ju 'aːrɪn ə 'bæb 'muːd // 'aːnt ju //
5. // iː 'kʊb biː 'raɪʔ aɪ 'spəʊz // bə 'ʃiː 'sed ɪʔ 'staːts ɒm 'mʌndeɪ //

## Activity 4

Transcribe the following into broad phonemic script (mark word stress and tone unit boundaries as above):

(a) Can you peel the rest of the carrots then wash the lettuce, please.
(b) I'm afraid the number's engaged, can you try again later.
(c) Apparently, the England team were losing as usual.
(d) Please don't panic. I'm sure the doctor's on his way.
(e) Could I have a prawn salad and a glass of sparkling water.

## Transcribing conversational speech

Now you can put into practice everything you have learned about the pronunciation of normal fluent speech.

## Activity 5

Write out the following dialogue in normal English script:
Mark any features of connected speech, that is, assimilations, elisions, contractions or linking.

A: // ðə pə'liːs əv bɪn 'æskɪŋ 'kwestʃənz ə'gen// ə'baʊt 'ðæt 'rɒbəri//
B: // 'wɒt 'rɒbəri// ə jə 'tɔːkɪŋ ə'baʊt//tʃuːə ɪ ə jə 'tɔːkɪŋ ə'baʊt ‖ //

A: //ðə 'wʌn ɒn 'sætədi// frəm ə 'ʃɒp ɪm 'meɪn 'striːt// aɪ 'təʊld jə 'lɑːs 'naɪt // rɪ'membə//

B: //əʊ 'je // 'sɒri bət aɪ 'kʊdn̩t 'θɪŋk 'wɒt jə wə 'tɔːkɪŋ ə'baʊt//

A: //'əpærəntli// ðə 'rɒbəz gɒt ə'weɪ wɪθ 'hɑːf ə 'mɪljən//

B: // 'wɒt // 'paʊnz//

A: // 'nəʊ// 'peəz ə 'ʃuːz//

## Activity 6

◀ Listen and transcribe the following into broad phonemic script (mark word stress and tone unit boundaries as above). Remember to note any features of connected speech that you hear.

A: Where have you been?

B: I've been waiting here for ages. Don't tell me that Peter's not coming again. I've had enough of him.

A: Don't panic. He's on his way. He sent me to find you and tell you that you should take a taxi and meet him at Maxim's.

B: What's happening at Maxim's?

A: I don't know but the food's good.

# Prosodic analysis

Now you can practise analyzing suprasegmental features of natural speech, rather than segmental or phonemic transcription. Focus on how the speakers chunk speech into tone units through the use of pauses, stress placement and tonicity. Try to note also whether they use a falling (\) or rising (/) tone at the end of tone units. Use the symbols in the key below to mark up your transcription.

## Transcription conventions

| | | |
|---|---|---|
| // | = | thought group boundary |
| **bold** | = | tonic or nuclear stress |
| ' | = | stressed syllable |
| - | = | pause |
| \ | = | falling tone |
| / | = | rising tone |

## Activity 7

◀ Listen to each of the six recordings and try to do your own suprasegmental analysis. Listen as many times as you like and:

(1) Write down what you hear – word for word (don't write phonemically)
(2) *When you've written all the words down, listen again several times and mark pauses*
(3) *Now listen again and mark all the stressed words*
(4) *Listen again and mark tonic words*
(5) *Finally, listen again and decide if the final word before each pause has a falling or rising tone*
(6) *When you've done as much as you can, look at the transcription, compare it with your own and listen to the recording while reading.*

Recording 1
Recording 2
Recording 3
Recording 4
Recording 5
Recording 6

# Pronunciation in the Classroom 13

## Introduction

In this chapter we will look at some of the practicalities of teaching pronunciation in the classroom and consider some techniques and activity types that can be used to teach the various elements of pronunciation.

Learning to pronounce a language is a very complex task and as with any other area of language learning there are techniques and activities which can facilitate the process. First of all however it is worth spending some time 'setting the scene' for effective pronunciation acquisition. This involves: (a) building an awareness and concern for pronunciation, (b) explaining the components parts of pronunciation and how they fit together and (c) outlining the pronunciation sub-skills learners need to develop.

## Setting the scene for effective pronunciation learning

### (a) Building an awareness and concern for pronunciation

In Chapter 1 we considered why pronunciation is important from a teaching point of view but this needs to be conveyed to the learner as well. It is essential that pronunciation is seen as a major contributor to successful spoken communication and that no-one learning a language can be expected to be understood with poor pronunciation skills. Teachers need to help their students recognize poor pronunciation and motivate them to improve. Furthermore, it is important to clarify the emotional and attitudinal aspects of pronunciation learning, in order to set clear, achievable and appropriate goals.

### (b) Explaining the components parts of pronunciation and how they fit together

As we have seen in this book there are many components to pronunciation but we could summarize these under the following areas:

   (i) phonemic distinctions
   (ii) syllable structure

(iii) word stress
(iv) features of connected speech
(v) intonation patterns.

Traditionally, pronunciation courses start with the smallest elements, that is the individual sounds or phonemes and work up towards the larger elements such as word stress, features of connected speech and finally intonation patterns. It can therefore seem to the learner that these are separate, unconnected components. However, it can make pronunciation learning more meaningful to explain that there is more to pronunciation than individual sounds and that these different components are inter-related and work together. For instance, the teacher can explain that the syllable is the basic unit of rhythm in English and typically has a central vowel. Understanding the alternation of stressed and unstressed syllables will enhance listening comprehension by making learners aware of those parts of speech which are highlighted and those which are de-emphasized. A connection can also be made between the rhythmic structure of English and vowel quality and the fact that stressed vowels are clearer and longer than their unstressed counterparts, which are typically reduced to schwa. This will in turn help learners hear and produce word stress patterns accurately.

### (c) Outlining the pronunciation sub-skills learners need to develop

Just as we looked at the various sub-skills that the pronunciation teacher needs to develop, it can also be helpful to consider the skills that the learner needs to acquire in order to master the various elements of pronunciation. These can be described as follows:

(i) *noticing* – pronunciation elements in speech, similarities and differences between L1 an L2 pronunciation
(ii) *discriminating* – between L1 and L2 elements, between correct and incorrect elements
(iii) *imitating* – sounds and other elements of pronunciation accurately
(iv) *reproducing* – elements without prompting
(v) *contextualizing* – individual elements within a stream of speech
(vi) *generating* – pronunciations in new contexts
(vii) *correcting* – their own inaccurate sounds and patterns.

Learners cannot be expected to produce sounds or patterns that they do not hear. We have seen that just as learners need help **noticing** grammatical forms explicitly, in the same way they benefit from being explicitly taught phonological forms to help them become aware of the differences between their own productions and those of L1 and proficient L2 speakers.

Numerous studies have suggested that many L2 production difficulties are rooted in perception. Evidence also indicates that appropriate perceptual training can lead to automatic improvement in production. For instance, work by Bradlow et al. (1996) has shown that when Japanese learners are trained to perceive the /r/-/l/ distinction, their productions may automatically improve, even when no production training is provided. This empirical finding supports the intuitive practice of using perceptual training tasks such as **discrimination** and identification exercises in the classroom. A traditional way of approaching the area of teaching sounds is therefore to begin with awareness raising activities.

**Imitation** is an essential part of L1 speech acquisition in order to develop the automatic motor skills required to produce and reproduce sounds. In the same way, the articulation of new L2 sounds requires the formation of new muscular habits and the ability to mimic has been reported as having a significant influence on second language pronunciation (Suter 1976, Purcell and Suter 1980). Given time and practice, such habits can be acquired but they can also slip if the learner's attention is deviated, for instance to a focus on content rather than form. Consequently an imitation stage using relatively de-contextualized drills and other repetition exercises may be important to develop new motor skills.

The L2 listener may not have the ability to perceive speech in the same way the L1 speaker does. The L2 listener is constantly influenced by the inventory of acoustic cues from their L1. For this reason the L2 learner should not be expected to gauge the accuracy of their own pronunciation until their **production** of L2 sounds has reached an acceptable proximity to the target.

A common problem for learners is that they can reproduce individual sounds or prosodic patterns accurately in isolation but as soon as they put them into the larger **context**, that is into connected speech, pronunciation errors occur again. It is therefore important that learners are given the opportunity to practice producing forms both in isolation and in a larger speech context.

As with other areas of language learning, the proof of mastery of the linguistic system, in this case of the phonological patterns and rules, is the ability to **generate** new pronunciations of unknown words or phrases, rather than simply reproduce what has been learned before. A variety of problem-solving or rule-deducing activities can be used to encourage this stage of phonological development.

Ultimately, the aim of the teacher is to become redundant in terms of modelling and monitoring target pronunciation forms and for the learner to be able to recognize and **correct** their own errors themselves. Encouraging self and peer or group-monitoring from a relatively early stage can facilitate this process of self-diagnosis and correction.

We will now look at a range of activities and techniques which can be used to help learners acquire the various components of English pronunciation. It is important to remember however that before embarking on any of these, choices will have been made about what aspects of pronunciation are teaching priorities and which are not.

## Voice quality

Voice quality is not an area that is frequently considered part of pronunciation training but we saw in Chapter 3 that there are arguments for introducing it early on in pronunciation teaching as a way of helping learners use their intuitive knowledge of what a 'foreign' language sounds like in a holistic approach to learning new sounds.

Various suggestions have been made about how to incorporate voice quality work into pronunciation teaching with a view to sensitizing learners to its importance and helping them graduate to more L2 articulatory settings. Thornbury (1993), for example has lots of practical and engaging activities and Evans and Jones (1995) present an interesting approach looking particularly at the link between voice quality and emotions or attitudes.

Some initial exercises are outlined below:

(1) Write down a few everyday phrases in your L1. Translate them into English. Articulate the phrases in L1 and in English without speaking aloud. Get someone to guess whether you are speaking English or not.

(2) Now say the phrases aloud, first in your L1 then in English. Get someone to explain any differences in voice quality between the two, for example, eg volume, hissing quality, nasal quality, length of sounds.

(3) Make a list of cognates in your L1 and English ( e.g. publicity (English) – publicidad (Spanish). Try to exaggerate the vocal setting features of the two languages.

(4) Write a phrase or sentence in your L1. Now try to say it aloud with an English 'accent'. Try to notice the adjustments you make to your articulatory settings.

(5) Write a phrase or sentence in English. Now try to say it aloud with an L1 'accent'. Try to notice the adjustments you make to your articulatory settings.

## Articulation

Again this is not an area that is generally covered explicitly in pronunciation teaching but these sorts of 'warming up' exercises, as in Activity 1 (which are typically used by drama and speech coaches) can help students relax and enjoy the process of getting into the sound and feel of a foreign language:

---

### Activity 1

Try these exercises yourself:

### Breathing and relaxation

Sitting comfortably:

- drop the head gently forward onto the chest
- reverse the movement letting the head fall slowly backwards, mouth open
- incline the head gradually from side to side, keeping the shoulders still
- slowly raise the shoulders towards the ears then lower the shoulders
- put your hands behind your head, with the elbows well back
- breathe in deeply through the nose and breathe out very slowly through the mouth
- breathe in deeply through the mouth and let the breath out gradually through the mouth while making an 'mm' sound. First let the breath out on a count of six, then, eight and then extend as long as you can.

⇨

After doing the 'breathing and relaxation' exercises;

- drop the jaw open gently, as wide as possible
- stretch the lips into a wide smile
- round the lips tightly.

## Voicing

1. Whisper 'he'. Place your fingertips lightly on your throat. Notice the lack of vibration. Now say 'he' aloud and notice the vibration. You can notice the same contrast by saying 'sip' and then 'zip'

## Jaw Position

2. Say 'meet' – notice the position of the jaw. It is almost closed. Now say 'mat'. Can you feel the difference?

Now practise saying 'meet', 'mat', 'meet', 'mat' several times

Now say 'two'. Is the jaw open or closed?

Now say 'tar' What position is the jaw in?

Now say 'two', 'tar', 'two', 'tar' several times

Now try saying 'meet' with your jaw open and 'mat' with your jaw closed.

Say ' I'. Where is the jaw position at the beginning and at the end?

Try saying 'I' but reversing the jaw positions. Is it difficult?

## Lips

Whisper 'tea'. What position are the lips in?

Why do photographers ask us to say 'cheese' when taking a photograph?

Say 'two'. What position are the lips in?

Say 'two', 'tea', 'two', 'tea' several times

Try to say 'tea' with rounded lips. It should sound more like the French sound in 'une'

Try to say 'two' with spread lips. Is it difficult?

## Tongue

Say the sound 'tea' again. Is the tongue low or high in the mouth?

Now say 'two' again. Which part of the tongue is raised?

Say 'tea', 'two', 'tea', 'two' several times and notice the position of the tongue.

Say 'boy'. What happens to the tongue?

## Length

What do the vowels in these words have in common?

bird, bard, board, bead, brood

What do these vowels have in common?

bit, bet, bat, hot, but, boot

Now say these words:

| | |
|---|---|
| bat | bad |
| bit | bid |
| back | bag |
| luck | lug |

Are the vowels the same length in each pair?

# Pronunciation activity types and techniques

## Teaching sounds

---

### Activity 2

(a) What difficulties do your learners have in pronouncing individual sounds?

(b) How do you help them?

(c) Do you know enough about the L1 and L2 language phonologies to be able to diagnose segmental pronunciation problems?

(d) How might you help learners who have difficulties with the following contrasts?

/b/p/ – 'pin', 'bin' and /t/d/ 'tin', 'din'

---

There is no doubt that at some stage the teacher will need to concentrate on accurate sound production. As teachers, we are all aware of technical tips to help learners produce certain sounds. However in some areas, notably in the production of vowels and some consonants, technical information is of relatively little use, as illustrated satirically in Figure 13.1.

**Figure 13.1** 'Technical' instructions on the articulation of 'th' (retreived from http://www.lgpcards.com)

In fact, it is more difficult to learn accurate vowels than consonants, probably because there are no distinct points of contact between articulators, unlike with consonants. Also, as we have seen, research suggests that introduction to vowel distinctions may be more efficiently accomplished through listening tasks whereas consonants tend to be mastered more efficiently through speaking tasks (Fucci et al. 1977, Leather 1983, Chun 2002).

We have also seen that research findings show the importance of perceptual training tasks such as discrimination and identification in order to facilitate productive skills. A traditional way of approaching the area of teaching sounds is therefore to begin with awareness raising activities. We do not usually pay conscious attention to the sounds of the language we speak and it can therefore require a great deal of concentration to do so. In addition learners may tend to hear the sounds of English in terms of the sounds of their own L1. Based on the sub-skills outlined earlier, a typical teaching sequence might therefore be based on the following Listening, Imitation, Production (LIP) approach:

*Listening* – Activities such as those involving minimal pairs (see below) to encourage learners to hear the sounds correctly. For example, learners can be asked to listen to words which differ in just one phoneme, for example, (pin/bin) and then be asked to say whether they are the same or different. This is often not as easy as it sounds.

*Imitation* – Here the role of the teacher is to produce accurate models for the learners to imitate and also to give feedback on how they are doing. Sometimes learners are unable to tell whether they are getting a sound right or wrong, especially if they have difficulty hearing it in the first place. Indeed, imitation is probably the most widely used technique but it does not guarantee accurate production. The technique perhaps tends to work more effectively with young learners. For remedial purposes with older learners imitation approaches may not be sufficient to change habits of pronunciation that have fossilized. When presenting an utterance for imitation by learners back-chaining has been found to be a useful technique.

*Production* – We can only really say that students have learnt a sound when they produce it accurately on their own when engaged in free speaking. It is important to remember that learning to pronounce sounds correctly is a gradual process of approximation. Even after getting it right on one occasion, learners may subsequently get it wrong and will need to keep on trying until they can consistently produce the correct sound accurately.

All sorts of variables are at work in pronunciation learning: confidence, motivation, perception, memory, muscular movement and control. Using sounds to make meaning involves the development of automaticity in connected sound production. Students need accurate models, time, practice, encouragement, revision and more time.

## Teaching tips

### Modelling

In order for the learner to first notice a sound and then discriminate between contrasting phonemes and finally produce such sounds themselves, they need to be provided with an accurate and consistent model. The teacher can obviously provide this model if they feel (a) confident they can produce the sounds in the required target form (i.e. BBC English or some alternative standard accent) and (b) can reproduce the target form consistently without noticeably changing other elements of pronunciation such as pitch movement, vowel quality or stress placement. Alternatively, a recorded speech sample could be used, for instance from a pronunciation course or a media recording from a source such as the television or internet.

### Visual aids

Research suggests that there are advantages in combining visual with audio input for pronunciation training and that this combined modality is superior to audio input only (Hardison 2002). It also appears that sounds that are relatively visible might be easier to learn than those which are less visible. For instance, a study by Markham and Nagano-Madsen (1996) found that voiced stops and fricatives tended to be worse produced the further back (so less visible) their articulation in the oral cavity. Consequently, it can be helpful to use visual as well as auditory input to show place and manner of articulation for those sounds that can be demonstrated visually. For example, articulations involving the lips (/p/, /b/ /m/) and teeth (/f/ /v/) and tip of the tongue (/t/, /d/, /n/, /ð/, /θ/). Also, lip rounding (e.g. for /w/ /u:/) can also be demonstrated visually. All of these sounds can be easily 'seen' as well as 'felt'.

For sounds that are less easily visible, diagrams showing a cross-section of the vocal tract and articulators are typically used, as in Figure 13.2.

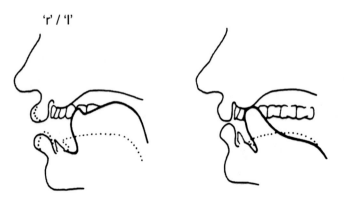

**Figure 13.2** Articulation of /r/ and /l/ (from 'Speaking Clearly' Rogerson and Gilbert 1990:96)

However, being shown a two-dimensional diagram of the inside of the mouth does not automatically lead to correct production of such sounds and can actually be quite confusing for some learners. A more sophisticated approach involves the presentation of a video recording or the articulation of a sound together with an animated cross-sectional diagram and the possibility to hear the sound, as in this example (Figure 13.3) from the University of Iowa's phonetics website.

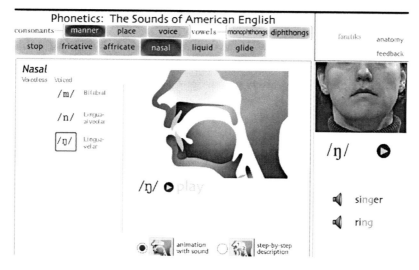

**Figure 13.3** University of Iowa's phonetics website (retrieved 15 October 2010 from http://www.uiowa. edu/~acadtech/phonetics/english/frameset.html)

Other, simpler visual aids can be used which can be equally effective in that they introduce a visual or kinesthetic element into the learning process. For instance, the use of rubber bands to illustrate the lengthening or shortening of vowels as in Figure 13.4.

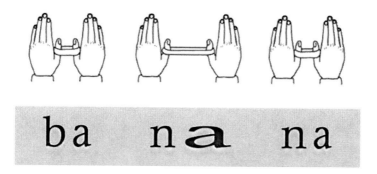

**Figure 13.4** Using rubber bands to show vowel length (from Gilbert 2008:38)

The main idea is to use as many visual, kinesthetic and auditory tools as possible to encourage pronunciation learning.

## Minimal pairs

Techniques designed to help learners hear and then produce individual sounds generally make extensive use of **minimal pairs**. As we have seen, these are pairs of words which differ in only one phoneme:

```
e.g. ship    sheep
     pill    Bill
     cut     gut
```

Minimal pairs are useful for a variety of activities. For example:

'Stop me if I change'

The teacher says minimal pairs in a series, changing from one word to the other at random. Learners have to clap or put their hands up when the teacher changes:

```
ship ship ship ship sheep sheep sheep ship etc.
                 (clap)            (clap)
```

In addition students can be asked to identify the odd one out, for example:

|   | a | b | c | d |
|---|------|-------|-------|-------|
| 1 | ship | sheep | sheep | sheep |
| 2 | cat | cat | cat | cat |
| 3 | sit | seat | seat | seat |
| 4 | hope | hope | hope | hop |
| 5 | pick | pick | peak | pick |

Students listen and note the latter of the odd one out.

## Simple recognition or perception

The teacher has a list of minimal pairs:

```
e.g. A       B
     ship    sheep
     bin     bean
     slip    sleep
```

Learners have two cards one with A and one with B. When the teacher pronounces a word learners have to hold up the appropriate card according to whether a word from list A or list B has been pronounced.

Once learners can hear contrasting sounds well, they can be asked to produce the minimal pair. They can first repeat the pair modelled by the teacher or heard in recording, then one student produces one member of the minimal pair and the teacher or other students identify it.

The next stage is to put the minimal pair into a wider stretch of speech, so for example, for the /v/ /w/ distinction. The individual sample words, 'veal' vs 'wheel' could be contextualized as:

    (a) Here's the veal
    (b) Here's the wheel.

Students could then be asked to practice saying sentences with a partner who has to decide which word ('veal' or 'wheel') was produced:

    (a) There's something wrong with this veal
    (b) There's something wrong with this wheel

It is important to try to make the context as meaningful as possible while avoiding complex language which might distract from focusing on the minimal pairs.

### Games

A variety of forms of phonemic Bingo has been produced but it is probably just as easy to make your own. Learners have cards with words or pictures on them and have to cover their word when the teacher calls it out. The first to cover the whole card is the winner.

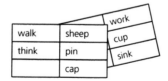

### Pairs practice

Pairs of students are given a sheet with a list of words on it. By talking and listening but not looking at each others' cards, each student must compare the list with that of their partner to work out whether the words are the same or different.

| A | B |
|---|---|
| 1. shrieck | 1. shrieck |
| 2. cheap | 2. chip |
| 3. shark | 3. shack |
| 4. batch | 4. bash |
| 5. lash | 5. lash |
| 6. match | 6. mash |
| 7. chin | 7. shin |
| 8. charm | 8. charm |
| 9. dish | 9. ditch |
| 10. perch | 10. birch |

## Bilingual minimal pairs

Bowen and Marks (1992) suggest using bilingual minimal pairs as a way of sensitizing learners to the differences between their own L1 and English. A series of near homophones are drawn up and learners have to say whether the teacher is pronouncing the word in their L1 or English.

| French | English | | Polish | English |
|--------|---------|---|--------|---------|
| tente | taunt | | tente | hell |
| attaque | attack | | klucz | clutch |
| tel | tell | | daj | dye |
| heure | her | | lot | lot |
| club | club | | kruk | crook |
| rage | raj | | mial | miaow |

The teacher then asks learners what the differences are between the Polish/French and English pronunciations. According to Bowen and Marks, although at first learners describe the differences in very general terms such as English is softer, they can be guided to more subtle voice quality differences such as place of articulation and position of tongue and lips.

Such an exercise can be very useful since learners tend to fit what they hear in English into their own L1 sound system. This activity forces them to concentrate on the small but subtle differences between the two. Often where there is close proximity of sound there is greater difficulty in separating them.

It is important however not to overuse minimal pairs. The aim ultimately is to help learners produce sound contrasts in connected speech. One way of doing this is to create short dialogues with samples of the minimal pairs (/v/ /w/) embedded such as:

A: This van is going very fast.
B: Yes, I bet he's over the speed limit.
A: The police can ban you from driving for a year.
B: That would be very unfortunate.

A: Yes, I vote we tell him to stop.

(from 'Speaking Clearly' Rogerson and Gilbert 1990:92)

Ideally, extracts of fluent speech can also be used for listening and production practice. For example:

'There <u>w</u>ere many <u>V</u>iking <u>v</u>illages in <u>v</u>arious parts of north-east and <u>w</u>est England, and there are still <u>w</u>ords in our language <u>w</u>ith Scandina<u>v</u>ian origins'

(from 'Speaking Clearly' Rogerson and Gilbert 1990:93)

Again, it is important to make such contexualized examples as meaningful as possible.

---

### Activity 3

(a) Make a set of minimal pairs for learners who have difficulties with distinguishing between the vowel sounds in walk and work?

(b) How would you break up the diphthongs in the following words for teaching purposes?

boy      tower      bear      higher

---

## Possible teaching materials

Most pronunciation course books and materials provide exercises for practising sounds and sound contrasts. Well-known books which deal specifically with learning sounds include 'Ship or Sheep' (Baker 2006) and O'Connor and Fletcher's 'Sounds English' (1989). As explained earlier, it can be helpful to provide audio and visual input to reinforce learning, in which case the following resources might be useful:

*Pronunciation animations*: One of Cambridge University Press's ELT resource sites. http://www.cambridge.org/elt/resources/skills/interactive/pron_animations/index.htm

*Flash Animation Project*: This site contains animated diagrams of speech sounds for English, German and Spanish. Developed by the University of Iowa. http://www.uiowa.edu/~acadtech/phonetics/

*Pronunciation Power*: Online and CDbased pronunciation learning materials for English and other languages. http://www.englishlearning.com/

# Teaching syllables

Despite what would seem to be a worrying variety of reasons for people not to get the point straight away, most students do pick the idea of the syllable rapidly. Some useful teaching techniques include:

Using familiar words to introduce the concept and asking students to guess how many syllables there are in them. These can be cognates which are similar in many languages but not exactly the same. Preferably choose words which might have a different number of syllables in English compared with other languages. For example:

chocolate    secretary    important    restaurant

Similarly, words with one root but different word classes can be used:

| | | |
|---|---|---|
| ease | easy | easily |
| will | willing | willingly |

Depending on the level of the students, examples can be given of possible syllable structure, keeping the central vowel constant if possible, for example:

I
IN
PIN
SPIN
PINCH

Also, the frequent mismatch between spelling and pronunciation can be illustrated here. It can be shown that the number of phonemes in a syllable does not necessarily correspond to the number of letters in a written word. So, for instance:

| | | |
|---|---|---|
| eye | /aɪ/ | V |
| night | /naɪt/ | CVC |

You can then get students to make similar patterns. The most practical solution, however, is to use tapping exercises until students intuitively perceive syllables in an English sense.

Important areas to work on, once students have grasped the basic concept of the English syllable, are (a) grammatical endings and the additional syllable rule (i.e. regular past tense verbs ending in /t/ or /d/ the final 'ed' is pronounced as an extra syllable; plural ending 'es' is pronounced as a extra syllables after words ending in sibilants (see Chapter 7) and (b) the effect of silent vowels on the number of syllables in a word (e.g. veg(e)table, secret(a)ry).

### Possible teaching materials

Some useful activities on syllables can be found in Hancock's (2003) 'English Pronunciation in Use', chapter 21 as well as in Gilbert's (2005) Clear Speech, chapter 1 and Rogerson and Gilbert's (1990) 'Speaking Clearly', chapter 1.

# Teaching stress and rhythm

Gilbert (2008:8) claims that it is very inefficient to teach individual sounds without first of all, establishing some basic understanding of the English system of rhythm and melody. Without this understanding of English prosody, she suggests, learners will end up practising English sounds in their L1 rhythm. She also suggests that if time teaching pronunciation is limited, it is best to concentrate on developing an understanding of the core system of rhythm and stress together with whichever phonemes are critical for the particular learners, rather than spending the majority of time on covering all the phonemes of English.

Rhythm and stress are obviously areas that lend themselves well to using visual and kinesthetic tools to support teaching and learning.

# Word stress

(a) As we have said before, it is important to get students into the habit of learning stress when they learn new vocabulary. They can be helped by deciding on a marking system to write stress patterns down. This can be simply using the conventional /'/ diacritic before the stressed syllable or a more 'visual' code can be used such as:

or:

engiNEER    revoLUtion

■■■    ■■■■
engineer    revolution

(b) Again, get students to compare 'international' words such as hotel, telephone, computer, etc. in the learners' own language to sensitize them to this whole area.

(c) Clap or tap the stress – exaggerate to help learners hear the constrast between strong and weak syllables.

(d) Hum the stress – ti tum ti tum

e.g.  He's gone to town
       ti    tum ti    tum

(e) Use exercises such as the ones below:-

  (i) *Sort this shopping list into columns according to the stress pattern:*

| tomatoes | carrots | potatoes | pizza | chicken |
| bananas | cornflakes | butter | vegetables | apples |
| cabbage | spinach | lettuce | broccoli | celery |

  (ii) *Which of the following words is the odd one out and why?*

  ○  (a) Station
  ○  (b) Relation
  ○  (c) Information
  ○  (d) Relate

*Possible teaching materials*

Most pronunciation teaching books contain a section on teaching word stress but Hancock's 'English Pronunciation in Use' (2003, units 28–31) is both thorough and accessible. Similarly, Underhill's 'Sound Foundations' has some interesting ideas for teaching word stress using Cuisienaire rods (1994:154–6). Word stress is an area where visual and auditory presentation can aid learning and some of the online multimedia resources on word stress (e.g. Pronunciation Power, which is available from http://www.englishlearning.com/) can be helpful.

## Teaching rhythm

There are many useful activity types for teaching learners first to hear and then produce English rhythmic patterns. These often rely on the same visual or kinesthetic tools we have suggested under 'word stress'.

Some examples include:

(a) 'same or different' (rhythm of words and phrases)

• ○ • • ○•   • ○ • • ○ •

e.g. 'computerization'      'he works at the station'

(b) expanding headlines/messages

e.g. 'SEND MONEY – BOUGHT BIKE'
please SEND me some MONEY 'cos I've BOUGHT a BIKE

(c) using strongly rhythmical material such as songs, poems and limericks.

e.g. There was an Old Man with a beard,
Who said, 'It is just as I feared!
Two Owls and a Hen,
Four Larks and a Wren,
Have all built their nests in my beard!' (Edward Lear 1846)

*Possible teaching materials*

Carolyn Graham's 'Jazz Chants' (1978) is a collection of chants and poems in which everyday language is set to jazz rhythms to demonstrate the rhythm and intonation patterns of English (see Figure 13.5). Jazz chants can also help learners emphasize prominent syllables and minimize weak syllables. Such activities can help learners get the 'feel' of English rhythm and the enjoyment of practising through pair or group work but it is important to point out that everyday speech is not as inherently rhythmic as in such literary or contrived examples.

**NOTES**

◆ This chant provides practice in the simple present question. *Do you know . . . ?* and the emphatic short response *Yes, of course I do.*

◆ Call students' attention to the rising Yes/No question intonation in *Do you know Mary?* and *Do you know her little brother?* versus the falling *Wh-* question intonation pattern of *Mary who?* Also, point out that the *h* sound in *her* is dropped when we say *know her* and *and her.*

◆ Do You Know Mary? may be used for practice in negative short answers plus follow-up questions in question-response combinations such as *Do you know Mary? No, I don't. Do you?* Have students listen for and practice the rising intonation of the follow-up questions.

◆ Once students are familiar with the chant, have them practice it, substituting their own names and the names of their family members.

## 2 Do You Know Mary?

Do you know Mary?
   Mary who?
Mary McDonald.
   Of course I do.

Do you know her little brother?
   Yes, of course I do.
   I know her brother
   and her mother
   and her father, too.

Do you know her older sister?
   Yes, of course I do.
   I know her older sister, Betty,
   and her younger sister, Sue.

Do you know her Aunt Esther?
   Yes, of course I do.
   I know her aunts and her uncles
   and her cousins, too.

Do you know her husband, Bobby?
   Yes, of course I do.
   I know her husband and his brother
   and his father, too.

**Figure 13.5** Sample 'jazz chant' (from Graham 1978)

Another useful source of teaching materials for rhythm practice is Colin Mortimer's 'Elements of Pronunciation' (1985). The book contains a series of recorded dialogues with a 'listen-and-repeat' section, followed by a recording of the dialogue at natural speed, and then a version with pauses to allow intensive practice. The materials could be criticized for perpetuating the 'stress-timing' myth and because the complexity of the vocabulary sometimes detracts from the focus on pronunciation but the simplicity and effectiveness of the exercise format compensated for these defects.

## Teaching connected speech

As we saw earlier, it is important that learners see the relationship between rhythm and other aspects of pronunciation: the connection 'downwards' on smaller elements of pronunciation such as the reduction of unstressed vowels and the influence 'upwards' on larger elements such as contractions, elisions and linking. Some activity types include:

(a) Getting learners to deduce 'rules' as to how words link by giving learners examples to categorize. For instance, by linking sound:

| here is    | who are    | she is     | know if |      |
|------------|------------|------------|---------|------|
| we ought   | there are  | are in     | may I   | do I |

| Linking 'r' | Linking 'y' | Linking 'w' |
|-------------|-------------|-------------|
|             |             | do I        |

(b) Deciding some sort of notation for linkage

e.g.  Pay‿attention

(c) Marking linking on familiar phrases (e.g. 'not at all', 'shut up').

(d) Marking potential links on tapescripts of songs, poems, etc.

(e) Crossing out the letter(s) which 'disappear' in the following sentences:

I don't want to
The next day
Sit down
Mind the doors

(f) 'Rhymalogues' – Morley's (1979) idea of using rhyming exchanges to practise contractions and reductions can be useful, enjoyable and easily memorable. For instance:

Q:  What did you do, Lou? (Whaddja do Lou?)
A:  I lost my pen, Ben
Q:  When's the play, Ray?
A:  It's at eight, Kate
Q:  Where did you go, Joe? (Wheredja go, Joe?)
A:  To the play

May from Morley (1979)

(g) Mini-dictations – It can be useful to get students into the habit of doing 'mini-dictations' at the beginning of class. The teacher says about ten discrete sentences based on everyday phrases. Each phrase is repeated twice with the same stress and intonation patterns. Students then check with each other before getting feedback from the teacher on the correct version. The class then discusses what aspects of connected speech they heard or didn't hear. For example:

When did he go
Do you (djə/ know if he is coming this ‿afternoon

(h) Listening for contractions and weak forms in various styles of spoken English

e.g. radio news, informal dialogues, speeches

(i)  Changing formal written messages to informal spoken messages:

e.g. 'What time do you want to meet?' – what time 'djə wannə' meet

(j)  Backchaining is a popular device used in repetition practice. Students listen to the teacher presenting a 'difficult' utterance, as in the example above:

'Do you know if he's coming this afternoon'

If it is difficult for students to reproduce, the teacher breaks it down from the end:

afternoon
this afternoon
coming
he's coming
he's coming this afternoon etc.

eliciting repetition each time. This builds confidence and enables the students to repeat successfully.

## Possible teaching materials

The pronunciation books in the 'Headway' series (Bowler and Cunningham 1999 onwards) have some good ideas for activities in this area. Similarly, Hancock's (2003) 'English Pronunciation in Use' has several useful units on contractions and weak forms. Rogerson and Gilbert's (1990) 'Speaking Clearly' and Gilbert's (2001) 'Clear Speech' also have units covering linking, reductions and contractions.

# Teaching accentuation and focus

Students should be introduced to these suprasegmental aspects of pronunciation as early as possible and they should be related to other aspects of language learning such as listening, speaking and reading practice (see 'Integrating pronunciation teaching' section).

After initially introducing the key concepts in a fairly controlled way, activities involving longer stretches of natural speech should be used as much as possible as it is through exposure to these longer extracts of language that the relationship between suprasegmentals and meaning becomes evident.

## Basic stress pattern

Many of the activity types listed above can be modified to focus on basic stress patterns in stretches of speech, developing awareness of and ability to produce stressed and unstressed words and emphasize the focus word in a thought group. A variety of spoken texts, voices and accents should be used if possible.

Simple dialogues can be used to introduce the basic stress pattern. For instance:

A: 'What's the **'matter**?
B: I've 'lost my **'keys**
A: 'Where did you **'put** them?
B: If I **'knew** that, I would have **'found** them!

Audio and video recordings of TV or radio broadcasts can be used for students to practise either (a) using a transcript to predict where stressed and focus words will go before listening to the recording or (b) listening first and then marking where stress and focus falls.

Students can be asked to rehearse and then speak or record similar short dialogues or speech extracts making sure they use appropriate accentuation.

### *Emphatic and contrastive stress*
Activities can be done to practise marking emphatic or contrastive stress. For example:

A: Excuse me, I think your in <u>my</u> seat.
B: Sorry but it says <u>7A</u> on my boarding card.
A: Oh, er . . . right. I asked for a <u>window</u> seat, you see . . .
B: Yeah, so did I. What's <u>your</u> seat number?
A: Let's see . . . Oh it's <u>8</u>A.
B: So, I guess your in the seat <u>behind</u> me.
A: Oh yes. <u>Sorry</u> about that.

(from 'English Pronunciation in Use' Hancock 2003)

## Teaching intonation

It should be obvious from earlier chapters that intonation is seen as an area of pronunciation that needs to be treated with some caution as far as teaching is concerned. This does not mean that it should be ignored entirely but it is suggested that more time will be profitably spent on developing receptive and productive skills regarding the placement of thought group boundaries and nuclear stress than on tone choice.

Activities can be done so that learners can identify thought groups and mark boundary pauses and nuclear stress. Again, listening to a variety of speech types and voices can help students identify falling and rising tones and possibly fall-rise tones. Careful modelling and imitation are still very helpful techniques. As with any area of pronunciation, noticing and discriminating activities should come before repetition and finally production of new speech.

### *Listening activities*
Gilbert makes the link between an understanding of English prosody and listening comprehension, stating that 'Without a sufficient, threshold-level mastery of the English prosodic

system, learners' intelligibility and listening comprehension will not advance, no matter how much effort is made drilling individual sounds (Gilbert 2008:8).

An effective teaching method would be in three stages:

(1) pre-listening study of text, where students are asked to predict which words or syllables are prominent; how the text would divide into tone units, and which tone types are likely to occur
(2) discussion of text, tone group by tone group (see example below)
(3) listening to a reading of the text, identifying tone groups, prominent syllables and tone types.

Chapman's study (2007:7) confirms that such pre-listening activities can greatly assist learners to identify intonation patterns when they finally come to listen to spoken text.

## Using transcripts

As with the other areas of pronunciation getting learners to hear the intonation patterns might be a first step. Techniques mentioned previously can be used such as predicting intonation patterns on transcripts before listening to speech or marking intonation after listening. Generally speaking, it is useful to get students to mark:

- thought group boundaries and or pauses
- nuclear stress placement
- fall or rise tone on the nucleus.

As, for example in the transcription activities in Chapters 11 and 12, such as this:

## Recording 2

//'my 'name is ˎ 'Simon //- and I was 'born in ˎ 'Tanza'nia // - I 'grew 'up in 'many
ˎ'different 'countries //- I have 'lived in the 'east ˎ'midlands //for the 'past 'fifteen ˎ'years//

(Activity 7, Chapter 12)

## Production activities

Students also need to use intonation interactively and not simply mimic melodic patterns. Therefore, an essential part of teaching the communicative value of intonation is to use exercises in which the listener's answers depend on noticing the speaker's choice of focus word. Such tasks give each student many opportunities to practice both speaking and listening. They also provide students with the opportunity to receive immediate, practical feedback.

Furthermore, changing students' partners from time to time aids learning to accommodate variations in speech.

For example:

> Have students read the following sentences, then take turns challenging a partner. Student A says question (a) or (b).
> Student B says the matching answer.
>
> > a: Were you in the bank on *Friday*? No, I was there Saturday.
> > b: Were you in the *bank* on Friday? No, I worked Friday.
> > a: Were *you* in the bank on Friday? No, but my sister was.
> > b: Were you *in* the bank on Friday? No, but I was near it.
>
> (from Rogerson and Gilbert 1990:49)

## 'Chunking' speech

It is important for learners to hear and then learn to produce speech in 'chunks' of related information or thought groups. This can not only aid their comprehension but also make them sound much more natural and fluent. A range of activities can be done to practise chunking, such as:

> 1. (4 x 3) + 6 = (answer 18)
> 2. 4 x (3 + 6) = (answer 36)
>
> A: The man and the woman dressed in black, came out of the restaurant. (both were in black)
> B: The man, and the woman dressed in black, came out of the restaurant. (the woman was in black)
>
> – a student gives the answer depending on how the numbers or words were 'chunked'

'*Shadowing*' of the teacher or of a recorded piece of speech is another technique. The learner tries to copy a spoken sentence by repeating it aloud or whispering it a second or so after the target speaker. Teachers can also help identify pauses or pitch rise of fall by the use of a hand gestures.

Listening to spontaneous speech is probably too challenging for the initial stages of studying prominence and intonation. More manageable would be the prepared speech of actors or newsreaders in recorded material, such as radio programmes.

*Reading aloud* is often decried as old-fashioned, but is an invaluable way to focus on prominence and intonation. A reading passage can be used to divide text into thought groups. Having divided a text into thought groups, learners can also be asked to predict where sentence stress should fall. Placement of the nucleus involves deciding what is significant 'new' material, what is already 'given' in the text and therefore non-prominent, what is contrastive within the text, and what might require special emphasis, for example in spoken dialogue. Narratives often involve the repetition of characters' names and other details of the story, providing opportunities to demonstrate the de-stressing or 'non-prominence' of repeated material, which often results in the nucleus being moved within a thought group. Tapping with pencil or fingers on a desk while speaking sentences aloud would help learners get accustomed to the idea of prominent syllables, with perhaps an extra loud tap for the nuclear syllable.

## Drama techniques

Often learners are reluctant to use a wide voice range when speaking English, fearing that they sound 'silly'. Techniques traditionally used to train actors are suggested by Wessels and Lawrence (1992:32) as being useful for the teaching of intonation. They offer a range of such techniques in their article.

Below is one which can be used to raise awareness of pitch. Get learners to chant or sing in rising or falling pitch:

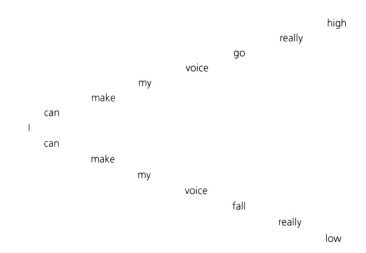

Similarly, using literature such as reading poems or plays to practise speaking dramatically can be very effective and enjoyable.

In a similar vein, students should be given the opportunity to 'excel' or 'put on their best pronunciation' (Kenworthy 1987:122) from time to time. This involves having time to prepare, rehearse and present, preferably in front of an audience. One way of doing this is by preparing 'voice overs' or commentaries for a short video, TV or film sequence, for instance for part of a weather forecast or news broadcast. For instance, students could be given the video sequence and asked to prepare a scripted commentary. They should listen to the sequence as often as they like and mark nuclear stress, pauses and final rise and fall tones before thought group boundaries. They can then rehearse giving the voice over until they are happy with their delivery and then present the sequence and commentary to an audience.

There are of course many other types of activities that can be used to practise intonation patterns, traditionally involving discrimination and production of pitch patterns. Relatively recently, the use of multimedia has been exploited in this area so that for instance it is possible to record and view a spectographic analysis of your own pitch movements, as shown in Figure 13.6.

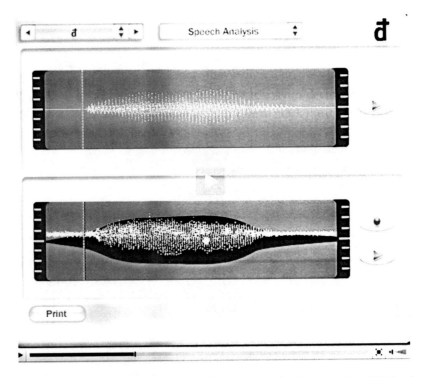

**Figure 13.6** Sample spectographic analysis of speech (from Pronunciation Power; retrieved 15 October 2010 from http://www.englishlearning.com/demos/flv_pp2_overview.html)

Or, more interactive tasks where students have to manipulate pitch movements to correspond to a recorded utterance, as in this example (Figure 13.7) from David Brett's website:

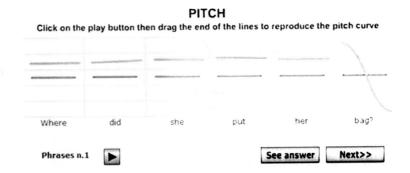

**Figure 13.7** Sample of interactive pitch contour activity (From David Brett's website http://davidbrett.uniss.it/index)

However, many students and teachers find these quite difficult to hear and reproduce.

Using a discourse intonation approach enables teachers and researchers to analyse speakers' choice of tone, prominence and key in naturally occurring speech. However, it has had limited impact on pronunciation teaching materials to date. As mentioned earlier, the most ambitious attempts have been Bradford's book 'Intonation in Context' (1988) and Brazil's own 'Pronunciation for Advanced Learners of English' (1994) both of which tried to apply the whole discourse intonation model to pronunciation production. More limited applications were made in Rogerson and Gilbert's (1990) 'Speaking Clearly' which, for instance, introduced the concept of 'key' to the division of speech into 'thought groups'. More recently, materials writers (e.g. Bowler and Cunningham 1999, Gilbert 2001, Hancock 2003) have focused more on teaching the concept of prominence productively while developing awareness of tone choice receptively.

# Conclusion

There are many other exercises types and techniques could be used to teach each of these pronunciation elements and those covered here are only a sample. There are now many useful and interesting pronunciation teaching materials available including textbooks, CDs and both commercial and free online courses and resources. The main thing is for the teacher to instil concern and a sense of enthusiasm for pronunciation in learners. To this end, the use of humour and drama are important tools for pronunciation teaching along with the inclusion of visual and kinesthetic elements to add variety to audio input.

# Key points

- Drills and other repetition exercises may be important to develop new motor skills, particularly regarding the articulation of new sounds.
- Providing learners with a variety of speakers is helpful.
- Perceptual training can result in significant improvement in production.
- Stress timing may be a myth in empirical terms but the concept of alternating strong and weak syllables is fundamental to English speech rhythm and a very important concept for learners to grasp.
- It is probably more beneficial to spend time teaching thought group division and nuclear stress placement than tone choice.
- L2 pronunciation learners 'hear' a new language through their L1 filter. This can be an advantage as well as a disadvantage by using the L1 sounds as a reference point for comparison and similarity where possible.

## Further reading

Cooper, R. (1990) 'Pronouncing on video', *Professional English Teacher,* 11 (2), 50.

Ferst, P. and Linehan, A. (1997) 'From speech bubbles to soap bubbles', *Modern English Teacher,* 6 (2), 32–5.

Gilbert, J. (1978) 'Gadgets: Non-verbal tools for teaching pronunciation', *CATESOL Occasional Papers,* 4, 68–78. Also in Brown, A. (ed., 1991) *Teaching English Pronunciation: A Book of Readings.* London: Routledge.

Jones, R. H. (1997) 'Beyond "listen and repeat": Pronunciation teaching materials and theories of second language acquisition', *System,* 25 (l), 103–12.

MacCarthy, P. (1976) 'Auditory and articulatory training for the language teacher and learner', *ELT Journal,* 30, 212–19. Also in Brown, A. (ed., 1991) *Teaching English Pronunciation: A Book of Readings.* London: Routledge, pp. 299–307.

Marks, J. (1992) 'Making pronunciation visible', in Brown, A. (ed.) *Approaches to Pronunciation Teaching.* London: Macmillan & The British Council.

Wennerstrom, A. K. (1992) 'Content-based pronunciation', *TESOL Journal,* 1 (3), 15–18.

Wessels, C. and Lawrence, K. (1992) 'Using drama voice techniques in the teaching of pronunciation', in Brown, A. (ed., 1991) *Teaching English Pronunciation: A Book of Reading.* London: Routledge, pp. 29–37.

Willis, K. (1993) 'A "new look" phonemic chart', *Professional English Teacher,* 13 (3), 35–6.

# Pronunciation Teaching: Some Questions Answered

## Introduction

Despite the value many learners put on pronunciation proficiency (Derwing and Rossiter 2002), teachers and trainers are often daunted by the prospect of teaching pronunciation and may consequently either undervalue or overlook this area of language teaching. Most English language teachers will happily teach grammar and vocabulary in the classroom, although few would consider themselves expert linguists in the fields of syntax or semantics. Why are the same teachers so wary of teaching pronunciation in the classroom?

Is it because the theoretical body of knowledge of phonetics and phonology seems so far removed from practical classroom applications? Is it because teachers and trainers are unclear about what can actually be achieved by pronunciation teaching? Especially given the current popularity of the communicative approach with its emphasis on fluency and communicative proficiency, it is hard to see where a traditional 'bottom-up' approach to pronunciation teaching based on the articulation of individual segments fits in. Is it because teacher educators are unclear about the specific knowledge and skills teachers need? Or is it because teachers, with limited contact time and pressures of syllabuses and exams, are not sure what to teach and how?

All of these questions are reflected for instance in the lack of systematic pronunciation syllabuses both in course documents and in textbooks, and the general lack of interest and analysis given to elements of pronunciation in oral proficiency assessment. Whatever the reason, or reasons for this neglect, it is important to help teachers focus more clearly on this aspect of oral skills development. Before considering these and other key questions relating to pronunciation teaching, it might be helpful to review some of the main historical developments in this area.

## Teaching Pronunciation – an overview

As with other aspects of language teaching, pronunciation teaching has been influenced by shifting trends and approaches in pedagogy over previous decades and even centuries. In the 1890s the development of the International Phonetic Alphabet (IPA), by Henry Sweet and his colleagues resulted in what was generally known as the *Reform Movement* in language teaching. This movement and the development of a system for describing and analysing the sound systems of languages did much to influence the teaching of pronunciation by advocating the following guidelines (Celce-Murcia et al. 1996:3):

- The spoken form of a language is primary and should be taught first
- The findings of phonetics should be applied to language teaching
- Teachers must have solid training in phonetics
- Learners should be given phonetic training to establish good speech habits.

Historically, the Reform Movement was very influential in the development of audiolingualism in the 1940s and 1950s. The emphasis on oral production in this approach led to the foregrounding of explicit pronunciation teaching through the behaviourist-based methods of imitation, repetition and drilling. In particular, teachers favoured using minimal pair contrasts, based on the phoneme as a minimally distinctive sound: a technique still much favoured by many teachers today.

The emergence of the cognitive approach in linguistics influenced by cognitive psychology and transformational-generative grammar (Chomsky 1959) resulted in a shift to viewing language primarily as rule-governed behaviour rather than habit formation. The outcome was the backgrounding of pronunciation teaching in favour of grammar and vocabulary because, it was argued that (1) native-like pronunciation was an unrealistic objective and could not be achieved (Scovel 2000); and (2) time would be better spent on teaching more learnable items, such as grammatical structures and words (Celce-Murcia et al. 1996).

The advent of the Communicative Approach in the 1980s saw yet another shift. The concentration on oral competence and communication brought pronunciation to the foreground again with the recognition that 'intelligible pronunciation is an essential component of communicative competence' (Morley 1994:488). However, the emphasis on meaningful communicative practice, made it difficult to justify the types of de-contextualized exercises and drills which had commonly been used for instance in teaching phonemic distinctions, such as minimal pairs practice. As mentioned earlier, the focus changed therefore towards a greater emphasis on suprasegmentals rather than segmentals as a means to enhancing intelligibility (Pennginton and Richards 1986).

The last decade has seen another shift in pedagogic climate, initiated partly by the rapid growth in the use of English as an International Language. Levis (2005:376) claims that, as a result, 'pronunciation theory, research and practice are in transition' again and that 'widely accepted assumptions such as the primacy of suprasegmentals, the supremacy of inner-circle models and the need for native instructors have been rightly challenged'.

Celce-Murcia et al. (1996:10) suggests that 'today we see signs that pronunciation instruction is moving away from the segmental/suprasegmental debate and towards a more balanced view'. Also, as we saw in Chapter 3, there is growing interest in the role of voice quality and underlying features such as tongue position, degree of jaw tension, spread or rounded lip position, and their contribution to the overall sound quality or accent of any particular language.

As we saw in Chapter 1, goals have also shifted historically in pronunciation teaching. In the days of audiolingualism, much pronunciation teaching was concerned with getting learners to produce sounds in order to approximate native speaker speech as closely as possible; termed the 'perfectionist tradition' by Brazil (1994). With the advent of more communicative approaches and the consequent emphasis on fluency as opposed to accuracy, there has been an increased awareness that intelligibility rather than native speaker pronunciation is a more realistic goal in language teaching for the majority of learners. Nevertheless, most researchers and teachers would also agree that ultimately a learner should not be discouraged from aiming at a near-native level of competence if they have a need, or an overwhelming desire, to do so.

Currently perhaps the most pressing debate in pronunciation teaching relates to the growing use of English as an international language, primarily between L2 speakers of English. As we saw in Chapter 1, this has led to a considerable amount of interest and research into the use of English as Lingua Franca and discussions about whether some fundamental assumptions about what and how we teach pronunciation should be reconsidered.

# Teaching pronunciation: some key questions

In the introduction we mentioned some questions which are commonly raised about pronunciation teaching. In the rest of this chapter, we will try to answer these and some other important questions that often confront pronunciation teachers.

(1) How do I decide what model and goals are appropriate for my learners?
(2) Can a NNS of English teach pronunciation effectively?
(3) What's more important: teaching segmental or suprasegmental aspects of pronunciation?
(4) Which approach is most effective for pronunciation teaching: bottom-up or top-down?
(5) Is it important for teachers and students to learn phonemic script?
(6) What skills and knowledge does the teacher need in order to teach pronunciation effectively?
(7) How do I decide pronunciation teaching priorities?
(8) How do I find time to teach pronunciation?
(9) How do I integrating pronunciation in specific language learning areas?
(10) How do I diagnose or assess a learner's pronunciation ability?
(11) Can technology enhance pronunciation teaching and learning?

## 1. How do I decide what model and goals are appropriate for my learners?

The issue of pronunciation models and goals has already been discussed in previous chapters. Clearly how learners themselves feel about their pronunciation is important. Brown (1992:6) following suggestions made by Kenworthy (1987) discusses the usefulness of questions such as those in Activity 1 in helping learners to reflect on how they feel about 'foreign' accents and 'good' pronunciation.

---

**Activity 1**

(1) Imagine you are talking in your first language to a NNS. The person doesn't speak your language very well and is difficult to understand. What do you do?

(2) What do you say when the NNS apologizes for their poor accent?

(3) How do you feel when a NNS pronounces your name wrong?

(4) How do you feel when you meet a NNS who speaks your language with a near perfect accent?

---

In answer to number 1, you probably seek to support the NNS's effort, to avoid threatening his or her face, to negotiate meaning as helpfully as possible. With question 2, when a NNS apologizes for a poor accent, many native speakers tend to offer re-assurance. Regarding question 3, mispronunciation of a name tends to be glossed over but it can be a source of irritation if such mispronunciation is long term. On question 4, there may be some ambivalent reactions. Many native speakers would be very impressed and appreciative, however, some may feel that a NNS with a near perfect L1 accent is getting 'too close for comfort' to the native speaker 'in-group' and feel more comfortable with an identifiable 'foreign' accent. Furthermore, politeness faux pas resulting from pragmatic failures are possibly easier to tolerate when there is an accent than when there is no foreign accent. Of course, these are generalizations and the choice of model and goal should be made carefully in light of learner needs and teaching context.

It is important that teachers are aware that pronunciation can be a more sensitive area of language learning than other areas such as grammar and vocabulary in that it involves modification of accent which can raise issues of attitude and identity. Research suggests that NNS teachers are rather ambivalent when discussing pronunciation goals and models and while many might be willing to consider ELF goals for students, many teachers strongly adhere to NS pronunciation norms themselves (Jenkins 2005, Sifakis and Sougari 2005, Kuo I-Chun 2006). This is in line with previous views (Kenworthy 1987, Roach 2000) about the need for teachers to acquire a high level of proficiency in target language pronunciation. The fact that many learners also maintain this aim despite the arguments put forward for a more restricted international English goal perhaps reflects concern for performance and proficiency as well as intelligibility as a goal in pronunciation (Timmis 2002, Kuo I-Chun 2006). Perhaps rather than focusing on the irrelevance of achieving native-like accents, teachers should emphasize the fact that learners can acquire a high level of proficiency in terms of fluency and intelligibility regardless of the accent used to do so.

## 2. Can a NNS of English teach pronunciation effectively?

Commonly, non-native English-speaking teachers (non-NESTs) have been awarded lower professional status than native English speaking teachers (NESTs), both by other teachers and by students (Medgyes 1992). However, the legitimacy of the NNS teacher has been a topic of much discussion in recent decades resulting in overwhelming support to improve their status (Widdowson 1994, Jenkins 2000). Many arguments have been proposed in support of NNS teachers including the fact that while NS teachers may have an advantage in terms of cultural and (possibly) linguistic knowledge and intuitions, they are not necessarily better language instructors. Seidlhofer (1999:238) also makes the point that the NNS teacher 'knows the target language as a foreign language' and that sharing this language learning experience with their students should be seen as 'the basis for non-native teachers' confidence, not their insecurity' (1999:238).

With regard to the teaching of pronunciation, the situation is of course rather more complicated, particularly with regard to pronunciation models. It would be naive to dismiss the fact that the NS teacher in the EFL classroom is better placed to provide a native English model (assuming that the teacher has the required accent within their repertoire). However, being able to provide a model is not the same thing as being able to teach learners how to acquire it. Gilbert (2008:43) echoes the same point:

> The disadvantage of non-native speaking teachers is that they tend to lack confidence in their own model. They often don't realize that native speaker teachers have quite a different disadvantage: they are unaware of what kinds of elements are difficult. Native speakers tend to assume that all aspects of spoken English (e.g., the uses of pitch and timing) are simply a natural part of human language, so they sometimes hurry over important matters. Non-native speakers, on the other hand, know from their own experience what aspects of spoken English require extra care. If the non-native speaking teacher has good listening recognition skills and a grasp of the Prosody Pyramid structure of English, then remaining elements of an L1 accent are of little importance.

Jenkins (2000) also argues that although NS teachers may be able to provide a NS model, they are not likely to have the detailed phonological knowledge of the learners' L1 pronunciation system that is required to facilitate the acquisition of the target accent. Furthermore, in a ELF rather than EFL context, the acquisition of a native accent may be less relevant or appropriate. Jenkins (2000) argues that in such cases the L2 learning experience and L1 background of the NNS pronunciation teacher has a distinct advantage.

### Activity 2

Where do you stand on this NEST vs non-NEST debate?

## 3. What's more important: teaching segmental or suprasegmental aspects of pronunciation?

We have already seen that priorities have shifted historically between teaching segmental or suprasegmental aspects of pronunciation. Although there has been an increasing emphasis on teaching suprasegmentals in many pronunciation materials in recent years, the merit of this focus is only partially supported by research. For instance, it appears that deviance in the pronunciation of suprasegmentals can cause considerable difficulty for NS listeners, however, segmental errors seem to have a much greater impact in intelligibility in ELF contexts (Derwing and Munro 1995, Jenkins and Setter 2005).

Leather (1999), for example, suggests native speaker listeners pay more attention to suprasegmentals than segmental accuracy. Also, some research by Anderson-Hsieh et al. (1992) found overall prosody (as opposed to segmental or syllable structure errors) had a greater influence on pronunciation rating for standardized spoken language tests. Similarly, Derwing and Munro (1997:15) conclude that 'improvements in NNS comprehensibility, at least for intermediate and high-proficiency learners, is more likely to occur with improvement in grammatical and prosodic proficiency than with a sole focus on correction of phonemic errors'.

In contrast, Jenkins (2000:155), in her data of NNS-NNS interactions, found that 'for EIL, and especially for NBESs (non-bilingual English speakers), the greatest phonological obstacles for mutual intelligibility appear to be deviant core sounds in combination with misplaced and/or mispronounced nuclear stress'. She found the majority of communication breakdowns were due to segmental errors (or segmental combined with nuclear stress errors).

In general it appears then that it might be more important for EFL learners, who will be communicating with native English speakers, to give more attention to suprasegmental aspects of pronunciation than ELF learners who might be better improving segmental accuracy primarily.

## 4. Which approach is most effective for pronunciation teaching: bottom-up or top-down?

While language teaching in general increasingly acknowledges the significance of context in interpreting meaning, it appears that bottom-up processing might be important for pronunciation learners, particularly at lower levels of proficiency. Because non-fluent L2 speech inevitably contains L1 transfer errors, low level listeners tend to process speech based largely on bottom-up rather than top-down strategies. Field agrees that, particularly in initial stages, learners tend to find individual sounds and words more concrete than higher level units and advocates what he calls a 'signal-based approach' (2004:332) to listening. This involves using bottom-up processing in listening activities rather than trying to extract information from the broader context.

Jenkins further claims that, in multilingual settings, due to the lack of shared sociocultural knowledge, learners rely more heavily on the acoustic signal: 'this in turn diverts cognitive resources away from features of the context, which are thence not available to compensate for any limitations in speech perception or production' (2000:83). In other words, a vicious circle arises whereby the articulation of sounds becomes paramount to intelligibility. Jenkins found that this creates problems which are difficult to resolve because the NNSs primarily use bottom-up processing strategies and seem unable to compensate for pronunciation errors by using contextual or syntactic information, especially in situations of processing overload.

Nevertheless, this should not deter from the importance of top-down processing for efficient listening comprehension, particularly for higher level learners.

Gilbert (2008:3) makes the point that aspects of prosody, such as pitch movement, nuclear stress and rhythm act as 'road signs' in spoken interaction, signalling to the listener which parts of speech are more, or less, important and indicating connections with what has gone before and what is coming next. Gilbert (2008:3) claims that 'Students who are taught about English prosodic patterns often report improved understanding of speech on TV, in movies, and in face-to-face conversation'. So, it seems that both bottom-up and top-down approaches are important and that the choice of one or the other will depend on the aspect of pronunciation which is being focused on and the level of the particular student or group of students.

## 5. Is it important for teachers and students to learn phonemic script?

Learning phonemic script can appear quite daunting for both teachers and learners but it does have several advantages for both. Here are some of the main ones:

- It is particularly useful for languages like English (or French) which have inconsistent spellings, as it highlights the fact that there is frequently an inexact sound-spelling correspondence in words.
- It raises learners awareness of the number of phonemes in English, particularly in the area of vowels.
- The pronunciation of words in isolation is very different from how they appear in connected speech. Using phonemic transcription enables us to show these features much more precisely than would be possible with traditional spelling.
- Once learnt, it provides a useful 'shorthand' and shared reference point for teacher and learners which can be used, for instance, for error correction.
- It is impossible to refer to sounds such as the schwa without it.
- It helps learners make the most of learner's dictionaries (Tench 1992).

## 6. What skills and knowledge does the teacher need in order to teach pronunciation effectively?

To be an effective teacher of pronunciation, both practical skills and theoretical knowledge of the subject area are required.

## *Practical skills*

The practical teaching skills are basically of two sorts:

(a) perceptual – for example, the ability to hear and recognize sounds (in isolation and in connected speech) and prosodic patterns
(b) productive – for example, the ability to reproduce individual sounds and prosodic patterns

Teachers need to become skilled in recognizing, analyzing and suggesting correction for pronunciation errors. In order to do this they need to be able to provide consistent models of the correct form and clear, accessible explanations. They should also be able to provide a suitable context for the pronunciation feature rather than treat it purely in isolation and integrate pronunciation work with other language areas when relevant. Finally, they need to be able to monitor learners' progress and give regular feedback as a means of maintaining motivation. In summary, the teacher needs to be skilled in the following areas:

(a) *recognition* – noticing of error
(b) *analysis* – of source of error
(c) *discrimination* – between error and acceptable form (e.g. 'often' – can be /ˈɒftən/ or /ˈɒfən/
(d) *imitation* – the ability to reproduce sounds accurately and provide a consistent model
(e) *contextualization* – ability to provide contextualized forms, spontaneously
(f) *explanation* – of rules and patterns (systematically and non-technically)
(g) *integration* – the ability to relate pronunciation to other language areas (e.g. grammar, spelling, listening and speaking)
(h) *monitoring* – the ability to give feedback and assess progress.

---

### Activity 3

Which of the above skills do you think you possess, if you are a pronunciation teacher?

---

Perhaps the most fundamental skill the teacher needs is the ability to perceive and produce sounds both in isolation and in connected speech. Teachers need not only have this skill themselves but also be able to develop it, if necessary, in their learners as well.

## *Knowledge of phonetics and phonology*

As we say in Chapter 1, a knowledge of the 'building blocks' (phonetics) and the 'system' (phonology) underlying pronunciation can be a great support for the development of practical teaching skills. This knowledge includes an awareness of significant differences between

L1 and L2 phonological systems, for example, in phoneme contrasts, syllable structure or distinctive features. It also includes the ability to identify, in phonetic or phonological terms, the nature of a pronunciation problem, for example, place or manner of articulation, stress placement or pitch movement.

Its application can help the teacher in several ways:

- understand the needs and likely difficulties of learners or groups of learners :
- discriminate between errors and acceptable forms (e.g. UK/UK 'car' /ˈkɑː/v /kɑːr/)
- find the most effective, and efficient way to correct errors
- select appropriate material and an appropriate model, or models
- set realistic goals
- decide priority areas for teaching and learning

### Level of teacher competence

Again, this issue was considered in Chapter 1 where we concluded that pronunciation teachers need to provide a clear, consistent pronunciation model with at least receptive competence in one more standard NS varieties: the chosen variety would depend on the teacher's own linguistic background and on the needs of the learners.

It can be helpful to consider competence as consisting of two areas, 'receptive' and 'productive' and define different goals for each. 'Receptive' competence would necessitate a near-native level of comprehension, including the ability to recognize and analyze major standard accents such as RP, Standard American or Standard Australian. 'Productive' competence, meanwhile, would require a level of pronunciation which would provide students with an accurate, consistent and relevant model through the ability to produce essential segmental and prosodic features and contrasts of English. In order to achieve this level of competence, trainee teachers need to be given as much opportunity as possible for self assessment and pronunciation development.

## 7. How do I decide pronunciation teaching priorities?

### Activity 4

Look at this list of key elements in pronunciation? Put them in order of teaching priority.

| | | | |
|---|---|---|---|
| phonemes | reductions | consonant clusters | tone choice |
| syllables | linking | key | |
| word stress | rhythm | thought groups | |
| weak forms | nuclear stress | contractions | |

Learners may well be aware of some of their own pronunciation difficulties but they will not be able to tell how important they are. It is therefore the teacher's role to decide a plan of action: to decide which areas of pronunciation to prioritize and which to leave well alone. In this sense, pronunciation teaching is not different to other areas of language teaching in that it requires teachers to decide priorities based on the needs and wants of their learners in light of the contexts in which they will use English.

Needs obviously depend on several factors, including the learners purpose for learning English (e.g. for professional purposes, to pass an exam), whether English will be used for local or international communication (and consequently whether a local standard or international standard accent will be appropriate) and what constraints there are (e.g. amount of time and resources available).

Another important consideration related to needs is, depending on the learner's entry level of pronunciation and the purpose for learning English, whether the primary goal is to increase *intelligibility*, to increase *fluency* or to increase *impact*, or a combination of the three. Various elements of pronunciation, from individual sound contrasts to non-segmental, prosodic features contribute to the perception of these three qualities.

To give operational definitions of these qualities: *intelligibility* can be defined as the speaker's ability to be understood by the listener, both as the speaker intended and the listener expected : *fluency* can be defined both as 'temporal fluency', that is, continuity of speech in terms of lack of hesitations, appropriate pausing and speed, and 'semantic fluency', that is, facility of recalling words and expressing ideas: *impact* can be defined as the ability to make an impression on one's audience. A speaker may be intelligible to a listener without being very fluent. Similarly, a speaker may be intelligible and fluent without having much impact. All in all, the ultimate goal must be for learners to communicate effectively in required situations.

In order to achieve such a goal, teachers need to be able to select specific elements of pronunciation as teaching priorities and they need to have a set of criteria on which to base such selections.

### *Criteria for deciding pronunciation priorities*

One concept that can be important in selecting pronunciation teaching priorities is **functional load**. We introduced this concept in Chapter 6, explaining how functional load refers to the amount of work two phonemes do to distinguish word meaning, that is, the importance of phoneme distinctions in minimal pairs (King 1967). It can be used to prioritize the teaching of phoneme contrasts according to their importance in English pronunciation. Ranking is based on the *frequency* of occurrence of minimal pairs and the *stability* of contrasts across regional varieties (see Catford 1987, Brown 1991). For example, the /l/ /n/ distinction occurs frequently in both initial and final position in minimal pairs (e.g. 'light' vs 'night' and 'sill' vs 'sin') and is not subject to regional variation. This contrast would therefore be afforded a 'high' functional load. However, the /ð/ /d/ contrast distinguishes relatively few minimal pairs and does not occur in some regional accents. It would therefore be considered a 'low' functional load contrast.

It appears that high functional load errors have the greatest impact on listeners' perceptions of accentedness and comprehensibility of L2 speech (Munro and Derwing 2006). Consequently, functional load is a useful tool to help select pronunciation teaching priorities.

There are of course other criteria which are important in deciding teaching priorities. For example, if a learner is unaware of the relationship between voicing and syllable length and makes little distinction between 'peas' and 'peace' or 'back' and 'bag', this error may affect *intelligibility* and should therefore be given high priority. On the other hand, a learner may not be able to distinguish /l/ and /ɫ/ but the effort involved in making an improvement would be greater than the result achieved, in other words it would be considered a *low return on investment* and would therefore be given low priority. A further criterion could be that the production of an error, such as /s/ instead of /θ/ ('sink' vs 'think'), which may not cause an intelligibility problem and therefore requires a low *degree of tolerance* by the listener. Another criterion for selection might be dependent on the learner's *end purpose* for studying English. For example, someone who can produce words and phrases with reasonable accuracy and fluency but who does not make very much contrast between stressed and unstressed syllables may be competent enough to carry out a good variety of face-to-face interactions in English but not have enough clarity or impact to be a TV news announcer.

These criteria are described in Table 14.1, which outlines how they could be used to help the teacher assess whether a particular pronunciation error should be given 'high' or 'low' priority (to adopt the terms used by Kenworthy, 1987).

**Table 14.1** Criteria used to decide pronunciation teaching priorities

| Criteria | Reason | Priority | Example |
|---|---|---|---|
| **Intelligibility** | The error causes communication breakdown | High | voicing and syllable length ('pea<u>ce</u>' vs 'pea<u>s</u>') |
| | The error does not affect intelligibility | Low | • /d/ v /ð/ as in 'dis' and 'this'<br>• 'wrong' tone choice |
| **Functional load** | The error is a frequently occurring contrast or feature: it would make understanding 'uncomfortable' | High | Confusion between /e/ in 'bet' and /æ/ in 'bat' |
| | This feature or contrast occurs rarely or not in some varieties of English | Low | Use of retroflex[ɽ] or uvular [ʀ] instead of English post-alveolar approximant /r/ as in 'tree' |
| **Degree of tolerance** | The error is a source of 'irritation' for the listener and requires a high degree of tolerance | High | • Overuse of final rising tone on statements etc.<br>• Incorrect word stress (e.g. 'develop rather than de'velop') |
| | Listeners are used to, or accept this feature of foreign or regional accent | Low | Lack of discrimination between use of light /l/ e.g. 'lip' and dark /ɫ/ (e.g. 'eel') |

**Table 14.1** Cont'd

| Criteria | Reason | Priority | Example |
|---|---|---|---|
| **Return on investment** | The effort involved merits the result achieved | High | • Nuclear stress placement<br>• Thought group divisions |
| | The effort involved is greater than the "return" | Low | Attitudinal functions of tone choice |
| **End-Purpose** | The error would prevent reaching the level of competence required | High | Lack of lengthening of vowels in stressed syllables (for language teachers) |
| | The feature will not interfere with achieving the target | Low | Lack of use of schwa for speakers in EIL contexts |

## 8. How do I find time to teach pronunciation?

Many teachers and researchers have realized that a lot less pronunciation goes on in language classrooms than they would have hoped and that pronunciation 'gets too small a piece of the language teaching pie' (Levis 2006:197). This is however hardly surprising given the pressure on most teachers to concentrate on other key areas of language learning, such as listening and writing and the lack of importance placed on pronunciation in English examinations and tests. As we saw earlier, pronunciation accounts for 5–6 per cent of the scores for most of the Cambridge English examinations and many teachers find that pronunciation is not assessed at all on their local examinations or syllabus. Despite this, most teachers and learners know that without a reasonable mastery of pronunciation, being understood and understanding others is almost impossible. The problem then is how to find time and how to prioritize pronunciation teaching.

One possible solution is to suggest integrating pronunciation into other teaching areas. There are several reasons for this:

(1) Constraints (syllabus, exams, teaching pattern) on time make it difficult to teach pronunciation as a separate subject.
(2) Pronunciation relates to areas such as grammar, vocabulary, listening.
(3) The principle of 'little and often' may be more beneficial than spending long periods solely on pronunciation.
(4) Learners can see that pronunciation is an integral part of language learning.

Indeed, the benefits of integrating the teaching and learning of pronunciation have been highlighted in recent years (Pennington 1989, Dalton and Seidlhofer 1994, Underhill 1994, Celce-Murcia et al. 1996). Nevertheless, teachers may still be unsure exactly how to integrate pronunciation with other language components and skills while ensuring that pronunciation work is seen as systematic, relevant and effective.

# 9. How do I integrate pronunciation in specific language learning areas?

## Vocabulary

No matter what type of work is being done regarding vocabulary, it provides opportunities to work on the pronunciation of words. Learning new vocabulary should incorporate learning the pronunciation of a new word. For instance, with the word 'occasionally' students should know which syllable is stressed, where the schwa sounds are and if there are any possible sound reductions or assimilations, that is, 'ally' – 'ly'.

### Phonemes

It is obvious that the sound segments of words should be an area of focus. Here are some possible activity types:

    (i) finding sounds

        e.g. with a section of reading or listening text, pick out words with the /ʃ/ phoneme or underline all the schwa /ə/ sounds

    (ii) grouping sounds

        e.g. take 5–10 new vocabulary items and get students to group them according to the vowel in the stressed syllable (im'mediate, 'recent = /iː/)

    (iii) phoneme chart (see Underhill 1994) – a wall chart can help students and teachers

        – pick up on mispronunciations at any time
        – set goals for individual learners (e.g. 3–4 'problem' sounds)

### Consonant clusters

Clusters can be problematic for many learners. Being able to predict clusters and finding coping strategies are important aspects of vocabulary learning.

    (i) predicting difficult sound groups:

        e.g. 'textbooks'

    (ii) finding strategies for simplifying clusters:

        e.g. missing out middle consonant

### Word stress

It is important for learners to consider word stress patterns as part of learning new words. Possible activities include:

    (i) recording/listing new vocabulary according to stress patterns
    (ii) predicting stress patterns of unknown multisyllabic words

        e.g. predicting rules for words with affixes, such as '..al' or '..ic'

## Connected speech

Again, even at individual word and phrase level, work can be done on the modifications that occur in fluent natural speech. For instance:

(i) marking common simplifications of words, expressions and collocations

e.g. p(e)rhaps, nice 'n easy, a piece of cake

## Spelling

When learning new words, the teacher can consolidate sound/spelling rules:

(i) predicting spelling or pronunciation of new words:

e.g. surnames, place names

(ii) marking 'silent' letters:

e.g. walk, knee, thumb

(iii) guessing spelling rules:

e.g. final /e/ – spit – spite; kite – kite

(iv) 'colour-coding' phonemes:

e.g. 'a' in want, 'ou' in cough and 'o' in hot – are all same phoneme /ɒ/

## *Grammar*

There are often rules linking phonology and grammar in languages, which native speakers know intuitively but are not generally aware of until they are pointed out. Many of these rules have been discussed in more detail in earlier chapters. An awareness of such rules, at various phonological levels, from phonemes to intonation, can be helpful for language learners.

## Phonemes

(i) learning irregular past tense forms:

e.g. put-put-put      speak-spoke-spoken
     cut-cut-cut        steal-stole-stolen

(ii) distinguishing between negative and affirmative forms:

e.g. 'can' /kæn/ vs 'can't' /kɑ:nt/

## Word stress

(i) marking word classes:

e.g. 'MANager', 'manaGErial'
     'Rebel', 'reBEL'
     'loudSPEAker', 'SUITcase'

## Syllables

(i) plurals and past tense endings:

    e.g. pronunciation rules for final syllables:
        - 'rose', 'roses' /ɪz/
        - 'want', 'wanted' /ɪd/

## Connected speech

(i) marking structure and content words in sentences:

    e.g. can you '<u>meet</u> me at the '<u>station</u> at '<u>twenty</u> to' <u>nine</u>

(ii) marking contractions and linking in complex verb forms:

    e.g. 'If <u>I'd</u> 'known about the 'party <u>I'd</u> 've 'come'

(iii) marking weak forms:

    e.g. 'What are you looking <u>at</u>?
        "I'm looking <u>at</u> your hat.

(iv) Recognizing accentuation patterns:

    (a) expanding newpaper headlines

        e.g. MAN HURT IN BLAST

    (b) changing accentuation and meaning:

        e.g. I thought it was going to RAIN
            I THOUGHT it was going to RAIN

    (c) accentuation vs word order

        e.g. I wanted the RED book
            It's the red book I wanted

## Intonation

(i) marking pauses and pitch movement ('oral punctuation')

    (a) distinguishing 'thought group' boundaries:

        e.g. (2+3) x 5 = ?
            2 + (3 x 5 ) = ?
            the number is 001 44 904 411848

    (b) distinguishing restrictive and non-restrictive clauses:

        e.g. The women, who had long black dresses, danced wonderfully
            The women who had long black dresses, danced wonderfully

    (c) distinguishing main and subordinate clauses:

        e.g. In Hong Kong, so I've been told, they drive on the left.
            Don't tell anyone but he's been sacked.

(ii) using tag questions:

    e.g. falling tone = stating, getting agreement
      e.g. it's Thursday today, ˎisn't it

    e.g. rising tone = checking information that is shared
      e.g. that's your sister, ˎisn't it

## Speaking

Pronunciation is obviously part of developing speaking skills. However, the pressures of speaking, planning what to say, choosing the right words and grammatical forms, leave little mental space to concentrate on pronunciation as well. Therefore, it is important for the teacher to take a systematic approach to any pronunciation work. Learners need self-monitoring strategies and opportunities to practice these strategies if improvements are to follow. When a learner starts to correct his or her own pronunciation mistakes while speaking it is a sure sign that self-monitoring is taking place.

It is similarly essential for the teacher to decide whether a pronunciation activity is focusing primarily on increasing *accuracy* or *fluency*. Also, in any speaking activities concentrating on pronunciation it is important that:

(a) a particular element/s of pronunciation is being worked on
(b) students do lots of practice first and then self/group monitoring and evaluation

*Accuracy practice* – the articulation of specific segmental or prosodic features:

  (i) 'shadowing'/recording:

    i.e. imitation or recording of stretches of speech paying particular attention to one feature:
    e.g. 'schwa', linking, consonant clusters

  (ii) oral dictation:

    i.e. one student gives a short dictation to a group of other students - they then check for specific difficulties, such as use of 'schwa', focus words

*Fluency practice* – the use of phonological features to increase fluency or impact: Students prepare a section of speech by marking pauses, focus words, linking, weak syllables, etc.

  (i) dialogues

    i.e. using a range of dialogues, such as sections of plays, textbook dialogues, news reading

  (ii) monologues

    e.g. news/ weather forecasts; telephone messages

*Reading Aloud* – As we have said, although this has generally viewed negatively by many teachers and methodologists as it can encourage hesitant, unnatural speech, it can be useful if well-directed and carefully-monitored. The section of text needs to be appropriate for reading aloud (e.g. part of a news broadcast or formal speech) and prepared for pronunciation features (as outlined above) before speaking.

## Listening

Listening and pronunciation go hand-in-hand and the extent to which one affects the other cannot be underestimated. Pronunciation training can greatly improve listening skills while focused listening practice can enhance pronunciation awareness.

As with speaking practice, it is important to decide if the focus is on listening accurately (i.e. intensive listening) or fluently (extensive listening). In listening practice, concentrating on pronunciation, it is often useful to use scripts to predict or mark phonological features.

*Accuracy practice* – the recognition/discrimination of specific segmental or prosodic features

    (i) dictation:

        e.g.  marking schwa, marking links, marking phonemes
        e.g.  guessing unknown words by number of syllables, stress placement

    (ii) using scripts:

        e.g.  predicting/marking features, such as vowel reductions, weak forms

*Fluency practice* – using phonological signals such as pitch change, pauses, focus to follow the structure of speech,

    (i) note-taking:

        e.g.  listening and taking notes to follow the structure of a talk

    (ii) message writing:

        e.g.  taking a telephone message to get key information

## Reading

Pronunciation can help improve reading techniques. For instance, slow readers:

- may have difficulties recognizing the written form of words, such as 'cough' or 'tough'
- may be reading word by word rather than focusing on content words and skimming less important information
- may not be using punctuation to chunk the text into 'message blocks' or 'thought groups'.

Reading can also improve pronunciation skills.

It can be very helpful to use the transcripts in textbooks (e.g. for dialogues, monologues) as the basis of pronunciation practice. There are three main sorts of activities that learners can do:

(1) Marking activities – learners have a transcript and listen to the dialogue/monologue and mark specific features of pronunciation
(2) Scripting activities – learners first read the transcript, without hearing the spoken text and predict where specific features of pronunciation might occur
(3) Reading activities – learners read the transcript and listen to the spoken text at the same time.

Examples of activities include:

- marking focus and/or content words
- scripting where pauses would go if the text were read
- reading at the same time as listening to the text – this activity has two advantages:
  o it forces the student to try and read at the same time as the speaker (and therefore to concentrate on content words)
  o it helps the student relate the written spelling of words to the spoken form.

## 10. How do I diagnose or assess a learner's pronunciation ability?

Before being able to use specific criteria to evaluate the importance of pronunciation errors, the teacher needs to make a diagnosis of a learner's oral English and their level of pronunciation proficiency. There are different ways of doing this but perhaps the most obvious are either collecting an individual speech sample or carrying out some sort of formal test. Whichever form of diagnosis of pronunciation is chosen, it should be used alongside other important information gathered regarding a student's potential for pronunciation improvement, that is information about learner variables such as motivation, attitude, age, language learning background and purpose for learning English, as discussed in Chapter 1.

### Collecting a speech sample

The main decision to make is whether to collect a sample of spontaneous speech or to record a learner reading some text aloud. There are advantages and disadvantages of each. Reading aloud is not a task that we have to do very often and it can make speakers rather anxious as well as causing them to produce more errors than usual (Hammerley 1982). On the other hand, using a planned text means the speech sample is consistent and can more easily be compared. Using spontaneous speech can also be problematic in that some speakers are more at ease speaking 'spontaneously' than others and the variability of the samples makes it more difficult to compare speakers. On balance, it is probably best to use a bit of both.

### Judging the sample

Research findings (Smith and Bisazza 1982) suggest that impressionistic or subject evaluations of intelligibility are just as accurate and dependable as objective assessments (based on carefully designed procedures and statistical measurement). It also appears that listeners can rank a group of speakers in order of intelligibility and the results tend to agree with other objective ranking methods. This means that the teacher does not need to get involved in complicated testing procedures in order to evaluate a learner's intelligibility. However, it is important to bear in mind that teachers or other 'language experts' are probably not the best judges of intelligibility. This is partly because they are used to, and therefore tend to accommodate to, their students' speech: in which case they may be too lenient in their assessment. Alternatively, it has been suggested that teachers can be more critical than the average layperson with regard to evaluating the intelligibility of NNS. In either case, it would seem that the best judges are people who are not overly familiar with non-native speech or with the speakers themselves.

Judges can be given some sort of scoring sheet, for instance a simple scale (e.g. 1–5) glossed as 'very difficult' to 'very easy' to understand. Once judges have evaluated each speaker they could then be asked to rank the speakers in order of difficulty, again using a simple ranking format as in Figure 14.1.

You will hear ....different speakers. Give each one a score from 1 to 5 depending on how easy or difficult they are to understand (1 = very easy, 5 = very difficult)

|  | 1 | 2 | 3 | 4 | 5 |
|---|---|---|---|---|---|
| Speaker 1 |  |  |  |  |  |
| Speaker 2 |  |  |  |  |  |
| Speaker 3 |  |  |  |  |  |
| Speaker 4 |  |  |  |  |  |
| Speaker 5 |  |  |  |  |  |

**Figure 14.1** Sample scoring sheet

## Analyzing the results

The judges' evaluations can then be used as the basis of a more detailed analysis of pronunciation difficulties underlying the intelligibility scores. If time permits, it should be possible for the teacher to pinpoint the sources of unintelligibility in terms of specific segmental or suprasegmental features. To facilitate this it can be helpful to compile an individual pronunciation assessment sheet for each student as in the example (Figure 14.2). This can be used for diagnostic purposes, to plan a pronunciation syllabus for a group of learners based on the analysis. However, it can also be used to assess progress in pronunciation proficiency if records are kept so that both teacher and students can compare results over a period of time. Such assessments can also provide a realistic evaluation either for students who tend to overestimate their level of intelligibility or for those who need reassurance that their pronunciation is actually better than they thought. Further examples of similar pronunciation 'profiles'

*(A). Background information (learner variables)*

Name . . . . . . . . . . . . . . . . . . . . . . . . . . . . . . . . . . . . . . . . . . . . . . . . . . . . . . .
Age . . . . . . . . . . . . . . . . . . . . . . . . . . . . . . . . . . . . . . . . . . . . . . . . . . . . . . . . .
Length of residence . . . . . . . . . . . . . . . . . . . . . . . . . . . . . . . . . . . . . . . . . . .
First language . . . . . . . . . . . . . . . . . . . . . . . . . . . . . . . . . . . . . . . . . . . . . . . . .
Other languages spoken . . . . . . . . . . . . . . . . . . . . . . . . . . . . . . . . . . . . . . . . .
Education . . . . . . . . . . . . . . . . . . . . . . . . . . . . . . . . . . . . . . . . . . . . . . . . . . . . .
Occupation . . . . . . . . . . . . . . . . . . . . . . . . . . . . . . . . . . . . . . . . . . . . . . . . . . .
Frequency of use of English . . . . . . . . . . . . . . . . . . . . . . . . . . . . . . . . . . . . . .
End purpose for learning English . . . . . . . . . . . . . . . . . . . . . . . . . . . . . . . . . .
Other English proficiency levels/scores . . . . . . . . . . . . . . . . . . . . . . . . . . . . .
Level of motivation (1= low, 5 = high) . . . . . . . . . . . . . . . . . . . . . . . . . . . . .

*(B). General assessment of speech*

| clarity | very intelligible ◄—————————————————————► unintelligible |
|---|---|
| speed | very slow ◄—————————————————————► very fast |
| fluency | very fluent ◄—————————————————————► disfluent |
| Voice range | very wide range ◄—————————————————————► very narrow range |
| volume | very high ◄—————————————————————► very low |
| Voice quality | very obviously L1 ◄—————————————————————► very obviously L2 |
| impact | very low ◄—————————————————————► very high |

*(C). Detailed assessment of pronunciation*

| **Suprasegmentals** | 1 (very weak) | 2 | 3 | 4 | 5 (very strong) |
|---|---|---|---|---|---|
| thought group division | | | | | |
| nuclear stress placement | | | | | |
| tone choice | | | | | |
| rhythm & prominence | | | | | |
| word stress | | | | | |
| linking | | | | | |

*Segmentals*

| **Consonants** | substitution | omission | articulation |
|---|---|---|---|
| plosives | | | e.g. /p/ not always aspirated initially |
| fricatives | | e.g. /faɪ/ for /faɪv/ | |
| affricates | e.g. /tʃ/ for /dʒ/ | | |
| approximants | | | uvular /r/ |
| laterals | | | /l/ is lip rounded |
| clusters | e.g. /st/ for /str/ | | |

| **Vowels** | articulation | length | substitution |
|---|---|---|---|
| Short vowels | | /bet/ and /bed/ – no length distinction | /iː/ for /ɪ/ in 'pin' |
| Long vowels | /iː/ is lip-rounded | | |
| diphthongs | | | Pure vowel [o] instead of /əʊ/ |
| reduction | | | full vowels in unstressed syllables (e.g. 'be'tween') |

**Figure 14.2** Individual Pronunciation Assessment

can be found in two American English pronunciation textbooks, Gilbert's 'Clear Speech' (2005:96) and Avery and Ehrlich's 'Teaching American English Pronunciation' (1992:182).

It is of course possible to take a more holistic approach to assessing pronunciation proficiency, based on an overall impression rather than analysing specific features of pronunciation. This approach is adopted in Morley's 'Speech Intelligibility Index' (Figure 14.3) which she advocates for assessing the intelligibility of a student's speech sample. Using this index, speech can be scored on one of six levels from level one ('basically unintelligible' that is, 'accent precludes functional oral communication') to level six ('speech is near-native' that is, 'accent is virtually non-existent' (Morley 1991:502).

Speech Intelligibility Index: Evaluation of Student Communicability

From Rapid *Review of English Vowels and Selected Prosodic Features* by Joan Morley, in press, Ann Arbor: The University of Michigan Press. Copyright by The University of Michigan Press. Adapted by permission.

| Level | Description | Impact on Communication |
|---|---|---|
| 1 | Speech is basically unintelligible; only an occasional word/phrase can be recognized. | Accent preludes functional oral communication. |
| 2 | Speech is largely unintelligible; great listener effort is required; constant repetitions and verifications are required. | Accent causes severe interference with oral communication. |
| | Communicative Threshold A | |
| 3 | Speech is reasonably intelligible, but significant listener effort is required due to speaker's pronunciation/grammatical errors which impede communication and cause listener distraction; ongoing need for repetitions and verifications. | Accent causes frequent interference with communication through the combined effect of the individual features of mispronunciation and the global impact of the variant speech pattern. |
| 4 | Speech is largely intelligible; while sound and prosodic variances from NS norm are obvious, listeners can understand if they concentrate on the message. | Accent causes interference primarily at the distraction level; listener's attention is often diverted away from the content to focus instead on the novelty of the speech pattern. |
| | Communicative Threshold B | |
| 5 | Speech is fully intelligible; occasional sound and prosodic variances from NS norm are present but not seriously distracting. | Accent causes little interference; speech is fully functional for effective communication. |
| 6 | Speech is [Page 502 of TESOL Quarterly, Vol. 25, No. 3, Autumn, 1991] is virtually nonexistent. features of divergence from NS can be detected; near-native sound and prosodic patterning. | |

*Notes on speech evaluation:*
1. Elicit a speech sample of several minutes. The sample should be sustained impromptu speech, not just answers to simple questions or rehearsed biographical comments. The sample should be spontaneous speech, perhaps on a topic such as: (a) What are your career plans in the next 5 years? (b) What makes your life interesting? (c) What makes a happy

**Figure 14.3** Morley's Speech Intelligibility Index

## *Formal tests*

As we have seen, pronunciation is a much more psychologically sensitive area of language learning than for instance grammar or vocabulary and it is particularly difficult to score objectively. As we have also mentioned, there are two sides to pronunciation, production and reception, and a comprehensive test requires both a speaking and listening element.

There are few examples of formal tests which are aimed specifically at measuring pronunciation ability and which cover both these elements. Many well-established tests of general language proficiency, such as the Cambridge examinations, IELTS and RSA include some reference to pronunciation skills but typically pronunciation does not play an important role. Szpyra-Kozłowska et al. (2005) found that the Cambridge examinations only allocate 5–6 per cent of the total score to pronunciation.

One of the problems with such tests is the ambiguity of the assessment criteria. For instance, commonly, the main criteria are 'intelligibility' and 'accent', as can be seen in the pronunciation descriptors from the five core Cambridge English tests:

- KET (Key English Test) – pronunciation is heavily influenced by L1 features and may at times be difficult to understand;
- PET (Preliminary English Test) – pronunciation is generally intelligible, but L1 features may put a strain on the listener;
- FCE (First Certificate in English) – although pronunciation is easily understood, L1 features may be intrusive;
- CAE (Certificate in Advanced English) – L1 accent may be evident but does not affect the clarity of the message;
- CPE (Certificate of Proficiency in English) – pronunciation is easily understood and prosodic features are used effectively; many features, including pausing and hesitation, are 'native-like'.

It is clear that use of such criteria is largely impressionistic and open to interpretation. As far as accent is concerned, a judgement like 'little accent' is very vague unless broken down. Also, research shows that there is no clear link between accent and intelligibility and even heavily-accented speech can be readily intelligible if the listener is familiar with that accent (Smith and Bisazza 1982). Similarly, regarding 'intelligibility', Jenkins (2000) and Kenworthy (1987) argue that native speakers or teachers are not necessarily the best judge in situations where English is used for international communication. In such contexts, Jenkins claims that intelligibility should be judged on the success of the interaction between the interlocutors themselves rather than external judges: 'Clearly in testing pronunciation, greater account than this must be taken of the "candidate interface": the ways in which they adapt their pronunciation to facilitate one another's understanding, and the extent to which they successfully achieve mutually intelligible pronunciation' (Jenkins 2000:213).

There are also some written tests which aim specifically at assessing receptive pronunciation skills, as in the pronunciation textbooks 'Speaking Clearly' (Rogerson and Gilbert 1990) and 'Clear Speech' (Gilbert 2005). In both books, a case is made for the close relationship in pronunciation ability between listening and speaking English. Gilbert (2008:44) makes the point that using tests to diagnose pronunciation difficulties or measure progress for pedagogic purposes is different to implementing objective tests for research purposes. In the latter, she claims that 'teaching to the test' detracts from test reliability whereas in the former it is essential to teach what is being tested: 'The test must measure what we are going to teach. Put another way, the curriculum that is going to be presented, including prioritizing of topics, must be directly addressed in the pre-testing.'

There have been some attempts to produce automated online tests but the technical complexity of creating such tests has resulted in the focus being primarily on the acoustic analysis of phonemes. As a result, most of these are to date of little interest to the pronunciation teacher.

## 11. Can technology enhance pronunciation teaching and learning?

Increasingly teachers and learners are making use of computer technology to enhance language learning and this includes pronunciation practice. However, compared with other language areas, computer-assisted pronunciation teaching, or CAPT, 'remains in its infancy in many ways' (Levis 2006:184). Levis points out that this is disappointing given the potential of computer technology to facilitate pronunciation learning. For instance, computers can provide endless opportunities for repetition and practice of sounds, individualized feedback, listening practice, visual support to enhance articulation and, in some cases, the chance to record and compare the student's pronunciation against a model version. Also, given that many teachers feel under-prepared to teach pronunciation and have insufficient lass time to dedicate to it, CAPT seems to offer many advantages (2009).

Many pronunciation textbooks and dictionaries now include an audio CD for listening practice. Some of these, such as the latest edition of the Daniel Jones English Pronouncing Dictionary (Roach et al. 2003), enable the learner to record and compare their own pronunciation with the dictionary version, as well as providing spoken samples of every dictionary entry.

Technological developments in the last ten years have seen the emergence of more sophisticated pronunciation learning software applications and interactive websites. Some of these, such as Pronunciation Power are available in hybrid formats, that is, both as a CD-ROM and downloadable from the internet. The Pronunciation Power application, makes extensive use of multimedia to provide a highly interactive and engaging pronunciation learning environment (Figure 14.4), covering both segmental and suprasegmental features, as well as a pronunciation test which is individually marked and returned by a teacher.

Some of these applications are underpinned by extensive academic research, so ensuring greater accuracy of phonological descriptions than some of the more commercially-driven counterparts. Good examples are Kaltenboeck's (2002) CD-ROM for the teaching of intonation,

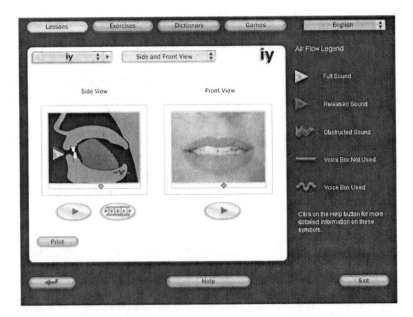

**Figure 14.4** Screenshot from Pronunciation Power

Protea Textware's 'Connected Speech' which consists of three CD-ROMs focusing on connected speech in Australian, American and British English and Caudwell's (2002–2003) online 'Streaming Speech' dealing with many features of fluent natural speech in British English.

There is also an increasing amount of pronunciation material available solely online via the internet, much of which is free to use. As with any unedited materials, a degree of caution and criticality is needed to select the best of these websites. There are some interesting and information-rich resources which have been developed by various academic departments, such as *UCL, Iowa* or teaching organizations (*LLAS*). There are also some commendable sites created and maintained by enthusiastic individuals (e.g. *Brett*, Maidment, Powers) Brett's multimedia, interactive resources are particularly engaging both for teachers and students.

One of the key concerns for computer-based pronunciation learning, as with classroom-based learning, is whether or not it is effective. There is some evidence that CAPT can be effective in pronunciation learning. For instance, Hirata (2004:372) found that 'subjects who participated . . . acquired a generalized ability to produce and perceive Japanese words contrasting in pitch and duration' and Wang and Munro (2004) found that computer-based training improved learners' ability to perceive vowel contrasts over time.

However, one of the challenges for Computer-Assisted Language Learning (CALL) in general and perhaps CAPT in particular, is providing adequate feedback and interactivity. The novelty of online 'drag and drop' or 'odd-one-out' activities soon wears thin unless supported by pedagogically sound feedback or support. More generally, it is essential that a concern for technological innovation is not at the expense of sound pedagogic practice. As Neri et al.(2002a:442) report 'many authors describe commercially available programs as fancy-looking systems that may at first impress student and teacher alike, but eventually fail to meet sound pedagogical requirements'.

It is largely these areas of interactivity and providing intelligent feedback that is problematic for pronunciation learning and other areas of language learning (Rogerson-Revell 2007). For instance, to date, it is very difficult to provide accurate automated speech recognition (ASR) feedback on non-native speech samples. One application that does seem to have had some success in this area, is 'Connected Speech' (Protea Textware 2007) which gives learners feedback on their pronunciation using speech recognition.

Despite some of the shortcomings mentioned here, as technologies continue to advance their applications for pronunciation teaching and learning will improve. In the meantime, CAPT still have several features to offer:

- It is tireless and patient
- It can provide repetitively consistent speech models
- It can provide a variety of voices
- It can encourage learner autonomy
- It enables visual as well as audio input and feedback.

## Conclusion

For many students of English the real challenge to mastery of the language is not the grammar, not the vocabulary but the pronunciation. It is an area traditionally thought of as 'difficult' and frequently ignored by teachers and learners alike. Nevertheless, it leads to breakdowns in communication and once fossilized, poor pronunciation is immensely difficult to remedy. With the advent of more communicative methodologies, dedicated pronunciation coursebooks and interactive resources, a principled and engaging approach to teaching pronunciation can be adopted. The important thing is that pronunciation should not be relegated to a five minute slot at the end of a lesson but integrated into all aspects of teaching.

## Further reading

Brown, P. C. (2001) 'The interactive dictation', *The Language Teacher,* 25 (7), 27–8.

Cauldwell, R. T. (1996) 'Direct encounters with fast speech on CD audio to teach listening', *System,* 24/4, 521–8.

Chela-Flores, B. (2001) 'Pronunciation and language learning: An integrative approach', *IRAL,* 39 (2), 85–101.

De Bot, C. L. J. (1980) 'The role of feedback and feedforward in the teaching of pronunciation – an overview', *System,* 8, 35–45.

Derwing, T. and Munro, M. (2005) 'Second language accent and pronunciation teaching: A research-based approach', *TESOL Quarterly,* 39 (3), 379–97.

Gilbert, J. (2008) *Teaching Pronunciation: Using the Prosody Triangle*. New York: Cambridge University Press.

Leather, J. (1983) 'Second-language pronunciation learning and teaching, State of the art review article', *Language Teaching*, 16, 198–219.

Levis, J. (2005) 'Changing contexts and shifting paradigms in pronunciation teaching', *TESOL Quarterly*, 39 (3), 369–78.

Levis, J. (2006) 'Pronunciation and the assessment of spoken language', in Hughes, R. (ed.) *Spoken English, Applied Linguistics and TESOL: Challenges for Theory and Practice*. New York: Palgrave Macmillan, pp. 245–70.

MacDonald, D., Yule, G. and Powers, M. (1994) 'Attempts to improve English L2 pronunciation: The variable effects of different types of instruction', *Language Learning*, 44 (1), 75–100.

Molholt, G. (1992) 'Visual displays develop awareness of intelligible pronunciation patterns', in Brown, A. (ed.) *Approaches to Pronunciation Teaching*. London: Macmillan and The British Council, pp. 138–51.

Morley, J. (1991) 'The pronunciation component in teaching English to speakers of other languages', *TESOL Quarterly*, 25, 481–520.

Pennington, M. C. (1989) 'Teaching pronunciation from the top down', *RELC Journal*, 20, 20–38.

Pennington, M. C. and Richards, J. C. (1986) 'Pronunciation revisited', *TESOL Quarterly*, 20, 145–50.

Stevick, E. W. (1978) 'Toward a practical philosophy of pronunciation: Another view', *TESOL Quarterly*, 12, 145–50. Also in Brown, A. (ed., 1991) *Teaching English Pronunciation: A Book of Readings*. London: Routledge.

Tench, P. (1992) 'Phonetic Symbols in the Dictionary and in the Classroom', in Brown, A. (ed.) *Approaches to Pronunciation Teaching*. London: Macmillan, pp. 90–102.

Yule, G. and MacDonald, D. (1995) 'The different effects of pronunciation teaching', *IRAL*, 33 (4), 345–50.

# Pronunciation Problem Areas  15

## Introduction

At the beginning of this book we considered some of the features that can influence L2 pronunciation acquisition and saw the phonological transfer from the L1 is a major factor. We also saw, in Chapter 14, that an important aspect of the pronunciation teacher's skills and knowledge is an awareness of significant differences between the L1 and L2 phonological systems. As Rivers (1968:131) states, 'Unless the teacher understands how the student is using his speech organs in producing a native language sound and what he should be doing to reproduce the foreign language sound acceptably, he cannot help the student beyond a certain stage of earnest but inaccurate imitation.'

Obviously, the non-native English teacher has an advantage here in a monolingual classroom where they share the students' L1. However, many teachers work in multilingual classrooms with students from a wide range of language backgrounds in which case it is difficult to develop a deep or comprehensive knowledge of all the learners' phonological systems. Nevertheless, it is helpful for the teacher to be aware of some of the key phonological differences between the L1 and English in order to help diagnose and remedy pronunciation problems. This chapter provides an overview of some of these phonological differences and potential pronunciation difficulties for L1 speakers of various languages. Inevitably, this overview is limited in the amount of detail and the languages it covers and the phonological differences described will not be problematic for all learners. The references at the end of the chapter are provided for those who would like to investigate such differences further or research the phonological systems of other languages.

We begin by considering some common areas of pronunciation difficulty in English and then look at language-specific pronunciation problems. You are reminded to refer to Chapter 13 for techniques and activities to deal with problem areas and to look at the individual chapters (e.g. Chapter 5, 'Vowels') for further details. It should also be remembered that the differences presented here are 'descriptive' rather than 'prescriptive' in terms of what should be taught. It is the teacher's job, in the light of their knowledge of the learners' needs and abilities to decide on pronunciation teaching priorities (see Chapter 14, section 7).

# Common pronunciation problem areas

## Vowels

It is unsurprising that vowels can be problematic for many L2 learners as English has more vowels than most other languages. Many of the world's languages have only five vowels (e.g. Spanish and Japanese) compared with the 20 (including diphthongs) in BBC English. The main problem areas are covered below.

### Tense vs lax

The lack of distinction between tense and lax vowels (e.g. /ɪ/ /iː/) is a very common problem. For instance, the vowel in 'Pete' and 'pit' may sound the same with learners producing a vowel sound somewhere between the two.

### Schwa

Again, many languages do not have reduced vowels in unstressed syllables so the concept of 'schwa' is foreign to learners from such language groups.

### Mid and open vowels

English has a lot of mid and open vowels compared with many other languages and these can be difficult for learners to distinguish (e.g. /e/ /æ/ /ʌ/ /ɑː/).

> **Tip**
>
> /e/ v /æ/ Get students to sit resting their jaw on their hand with their elbow on a table. Ask them to say the English vowels /e/ and /æ/ and feel the jaw pushing their hand down, showing that the /æ/ sound is lower down or more open in the oral cavity.
>
> /ʌ/ v/ ɑ/. Use the 'jaw' exercise again to get students to feel the movement between more mid and open vowels.

### Diphthongs

Again English has a lot of diphthongs (up to 8 in BBC English) in comparison to some other languages. These may be replaced by a pure vowel or monophthong by learners. Alternatively, the way diphthongs are articulated in English, with the nucleus coming first, followed by the glide, may be reversed in other languages.

> **Tip**
>
> The usual way to help learners produce diphthongs is by getting them to say the two parts of the diphthong separately first and then gradually get them to speed up the articulation so that they run together (e.g. /ɪ/ + /ə/ = / ɪə/).

# Consonants

Difficulties can arise if English phonemes do not exist in the L1. For instance, some learners may not have the /p/, /b/ phonemes in their first language, such as Arabic, which has no /p/ sound. In others, English phonemes may only be allophones. For example, in Spanish, /d/ /ð/ are allophones of /d/. As a result, some learners may not readily perceive the distinctive quality of /ð/ in English and misuse it in place of /d/ or even /θ/, which exists as a phoneme in Spanish. French does not have /θ/, /ð/ so learners may have difficulty acquiring and maintaining this pair of phonemes. Alternatively, the same phonemes may exist but not in the same position in a word as in English (g /s/ before /m/ /n/ or /l/ at the beginning of a word is pronounced /z/ in Greek).

Furthermore, the features that make phonemes distinctive in English, such as voicing, aspiration, vowel length preceding voiced stops may not be the same in the learner's L1. Some of the most common problem areas are listed below.

## Aspiration

Many languages do not aspirate the voiceless stops /p/, /t and k/ at the beginning of words. So, 'pin' may sound like 'bin' and 'cot' like 'got' and 'ten' like 'den'.

---

### Tip

Focus on the production of aspiration in syllable-initial //p/, /t/ and k/ by making students aware of the 'puff of air' that accompanies the release of the consonant. Use a piece of paper, or the palm of the hand, held in front of the mouth so that students can feel the puff of air produced for the voiceless stops.

Alternatively, get students to put a /h/ before the vowel and then add the voiceless stop before it. For example:

| | |
|---|---|
| 'ay' | 'ow' |
| 'hay' | 'how' |
| 'p(h)ay' | c(h)ow' |

---

## Voiced consonants

Voicing is a distinctive feature of English consonants and we have a lot of voiced/voiceless pairs such as /t/ vs /d/, /p/ vs /b/ and /tʃ/ vs /dʒ/.

## Voiced fricatives

Many students are unable to distinguish between voiced and voiceless fricatives and may have difficulty producing the voiced version, for instance producing /ʃ / for /ʒ/ or /f/ for /v/.

> **Tip**
>
> As vowels are always voiced, get students to say a prolonged 'ah' sound and feel the vibration in their throat. Then ask them to add a /z/ sound, continuing the voicing ('aaaazzzz'). Student can then be given a range of minimal pair and other discrimination activities to practice distinguishing voiced and voiceless sounds.

## Affricates

The English affricates /tʃ/ /dʒ/ may not exist in the student's L1. So, /ʃ/ may be substituted for /tʃ/ (e.g. 'ship' rather than 'chip') and /ʒ/ as in 'pleasure' may be substituted for /dʒ/ 'joke'.

> **Tip**
>
> Example: 'ship' vs 'chip' – get students to say 'ship' and then say 't' and then add the two together 't + ship' = 'chip'. Alternatively, get students to say /ʃ/ as in 'ship' and then put the tip of the tongue on the tooth ridge, as for /t/ and repeat the sound, producing /tʃ/.

## Dental fricatives

Many languages do not have the dental fricatives /θ/ /ð/ and students may use either /t/ or /s/ for /θ/ and /d/ or /z/ for /ð/.

> **Tip**
>
> Get learners to move the tongue further forward, pushing the tip of the tongue between the teeth. Practising pairs such as 'tin', 'thin' or 'fort', 'fourth' can help learners feel the difference in articulation between dental and alveolar sounds (and the fact that /t/ is a stop while /θ/ is a continuant.

## Voiced final consonants and vowel length

Again, the lengthening of the vowel before a final voiced consonant is an important phonetic feature of English. It is important for students to hear and then be able to produce the difference in vowel length before voiced and voiceless consonants. For example:

| final voiced consonant (longer vowel) | Final voiceless consonant (shorter vowel) |
| --- | --- |
| leave | leaf |
| bad | bat |
| bag | back |

## Consonant omission or insertion

In some languages, such as French, /h/ is not pronounced at the beginning of words and students will therefore have difficulties when it occurs in this position in English words, either pronouncing it when it is silent (e.g. 'hour', 'honest') or omitting it when it is pronounced (e.g. 'his', 'hear').

> **Tip**
>
> To eliminate the 'silent' letter, practise linking exercises, linking vowel to consonant and consonant to vowel (e.g. the (y) (h)our).

## Syllable structure

The CVC syllable structure of English can be problematic for learners whose L1 has a different structure, typically the CV structure which is 'an absolute universal in the languages of the world' (Carlisle 2001:2).

We have seen (in Chapter 7) how the structure of syllables in English results in common and complex consonant clusters in individual words and across word boundaries. These can are often cause difficulties for learners of English. Examples such as:

the physi<u>cs b</u>lock
ho<u>ld t</u>ight
nex<u>t Th</u>ursday
nex<u>t F</u>riday

can attract an extra vowel. Some Arabic speakers may include glide vowels in next Thursday /nɪkest θɜːrɪzdeɪ/ to assist their articulation. Chinese learners have a tendency to omit post-vocalic consonants because Chinese has a CV syllabic pattern. As a result, 'hold tight' may be perceived and produced as /həʊ taɪ/.

> **Tip**
>
> Native speakers of English often simplify such clusters anyway and this can be pointed out to learners. However, they need to know which parts of the cluster can be omitted, that is usually the middle consonant (e.g. 'hol(d) tight').
>
> Initial consonant clusters can be problematic if they do not occur in the L1, such as /sk/ in Spanish. In many cases, learners will insert an additional vowel, for example 'eschool'.

> **Tip**
>
> Again, either practise linking such as 'his school' or for more complex vowel insertions as in 'sekeru' (a screw) practise breaking the word down into syllables and back chaining, for example 'ru' – 'cru' – 'as' – 'asc' – 'ascru'

## Word stress

Learners frequently have difficulty with word stress for several reasons:

(a) Although, as we have seen, there are rules for word stress (see Chapter 9), there are also a considerable number of exceptions.

(b) It is generally true to say that stress patterns in English vary more than in many other languages.

(c) There may be interference from the learner's L1. This is particularly true of 'international' words, that is cognates. For example:

| | |
|---|---|
| 'nervous (English) | nervi'oso (Spanish) |
| 'restaurant (English) | restau'rant (french) |
| elec'tricity (English) | elettricità (Italian) |

So, for example, Italian learners of English may try to fix stress on the penultimate syllable in every multisyllabic word. French learners of English may use their L1 stress, patterns in words like:

'possible and pronounce it pos'sible

Consider also the difficulties of shifting stress patterns in related words:

| | |
|---|---|
| inflam'mation | in'flammatory |
| 'residence | resi'dential |
| pho'nology | phono'logical |

and then, the apparent consistencies:

soci'ologist    soci'ology    soci'ological

## Tip

Give students 'problem solving' groups of words to sort according to stress patterns. Use visual or mnemonic devices to help learners remember the stress placement of new vocabulary items.

## Nuclear stress

Many languages use a system similar to English for nuclear stress placement. However, the phonetic characteristics of stress may be different. For example, pitch change is more significant than vowel length in 'pitch-accented' languages like Japanese.

The principal stress in an utterance, that is the nucleus, is highly mobile in English. This is not the case in some languages, such as French where changes of word order may be needed to emphasize the nucleus. Also, in English, nuclear stress and word stress are very much interrelated so that the stress in a word may be more or less pronounced depending on its role in the sentence.

## Tip

It may be necessary to exaggerate both length and loudness to get the degree of stress necessary for English.

# Rhythm

This is a key issue for second language learners whose first language may tend towards syllable rather than stress-timing (e.g. French or Spanish). For learners from such an L1 background, it is important to emphasize the difference between stressed and unstressed syllables and vowel reduction in the unstressed syllables. Learners with an L1 which does not have such reduced, unstressed syllables will be unfamiliar with the related effects of phoneme modification (such as assimilation, elision and linking) in fluent connected speech.

## Tip

Rote learning of lists of words such as days of the week or months of the year can be helpful.
Use a variety of rhythmic material, such as limericks poems and chants (see Chapter 13) for further ideas.

# Intonation

There are a number of features that can cause difficulty. First of all, how utterances are divided into thought groups. Some learners may seek to make thought groups too long. Also, although all languages have to chunk speech into meaningful segments, intonation may not play such an important role in this as it does in English. For instance, some languages use clause-final particles to mark thought group boundaries (e.g. Cantonese, Korean).

There may also be a narrower pitch range in the learner's L1 so that the voice sounds rather flat or even when speaking English. Another common difficulty is the tendency to keep the pitch high in mid utterance, rather than use low falling pitch as in English.

Pre-nuclear intonation patterns vary considerably between languages. In BBC English, the most common pattern in a series of falling levels. Some Scandinavian languages, such as Norwegian and Swedish tend to use a series of glides upwards, which can sound over-enthusiastic or even comical to English ears. However, the most inappropriate pattern is a sequence of low level pitch over a series of syllables which can sound either bored or surly (Cruttenden 2008:325).

In addition, the complex functions of intonation, including its attitudinal, informational and pragmatic functions gives English a rich inventory of tones to convey the implications of an utterance. Intonation may not have such complex functions in some other languages.

## Tip

Any common phrases or short dialogues can be used for frequent intonation practice. Also, many of the activities suggested in Chapter 13, such as the use of drama and voice overs can be used for more targeted practice.

# Language-specific pronunciation difficulties

## Arabic

There are many varieties of Arabic, both within and between countries and some of these are not mutually intelligible. However, most speakers are familiar with the pronunciation of the standard dialect, Classical Standard Arabic (Figure 15.1).

### Consonants

| CONSONANTS (PULMONIC) | Bilabial | Labiodental | Dental | Alveolar | Postalveolar | Retroflex | Palatal | Velar | Uvular | Pharyngeal | Glottal |
|---|---|---|---|---|---|---|---|---|---|---|---|
| Plosive | b | | | t d | | | | k ɡ | q | | ʔ |
| Nasal | m | | | n | | | | | | | |
| Trill | | | | r | | | | | | | |
| Tap or Flap | | | | ɾ | | | | | | | |
| Fricative | | f | θ ð | s z | ʃ | | | | x ʁ | ħ ʕ | h |
| Affricate | | | | | dʒ | | | | | | |
| Lateral fricative | | | | | | | | | | | |
| Approximant | | | | | | | j | | | | |
| Lateral approximant | | | | l | | | | | | | |
| Where symbols appear in pairs, the one to the right represents a voiced consonant. | | | | | | | | | | | |

**Figure 15.1** Arabic consonant chart

/p/ vs /b/ – Arabic speakers tend to produce /p/ with no aspiration so l /p/ may sound like /b/, for example 'bebsi' for 'Pepsi'.

No affricates /tʃ/ /dʒ/ – /ʃ/ may be substituted for /tʃ/ (e.g. 'ship' rather than 'chip') and /ʒ/ as in 'pleasure' may be substituted for /dʒ/ 'joke'.

No dental fricatives /θ/ /ð/ – students may use either /t/ or /s/ for /θ/ and /d/ or /z/ for /ð/

/r/ – Arabic learners will tend to use their native trilled or rolled /r/ when speaking English

/l/ in Arabic is very 'clear' and is made with the tip of the tongue.

### Vowels

There are more vowels in English than in Arabic so learners will tend to substitute their own smaller number of vowels for English vowels (Figure 15.2).

/ɪ/ /e/ confusion – as in 'bit', 'bet'

/e/ /æ/ /ʌ/ confusion – as in 'pet', 'pat', 'put'

/ɔː/ /əʊ/ confusion – as in 'bought', 'boat' (learners tend to use a pure vowel [o] for both.

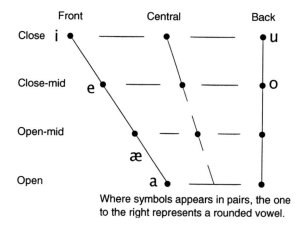

Where symbols appears in pairs, the one
to the right represents a rounded vowel.

**Figure 15.2** Arabic vowel chart (adapted from Maddieson 1984).

There are no diphthongs in Arabic.

Schwa does occur (e.g. in 'Mohammed') but is not so frequent or varied as in English.

### Syllable structure

Words do not begin with vowels in Arabic: a glottal stop always precedes the vowel. This may give initial vowels a very 'back' or gutteral quality.

Three element consonant clusters may be problematic, at the beginning and end of words, for example, 'street', 'against'. Typically, a vowel may be inserted, as in 'again-est'.

### Word stress

Word stress placement is similar to English in that multisyllabic words have stressed and unstressed syllables. However, the rules for word stress placement differ and are more regular which can cause problems. For example, Arabic speakers will tend to stress a final syllable if it ends in a vowel followed by two consonants, as in 'comfort'.

### Rhythm

Arabic lies towards the 'stress-timed' end of the 'stress' vs 'syllable' timed scale. However, unstressed vowels are not as reduced as in English so the contrast between stressed and unstressed syllables may not be so clear.

### Intonation

Accentuation works in a similar way in Arabic and English with content words being stressed and function words unstressed. However, emphasis is usually done through word order rather than contrastive stress. Pitch movement may be within a smaller range but is not generally problematic for language learners.

## Chinese

As with Arabic, there are many varieties of Chinese. The focus here is on the two main standard varieties, Cantonese (spoken in Hong Kong and Canton, southern China) and Mandarin, the national language (spoken in the capital, Beijing, and most of China and Taiwan). Many of the English pronunciation problems are shared (Figure 15.3).

### Consonants

| CONSONANTS (PULMONIC) | Bilabial | Labiodental | Dental | Alveolar | Postalveolar | Retroflex | Palatal | Velar | Uvular | Pharyngeal | Glottal |
|---|---|---|---|---|---|---|---|---|---|---|---|
| Plosive | p | | | t | | | | k | | | |
| Nasal | m | | | n | | | | ŋ | | | |
| Trill | | | | | | | | | | | |
| Tap or Php | | | | | | | | | | | |
| Fricative | | f | f | s | | ʂ ʐ ç | | | x | | |
| Affricate | | | | ts | | tʂ | oç | | | | |
| Lateral fricative | | | | | | | | | | | |
| Approximant | | | | | | | j | | | | |
| Lateral approximant | | | | l | | | | | | | |

☐ These consonants occur in Mandarin only

**Figure 15.3** Chinese consonant chart

There are only six possible final consonants in Chinese, the nasals /n/ and /ŋ/ and also /m/ in Cantonese and the three voiceless plosives /p/, /t/ and /k/, although these sounds are unreleased at the end of words in Chinese. This results in words such as 'pat' or 'king' is that the end of the word sounds swallowed. This is not necessarily a problem with final unvoiced plosives as many L1 English speakers do this in fluent speech, however, more importantly, there is little lengthening of the vowel before a final voiced consonant so little distinction between words such as 'pat' vs 'pad'.

There is no /θ/ in Chinese and /θ/ and /t/ or /f/ may be substituted, with /d/ or /v/ for /ð/. However, in Cantonese there is no /v/ sound.

> /tʃ/ /dʒ/ – only the voiceless phoneme exists in Chinese (e.g. 'choy'), so learners may have difficulty distinguishing, for example between 'chill' and 'Jill'.
> /b/ /d/ /g/ – voiceless plosives do not occur at the end of words.
> /z/ and /ʒ/ do not exist in Chinese and may be replaced by /ʃ/, for example, 'zoo' – 'shoe'
> /s/ and /ʃ/ are allophonic variants in Cantonese, so 'Sue' and 'shoe' may not be distinguished.
> /r/ and /l/ and /n/ – this is a common problem both in terms of production and perception.

Word final – /l/ may sounds like /r/ (e.g. 'fall' – 'four').

Word initial – /r/ may be substituted for /l/ (e.g. 'raw' – 'law'), /l/ may be substituted for /n/ (e.g. 'light' – 'night')

In clusters – 'blue' may sound like 'brew' or 'fly' like 'fry'.

## Vowels

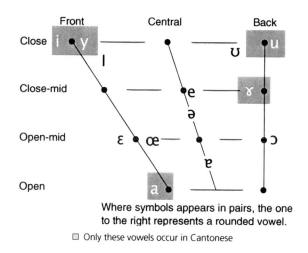

Where symbols appears in pairs, the one to the right represents a rounded vowel.

☐ Only these vowels occur in Cantonese

**Figure 15.4** Chinese vowel chart (adapted from Maddieson 1984 and Lyovin 1997)

As with many languages, the distinction between tense and lax vowels does not exist in Chinese and Chinese learners of English will tend to produce sounds between the two (Figure 15.4).

/e/ /æ/ /ʌ/ /ɑ/ – again, like many other language groups, distinguishing between these sounds may be problematic.

/ʊ/ u/ distinction can be problematic – as it is for some L1 speakers with non-BBC accents.

/ɪ/ and /iː/ both exist in Chinese but there are restrictions on which consonants can follow them.

## Syllables

Syllables are typically CV in structure although a CVC structure is possible.

Consonant clusters can be particularly difficult as they are very rare in Chinese. Consonant deletion is the most common strategy used by learners to avoid such clusters (as native speakers do in some cases).

Word initial clusters – deletion of /r/ following initial /b/ or /p/ (e.g. 'bring' – 'bing')

Word medial clusters – /r,/, /l/, /t/, /d/, /f/ and /v/ are frequently deleted after a vowel (e.g. 'silver' – 'siver')

### Rhythm

The main difference between Cantonese and Mandarin is their rhythm. Mandarin is closer to the 'stress-timed' end and Cantonese to the 'syllable-timed' end of the stress vs syllable-timed continuum. Cantonese speakers in particular may sound quite 'stacatto' when speaking English, however, English rhythm is problematic for both Cantonese and Mandarin learners.

### Intonation

Chinese is a tone language and that includes all its varieties. This means a change in pitch on a word can changes its lexical meaning. Also, pitch changes occur over a syllable or word rather than a stretch of speech so practice may be needed in the perception of pitch movement over thought groups.

## French

Although semantically French and English have much in common (as many vocabulary items are shared as a result of the Norman conquest in the eleventh century), there are considerable phonological differences between the two languages.

### Consonants

Most English consonant sounds have equivalents or near equivalents in French (Figure 15.5). However there are a few differences that could create problems for learners.

| CONSONANTS (PULMONIC) | Bilabial | Labiodental | Dental | Alveolar | Postalveolar | Retroflex | Palatal | Velar | Uvular | Pharyngeal | Glottal |
|---|---|---|---|---|---|---|---|---|---|---|---|
| Plosive | p  b | | | t  d | | | | k  g | | | |
| Nasal | m | | | n | | | ɲ | ŋ | | | |
| Trill | | | | | | | | | | | |
| Tap or Flap | | | | | | | | | | | |
| Fricative | | f  v | | s  z | ʃ  ʒ | | | | ʁ | | |
| Affricate | | | | | | | | | | | |
| Lateral fricative | | | | | | | | | | | |
| Approximant | | | | | | | j | | | | |
| Lateral approximant | | | | l | | | | | | | |
| Where symbols appear in pairs, the one to the right represents a voiced consonant. | | | | | | | | | | | |

**Figure 15.5** French consonant chart

In French, /θ/, /ð/, /tʃ/, /dʒ/, /h/ and /ŋ/ do not occur.
/s/ and /z/ may be substituted for /θ /, /ð/ respectively.
/ʃ/ and / ʒ/ may similarly be substituted for /tʃ/, /dʒ/,

The letter 'h' exists in French (e.g. 'heure', 'hopital') but is not pronounced, so many learners omit the English /h/ sound, while others, being aware of this difference between L1 and L2, overcompensate by inserting the sound where /h/ is usually silent in English (e.g. 'honest', 'hour').

French /r/ is a more uvular sound than English /r/ so a Francophone learner may try to articulate /r/ too far back in the mouth.

The phonemes /p/, /t/ and /k/ are usually not aspirated in French.

## Vowels

French also has a large number of vowel sounds: up to 13 oral and four nasal, depending on the dialect (Figure 15.6). However, only six of these sounds are shared with English. (Swan and Smith 2001).

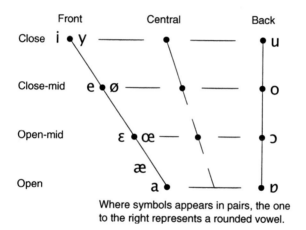

**Figure 15.6** French vowel chart (adapted from Handbook of the International Phonetic Association 1999)

In addition, French does not usually distinguish between the tense (long), and lax (short) vowel pairs, but rather uses a sound that is somewhere between them, but closer to the tense vowel.

For this reason /ɪ/ is often pronounced as /i:/ and /u:/ as /y/.

The diphthong /eɪ/ is sometimes produced as /e/.

Some learners have difficulty distinguishing between some or all of /e/, /æ/, /ʌ/ and /ɑ/.

## Word stress

Word stress is not usually marked in French dictionaries and stress is not essential to the phonological structure of the word which makes it very different from English and many other European languages. Unlike the variable or mobile stress of English, French word stress is usually predictable, with stress on the final syllable (or the penultimate syllable if the last syllable contains schwa). A learner may be unsure of where to place stress in English words, or may place it incorrectly on the final syllable because of the influence of French. This is particularly difficult for cognate words such as 'restaurant'.

### Syllables

French does have unstressed syllables, however the vowels in them are not generally as reduced or shortened as in English. This is different from English in which unstressed syllables most often have the vowel replaced with /ə/ and sometimes with /i/.

Learners may stress syllables containing syllabic consonants so that *didn't* might sound like '*di -dent*'.

### Rhythm

Although French does have rhythmic groups, the rhythm it is quite different to English and is considered by some to be syllable-timed. Even though French has a scwha vowel, French students may not reduce unstressed syllables to the extent that is necessary to create an English rhythmic pattern, giving each syllable in a sentence equal or near-equal prominence and therefore create a stilted rhythm, unlike natural English.

### Intonation

Although English and French share similar intonation patterns, the tendency to stress the final syllable in a thought group changes the sound and rhythm of English. Also the general pitch range seems somewhat narrower with less use of gliding pitch contours. This can give the impression of lack of interest or involvement.

The concept of contrastive stress does exist in French however learners still tend to have problems de-accenting repeated or 'old' information in a message.

## German

German and English both come from the germanic group of language families and share many pronunciation features, particularly at suprasegmental levels. There are a lot of differences between regional and national varieties of German. Normally educated northern German is taken as a model or standard in the media.

### Consonants

German shares many consonants with English including a non-rhotic /r/ / ð/ and /θ/ do not occur in German and may substitute /z/ and /s/ respectively (Figure 15.7).

/w/ may be problematic – German speakers may substitute /v/ for /w/ (e.g. 'vest' for 'west').
/r/ tends to be uvular in northern German (which is too far back) and trilled in southern German (which is too far forward).

| CONSONANTS (PULMONIC) | Bilabial | Labiodental | Dental | Alveolar | Postalveolar | Retroflex | Palatal | Velar | Uvular | Pharyngeal | Glottal |
|---|---|---|---|---|---|---|---|---|---|---|---|
| Plosive | p  b | | | t  d | | | | k  g | | | |
| Nasal | m | | | n | | | ɲ | ŋ | | | |
| Trill | | | | | | | | | R | | |
| Tap or Php | | | | | | | | | | | |
| Fricative | | f  v | | s  z | ʃ  ʒ | | | x | | | h |
| Affricate | | pf | | ts | | | | | | | |
| Lateral fricative | | | | | | | | | | | |
| Approximant | | | | | | | j | | | | |
| Lateral approximant | | | | l | | | | | | | |
| Where symbols appear in pairs, the one to the right represents a voiced consonant. | | | | | | | | | | | |

**Figure 15.7** German consonant chart

Final voiced stops, fricatives and affricates (e.g. /b/, /v/ /dʒ/. German speakers will typically produce voiceless versions at the end of words (e.g. /p/, /f/, /tʃ//dʒ/ does not exist in German and may be replaced by /tʃ/.

## Vowels

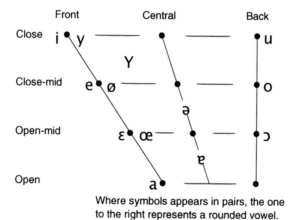

Where symbols appears in pairs, the one to the right represents a rounded vowel.

**Figure 15.8** German vowel chart (adapted from Maddieson 1984)

/æ/ /e/ confusion (e.g. 'ban' vs 'Ben')
/ʌ/ does not exist in German
Diphthongs /eɪ/ ('say') and /əʊ/ ('sew') may be produced as long monphthongs (Figure 15.8).

## Word stress

As with English, German tends to put the stress on the first syllables in two-syllable words. Suffixes in German can also alter word stress patterns as in English, so this should not be a problem area, except in cases where the rules are different (e.g. English con'servative is conserva'tive in German and 'legal in Engish is le'gal in German).

## Rhythm

Vowel reduction and rhythm are similar in German and English and are not generally problematic.

## Intonation

Intonation patterns are also quite similar in both languages. In northern German a similar pattern is common but with glides replacing levels, which can sound aggressive if over used (Cruttenden 2008).

# Greek

Again, there is considerable dialectal variation in Greek.

## Consonants

| CONSONANTS (PULMONIC) | Bilabial | Labiodental | Dental | Alveolar | Postalveolar | Retroflex | Palatal | Velar | Uvular | Pharyngeal | Glottal |
|---|---|---|---|---|---|---|---|---|---|---|---|
| Plosive | p   b | | | t   d | | | | k   g | | | |
| Nasal | m | | | n | | | | | | | |
| Trill | | | | | | | | | | | |
| Tap or Flap | | | | ɾ | | | | | | | |
| Fricative | | f   v | θ   ð | s   z | | | | x   ɣ | | | |
| Affricate | | | | ts  dz | | | | | | | |
| Lateral fricative | | | | | | | | | | | |
| Approximant | | | | | | | j | | | | |
| Lateral approximant | | | | l | | | | | | | |
| Where symbols appear in pairs, the one to the right represents a voiced consonant. | | | | | | | | | | | |

**Figure 15.9** Greek consonant chart

There is little aspiration of initial /p/, /t/, /k/ (Figure 15.9).

Devoicing of final voiced stop, fricatives and affricates (e.g. 'bat' for 'bad', 'rish' for 'rich', 'bays' for 'beige').

Nasals (/n/, /m/ and /ŋ/) can be problematic. They tend to be deleted or inserted in certain conditions (see 'syllables').

Voiceless stops /p/, /t/ and /k/ are voiced following nasals. So, some consonant clusters can be problematic, particularly /mp/ /nt/ and /nk/ both for production and reception. For instance, learners may mishear 'symbol' for 'simple' or 'sender' for 'centre' or 'angle' for 'ankle'. Alternatively, 'finger' may be misheard as 'figure' or 'hand' as 'had'.

/s/ /ʃ/ confusion (e.g. 'sip' vs 'ship').
/s/ /z/ – learners may replace voiceless sibilant /s/ with /z/ in initial position (e.g. 'zleep' for 'sleep').
/z/ /ʒ/ confusion (e.g. 'lizard', 'leisure').
/tʃ/ /dʒ/ (e.g. 'check' – 'jet') may be devoiced to 'ts' and 'dz'.

## Vowels

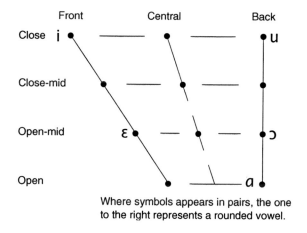

Where symbols appears in pairs, the one to the right represents a rounded vowel.

**Figure 15.10** Greek vowel chart (adapted from Maddieson 1984)

Difficulty distinguishing tense vs lax vowels (e.g. 'bit' vs 'beat') (Figure 15.10).
Confusion between /æ/ /ʌ/ and /ɑ:/ (e.g. 'hat', 'hut', 'hard').
/ɔ:/ /ʌ/ /ʊ/ confusion (as in 'bought', 'but', 'book').
Greek has no diphthongs and no schwa.

## Syllables
There are no final consonant clusters in Greek and few final single consonants. Learners may tend to insert a vowel with words ending in a consonant (particularly /p/, /t/ and /k/). So a noun like 'big' could be confused with the adjective 'bigger'.

## Rhythm
Greek is towards the syllable-timed end of the rhythm continuum. Northern dialects have more vowel reduction than southern dialects of Greek which tends to sound more syllable-timed.

## Intonation

Pitch range may be perceived as narrower in Greek.

Contrastive stress may be problematic.

# Italian

Italian is a romance language, along with, for example, French, Spanish and Portuguese. While it shares a lot lexically with these languages, there are some considerable phonological differences.

## Consonants

| CONSONANTS (PULMONIC) | | | | | | | | | | | |
|---|---|---|---|---|---|---|---|---|---|---|---|
| | Bilabial | Labiodental | Dental | Alveolar | Postalveolar | Retroflex | Palatal | Velar | Uvular | Pharyngeal | Glottal |
| Plosive | p  b | | | t  d | | | | k  g | | | |
| Nasal | m | | | n | | | ɲ | | | | |
| Trill | | | | r | | | | | | | |
| Tap or Php | | | | | | | | | | | |
| Fricative | | f  v | | s  z | ʃ | | | | | | |
| Affricate | | | | ts  dz | tʃ  dʒ | | | | | | |
| Lateral fricative | | | | | | | | | | | |
| Approximant | | | | | | | | | | | |
| Lateral approximant | | | | l | | | ʎ | | | | |
| Where symbols appear in pairs, the one to the right represents a voiced consonant. | | | | | | | | | | | |

**Figure 15.11** Italian consonant chart

/θ/ /ð/ do not exist in Italian (Figure 15.11). /θ/ may be replaced with /f/, /s/ or /t/ (e.g. 'fin' for 'thin') and /ð/ by /v/, /z/ or /d/ (e.g. 'van' for 'than').

/ʒ/ (as in 'measure') does not exist and may be replaced by /ʃ/ or /dʒ/.

Initial /h/ may be omitted (e.g. 'art' for 'heart').

Insufficient aspiration of word initial /p/, /t/ /k/, so a word like 'pin' could sound like 'bin'.

Word final stops /p/ /t/ /k/ and /b/ /d/ /g/ may be followed by a short vowel sounds (e.g. 'big' sounds like 'bigger', 'rub' like 'rubber').

/s/ may be replaced by /z/ before initial consonants /m/ /l/ /n/ (e.g. 'zlip' for 'slip', 'znip' for 'snip').

## Vowels

Vowel lengthening rules are different in English and Italian (Figure 15.12). The main problems resulting from this are that:

The vowel in words ending in a vowel may be too short.

Vowels in words ending in a voiced consonant or sibilant may be too short, so, for example 'sad' may sound like 'sat' and 'cause' like 'course'.

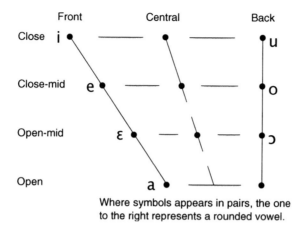

Where symbols appears in pairs, the one
to the right represents a rounded vowel.

**Figure 15.12** Italian vowel chart (adapted from Agard and Di Pietro 1965)

Difficulty distinguishing tense vs lax vowels (e.g. 'bit' vs 'beat') – /ɪ/ does not exist in Italian.
Confusion between /æ/ and /e/ (e.g. 'bad' and 'bed'). /æ/ does not exist in Italian.
/æ/ /ʌ/ and /ɑ:/ (e.g. 'hat', 'hut', 'hard') confusion.

## Syllables

Consonant clusters can be problematic. Initial clusters are difficult if they contain consonants that are 'new' to Italian learners such as /θ/ in 'through' or clusters that do not exist in Italian, such as /sl/ in 'sleep' will become 'zleep'.

Final clusters do not occur in Italian. Consonant deletion is a common strategy as is vowel insertion. The same strategies may be used for medial clusters in the middle of words or at word boundaries (e.g. 'top prize' – /tɒpəpraɪzə/).

## Word stress

Word stress is mobile in Italian as in English, however there will be cases where word stress rules are different in the two languages, especially in cognates such as 'nation vs na'zione and a'bility and abili'ta.

## Rhythm

Vowels are not weakened in unstressed syllables in Italian so the rhythm sounds very different to English. Function words, for example, may be over-prominent.

# Japanese

Japanese is spoken by over 130 million people. It is a member of the Japonic language family which has a number of rather undefined relationships with other languages. It has a relatively small sound inventory and is a tonal language.

## Consonants

| CONSONANTS (PULMONIC) | Bilabial | Labiodental | Dental | Alveolar | Postalveolar | Retroflex | Palatal | Velar | Uvular | Pharyngeal | Glottal |
|---|---|---|---|---|---|---|---|---|---|---|---|
| Plosive | p  b | | | t  d | | | | k  g | | | |
| Nasal | m | | | n | | | | ŋ | | | |
| Trill | | | | | | | | | | | |
| Tap or Php | | | | ɾ | | | | | | | |
| Fricative | ɸ | | | s  z | ʃ | | ç | | | | h |
| Affricate | | | | ts | tʃ  dʒ | | | | | | |
| Lateral fricative | | | | | | | | | | | |
| Approximant | | | | | | | j | | | | |
| Lateral approximant | | | | | | | | | | | |
| Where symbols appear in pairs, the one to the right represents a voiced consonant. | | | | | | | | | | | |

**Figure 15.13** Japanese consonant chart

/b/v/ confusion (e.g. 'berry' for 'very').

/θ/ /ð/ do not exist in Japanese (Figure 15.13). /θ/ may be replaced with /s/ or /t/ (e.g. 'tin' for 'thin') and /ð/ by /z/ or /d/ (e.g. 'dan' for 'than').

/f/ does not exist in Japanese so 'fit' may sounds like 'hit'.

/l/ and /r/ confusion for production and perception. Japanese has one vowel between to two. So, 'arrive' may sounds like 'alive' and 'right' like 'light'.

/ʃ/ does not occur before /e/ or /eɪ/ in Japanese, so words such as 'shame' or 'shell' may be problematic.

## Vowels

Japanese only has five vowels so the large number of English vowels can be problematic. Japanese has 'double vowels' where two vowels together are twice as long as two normal vowels (e.g. 'ee' – yes) (Figure 15.14).

/ɪ/ does not exist in Japanese and /iː/ may be substituted (e.g. 'beat' for 'bit').

/uː/ /ʊ/ contrast can be confusing as /ʊ/ does not exist in Japanese.

/æ/ /ʌ/ and /ɑː/ ('hat', 'hut', 'hard') confusion.

/ɒ/ /ɔː/ confusion, so learners may substitute 'cot' for 'caught'.

## Syllables

Japanese is a mora-timed language. A 'mora' is similar to a 'syllable' but can vary in weight (there are 'light' and 'heavy' syllables) and differences in vowel length.

Japanese has a predominantly CVV or CVCV syllable structure, so closed CVC syllables can be problematic.

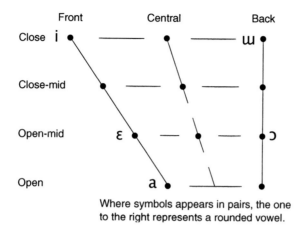

Where symbols appears in pairs, the one
to the right represents a rounded vowel.

**Figure 15.14** Japanese vowel chart (adapted from Maddieson 1984)

Japanese de-voices the vowels /i:/ and /u:/ between voiceless consonants or between voice-less consonant and silence (as at the end of a word). Therefore, a Japanese version of the name Hiroshi or Yoshiko is apt to sound like two syllables.

Japanese counts nasals (n, m and ng) as syllables, with the result that a word like 'insutanto' (the Japanese version of 'instant') will sound like a six-syllable word to a Japanese learner.

There are very few consonant clusters in Japanese in initial or final position. Clusters may be broken up by vowel insertion (e.g. 'ski' – 'suki', 'screw' – su-ku-ru').

### Rhythm

Japanese is syllable-timed and there is not schwa sound which means the vowel reduction which is necessary to produce an English rhythm is not present.

### Intonation

Because of the equal distribution of syllable stress in Japanese, the concept of nuclear stress and focus may be difficult. Also, pitch tends to be a more important indicator of stress place-ment than length, unlike in English, although pitch movement is unlikely to cause intelligibil-ity problems.

One potential area of difficulty is that pitch range varies considerably between the sexes in Japanese, so attempts to impose an English use of pitch may cause embarrassment or reluc-tance. For instance, in Japanese, only women use higher pitch to signal politeness while men use a much lower pitch (Loveday 1981).

## Hindi/Urdu

Modern Hindi is the official language of India while Urdu is the national language of Pakistan. Hindi and Urdu are phonologically similar, both belonging to the Indo-Aryan group of languages, and speakers of both these and other Indian languages from the same language group (e.g. Punjabi, Sanskrit, Gujarati) may share similar pronunciation problems.

## Consonants

| CONSONANTS (PULMONIC) | Bilabial | Labiodental | Dental | Alveolar | Postalveolar | Retroflex | Palatal | Velar | Uvular | Pharyngeal | Glottal |
|---|---|---|---|---|---|---|---|---|---|---|---|
| Plosive | p    b |  |  | t    d |  | ʈ    ɖ |  | k    g |  |  |  |
| Nasal | m |  |  | n |  |  |  | ŋ |  |  |  |
| Trill |  |  |  |  |  |  |  |  |  |  |  |
| Tap or Php |  |  |  | ɾ |  | ɽ |  |  |  |  |  |
| Fricative |  | f |  | s    z | ʃ |  |  |  |  |  | h |
| Affricate |  |  |  |  | tʃ  dʒ | tʂ  dʐ |  |  |  |  |  |
| Lateral fricative |  |  |  |  |  |  |  |  |  |  |  |
| Approximant |  | ʋ |  |  |  |  | j |  |  |  |  |
| Lateral approximant |  |  |  | l |  |  |  |  |  |  |  |
| Where symbols appear in pairs, the one to the right represents a voiced consonant. | | | | | | | | | | | |

**Figure 15.15** Hindi/Urdu consonant chart

Confusion of voiceless stops /p/, /t/, /k/ with voiced stops /b/ /d/ /g/. Hindi/Urdu speakers tend to perceive English unaspirated voiceless stops p/, /t/, /k/ as voiced counterparts /b/ /d/ /g/, because Indian versions are produced with much more aspiration than English equivalents (Figure 15.15).

> /f/p/ confusion (e.g. 'fair', 'pair') and voiced equivalents /v/ /b/ (e.g. 'very', 'berry').
> /v/ and /w/ ('vet', 'wet') may be confused in perception and production.
> /θ/ /ð/ do not occur and may be replaced with a heavily aspirated /t/ and /d/ respectively.

## Vowels

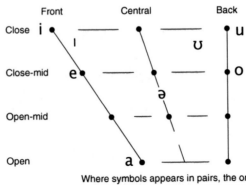

Where symbols appears in pairs, the one to the right represents a rounded vowel.

**Figure 15.16** Hindi/Urdu vowel chart (adapted from Kelkar and Maddieson 1984)

/e/ /æ/ confusion (Figure 15.16). Hindi and Punjabi speakers tend to substitute /e/ for /æ/ as in 'bed', 'bad'.

Difficulty with tense/lax distinction in /eɪ/ v /e/.

## Syllables

Final consonant clusters can be problematic. Either vowel insertion or consonant deletion may be used (e.g. 'tax' for 'taxed' or 'walk-ed' for 'walked').

## Word stress

Word stress placement in fairly regular in Hindi and Urdu and typically on the first syllable, which can be problematic for learners of English.

## Rhythm

Hindi and Urdu are both considered 'syllable-timed' languages. There is no schwa in either language, so vowel reduction does not occur.

## Intonation

Pitch rather than length is the main marker of accentuation so speakers of both Hindi and Urdu may have difficulties perceiving and producing characteristic stress patterns of English.

# Polish

Polish is one of the Slavic group of languages, along, for example, with Czech, Slovak, Ukrainian and Russian, which share similar pronunciation problems.

## Consonants

Polish has a large and complex consonant system with many retroflex, palatal and velar sounds (Figure 15.17).

| CONSONANTS (PULMONIC) | Bilabial | Labiodental | Dental | Alveolar | Postalveolar | Retroflex | Palatal | Velar | Uvular | Pharyngeal | Glottal |
|---|---|---|---|---|---|---|---|---|---|---|---|
| Plosive | p b | | t  d | | | | | k  g | | | |
| Nasal | m | | n | | | | | ŋ | | | |
| Trill | | | | r | | | | | | | |
| Tap or Php | | | | | | | | | | | |
| Fricative | | f  v | s  z | | ʃ  ʒ | | | | | | |
| Affricate | | | ts  dz | | tʃ  dʒ | | | | | | |
| Lateral fricative | | | | | | | | | | | |
| Approximant | | | | | | | j | | | | |
| Lateral approximant | | | | l | | | | | | | |
| Where symbols appear in pairs, the one to the right represents a voiced consonant. | | | | | | | | | | | |

**Figure 15.17** Polish consonant chart

Initial phonemes /p/, /t/ and /k/ are not aspirated in Polish.

Word final voiced stops, fricatives and affricates will be devoiced.

/w/ /v/ confusion. Polish speakers will tend to substitute /v/ for /w/ (e.g. 'vest' for 'west').

/θ/ /ð/ do not exist in Polish. /θ/ may be replaced with /t/ (e.g. 'tin' for 'thin') and /ð/ by /d/ (e.g. 'dan' for 'than').

/l/ /w/ confusion at the end of words and syllables. Polish speakers will produce a lip rounded sound rather than a dark /l/, so, 'goal' may sound like 'go'.

## Vowels

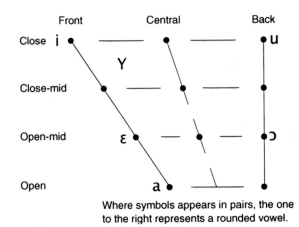

Where symbols appears in pairs, the one
to the right represents a rounded vowel.

**Figure 15.18** Polish vowel chart (adapted from Urbanska (ed.) 1977)

Polish has six oral monophthongs and two nasal vowels (Figure 15.18).

Difficulty distinguishing tense vs lax vowels (e.g. 'bit' vs 'beat') – /ɪ/ does not exist in Polish.

/æ/ may be confused with /ʌ/ and /e/ (e.g. 'ban', 'bun', 'ben'), /e/ may be substituted for both the others.

## Syllables

Polish, like other Slavic languages, permits complex consonant clusters.

## Word stress

Predominantly, word stress is placed on the penultimate syllable in Polish which may cause problems.

## Rhythm

Polish falls towards the 'syllable-timed' end of the stress vs syllable-timed continuum. There is no schwa, so vowel reduction does not occur.

# Spanish

As with Chinese, there are many differences between regional and national varieties of Spanish but most of the difficulties mentioned here are common across varieties.

## Consonants

| CONSONANTS (PULMONIC) | | | | | | | | | | | | |
|---|---|---|---|---|---|---|---|---|---|---|---|---|
| | Bilabial | Labiodental | Dental | Alveolar | Postalveolar | Retroflex | Palatal | Velar | Uvular | Pharyngeal | Glottal |
| Plosive | p | | | t | | | | k  g | | | |
| Nasal | m | | | n | | | ɲ | | | | |
| Trill | | | | r | | | | | | | |
| Tap or Flap | | | | ɾ | | | | | | | |
| Fricative | β | f | θ ð | s | | | | x ɣ | | | |
| Affricate | | | | | ʧ | | | | | | |
| Lateral fricative | | | | | | | | | | | |
| Approximant | | | | | | | j | | | | |
| Lateral approximant | | | | l | | | ʎ | | | | |
| Where symbols appear in pairs, the one to the right represents a voiced consonant. | | | | | | | | | | | |

**Figure 15.19** Spanish consonant chart

/b//v/ confusion (e.g. 'berry' for 'very'). In Spanish there is a sound which is a sort of combination of the two sounds (Figure 15.19).

/θ/ /ð/. /ð/ may sound like /d/ (e.g. 'den' for 'then') and /θ/ only exists in European Spanish and may be replaced by /f/ or /s/ (e.g. 'sin' or 'fin' for 'thin').

/ʃ/ does not occur in many varieties of Spanish and may be replaced by /s/ or /ʧ/ (e.g. 'Sue' or 'chew' for 'shoe').

Little aspiration of initial /p/, /t/, /k/.

/y/ /dʒ/ confusion. Spanish speakers may substitute /dʒ/ for /y/ (e.g. 'use' for 'juice' or 'gel' for 'yell').

Word final nasals (/m//n/ and /ŋ/). In some dialects these sounds are interchangeable at the ends of words (e.g. 'sing' may be pronounced as 'sin' or 'sim').

## Vowels

There are only five monophthongs and four diphthongs in Spanish and there is no variation in length in Spanish vowels (Figure 15.20).

Difficulty distinguishing tense vs lax vowels (e.g. 'bit' vs 'beat') – /ɪ/ does not exist in Spanish.

/e/ /æ/ confusion. /e/ may be used for both (e.g. 'bet' for 'bat').

/ʌ/ does not exist in Spanish. 'Must' may sound like 'mast' or 'most'.

/aɪ/ /eɪ/ confusion. Although both diphthongs occur in Spanish, there may be spelling interference, so, for example a word like 'main' /meɪn/ may be pronounced /maɪn/.

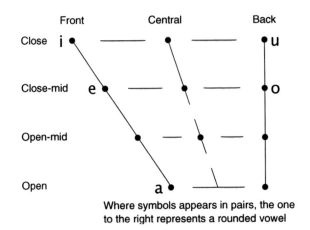

Where symbols appears in pairs, the one
to the right represents a rounded vowel

**Figure 15.20** Spanish vowel chart (adapted from Maddieson 1984)

## Syllables

Spanish and English share many consonant clusters but 'new' clusters may be problematic.

Spanish speakers may have difficulties with consonant clusters at the end of words, omitting the final consonant (e.g. 'hol' for 'hold' or 'las' for 'last').

Spanish speakers tend to pronounce all past tense 'ed' endings as an additional syllable (e.g. 'laugh-ed').

Word initial clusters starting with /s/ (e.g. 'scream', 'sport'). Learners will tend to insert a vowel before the 's', for example 'escream' or 'a good school' /ə gʊd ɪskuːl/.

## Word stress

Word stress in Spanish normally falls on the penultimate syllable. This can vary but if it does the movement is marked by an accent.

The concept of compound stress can be problematic for learners.

## Rhythm

Spanish falls towards the 'syllable' end of the stress vs syllable-timed continuum. There is no schwa, so vowel reduction does not occur.

## Intonation

Emphasis is produced rather through lexis or word order than pronunciation so the concept of contrastive stress can be problematic.

Pitch range tends to be narrower in Spanish.

# Turkish

Although Turkish uses essentially the same alphabet as English, its orthographic system, which employs to a large extent one-to-one letter-sound correspondence, can cause interference with English pronunciation.

## Consonants

Turkish has 20 consonants and shares many consonants with English (Figure 15.21).

| CONSONANTS (PULMONIC) | Bilabial | Labiodental | Dental | Alveolar | Postalveolar | Retroflex | Palatal | Velar | Uvular | Pharyngeal | Glottal |
|---|---|---|---|---|---|---|---|---|---|---|---|
| Plosive | p  b | | | t  d | | | c  ɟ | k  g | | | ʔ |
| Nasal | m | | | n | | | | | | | |
| Trill | | | | | | | | | | | |
| Tap or Flap | | | | ɾ | | | | | | | |
| Fricative | | f  v | | s  z | ʃ  ʒ | | | ɣ | | | h |
| Affricate | | | | | tʃ  dʒ | | | | | | |
| Lateral fricative | | | | | | | | | | | |
| Approximant | | | | | | | j | | | | |
| Lateral approximant | | | | l | | | ʎ | | | | |
| Where symbols appear in pairs, the one to the right represents a voiced consonant. | | | | | | | | | | | |

**Figure 15.21** Turkish consonant chart

/θ/ /ð/ do not occur in Turkish.

/v/ and /w/ may be confused in perception and production.

Turkish speakers tend to devoice /b/ /d/ /g/ and /dʒ/ at the end of words and syllables, so they sound like //p/ /t/ /k/ and /tʃ/ (e.g. 'mad' may sounds like 'mat' and 'litter' may sounds like 'lidder'. They will similarly not make the vowel lengthening necessary before final voiced sounds.

## Vowels

Turkish has eight vowels and no diphthongs. Vowels in Turkish tend to be shorted than in English and in some contexts vowels are elided (e.g. 'city' may sound like 'stee') (Figure 15.22).

Difficulty distinguishing tense vs lax vowels (e.g. 'bit' vs 'beat') – /ɪ/ does not exist in Turkish.

/æ/ may be confused with /ʌ/ and /ɑ:/ (e.g. 'ban', 'bun', 'barn').

/ɔ:/ /ɒ/ confusion (e.g. 'nought', 'not') both may be replaced with a vowel closer to /ɑ:/

/u/ /ʊ/ confusion.

/eɪ/ may be confused with /e/ (e.g. 'mate', 'met').

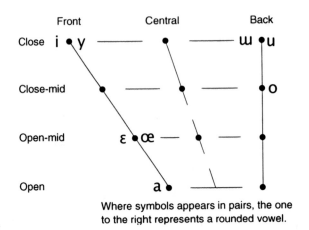

Where symbols appears in pairs, the one to the right represents a rounded vowel.

**Figure 15.22** Turkish vowel chart (adapted from Maddieson 1984)

## Syllables

Turkish shares many final consonant clusters with English. However, if the final consonant is a voiced plosive it may be problematic, as explained above (e.g. 'bulb' may sound like 'bulp').

Initial consonant clusters do not occur in Turkish. The most problematic initial clusters are those beginning with /s/, where vowel insertion is a common strategy ('step' becomes 'i-step' or 'si-tep').

## Word stress

As with English, word stress is mobile in Turkish so word stress should not be too problematic except where Turkish patterns are different to English. For example, stress is typically on the final syllable in many Turkish words, including nouns, pronouns, verbs, conjunctions and adverbs. In comparison, English nouns, main verbs and adjectives are front-stressed.

## Rhythm

There is no schwa so the vowel reduction which is necessary to produce an English rhythm is not present and the rhythmic pattern is generally much more even because of the tendency to pronounce each syllable clearly.

## Intonation

Pitch movement is rarely problematic. However, in negative sentences the syllable before the negative suffix is stressed which may sound overly insistent in English. Apart from this, sentence focus and accentuation works in a similar way to English.

**Fig 15.23** Overview of potential pronunciation problems by language group

| Language | Final voiced/voiceless stops (e.g. /t/ /d/) | Aspiration of initial plosives (e.g. /p/ /t/ /k/) | /θ/ /ð/ | /f/ /v/ /w/ | /s/ /z/ /ʃ/ /ʒ/ | /tʃ/ /dʒ/ | /h/ | /r/ | Consonant clusters | Tense/lax vowels (e.g. /ɪ/ /iː/ /ʊ/ /uː/) | /e/ /æ/ /ʌ/ | /ɔ/ /ɜː/ | /ə/ | Word stress | Rhythm and intonation |
|---|---|---|---|---|---|---|---|---|---|---|---|---|---|---|---|
| Arabic | ✓ | ✓ | ✓ | x | x | ✓ | ✓ | x | x | ✓ | ✓ | ✓ | x | x | ✓ |
| Chinese | ✓ | ✓ | ✓ | x | ✓ | ✓ | x | ✓ | ✓ | x | ✓ | ✓ | ✓ | ✓ | ✓ |
| French | ✓ | x | ✓ | ✓ | x | ✓ | ✓ | ✓ | ✓ | ✓ | ✓ | ✓ | x | x | ✓ |
| German | ✓ | ✓ | ✓ | ✓ | x | ✓ | x | x | x | x | ✓ |  | x | x | x |
| Greek | ✓ | ✓ | x | x | ✓ | ✓ | x | x | ✓ | ✓ | ✓ | ✓ | ✓ | x | x |
| Indian | ✓ | ✓ | ✓ | ✓ | x | x | x | x | x | ✓ | ✓ | x |  | ✓ | ✓ |
| Italian | ✓ | x | ✓ | ✓ | ✓ | x | ✓ | x | ✓ | ✓ | ✓ | x | ✓ | ✓ | ✓ |
| Japanese | x | ✓ | ✓ | x | x | x | x | ✓ | ✓ | ✓ | ✓ | ✓ | ✓ | ✓ | ✓ |
| Polish | ✓ | ✓ | ✓ | ✓ | ✓ | x | x | ✓ | x | ✓ | ✓ | x | ✓ | x | x |
| Spanish | ✓ | x | x | ✓ | ✓ | ✓ | x | ✓ | ✓ | ✓ | ✓ | x | ✓ | x | ✓ |
| Turkish | ✓ | ✓ | ✓ | ✓ | ✓ | ✓ | x | x | x | ✓ | ✓ | ✓ | ✓ | x | x |

# Further reading

## General contrastive studies

Campbell, G. (1991) *Compendium of the World's Languages.* London: Routledge.

Delattre, P. (1964) Comparing the vocalic features of English, German, Spanish and French, *IRAL,* 11 (2), 71–97.

*Handbook of the International Phonetic Association* (1999) Cambridge: Cambridge University Press.

Kaye, A. S. and Daniels, P. T. (eds) (1997) *Phonologies of Asian and Africa (Including the Caucasus).* Volumes I and II. Winona Lake, Indiana: Eisenbrauns.

Ladefoged, P. and Maddieson, I. (1996) *Sounds of the World's Languages.* Oxford: Blackwell.

Lyovin, A. V. (1997) *An Introduction to the Languages of the World.* New York: Oxford University Press.

Maddieson, I. (1984) *Patterns of Sound.* Cambridge: Cambridge University Press.

Swan, M. and Smith, B. (2001) *Learner English: A Teacher's Guide to Interference and other Problems,* 2nd edition. Cambridge: Cambridge University Press.

Yavas, M. (2006) *Applied English Phonology.* Oxford: Blackwell Publishing.

## Arabic

Azziz, Y. Y. (1974) 'Some problems of English consonant sounds for the Iraqi learner', *English Language Teaching Journal,* 28 (2), 166–8.

Watson, J. (2002) *The Phonology and Morphology of Arabic.* New York: Oxford.

## Chinese

Anderson, J. (1983) 'The difficulties of English syllable structure for Chinese ESL learners', *Language Learning and Communication,* 2 (1), 53–61.

Duanmu, S. (2000) *The Phonology of Standard Chinese.* New York: Oxford University Press.

## French

Fougeron, C. and Smith, C. L. (1999) 'French', in International Phonetic Association *Handbook of the International Phonetic Association: A Guide to the Use of the International Phonetic Alphabet.* Cambridge: Cambridge University Press, pp. 78–81.

Price, G. (1991) *An Introduction to French Pronunciation.* Oxford: Basil Blackwell.

Wenk, B. and Wioland, F. (1982) 'Is French really syllable timed?', *Journal of Phonetics,* 10, 193–216.

## Italian

Agard, F. and Di Pietro, R. (1965) *The Sound Structures of English and Italian.* Chicago: Chicago University Press.

D'Eugenio, A. (1977) 'Stress distribution in Italian and English word's', *IRAL,* 15 (2), 55–63.

Rogers, D. and d'Arcangeli, l. (2004) 'Illustrations of the IPA: Italian', *Journal of the International Phonetic Association,* 34 (1), 117–212.

## Turkish

Zimmer, K. and Orgun, O. (1999) 'Turkish', in *Handbook of the International Phonetic Association: A Guide to the Use of the International Phonetic Alphabet.* Cambridge: Cambridge University Press, pp. 154–6.

## Hindi/Urdu

Masica, C. (1991) *The Indo-Aryan Languages.* Cambridge: Cambridge University Press.

Ohala, M. (1999) 'Hindi', in International Phonetic Association, *Handbook of the International Phonetic Association: A Guide to the Use of the International Phonetic Alphabet.* Cambridge University Press.

# Spanish

Foster, D. W. (1968) 'A contrastive note on stress and equivalent structures in Spanish', *IRAL*, 6, (3), 257–66.

Stockwell, R. P. and Bowen, J. D. (1965) *The Sounds of English and Spanish*. Chicago: University of Chicago Press.

# German

Erdmann, P. (1973) 'Patterns of stress transfer in English and German', *IRAL*, 11, 229–41.

Wiese, R. (1996) *The Phonology of German*. Oxford: Oxford University Press.

# Greek

Efstathiades, S. (1974) *Greek and English phonology: A comparative investigation*, Thessaloniki: Aristoteleion Panepistēmion Thessalonikēs.

Petrounias, E. 'The pronunciation of "Greek" words in English'. Available online, retrieved 21 November 2009 from http://www.philology.uoc.gr/conferences/6thICGL/ebook/c%5Cpetrounias.pdf

# Polish

Gussman, E. (2007) *The Phonology of Polish*. Oxford: Oxford University Press.

Urbanska, I. (ed.) (1977) *A Handbook of Polish Pronunciation for English Learners*. Panstwowe Wydawrictwo, Naukowe: Warszawa.

# Japanese

Loveday, L. (1981) 'Pitch, politeness and sexual role', *Language and Speech*, 24, 71–88.

Thompson, I. (2001) 'Japanese speakers', in M. Swan and B. Smith (eds) *Learner English: A Teacher's Guide to Interference and other Problems*, 2nd edition. Cambridge: Cambridge University Press, pp. 296–309.

Wang, S., Higgins, M. and Shima, Y. (2005) 'Training English pronunciation for Japanese learners of English online', *The JALT CALL Journal*, 1 (1), 39–47. Available online, retrieved 31 October 2008, from http://jaltcall.org/journal/

Yamada, R. and Tokhura, Y. (1992) 'The effects of experimental variables on the perception of American English /r/ and /l/ by Japanese listeners', *Perception and Psychophysics*, 52, 376–92.

# References

## Chapter 1

Abercrombie, D. (1949) 'Teaching pronunciation', *English Language Teaching*, 3, 113–22.

Abercrombie, D. (1991) Teaching Pronunciation, In *Teaching English Pronunciation: A Book of Readings*. Ed. A. Brown. London and New York: Routledge, pp. 87–95.

Abercrombie, D. (1988) 'RP R.I.P', *Applied Linguistics*, 9 (2), 115–24.

Bex, T. and R. Watts (eds) (1999) *Standard English: The Widening Debate*. London: Routledge.

Collins, B. And Mees, I. M. (2003) *Practical Phonetics and Phonology*. London and New York: Routledge.

Cruttenden, A. (2008) *Gimson's Pronunciation of English* (7th edition). London: Hodder Education.

Crystal, D. (1995) *The Cambridge Encyclopedia of the English Language*. Cambridge: Cambridge University Press.

Crystal, D. (1997) *English as a Global Language*. Cambridge: Cambridge University Press.

Daniels, H. (1995) 'Psycholinguistic, psycho-affective and procedural factors in the acquisition of authentic L2 pronunciation', *Speak Out!*, 15, 3–10.

Davies, A. (2003) *The Native Speaker: Myth and Reality*. Clevedon: Multilingual Matters.

Dauer, R. (2005) 'The Lingua Franca Core: A new model for pronunciation instruction?' *TESOL Quarterly*, 39 (3), 543–50.

Gimson, A. C. (1977) 'Daniel Jones and standards of English pronunciation', *English Studies*, 58, 151–8.

Hartle, S. (2008) 'From the heart of the expanding circle', *IATEFL Voices*, 200, 6.

Hieke, A. E. (1985) 'A componential approach to oral fluency evaluation', *Modern Language Journal*, 69, 135–42.

Honey, J. (1989) *Does Accent Matter?* (2nd edition). Paris: Farrar Straus & Giroux.

James, C. (1998) *Errors in Language Learning and Use*. London: Longman.

Jenkins, J. (2000) *The Phonology of English as an International Language*. Oxford: Oxford University Press.

Jones, D. (1977) English Pronouncing Dictionary, 14th ed., revised by A. C. Gimson. London: Dent.

Kenworthy, J. (1987) *Teaching English Pronunciation*. Harlow, U.K.: Longman.

Krauss, R., Freyberg, R. and Morsella, E. (2002) 'Inferring speakers' physical attributes from their voices', *Journal of Experimental Social Psychology*, 38 (6), 618–25.

Kuo I-Chun. (2006) 'Addressing the issue of teaching English as a lingua franca', *ELT Journal*, 60 (3), 213–21.

Ladefoged, P. (2001) *A Course in Phonetics* (4th edition). New York: Harcourt Brace Jovanovich.

Mey, J. (ed.) (1998) *Concise Encyclopedia of Pragmatics*. Oxford: Elsevier Science.

Modiano, M. (1996) The Americanisation of Euro-English. *World Englishes*, 15 (2), 207–15.

Porter, P. A. and Garvin, S. (1989) 'Attitudes to pronunciation in EFL', *Speak Out!*, (5), 8–15.

Roach, P. (2000) *English Phonetics and Phonology* (3rd edition). Cambridge: Cambridge University Press.

Scherer, K. R. (1986) 'Vocal affect expression: A review and a model for future research', *Psychological Bulletin*, 99, 143–65.

Smith, L. E. and Nelson, C. (1982) 'International intelligibility of English: Directions and resources', *World Englishes*, 4 (3), 332–42.

Trudgill, P. (1999) 'Standard English: What it isn't', in Bex, T. and Watts, R. (eds) *Standard English: The Widening Debate*. London: Routledge, 117–28.

Widdowson, H. (1994) 'The Ownership of English', *TESOL Quarterly*, 28, 377–89.

# Chapter 2

Best, C. T. (1994) 'The emergence of native-language phonological influences in infants: A perceptual assimilation model', in Goodman, J. C. and Nusbaum, H. (eds) *The Development of Speech Perception*. Cambridge, Massachusetts: The MIT Press, pp. 167–224.

Brazil, D. (1997) *The Communicative Value of Intonation in English*. Cambridge: Cambridge University Press.

Broselow, E., Hurtig, R. and Ringen, C. (1987) 'The perception of second language prosody', in G. Ioup and S. H. Weinberger (eds) *Interlanguage Phonology*. Cambridge, MA: Newbury House, pp. 250–362.

Brown, A. (ed.) (1991) *Teaching English Pronunciation: A Book of Reading*. London: Routledge.

Brown. P. C. ( 2001) 'The interactive dictation', *The Language Teacher*, 25 (7), 27–8.

Carlisle, R. S. (2001) 'Syllable structure universals and second language acquisition. *International Journal of English Studies*', 1 (1), 1–20.

Carroll, J. B. (1962) 'The prediction of success in intensive foreign language training', in Glaser, R. (ed.) *Training research and education*. Pittsburgh: University of Pittsburgh Press, 87–136.

Caudwell, R. (2002–2003) 'Grasping the nettle: The importance of perception work in listening comprehension', Available online, retrieved 19 December 2009 from http://www.developingteachers.com/articles_tchtraining/perception1_richard.htm

Caudwell, R. and Hewings, M. (1996) 'Intonation rules in ELT textbooks', *ELT Journal*, 50 (4), 327–34.

Cenoz, J. and Lecumberri, L. (1999) 'The acquisition of English pronunciation: Learners' views', *International Journal of Applied Linguistics*, 9 (1), 3–17.

Daniels, H. (1995) 'Psycholinguistic, psycho-affective and procedural factors in the acquisition of authentic L2 pronunciation', *Speak Out!* 15, 3–10.

de Bot, K. (1986) 'The transfer of intonation and the missing database', in Kellerman, E. and Sharwood Smith, M. (eds) *Crosslinguistic Influence in Second Language Acquisition*. Pergamon: New York, pp. 110–19.

Derwing, T. and Munro, M. (2005) 'Second language accent and pronunciation teaching: A research-based approach', *TESOL Quarterly*, 39 (3), 379–97.

Dewaele, J. and Furnham, A. (1999) 'Extraversion: The unloved variable in applied linguistics research', *Language Learning*, 49 (3), 509–44.

Eckman, F. (1977) 'Markedness and the contrastive analysis hypothesis', *Language Learning*, 27, 315–30.

Eckman, F. and Iverson, G. (1994) 'Pronunciation difficulties in ESL: Coda consonants in English interlanguage', in M. Yavas. (ed.) *First and Second Language Phonology*. San Diego, CA: Singular Publishing Group Inc. pp. 251–65.

Ellis, R. (1994) *The Study of Second Language Acquisition*. New York: Oxford University Press.

Flege, J. E. (1987) 'A critical period for learning to pronounce foreign languages?', *Applied Linguistics*, 8, 162–77.

Flege, J. E. and Hillenbrand, J. (1984) 'Limits in phonetic accuracy in foreign language speech production', *Journal of the Acoustical Society of America*, 76, 708–21.

Flege, J. and Wang, C. (1989) 'Chinese subjects' perception of the word-final English/t/-/d/ contrast: Performance before and after training', *Journal of the Acoustical Society of America*, 6 (5), 1684–97.

Lenneberg, E. H. (1967) *Biological Foundations of Language*. New York: John Wiley & Sons.

Jenkins, J. (2000) *The Phonology of English as an International Language*. Oxford: Oxford University Press.

Jenkins, J. and Setter, J. (2005) 'State of the art review article: Pronunciation', *Language Teaching*', 38, 1–17.

Krashen, S. (1982) *Principles and Practice in Second Language Acquisition*. Oxford: Pergamon Press.

Ioup, G. (1984) 'Is there a structural foreign accent? A comparison of syntactic and phonological errors in second language acquisition', *Language Learning*, 34 (2), 1–17.

Ioup, G., Boustagi, E., El Tigi, M. and Moselle, M. (1994) 'Reexamining the critical period hypothesis: A case study of successful adult SLA in a naturalistic environment', *Studies in Second Language Acquisition*, 16, 73–98.

Lado, R. (1957) *Linguistics Across Cultures*. Ann Arbor: University of Michigan Press.

Levis, J. (1999) 'Training teachers to use English as a pronunciation resource', *Speak Out!* 24, 16–24.

Levis, J. (2005) 'Changing contexts and shifting paradigms in pronunciation teaching', *TESOL Quarterly*, 39 (3), 369–78.

Locke, J. L. (1993) *The Child's Path to Spoken Language*. Cambridge, MA: Harvard University Press.

Long, M. H. (1990) 'Maturational constraints on language development', *Studies in Second Language Acquisition*, 12, 251–85.

Major, R. C. (1987) 'A model for interlanguage phonology', in Ioup, G. and Weinberger, S. H. (eds) *Interlanguage Phonology*. Cambridge, Massachusetts: Newbury House, pp. 101–24.

Marks, J. (1999) 'Is stress-timing real?', *ELT Journal*, 53 (3), pp. 191–9.

McCarthy, P. (1991) 'Auditory and articulatory training for the language teacher and learner', in A. Brown. (ed.) *Teaching English Pronunciation: A Book of Readings*. London: Routledge, pp. 299–308.

Neufeld, G. and Schneiderman, E. (1980) 'Prosodic and Articulatory Features in Adult Language Learning', in Scarcella, R. and Krashen, S. (eds) *Research in Second Language Acquisition*. Rowley, MA: Newbury House.

Pennington, M. (1989) 'Teaching pronunciation from the top down', *RELC Journal*, 20, 20–38.

Polka, L. (1995) 'Linguistic influences in adult perception of non-native vowel contrasts', *Journal of the Acoustic Society of America*, 97, 1286–96.

Purcell, E. and Suter, R. (1980) 'Predictors of pronunciation accuracy: A reexamination', *Language Learning*, 30, 271–87.

Rogerson, P. and Gilbert, J. (1990) *Speaking Clearly*. Cambridge: Cambridge University Press.

Schmidt, R. W. (1977) 'Sociolinguistic variation and language transfer in phonology', in Ioup, G. and Weinberger, S. H. (eds) *Interlanguage Phonology*. Cambridge, MA: Newbury House.

Schneiderman, E., Bourdages, J. and Champagne, C. (1988) 'Second-language accent: The relationship between discrimination and perception in acquisition', *Language Learning*, 38, 1–19.

Scovel, T. (2000) 'A critical review of the critical period research', *Annual Review of Applied Linguistics*, 20, 213–23.

Selinker, L. (1992) *Rediscovering interlanguage*. London: Longman.

Setter, J. and Jenkins, J. (2005) 'Pronunciation', [State of the Art Review Article] *Language Teaching*, 38 (1), 1–17.

Spada, N. (1997) 'Form-focussed instruction and second language acquisition: A review of classroom and laboratory research', [State of the Art Article] *Language Teaching*, 30 (2), 73–87.

Suter, R. W. (1976) 'Predictors of pronunciation accuracy in second language learning', *Language Learning*, 26, 233–53.

Wenk, B. (1986) 'Crosslinguistic influence in second language phonology: Speech rhythms', in E. Kellerman and S. Sharwood (eds) *Cross-Linguistic Influence in Second Language Acquisition*. Oxford: Pergamon Press, pp. 120–33.

# Chapter 3

Dalton, C. and Seidlhofer, B. (1994) *Pronunciation*. Oxford: Oxford University Press.

Esling, J. (1978) 'The identification of features of voice quality in social groups', *Journal of the International Phonetic Association*, 7, 18–23.

Esling, J. and Wong R. (1983) 'Voice quality settings and the teaching of pronunciation', *TESOL Quarterly*, 17 (1), 89–95.

Esling, J. H. (1994) 'Some perspectives on accent: Range of voice quality variation, the periphery and focusing', in J. Morely (ed.). *Pronunciation Pedagogy and Theory: New Views, New Directions*. Alexandria, VA: TESOL, pp. 49–63.

Honikman, B. (1964) 'Articulatory settings', in Abercrombie, D., Fry, D. B., MacCarthy, P. A. D., Scott, N. C. and Trim, J. L. M. (eds), in Honour of Daniel Jones: Papers Contributed on the Occasion of his Eightieth Birthday, 12 September, 1961, Longman, London, pp. 73–84.

Jenkins, J. (2000) *The Phonology of English as an International Language.* Oxford: Oxford University Press.

Jones, R. and Evans, S. (1995) 'Teaching pronunciation through voice quality', *ELT Journal,* 49 (3), 244–51.

Kenworthy, J. (1987) *Teaching English Pronunciation.* London: Longman.

Laver, J. (1980) *The Phonetic Description of Voice Quality.* Cambridge: Cambridge University Press.

Laver, J. (1994) *Principles of Phonetics.* Cambridge: Cambridge University Press.

O'Connor, J. D. (1973) *Phonetics.* Harmondsworth: Penguin.

Pennington, M. (1996) *Phonology in English Language Teaching.* London and New York: Longman.

Thornbury, S. (1993) 'Having a good jaw: Voice setting phonology', *ELT Journal,* 47 (2), 126–31.

Trask, R. L. (1996) *Dictionary of Phonetics and Phonology.* London: Routledge.

# Chapter 4

Cruttenden, A. (2008) *Gimson's Pronunciation of English* (7th edition). London: Hodder Education.

Gimson, A. C. (1977) 'Daniel Jones and standards of English pronunciation', *English Studies,* 58, 151–8.

Gimson, A. C. (1994) *An Introduction to the Pronunciation of English.* London: Edward Arnold Ltd.

Jenkins, J. (2000) *The Phonology of English as an International Language.* Oxford: Oxford University Press.

Rogerson, P. and Gilbert, J. (1990) *Speaking Clearly: Pronunciation and Listening Comprehension for Learners of English.* Cambridge: Cambridge University Press.

# Chapter 5

Avery, P. and Ehrlich, S. (eds) (1987) *The Teaching of Pronunciation: An Introduction for Teachers of English as a Second Language.* Oxford: Oxford University Press.

Chun, D. (2002) *Discourse Intonation in L2: From Theory and Research to Practice.* Philadelphia: John Benjamins.

Cruttenden, A. (2008) *Gimson's Pronunciation of English* (7th edition). London: Hodder Education.

Dauer, R. (2005) 'The lingua franca core: A new model for pronunciation instruction?', *TESOL Quarterly,* 39 (3), 543–50.

Fucci, D. M., Crary, M., Warren, J. and Bondi, Z. (1977) 'Interaction between auditory and oral sensory feedback in speech regulation', *Perceptual and Motor Skills,* 45, 123–129.

Gilbert, J. (2001) *Clear Speech from the Start.* Cambridge: Cambridge University Press.

Hillenbrand, J. M. and Clark, M. J. (2000) 'Some effects of duration on vowel recognition', *Journal of the Acoustical Society of America,* 108, 3013–3022.

I-Chun, (Vicky) Kuo. (2006) 'Addressing the issue of teaching English as a lingua Franca', *ELT Journal,* 60 (3), 213–21.

Jackobson, R. and Halle, M. (1964) 'Tenseness and laxness', in Abercrombie, D., Fry, D. B., MacCarthy, P. A. D., Scott, N. C., Trim, J. L. M. (eds), in Honour of Daniel Jones: Papers Contributed on the Occasion of his Eightieth Birthday, 12 September, 1961, Longman, London, pp. 96–101.

Jenkins, J. (2000) *The Phonology of English as an International Language.* Oxford: Oxford University Press.

Jenner, B. (1995) 'On diphthongs', *Speak Out!* 15, 15–16.

Jones, D. (1917) *An English Pronouncing Dictionary.* London: Dent.

Leather, J. (1983) 'State of the art: Second-language pronunciation learning and teaching', *Language Teaching,* 16, 198–219.

Roach, P. ( 2000) *English Phonetics and Phonology.* Cambridge: Cambridge University Press.

## Chapter 6

Brown, A. (ed.) (1991) *Teaching English Pronunciation: A Book of Reading*. London: Routledge.

Catford, J. C. (1987) 'Phonetics and the teaching of pronunciation: A systemic description of English phonology', in J. Morley (ed.) *Current Perspectives on Pronunciation*. Alexandria, VA: TESOL, pp. 87–100.

Cruttenden, A. (2008) *Gimson's Pronunciation of English* (7th edition). London: Hodder Education.

Derwing, T. and Munro, M. J. (2005) 'Second language accent and pronunciation teaching: A research-based approach', *TESOL Quarterly*, 39 (3), 379–97.

Gilbert, J. (2008) *Teaching Pronunciation: Using the Prosody Triangle*. New York: Cambridge University Press.

Jenkins, J. (2000) *The Phonology of English as an International Language*. Oxford: Oxford University Press.

King, R. D. (1967) 'Functional load and sound change'. *Language* 43, 831–852.

Leahy, R. (1980) 'A practical approach for teaching ESL pronunciation based on distinctive feature analysis', *TESOL Quarterly*, 14 (2), 209–19.

Roach, P. (2000) *English Phonetics and Phonology*. Cambridge: Cambridge University Press.

Rogerson, P. and Gilbert, J. (1990) *Speaking Clearly*. Cambridge: Cambridge University Press.

## Chapter 7

Anderson, J. (1983) The difficulties of English syllable structure for Chinese ESL learners. *Language Learning and Communication*, 2 (1), 53–62.

Avery, P. and Ehrlich, S. (eds) (1987) *The Teaching of Pronunciation: An Introduction for Teachers of English as a Second Language*. Oxford: Oxford University Press.

Cruttenden, A. (1994) *Gimson's Pronunciation of English* (5th edition). London: Edward Arnold.

Dalton, C. and Seidlhofer, B. (1994) *Pronunciation*. Oxford: Oxford University Press.

Giegerich, H. J. (1992) *English Phonology: An Introduction*. Cambridge: Cambridge University Press.

Major, R. C. (1994) 'Chronological and stylistic aspects of second language acquisition of consonant clusters', *Language Learning*, 44, (4), 655–80.

Mehler, J. and Christophe, A. (1992) 'Speech processing and segmentation in natural languages', in Tohkura, Y., Vatikiotis-Bateson, E. and Sagisaka, Y. (eds) *Speech Perception, Production, and Linguistic Structure*. Tokyo and Amsterdam: Ohmsha and IOS Press, pp. 221–38.

Roach, P. (1991) *English phonetics and phonology* (2nd edition). Cambridge: Cambridge University Press.

Suenobo, M., Kanzaki, K. and Yamane, S. (1992) 'An experimental study of intelligibility of Japanese English', *IRAL*, 30 (2), 146–56.

## Chapter 8

Kenworthy, J. (1987) *Teaching English Pronunciation*. Harlow, U.K.: Longman.

## Chapter 9

Brown, A. (ed.) (1991) *Teaching English Pronunciation: A Book of Reading*. London: Routledge.

Crystal, D. (1988) *The English Language Today*. London: Penguin.

Cruttenden, A. (2008) *Gimson's Pronunciation of English* (7th edition). London: Hodder Education.

Dauer, R. (2005) 'The Lingua Franca Core: A New Model for Pronunciation Instruction?', *TESOL Quarterly*, 39 (3), 543–50.

Gilbert, J. (2005) *Clear Speech: Pronunciation and Listening Comprehension in North American English* (3rd edition). Cambridge: Cambridge University Press.

Gilbert, J. (2008) *Teaching Pronunciation: Using the Prosody Triangle.* New York: Cambridge University Press.

Grosjean, F. and Gee, J. (1987) 'Prosodic structure and spoken word recognition', *Cognition*, 25, 135–55.

Jenkins, J. (2000) *The Phonology of English as an International Language.* Oxford: Oxford University Press.

Kenworthy, J. (1987) *Teaching English Pronunciation.* Harlow, U.K.: Longman.

Vaughan-Rees, M. (1999) 'Word-stress rules', *Speak Out!*, 23, 38–9.

Wells, J. C. (2000) *Longman Pronunciation Dictionary* (2nd edition). Harlow: Pearson Education Limited.

# Chapter 10

Abercrombie, D. (1965) 'RP and local accent', in Abercrombie, D. *Studies in Phonetics and Linguistics.* Oxford: Oxford University Press.

Adams, C. (1979) *English Speech Rhythm and the Foreign Learner.* Mouton: The Hague.

Allen, G. D. (1975) 'Speech rhythm: Its relation to performance universals and articulatory timing', *Phonetics*, 3, 75–86.

Bolinger, D. (1981) 'Consonance, Dissonance, and Grammaticality: The Case of wanna', *Language and Communication*, 1, 189–206.

Brown, G. (1977) *Listening to Spoken English.* Cambridge: Cambridge University Press.

Cauldwell, R. (1996) 'Stress-timing: observations, beliefs and evidence, Eger,' *Journal of English Studies*, 1, 33–48.

Cruttenden, A. (1997) *Intonation* (2nd edition). Cambridge: Cambridge University Press.

Cruttenden, A. (2008), *Gimson's Pronunciation of English* (7th edition). London: Hodder Education.

Cutler, A. (1993) 'Segmenting speech in different languages', *The Psychologist*, 6, 453–455.

Dauer, R. M. (1983) 'Stress timing and syllable timing reanalysed', *Journal of Phonetics*, 11, 51–62.

Gilbert, J. (2008) *Teaching Pronunciation: Using the Prosody Triangle.* New York: Cambridge University Press.

Gimson, A. C. (1994) *An Introduction to the Pronunciation of English* (5th edition). Revised by A. Cruttenden (ed.). London: Edward Arnold.

Halliday, M. A. K. (1967) *Intonation and Grammar in British English.* The Hague: Mouton.

Hieke, A. E. (1984) 'Linking as a marker of fluent speech', *Language and Speech*, 27, 343–54.

Jenkins, J. (2000) *The Phonology of English as an International Language.* Oxford: Oxford University Press.

Klatt, D. (1975) 'Voice onset time, frication and aspiration in word-initial clusters', *Journal of Speech and Hearing Research*, 18, 686–705.

Ladefoged, P. (1982) *A Course in Phonetics* (2nd edition). New York: Harcourt Brace Jovanovich.

O'Connor, J. D. (1973) *Phonetics.* Harmondsworth: Penguin.

Roach, P. J. (1991) *English Phonetics and Phonology: A Practical Course* (2nd edition). Cambridge: Cambridge University Press.

Roach, P. J. (2000) *English Phonetics and Phonology: A Practical Course* (3rd edition). Cambridge: Cambridge University Press.

Taylor, D. S. (1981) 'Non-native speakers and the rhythm of English', *IRAL*, 14 (3), 219–26.

Wenk, B. J. (1985) 'Speech rhythms in second language acquisition', *Language & Speech*, 28, 157–75.

# Chapter 11

Avery, P. and Ehrlich, S. (1992) *Teaching American English Pronunciation.* Oxford: Oxford University Press.

Bradford, B. (1988) *Intonation in Context.* Cambridge: Cambridge University Press.

Bradford, B. (1997) 'Upspeak in British English, *English Today*, 51, 13.3, 33–6.

Brazil, D. (1994) *Pronunciation for Advanced Learners of English*, Cambridge: Cambridge University Press.

Brazil, D. (1997) *The Communicative Value of Intonation in English.* Cambridge: Cambridge University Press.

Brazil, D., Coulthard, M. and Johns, C. (1980) *Discourse Intonation and Language Teaching*. London: Longman.

Chafe, W. (1979) 'The flow of thought and the flow of language', in T. Givón (ed.) *Syntax and Semantics*, 12: *Discourse and Syntax*. New York: Academic Press, pp. 159–81.

Couper Kuhlen, E. (1986) *An Introduction to English Prosody*. London: Hodder Arnold.

Cruttenden, A. (1986) *Intonation*. Cambridge: Cambridge University Press.

Cruttenden, A. (1997) *Intonation* (2nd edition). New York: Cambridge University Press.

Cruttenden, A. (2008) *Gimson's Pronunciation of English* (7th edition). London: Hodder Education.

Crystal, D. (1969) *Prosodic Systems and Intonation*. Cambridge: Cambridge University Press.

Crystal, D. and Quirk, R. (1964) *Systems of Prosodic and Paralinguistic Features in English*. The Hague: Mouton.

Dalton, C. and Seidlhofer, B. (1994) *Pronunciation*, Oxford: Oxford University Press.

Du Bois, J.W. (1991) 'Transcription design principles for spoken discourse research', *Pragmatics* 1, 71–106.

Gilbert, J. (1993) *Clear Speech: Pronunciation and Listening Comprehension in North American English* (2nd edition). New York: Cambridge University Press.

Gilbert, J. (2008) *Teaching Pronunciation: Using the Prosody Triangle*. New York: Cambridge University Press.

Gimson, A. C. (1994) *Gimson's Pronunciation of English* (4th edition). Revised by A. Cruttenden. London: Arnold.

Halliday, M. A. K. (1970) 'Language structure and language function', in Lyons (ed.) *New Horizons in linguistics*. Harmondsworth: Penguin.

Jenkins, J. (2000) *The Phonology of English as an International Language*. Oxford: Oxford University Press.

Kaltenboeck, G. (2002) Computer-based intonation teaching: Problems and potential. *Talking Computers, Proceedings of the IATEFL Pronunciation and Computer Special Interest Groups*, pp. 11–17.

Kellerman, E. (1979) 'Transfer and non-transfer: Where we are now', *Studies in Second Language Acquisition*, 2, 37–57.

Kriedler, C. (1989) *The Pronunciation of English*. Oxford: Basil Blackwell.

Ladd, D. R. (1996) *Intonational Phonology*. Cambridge: Cambridge University Press.

Levis, J. (1999) 'The intonation and meaning of normal yes-no questions', *World Englishes*, 18 (3), 373–80.

McCarthy, M. (1991) *Discourse Analysis for Language Teachers*. Cambridge: Cambridge University Press.

Morley, J. (1991) 'The pronunciation component in teaching English to speakers of other languages', *TESOL Quarterly*, 25 (3), 481–520.

O'Connor, J. D. and Arnold, G. F. (1973) *Intonation of Colloquial English* (2nd edition). London: Longman

Palmer, H. (1922) *English Intonation*. Cambridge: Heffer.

Peters, A. M. (1977) 'Language learning strategies: Does the whole equal the sum of the parts?', *Language*, 53, 560–73.

Roach, P. (2000) *English Phonetics and Phonology* (3rd edition). Cambridge: Cambridge University Press.

Rogerson, P. and Gilbert, J. (1990) *Speaking Clearly*. Cambridge: Cambridge University Press.

Sweet, H. (1906) *A Primer of Phonetics*. Oxford: Oxford University Press.

Taylor, D. S. (1993) 'Intonation and accent in English: What teachers need to know', *IRAL*, 16 (1), 1–21.

Thomson, I. (1983) *Intonation in Use*. Oxford: Oxford University Press.

Wells, J. (2006) *English Intonation: An introduction*. Cambridge: Cambridge University Press.

# Chapter 13

Baker, A. (2006) *Ship or Sheep? Student's Book – An Intermediate Pronunciation Course*. Cambridge: Cambridge University Press.

Bowen, T. and Marks, J. (1992) *The Pronunciation Book: Student-Centred Activities for Pronunciation Work*. Burnt Mill: Longman.

Bowler, B. and Cunningham, S. (1999) *Headway Pronunciation Course.* Oxford: Oxford University Press.

Bradford, B. (1988) *Intonation in Context.* Cambridge: Cambridge University Press.

Bradlow, A., Pisoni, D., Yamada, R. A. and Tohkura, Y. (1997) 'Training Japanese listeners to identify English /r/ and /l/: IV. Some effects of perceptual learning on speech production', *Journal of the Acoustical Society of America,* 101 (4), 2299–310.

Bradlow, A. R., Torretta, G. M. and Pisoni, D. B. (1996) 'Intelligibility of normal speech I: Global and fine-grained acoustic-phonetic talker characteristics', *Speech Communication,* 20, 255–72.

Brazil, D. (1994) *Pronunciation for Advanced Learners of English Teacher's Book and Student's Book.* Cambridge: Cambridge University Press.

Chapman, M. (2007) 'Theory and practice of teaching discourse intonation', *ELT Journal,* 61 (1), 3–11.

Chun, D. (2002) *Discourse Intonation in L2: From Theory and Research to Practice.* Philadelphia: John Benjamins.

Evans, S. and Jones, R. (1995) 'Teaching pronunciation through voice quality', *ELT Journal,* 49 (3), 244–51.

Fucci, D., Crary, M., Warren, J. and Bondi, Z. (1977) 'Interaction between auditory and oral sensory feedback in speech regulation', *Perceptual and Motor Skills,* 45, 123–9.

Gilbert, J. (2001) *Clear Speech from the Start.* Cambridge: Cambridge University Press.

Gilbert, J. (2005) *Clear Speech: Pronunciation and Listening Comprehension in North American English* (3rd edition). Cambridge: Cambridge University Press.

Gilbert, J. (2008) *Teaching Pronunciation: Using the Prosody Triangle.* New York: Cambridge University Press.

Graham, C. (1978) *Jazz Chants.* New York: Oxford University.

Hancock, M. (2003) *English Pronunciation in Use.* Cambridge: Cambridge University Press.

Hardison, D. (2002) 'Computer-assisted second-language learning: Generalization of prosody-focused training', *Proceedings of ICSLP,* 2002, 1217–20.

Kenworthy, J. (1987) *Teaching English Pronunciation.* London: Longman.

Lear, E. (1846) *A Book of Nonsense.* London: Thomas MacLean.

Leather, J. (1983) 'State of the art: Second-language pronunciation learning and teaching', *Language Teaching,* 16, 198–219.

Markham, D. and Nagano-Madsen, Y. (1996) 'Input modality effects in foreign accent', in Bunnel, H. T. and Idsardi, W. (eds) *Applied Science and Engineering Laboratories.* Alfred E. duPont Institute.

Morley, J. (1979) *Improving Spoken English.* Ann Arbor, MI: University of Michigan Press.

Mortimer, C. (1985) *Elements of Pronunciation.* Cambridge: Cambridge University Press.

O'Connor, J. D. and Fletcher, C. (1989) *Sounds English.* Harlow: Longman.

Purcell, E. and Suter, R. (1980) 'Predictors of pronunciation accuracy: A reexamination', *Language Learning,* 30, 271–87.

Rogerson, P. and Gilbert, J. (1990) *Speaking Clearly.* Cambridge: Cambridge University Press.

Suter, R. W. (1976) 'Predictors of pronunciation accuracy in second language learning', *Language Learning,* 26, 233–53.

Thornbury, S. (1993) 'Having a good jaw: Voice setting phonology', *ELT Journal,* 47 (2), 126–31.

Wessels, C. and Lawrence, K. (1992) 'Using drama voice techniques in the teaching of pronunciation', in A. Brown (ed.) (1991) *Teaching English Pronunciation: A Book of Reading.* London: Routledge.

Underhill, A. (1994) *Sound Foundations: Learning and Teaching Pronunciation.* London: Macmillan.

# Chapter 14

Anderson-Hsieh, J., Johnson, R. and Koehler, K. (1992) 'The relationship between native speaker judgments of nonnative pronunciation and deviance in segmentals, prosody, and syllable structure', *Language Learning,* 42, 529–55.

Brazil, D. (1994) *Pronunciation for Advanced Learners*. Cambridge: Cambridge University Press.

Brown, A. (1991) 'Functional load and the teaching of pronunciation', in Brown, A. (ed.) *Teaching English Pronunciation: A Book of Readings*. London: Routledge, pp. 211–24.

Brown, A. (ed.) (1992) *Approaches to Pronunciation Teaching*. London: The British Council.

Catford, J. C. (1987) 'Phonetics and the teaching of pronunciation: A systemic description of English phonology', in J. Morley (ed.) *Current Perspectives on Pronunciation*. Alexandria, VA: TESOL.

Caudwell, R. (2002–2003) Grasping the nettle: The importance of perception work in listening comprehension. Retrieved December 19, 2009 from http://www.developingteachers.com/articles_tchtraining/perception1_richard.htm

Celce-Murcia, M., Brinton, D. and Goodwin, J. (1996) *Teaching Pronunciation: A Reference for Teachers of English to Speakers of other Languages*. Oxford: Oxford University Press.

Chomsky, N. (1959) 'Review of verbal behavior, by B. F. Skinner', *Language*, 35, 26–57.

Derwing, T. and Munro, M. (1997) 'Accent, intelligibility and comprehensibility: Evidence from four L1s'. *Studies in Second Language Acquisition*, 19, 1–16.

Derwing, T. and Munro, M. (2005) 'Second language accent and pronunciation teaching: A research-based approach', *TESOL Quarterly*, 39 (3), 379–97.

Derwing, T. and Rossiter, M. (2002) 'ESL learners' perceptions of their pronunciation needs and strategies', *System*, 30, 155–66.

Field, J. (2004) 'An insight into listeners' problems: Too much bottom-up processing or too much top-down?' *System*, 32, 363–77.

Gilbert, J. (2008) *Teaching Pronunciation: Using the Prosody Triangle*. New York: Cambridge University Press.

Hammerley, H. (1982) 'Contrastive phonology and error analysis', *International Review of Applied Linguistics*, xx/1.

Hirata, Y. (2004) 'Computer assisted pronunciation training for native English speakers learning Japanese pitch and durational contrasts', *Computer Assisted Language Learning*, 17 (3–4), 357–76.

Hughes, R. (ed.) (2005) *Spoken English, Applied Linguistics and TESOL: Challenges for Theory and Practice*. New York: Palgrave Macmillan.

Jenkins, J. (2000) *The Phonology of English as an International Language*. Oxford: Oxford University Press.

Jenkins, J. (2005) 'Implementing an international approach to English pronunciation: The role of teacher attitudes and identity', *TESOL Quarterly*, 39, 535–43.

Jenkins, J. and Setter, J. (2005) 'Pronunciation: State of the art review article', *Language Teaching*, 38, 1–17.

Kaltenboeck, G. (2002) Computer-based intonation teaching: Problems and potential. *Talking Computers, Proceedings of the IATEFL Pronunciation and Computer Special Interest Groups*, pp. 11–17.

Kenworthy, J. (1987) *Teaching English Pronunciation*. London: Longman.

King, R. D. (1967) 'Functional load and sound change', *Language*, 43, 831–52.

Kuo I-Chun. (2006) 'Addressing the issue of teaching English as a lingua franca', *ELT Journal*, 60 (3), 213–21.

Leather, J. (1999) Second-language speech research: An introduction. *Language Learning*, 49 (1), 1–37.

Levis, J. (2005) 'Changing contexts and shifting paradigms in pronunciation teaching', *TESOL Quarterly*, 39 (3), 369–78.

Levis, J. (2006) 'Pronunciation and the assessment of spoken language', in Hughes, R. (ed.) *Spoken English, applied linguistics and TESOL: Challenges for Theory and Practice*. New York: Palgrave Macmillan.

Medgyes, P. (1992) 'Native or non-native: Who's worth more?', *ELT Journal*, 46 (4), 340–49.

Morley, J. (1991) 'The pronunciation component in teaching English to speakers of other languages', *TESOL Quarterly*, 25, 481–520.

Morley, J. (1994) 'A multidimensional curriculum design for speech/pronunciation Instruction', in Morley (ed.) *Pronunciation Theory and Pedagogy: New Views, New Directions*. Alexandria, VA: TESOL Publications, pp. 64–91.

Munro, M. and Derwing, T. (2006) 'The functional load principle in ESL pronunciation instruction: An exploratory study', *System*, 34, 520–31.

Neri, A., Cucchiarini, C. and Strik, H. (2002a) Feedback in computer assisted pronunciation training: Technology push or demand pull? *Proceedings of International Conference on Spoken Language Processing* 2002 (1209–1212). Denver, CO. Available online, retrieved 16/09/09, from http://lands.let.kun.nl/literature/neri.2002.2.pdf

Roach, P. J. (2000) *English Phonetics and Phonology: A Practical Course* (3rd edition). Cambridge: Cambridge University Press.

Roach, P. J., Hartman, J. W. and Setter, J. E. (eds) (2003) *Daniel Jones' English Pronouncing Dictionary* (16th edition). Cambridge: Cambridge University Press.

Rogerson, P. and Gilbert, J. (1990) *Speaking Clearly*. Cambridge: Cambridge University Press.

Rogerson-Revell, P. (2007) 'Directions in e-learning tools and technologies and their relevance to online distance language education', *Open Learning*, 22 (1), 57–74.

Pennington, M. (1996) *Phonology in English Language Teaching*. London and New York: Longman.

Pennington, M. C. (1989) 'Teaching pronunciation from the top down', *RELC Journal*, 20, 20–38.

Pennington, M. C. and Richards, J. C. (1986) 'Pronunciation revisited', *TESOL Quarterly*, 20, 145–50.

Protea Textware. (2007) A pronunciation program that focuses on the suprasegmentals (British, North American and Australian versions). http://www.proteatextware.com.au/default.asp

Scovel, T. (1969) 'Foreign accents, language acquisition, and cerebral dominance', *Language Learning*, 19, 245–53.

Seidlhofer, B. (1999) 'Double standards: Teacher education in expanding circle', *World Englishes*, 18, 233–45.

Sifakis, S. and Sougari, A. (2005) 'Pronunciation issues and EIL pedagogy in the periphery: A survey of Greek state school teachers' beliefs', *TESOL Quarterly*, 39, 467–88.

Smith, L. and Bisazza, J. (1982) 'The comprehensibility of three varieties of English for college students in seven countries', *Language Learning*, 32 (2), 259–70.

Szpyra-Kozłowska, J., Frankiewicz, J., Nowacka, M. and Stadnicka, L. (2005) 'Assessing Assessment Methods: On the reliability of pronunciation tests in EFL'. Available online, retrieved 11.11.09 from http://www.phon.ucl.ac.uk/home/johnm/ptlc2005/pdf/ptlcp37.pdf.

Tench, P. (1992) 'Phonetic symbols in the dictionary and in the classroom', in Brown, A. (ed.) *Approaches to Pronunciation Teaching*. London: Macmillan.

Timmis, I. (2002) 'Native-speaker norms and international English: A classroom View', *ELT Journal*, 56, 240–9.

Underhill, A. (1994) *Sound Foundations: Learning and Teaching Pronunciation*. London: Macmillan.

Wang, X. and Munro, M. (2004) 'Computer-based training for learning English vowel Contrasts', *System*, 32 (4), 539–52.

Widdowson, H. (1994) 'The ownership of English', *TESOL Quarterly*, 28, 377–89.

# Chapter 15

Agard, F. and Di Pietro, R. (1965) *The Sound Structures of English and Italian*. Chicago: Chicago University Press.

Carlisle, R. S. (2001) 'Syllable Structure Universals and Second Language Acquisition', *International Journal of English Studies*, 1, 1–19.

Cruttenden, A. (2008) *Gimson's Pronunciation of English* (7th edition). London: Hodder Education.

*Handbook of the International Phonetic Association* (1999) Cambridge: Cambridge University Press.

Loveday, L. (1981) Pitch, politeness, and sexual role: An investigation. *Language and Speech*, 24, 71–88.

Lyovin, A. V. (1997) *An Introduction to the Languages of the World*. New York: Oxford University Press.

Maddieson, I. (1984) *Patterns of Sound*. Cambridge: Cambridge University Press.

Rivers, W. M. (1968) *Teaching Foreign-Language Skills*. Chicago: The University of Chicago Press.

Swan, M. and Smith, B. (2001) *Learner English: A Teacher's Guide to Interference and other Problems* (2nd edition). Cambridge: Cambridge University Press.

Urbanska, I. (ed.) (1977) *A Handbook of Polish Pronunciation for English Learners*. Panstwowe Wydawrictwo, Naukowe: Warszawa.

# Further Resources

This is a limited list of some useful websites, CDRoms and books for teaching and learning pronunciation. There are many more!

## Websites and CDRoms

*BBC Learn English* – Pronunciation section with lots of useful pronunciation resources including quizzes and downloads *http://www.bbc.co.uk/worldservice/learningenglish/grammar/pron/*

*Common mistakes in English by language background* Ted Powers website on common pronunciation errors by language group. *http://www.btinternet.com/~ted.power/phono.html*

*Connected Speech* by Protea Textware A pronunciation program that focuses on the suprasegmentals (British, North American and Australian versions). *http://www.proteatextware.com.au/default.asp*

*David Brett's* excellent interactive Flash-based resources for phonology and phonetics *http://davidbrett.uniss.it/*

*Easily confused phonetic symbols* John Wells' list of common errors when using the International Phonetic Alphabet. *http://www.phon.ucl.ac.uk/home/wells/confusables.htm*

*Ethnologue language atlas* A searchable web-based languages-of-the-world database from SIL international *http://www.ethnologue.com/web.asp*

*International Dialects of English Archive* (IDEA) online archive of accent and dialect samples designed for theatre and film artists

*International Phonetic Association* Phonetics information and resources (e.g. downloadable IPA charts and sound files). *http://www.langsci.ucl.ac.uk/ipa/*

*Longman Pronunciation Dictionary* by John Wells, including The Longman Pronunciation Coach CD-ROM. *http://www.pearsonlongman.com/dictionaries/LPD/video/LPD3.html*

*Paul Meier's Dialect Services* Fascinating online resources from the international voice and dialect coach. *http://www.paulmeier.com/index.html*

*Peter Ladefoged's phonetics resource page* includes language maps, IPA symbol search, sound index and a phonetics of English course. *http://hctv.humnet.ucla.edu/departments/linguistics/vowelsandconsonants/index.html*

*Phonetics Flash Animation Project* This site contains animated diagrams of speech sounds for English, German and Spanish. Developed by the University of Iowa. *http://www.uiowa.edu/~acadtech/phonetics/*

*Phonetics resources* a wide range of useful and interesting resources from the University of Aberdeen. *http://www.abdn.ac.uk/langling/resources/phonetics.html*

*Phonological Atlas of North America* This project documents changes in North American English dialects

*Phonology & Phonetics Review:* a practice and review unit for students of phonology and phonetics by Pamela Rogerson-Revell. UK Higher Education Authority's Subject Centre for Languages, Linguistics and Area Studies *http://www.llas.ac.uk/materialsbank/mb081/page_01.htm*

*Pronunciation animations* One of Cambridge University Press's ELT resources sites. *http://www.cambridge.org/elt/resources/skills/interactive/pron_animations/index.htm*

*Pronunciation Power* Online and CD Rom-based interactive pronunciation materials *http://www.englishlearning.com/*

*Pronunciation Tip of the Day* from University College London's Department of Speech, Hearing and Phonetic Sciences *http://www.phon.ucl.ac.uk/home/johnm/eptotd/tiphome.htm*

*Speech Accent Archive* hundreds of samples of English accents recorded with detailed transcriptions and notes on phonological features for each accent. *http://accent.gmu.edu/*

*Speech in Action* Richard Cauldwell's listening and pronunciation courseware based on recordings of unscripted speech *http://www.speechinaction.com/*

*Speech Internet Dictionary* Comprehensive dictionary of phonetics and phonology edited by John Maidment *http://www.phon.ucl.ac.uk/home/johnm/sid/sidhome.htm*

*Voice and Speech Sounds* lots of interactive voice and speech resources, including phonetics charts by Eric Armstrong, University of York, Canada. *http://www.yorku.ca/earmstro/index.html*

*Web Tutorials in phonetics* by John Maidment. Lots more from University College London's Department of Phonetics and Linguistics. *http://www.phon.ucl.ac.uk/resource/tutorials.html#phon*

## Pronunciation textbooks

Baker, A. (1981) *Ship or Sheep?* Cambridge: Cambridge University Press.

Bowen, T. & Marks, J. (1992) *The Pronunciation Book: Student-Centred Activities for Pronunciation Work.* Burnt Mill: Longman.

Bowler, B. and Cunningham, S. (1999) *Headway Pronunciation Course.* Oxford: Oxford University Press.

Bradford, B. (1988) *Intonation in Context.* Cambridge: Cambridge University Press.

Brazil, D. (1994) *Pronunciation for Advanced Learners of English.* Cambridge: Cambridge University Press.

Cook, V. (1979) *Using Intonation.* London: Longman.

Gilbert, J. (2005) *Clear Speech: Pronunciation and Listening Comprehension in North American English* (3rd edition). Cambridge: Cambridge University Press.

Graham, C. (1978) *Jazz Chants.* New York: Oxford University Press.

Hancock, M. (1995) *Pronunciation Games.* Cambridge: Cambridge University Press.

Hancock, M. (2003) *English Pronunciation in Use.* Cambridge: Cambridge University Press.

Hewings, M. (1993) *Pronunciation Tasks: A Course for Pre-intermediate Learners.* Cambridge: Cambridge University Press.

Mortimer, C. (1985) *Elements of Pronunciation.* Cambridge: Cambridge University Press.

O'Connor, J. D. (1976) *Better English Pronunciation* (2nd edition). Cambridge: Cambridge University Press.

O'Connor, J. D. and Arnold, G. F. (1963) *Intonation of Colloquial English.* London: Longman.

O'Connor, J. D. and Fletcher, C. (1989) *Sounds English.* Harlow: Longman.

Rogerson, P. and Gilbert, J. (1990) *Speaking Clearly.* Cambridge: Cambridge University Press.

Underhill, A. (1994) *Sound Foundations: Learning and Teaching Pronunciation.* London: Macmillan.

Vaughan-Rees, M. (1994) *Rhymes and Rhythm.* London: Macmillan.

Vaughan-Rees, M. (2002) *Test Your Pronunciation.* London: Penguin.

# Key to Activities and Reviews

## Chapter 3  Speech Sounds

### Key to Activities

---

**Activity 7**

We ask people to say 'cheese' before taking a photograph because the vowel sound 'ee' requires the lips to be spread very wide thus producing a sort of 'smile'.

---

**Activity 10**

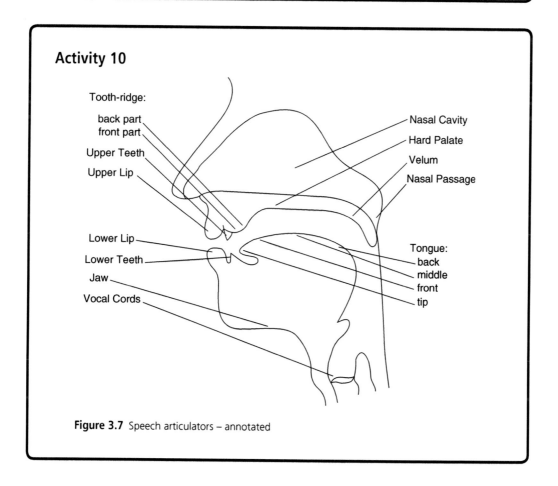

**Figure 3.7** Speech articulators – annotated

# Chapter 4 Consonants

## Key to Consonant Practice Activities

### Activity 1

| Place of articulation | | Bilabial | Labiodental | dental | Alveolar | Palato-alveolar | Palatal | Velar | Glottal |
|---|---|---|---|---|---|---|---|---|---|
| Manner of articulation | PLOSIVE | p b | | | t d | | | k g | |
| | FRICATIVE | | f v | θ ð | s z | ʃ ʒ | | | h |
| | AFFRICATE | | | | | tʃ dʒ | | | |
| | NASAL | m | | | n | | | ŋ | |
| | LATERAL | | | | l | | | | |
| | APPROXIMANT | ɯ | | | | r | j | | |

### Activity 2

| | | |
|---|---|---|
| (i) | a voiced bilabial plosive | bit |
| (ii) | a voiced labio-dental fricative | veer |
| (iii) | a voiceless palato-alveolar affricate | chin |
| (iv) | a voiceless alveolar plosive | tight |
| (v) | a voiced bilabial nasal | might |
| (vi) | a voiced bilabial approximant which can be called a semi-vowel also | weir |
| (vii) | a voiceless labio-dental fricative | fare |
| (viii) | a voiced dental fricative | then |
| (ix) | a voiceless palato-alveolar fricative | sure |
| (x) | a voiced velar plosive | got |

### Activity 3

| | | | |
|---|---|---|---|
| (i) | television | = | voiced palato-alveolar fricative |
| (ii) | shaking | = | voiceless velar plosive |
| (iii) | badger | = | voiced palato-alveolar affricate |
| (iv) | father | = | voiced dental fricative |
| (v) | dung | = | voiced velar nasal |
| (vi) | pushing | = | voiceless palato-alveolar fricative |
| (vii) | solid | = | voiceless alveolar lateral approximant |
| (viii) | regard | = | voiced velar plosive |
| (ix) | patchy | = | voiceless palato-alveolar affricate |
| (x) | reveal | = | voiced labio-dental fricative |

## Activity 4

| | | |
|---|---|---|
| white /w/ /t/ | clock /k/ /l/ / /k/ | edge /dʒ/ |
| pull /p/ /l/ | through /θ/ /r/ | vision /v/ /ʒ/ /n/ |
| chalk /tʃ/ /k/ | shell /ʃ/ /l/ | finger /f/ /ŋ/ /g/ |
| boxes /b/ /k/ /s/ /z/ | fifth /f/ /f/ /θ/ | wrong /r/ /ŋ/ |
| queue /k/ /j/ | cares /k/ /z/ | anger /ŋ/ /g/ |

## Activity 5

Then, the three young boys hid in the bushes until their pursuers passed by. At one point, the youngest began to groan in fear. The other two threw themselves on top of him and smothered the noise. The danger passed.

/ð/ is very common in initial position in function words such as 'then', 'this', 'the' and tends to occur intervocalically in content words like 'smother', 'mother', 'father'. /θ/ often occurs in initial position in content words such as 'throw', 'thin', 'think', 'thought'.

## Activity 6

/h/ cannot occur in final position in a word. /ŋ/ can only occur in final and medial position. /ʒ/ in 'measure' generally occurs in medial, intervocalic position, except for a few 'loan' words such as 'garage', 'rouge', 'beige'. /r/ does not occur in final position in RP.

# Chapter 5 Vowels

## Key to Activities

## Activity 1

(a) /uː/ is a back vowel
(b) / iː/ is a front vowel
(c) /ə/ is a central vowel

## Activity 2

| Front | Central | Back |
|---|---|---|
| /i:/ /ɪ/ /e/ / æ / | /ə/ /ʌ/ /ɜ:/ | /u:/ /ɔ:/ /ʊ/ /ɒ/ |

## Activity 3

Ideally, you would recognize that the front and back vowels are presented in a descending degree of closeness. If you have plotted them in the following way, you can begin to see the relationships they have to parts of the mouth:

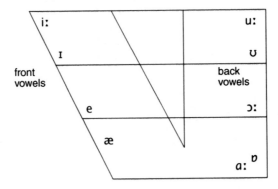

## Activity 25

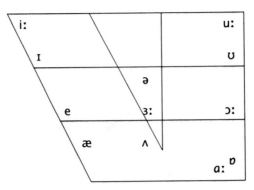

## Key to Vowel Practice Activities

### Activity 1

Examples are:

> got, sit, seat, sort, sat, gate, goat, part, put,     pool, cup, ago, fur, sight, toy, fear, fair, get, gout, poor.

### Activity 3

|     | A     | B     | C     | D     |
|-----|-------|-------|-------|-------|
| 1   | live  | love  | love  | love  |
| 2   | bed   | bed   | bud   | bed   |
| 3   | ran   | run   | ran   | ran   |
| 4   | barn  | barn  | barn  | bun   |
| 5   | hot   | hut   | hot   | hot   |
| 6   | born  | bun   | born  | born  |
| 7   | walk  | walk  | work  | walk  |
| 8   | room  | rum   | room  | room  |
| 9   | tale  | tale  | tale  | tell  |
| 10  | rat   | right | right | right |
| 11  | john  | join  | join  | join  |
| 12  | knee  | knee  | near  | knee  |
| 13  | very  | vary  | very  | very  |
| 14  | tow   | tow   | two   | tow   |
| 15  | hum   | home  | home  | home  |
| 16  | ground | grand | ground | ground |
| 17  | hurt  | hurt  | hurt  | hut   |
| 18  | pat   | pat   | pot   | pat   |
| 19  | said  | said  | sad   | said  |
| 20  | gate  | get   | get   | get   |

### Activity 4

(1) /ɒ/   /eɪ/   /ɪ/
(2) /ʌ/   /æ/    /ɒ/
(3) /ɪ/   /aɪ/   /ʊ/
(4) /ɔ:/  /ɑ:/   /e/

⇨

## Activity 4—Cont'd

(5) /ɜː/ /ɑː/ /e/
(6) /uː/ /e/ /eɪ/
(7) /ɪə/ /ɔɪ/ /əʊ/
(8) /aɪ/ /ɔɪ/ /iː/
(9) /aɪ/ /əʊ/ /eɪ/
(10) /ɔɪ/ /eɪ/ /aɪ/
(11) /æ/ /ɑː/ /uː/ /ʌ/
(12) /e/ /əʊ/ /ɪ/
(13) /ɔː/ /ɜː/ /ɑː/
(14) /ɪ/ /iː/ /ɔɪ/
(15) /ʊə/ /eə/ /ɪə/

## Activity 5

(a)

| cat /æ/ | seal /iː/ | cool /uː/ |
|---|---|---|
| share /eə/ | hill /ɪ/ | beer /ɪə/ |
| walk /ɔː/ | feel /iː/ | bin /ɪ/ |
| sank /æ/ | fur /ɜː/ | why /aɪ/ |
| far /ɑː/ | bird /ɜː/ | shot /ɒ/ |
| broad /ɔː/ | shore /ɔː/ | cut /ʌ/ |
| send /e/ | few /uː/ | pull /ʊ/ |

(b)

1. /uː/ in 'soon' – long, close, back, rounded
2. /ɪ/ in 'hill' – short, close, front, neutral
3. /ɒ/ in 'hot' – short, open, back, rounded
4. /ɜː/ in 'work' – long, mid-open, central, neutral
5. /iː/ in 'feet' – long, close, front, spread

## Activity 6

| window /ɪ/ /əʊ/ | roses /əʊ/ ɪ/ | information /ɪ/ /ə/ /eɪ/ /ə/ |
|---|---|---|
| woman /ʊ/ /ə/ | apples /æ/ /ə/ | tower /aʊə/ |
| women /ɪ/ /ə/ | usual /uː/ (/ʊ/) /ə/ | fire /aɪə/ |
| gentlemen /e/ /ə/ /ə/ | secretary /e/ /ə/ (/ə/) /i/ | idea /aɪ/ /ɪə/ |

## Activity 7

a. /aɪ/ (dive)  e. /eɪ/ (pain)
b. /ɔɪ/ (coin)  f. /ɪə/ (near)
c. /eə/ (hair)  g. /ʊə/ (pure)
d. /aʊ/ (now)  h. /əʊ/ (home)

# Chapter 6 Phonemes in Context

## Key to Activities

### Activity 1

| chop | ship | not minimal pair | Two phonemes (/ʃ/ v /tʃ/ and /ɒ/ v /ɪ/ are distinguished rather than one |
|---|---|---|---|
| right | rat | minimal pair | /aɪ/ v /æ/ are different phonemes |
| muggy | mucky | minimal pair | /g/ v /k/ are different phonemes |
| leisure | lesser | minimal pair | /ʒ/ v /s/ are different phonemes |
| pool | pull | minimal pair | /uː/ v /ʊ/ are different phonemes |
| other | author | not minimal pair | Two phonemes /ʌ/ v /ɔ:/ and /ð/ v /θ/ are distinguished rather than one |

### Activity 2

In (a) the [k] is heavily aspirated, unlike the other three examples. In (c) in final position, voiceless plosives such as [k] are regularly unexploded, or only partly exploded. So the release stage may be inaudible.

### Activity 3

fitness   fɪtˈnəs
picnic    pɪkˈnɪk
tractor   trækˈtə
hot dog   hɒtˈdɒg
midday    mɪdˈdeɪ

## Activity 4

Underline the position of potential glottal stops in the following phrases:

(1) Got that?
(2) Are you quite sure?
(3) He's a fitness instructor.
(4) Where's the kitten gone?

## Activity 5

The vowels in the stressed syllables in column 1 are shorter than in columns 2 and 3 as they precede a voiceless plosive, fricative or affricate:

| Short vowel | long vowel | long vowel |
|---|---|---|
| neat | knee | need |
| wheat | we | weed |
| light | lie | lied |
| piece | pea | peas |
| safe | say | save |

## Activity 6

(i) /p/ in 'pig' is heavily aspirated, unlike the other three examples, while /b/ in 'big' is not aspirated
(ii) neither /t/ nor /d/ is aspirated in mid position but /d/ is voiced and /t/ is voiceless. The preceding vowel is lengthened before the lenis consonant /d/.
(iii) neither plosive is aspirated in final position and voiceless plosives such as [p] are regularly unexploded, or only partly exploded. So the release stage may be inaudible. The preceding vowel is lengthened before the lenis consonant /g/.

## Activity 7

'Bill heard the loud bell just as light fell.'

## Activity 8

The /r/ is pronounced in the underlined cases:

| **1** | **2** | **3** |
|---|---|---|
| rare | rarely | rarer |
| ear | earplug | earring |
| tear | terror | terrorist |
| fear | fearful | fearing |

## Activity 9

| traitor | danger | character | tomorrow | |
|---|---|---|---|---|
| forget | accurate | alone | organize | appearance |

## Activity 10

many, funny, actually, misery, usual, poverty

meni, fʌni, æktjuəli (or æktʃuəli), mɪzəri, juːʒuəl, pɒvəti

# Key to Phoneme Practice Activities

1.

| (a) been | (b) fill | (c) cash | (d) shoot |
|---|---|---|---|
| mess | pool | thing | jam |
| full | bird | then | hung |
| fat | harm | yacht | sheep |
| much | cot | chuck | June |

| (e) joke | (f) mouth | (g) bike | (h) arrived |
|---|---|---|---|
| wear | shake | pace | aloud |
| size | fierce | fair | private |
| boil | show | voice | carvings |
| wierd | choke | shoulder | morning |

(i) joking     (j) forest
    willful          shallow
    woollen         mountain
    easy            finished
    derby          forgot

2.

|  |  | (i) | (ii) | (iii) |
|---|---|---|---|---|
| (a) | fox | /fɒx/ | /fɒks/ | /fɔ:ks/ |
| (b) | June | /ˈdu:n/ | /ˈdʒu:n/ | /ˈdʒʌn/ |
| (c) | double | /ˈdʌbl/ | /ˈdʊbel/ | /ˈdu:bl/ |
| (d) | idea | /ɪˈdɪə/ | /aɪˈdɪə/ | /aɪˈdɪɑ/ |
| (e) | only | /ˈonli:/ | /ˈaunli:/ | /ˈəunli/ |
| (f) | alarm | /əˈlɑ:m/ | /aˈlɑ:m/ | /æˈlɑ:m/ |
| (g) | menu | /ˈmenu:/ | /ˈmenju:/ | /ˈmenʊ/ |
| (h) | message | /ˈmesædʒ/ | /ˈmesedʒ/ | /ˈmesɪdʒ/ |

3. If you do not have a BBC English accent, you may have some differences in the vowels in words like 'laugh' (eg /læf/ rather than /lɑ:f/).

(a) /kæb/        (b) /fi:l/
(c) /lɑ:f/        (d) /kætʃ/
(e) /vɔɪs/        (f) /feə/
(g) /hɑ:m/       (h) /tʃʌk/
(i) /fʊl/        (j) /ðen/
(k) /hʌŋ/       (l) /ʃu:t/
(m) /bɜ:d/       (n) /nju:z/
(o) /ˈmju:zɪk/    (p) /dɪʃ/
(q) /kju:/        (r) /dʒɔɪn/

4.

(1) /ɒ/ /eɪ/ /ɪ/      (9) /aɪ/ /əʊ/ /eɪ/
(2) /ʌ/ /æ/ /ɒ/     (10) /ɔɪ/ /eɪ/ /aɪ/
(3) /ɪ/ /aɪ/ /ʊ/     (11) /æ/ /ɑ:/ /u:/ /ʌ/
(4) /ɔ:/ /ɑ:/ /e/    (12) /e/ /əʊe/ /ɪ/
(5) /ɜ:/ /ɑ:/ /e/    (13) /ɔ:/ /ɜ:/ /ɑ:/
(6) /u:/ /e/ /eɪ/    (14) /ɪ/ /i:/ /ɔ:/
(7) /ɪə/ /ɔɪ/ /əʊ/   (15) /ʊə/ /eə/ /ɪə/
(8) /aɪ/ /ɔɪ/ /i:/

5.

(1) She ran to the station /ʃi ræn tu ðə ˈsteɪʃən/
(2) What should she do now? /wɒt ʃəd ʃi du: naʊ/
(3) Can you give them a lift? /kən ju gɪv ðəm ə lɪft/
(4) Please look straight ahead. /pli:z lʊk streɪt əˈhed/
(5) Tell me when you've finished. /tel mi wen juv ˈfɪnɪʃd/

# Chapter 7  The Syllable

## Key to Activities

### Activity 1

(a) /ˈkærəktə/ (3)
(b) /ˈlaɪbrərɪ/ (3) but some people only pronounce 2) /ˈlaɪbrɪ/
(c) /əʊˈeɪsɪs/ (3)
(d) /ˈwedənzdeɪ/ (3)
(e) /bjuːtɪfli / (3), but you may have heard 4 /bjuːtɪfəli / in very 'careful' speech
(f) /pleɪn/ (1)
(g) /ˈɔːdɪnrɪ/ (3) but US pronunciation may be / ˈɔːrdənerɪ/-(4)
(h) /bɪˈheɪvjə/ (3)
(i) /sʌdn̩/ (2)
(j) /lɪtl̩, / (2)

### Activity 2

| | | | | | | |
|---|---|---|---|---|---|---|
| a. | /ptiːd/ | /pt/ not possible syllable initially | h. | /gwɪnk/ | Possible syllable |
| b. | /ŋɒsp/ | /ŋ/ not possible syllable initially | i. | /prɑːh/ | /h/ not possible syllable finally |
| c. | /slaɪp/ | Possible syllable | j. | /skwel/ | Possible syllable |
| d. | /pnɑːm/ | /pm/ not possible syllable initially | k. | /liːmg/ | /mg/ not possible syllable finally |
| e. | /glæn/ | Possible syllable | l. | /mrɔːk/ | Possible syllable |
| f. | /ʃrɒlts/ | Possible syllable | m. | /vwæk/ | /vw/ not possible syllable initially |
| g. | /ʒʌms/ | /ʒ/ not possible syllable initially | n. | /knaɪf/ | /kn/ not possible syllable initially |

### Activity 3

| | | pre-final | final | post-final 1 | post-final 2 |
|---|---|---|---|---|---|
| barged | bɑː | | dʒ | d | |
| patch | pæ | | tʃ | t | |
| alps | æ | l | p | s | |
| pinched | pɪ | n | tʃ | t | |
| seventh | seve | n | θ | | |
| rifts | rɪ | | f | t | s |
| against | əge | n | s | t | |
| judged | dʒʌ | | dʒ | | |
| lapsed | læ | | p | s | t |

## Activity 4

| helps | /helps/ | sixth | /siksθ/ |
|---|---|---|---|
| squash | /skwɒʃ/ | next | /nekst/ |
| spray | /spreɪ/ | boxes | /bɒksəz/ |
| twelfths | /twelfθs/ | reached | /riːtʃt/ |

| /plʌndʒd/ | plunged | /klaʊdz/ | clouds |
|---|---|---|---|
| /skrɪpts/ | scripts | /krʌnʃt/ | crunched |
| /græbd/ | grabbed | /θænkt/ | thanked |
| /spreɪd/ | sprayed | /riːtʃt/ | reached |

## Activity 5

(a) bottling     (2) /bɒt̩lɪŋ/ or /bɒtəlɪŋ/ (3) in slow, careful speech
(b) capital     (3) /kæpit̩l/ or /kæpitəl/
(c) kitten     (2) /kɪtn̩/
(d) carnation     (3) /kɑːneɪʃn̩/ or /kɑːneɪʃən/
(e) threatening     (2) /θretn̩ɪŋ/ or /θretənɪŋ/ (3) in slow, careful speech
(f) puzzle     (2) /pʌzl̩/
(g) gardener     (2) /gɑːdn̩ə/
(h) sudden     (2) /sʌdn̩/

## Activity 6

You will notice that the words can be divided into three groups according to the rule:

- If a verb ends in /t/ or /d/ the ending will be pronounced /ɪd/.
- If a verb ends in a voiceless sound, the past tense is pronounced /t/.
- If a verb ends in a voiced sound, the past tense is pronunounced /d/.

| /d/ | /t/ | /ɪd/ |
|---|---|---|
| robbed | helped | abated |
| poured | picked | lasted |
| pulled | laughed | wanted |
| banged | passed | ended |
| begged | washed | founded |
| loved | belched | boosted |
| loathed | | herded |
| buzzed | | potted |
| wedged | | roasted |
| pinned | | |
| massaged | | |
| rimmed | | |

## Activity 7

Again, you will notice a similar rule:

- If a noun ends in a sibilant sound (ie /s/ /z/ / ʃ/ /ʒ/ /tʃ/ or /dʒ/) the plural ending will be pronounced /əz/ or /ɪz/.
- If a noun ends in a voiceless sound, the plural is pronounced /s/.
- If a noun ends in a voiced sound, the plural is pronounced /z/.

| /s/ | /z/ | /ɪz/ or /əz/ |
|-----|-----|--------------|
| taps | cars | batches |
| bits | plums | pulses |
| sacks | tools | dishes |
| Plinths | ways | badges |
| caps | peas | houses |
| locks | prawns | garages |
| reefs | pans | |
| | pears | |
| | oars | |
| | rings | |
| | bids | |

# Chapter 8  Phonology Review 1

## Key to Activities

### A: Phonology Practice

## Activity 1

(1) Phonology is the study of the sounds patterns within a particular language, such as Chinese or English, or in a language variety, such as Cantonese Chinese or Indian English; while phonetics is the scientific description of speech sounds across languages, unrelated to a specific language.

(2) A phoneme is the smallest meaningful sound segment in a language.

(3) The hard palate is the hard part in the middle of the roof of the mouth.

(4) The nasal cavity is involved in the production of some vowels and consonants, as air can be exhaled through the nose as well as the mouth. With nasal consonants, most or all of the air is expelled through the nose (e.g. /m/, /n/ /ŋ/).

(5) Consonant sounds involve some degree of obstruction of the air flow by contact of the speech articulators, while vowels are created by changing the shape of the vocal tract but does not involve contact of the articulators.

(6) The larynx or voice box is the main phonatory organ and has a key role in many speech sounds.

## Activity 1—Cont'd

(7) It is easier to see the movement of some articulators (e.g. lips, teeth) involved in the production of consonants than in the production of vowels where there is no obvious contact between articulators. This is true of consonants produced in the front of the mouth (such as /m/ and /f/) but less so of consonants produced in the middle or back of the mouth (such as /ʒ/ or /ŋ/).

(8) In English, the lips are typically neutral, i.e. neither very spread or rounded and there is generally little jaw movement. There is a preference for centralized vowels (e.g. '<u>a</u>bout' ','b<u>utte</u>r'in English). There is frequent tapping of the tongue tip against the alveolar ridge (because of the high proportion of alveolar consonants) and a general lack of muscularity of articulations, due to the particular 'laxness' of English consonants.

(9) The three sections of the speech mechanism comprise the respiratory organs, the phonatory organs and the articulatory organs.

(10) A 'model' is a set of standard pronunciation forms for a particular accent which can be used as a point of reference or guideline with which to measure pronunciation appropriacy or accuracy. A 'goal' is the level which a learner's pronunciation aims to reach in order to facilitate effective communication.

## Activity 2

1. alveolar ridge
2. egressive
3. raised
4. nasalized
5. schwa
6. voiced
7. [ pʰ ] aspirated 'p' ,[ t̚ ] unreleased 't'
8. vibrate rapidly
9. co-articulation
10. vowel

## Activity 3

1. false – there are two.
2. true
3. true

4. false – there are more fricatives than plosives
5. false – vowels are voiced sounds
6. false – there are three /m, n, ŋ/
7. false – the longest possible English syllable is CCCVCCCC
8. false – syllable-initial voiceless plosives are aspirated
9. false – some do, such as 'window' /wɪndəʊ/
10. true

## Activity 4

1. /iː/
2. /uː/
3. /iː/ /ɪ/ /e/ /æ/
4. /eɪ/ /aɪ/
5. /ə/
6. /dʒ/
7. /m/
8. /z/
9. /p/
10. /h/

## Activity 5

1. televi<u>s</u>ion   = /ʒ/ voiced palato-alveolar fricative
2. sha<u>k</u>ing     = /k/ voiceless velar plosive
3. ba<u>dg</u>er      = /dʒ/ voiced palato-alveolar affricate
4. fa<u>th</u>er      = /ð/ voiced dental fricative
5. du<u>ng</u>        = /ŋ/ voiced velar nasal
6. pu<u>sh</u>ing     = /ʃ/ voiceless palato-alveolar fricative
7. so<u>l</u>id       = /l/ voiceless alveolar lateral approximant
8. re<u>g</u>ard      = /g/ voiced velar plosive
9. pa<u>tch</u>y      = /tʃ/ voiceless palato-alveolar affricate
10. re<u>v</u>eal     = /v/ voiced labio-dental fricative

## Activity 7

| Consonants | |
|---|---|
| plosives | p b t d k g |
| fricatives | f v s z θ ð ʃ ʒ h |
| affricates | ʤ ʧ |
| nasals | m n ŋ |
| approximants | r j w |
| laterals | l |

| Vowels | |
|---|---|
| Short vowels | ɪ e æ ʊ ɒ ʌ ə |
| Long vowels | i: u: ɑ: ɜ: ɔ: |
| diphthongs | aɪ ɔɪ eɪ aʊ əʊ ɪə eə ʊə |

## Activity 8

1. allophonic variation
2. free variation
3. [i] and [u]
4. non-rhotic
5. [ʰ]
6. 'button' [bʌtn̩]
7. In 'sang', the vowel is nasalized because of the following nasal consonant /ŋ/ [sæ̃ŋ]. In 'tenth', the first consonant in the cluster, /n/, is dentalized because of the following dental /θ/ [ten̪θ]
8. V i.e. a single vowel (e.g. 'eye')
9. CCCVCCCC – that is 3 syllable initial consonants (e.g. 'string" /strɪŋ/) and 4 syllable final consonants (e.g. 'twelfths' /twelfθs/
10. No, because the consonant cluster /fng/ is not possible in English and /dr/ is not possible in final position (although it is possible initially e.g. 'drive').

## B: Transcription practice – Key

## Activity 1

| | | | |
|---|---|---|---|
| 1. born | born | bun /bʌn/ | born |
| 2. knee | near /nɪə/ | knee | knee |
| 3. hum /hʌm/ | home | home | home |

⇨

| | | | |
|---|---|---|---|
| 4. sat | sat | sat | <u>set</u>  /set/ |
| 5. push | <u>bush</u>  /buʃ/ | push | push |
| 6. pull | pull | <u>pool</u>  /puːl/ | pull |
| 7. wet | wet | <u>vet</u>  /vet/ | wet |
| 8. rich | rich | <u>ridge</u>  /rɪʤ/ | rich |
| 9. support | <u>sport</u>  /spɔːt/ | support | support |
| 10. text | text | text | <u>texts</u>  /teksts/ |

## Activity 2

(a) (iii)
(b) (iii)
(c) (i)
(d) (iv)
(e) (i)

## Activity 3

| | |
|---|---|
| 1. /ʃuː/ | 1. shoe |
| 2. /bɪəd/ | 2. beard |
| 3. /leɪt/ | 3. late |
| 4. /həʊm/ | 4. home |
| 5. /fɪʃ/ | 5. fish |
| 6. /ʧiːz/ | 6. cheese |
| 7. /ʃɔː/ | 7. shore |
| 8. /feə/ | 8. fair |
| 9. ʃaʊə/ | 9. shower |
| 10. /tɑː/ | 10. tar |
| 11. /waɪəz/ | 11. wires |
| 12. /wɜːk/ | 12. work |
| 13. /wɔːkt/ | 13. walked |
| 14. /rɪʧ/ | 14. rich |
| 15. /gæp/ | 15. gap |
| 16. /rəʊd/ | 16. road |
| 17. /rɪʤ/ | 17. ridge |
| 18. /tjuːn/ | 18. tune |
| 19. /meɪd/ | 19. made/ maid |
| 20. /rɒŋ/ | 20. wrong |

## Activity 4

1. bread
2. sheep
3. light
4. lazy
5. button
6. breathing
7. leisure
8. tired
9. many
10. flowered
11. pretty
12. mission
13. finger
14. mature
15. bottle
16. lesson
17. reaches
18. fifth
19. boxes
20. shrank

## Activity 5

1. /θæŋkt/
2. /teksts/
3. /helpt/
4. /sɪksθs/
5. /skrɪpts/
6. /skwɒʃt/
7. /rɪsks/
8. /spreɪd/
9. /riːtʃt/
10. /klaʊdz/

## Activity 6

1. tunnel
2. frightened
3. necklace
4. women
5. mirror
6. few
7. failed
8. large
9. city
10. lose

## Activity 7

| əˈbaʊt | əˈgen | səˈpraɪz |
|--------|-------|----------|
| fəˈget | səˈdʒest | ˈstændəd |
| iːzi | ˈneɪtʃə | ˈkʌlə |
| ˈəʊnli | ˈhʌndrəd | ˈθʌrə |

# Chapter 9  Word Stress

## Key to Activities

### Activity 2

(a) Two-syllable verbs. ◀ Listen to the examples:

| Initial Syllable Stress | Final Syllable Stress |
|---|---|
| 'borrow, 'open, 'equal, 'enter, 'marry, 'follow, 'practice, 'deepen, 'happen, 'rummage | ap'ply, 'a'rouse, as'sist, at'tempt, ad'join, 'col'lect, in'sist, de'tract, de'clare, re'sist, ex'tend, sur'mise, de'sign, de'pend, in'vest, in'tend, re'fuse |

Rule: The 'rule' is that if the second syllable has a long vowel (e.g. apply) or ends in 2 consonants (e.g. collect) then that syllable is stressed.

If the second syllable ends in a short vowel like /ə, ɪ/ (e.g. marry) or ends in diphthong /əʊ/ as in borrow, then the first syllable is stressed. Only one syllable is said to be stressed despite the length, for example, of /əʊ/ in 'follow.

(b) Two-syllable adjectives. ◀ Listen to the examples:

| Initial Syllable Stress | Final Syllable Stress |
|---|---|
| 'merry, 'valid, 'eager, 'open, 'common, 'able, 'pretty, 'hollow, 'jolly, 'fallow, 'hopeless, 'final, 'careless, 'second | im'mune a'dept cor'rect ma'lign a'fraid mun'dance |

Rule:  The adjectives follow the same rule as the verbs.

(c) Two-syllable nouns. ◀ Listen to the examples:

| Initial Syllable Stress | Final Syllable Stress |
|---|---|
| 'hamster, 'limit, 'pocket, 'pencil, 'paper, 'mutton, 'table, 'mirror, 'panel, 'penny, 'honey, 'danger, 'cotton, 'shower, 'furrow | sa'loon can'teen po'lice gi'raffe re'port re'pose spit'toon |

Rule: If the last syllable has a short vowel or /əʊ/, it is unstressed and the initial syllable has the primary stress. Final syllable stress on nouns is quite rare in English and it is often related to borrowed words: e.g. la'goon, sa'loon

## Activity 3

◀ Listen to the examples:

1. di'gest
2. 'digest
3. 'conduct
4. con'duct
5. 'progress
6. pro'gress

## Activity 4

a.

| | | |
|---|---|---|
| calcu'lation | de'cision | re'action |
| re'lation | associ'ation | ope'ration |
| so'lution | distri'bution | tele'vision |

*Words ending in 'sion' or 'tion' place the stress on the penultimate (second from the last) syllable*

b.

| | | |
|---|---|---|
| eco'nomic | te'rrific | stra'tegic |
| 'logic | patho'genic | do'mestic |
| meta'bolic | sta'tistic | me'lodic |

*Words ending in 'ic' place the stress on the penultimate syllable*

c.

| | | | |
|---|---|---|---|
| bi'ology | bio'logical | 'policy | po'itical |
| pho'tography | photo'graphical | so'ciety | socio'logical |
| tech'nology | techno'logical | elec'ricity | e'lectrical |
| ge'ography | geo'graphical | uni'versity | mana'gerial |

*Words ending in 'al' and 'y' place the stress on the antipenultimate (third from the end) syllable*

d. ◀ Listen to the examples:

| | | | |
|---|---|---|---|
| perso'nality | /ˌpɜːsəˈnælɪti/ | antibi'otic | /ˌæntibaɪˈɒtɪk/ |
| computerti'sation | /kəmˌpjuːtəraɪˈzeɪʃn̩/ | 'surgical | /ˈsɜːdʒɪkəl/ |
| agri'cultural | /ˌægrɪˈkʌltjərəl/ | trans'mission | /ˌtrænsˈmɪʃn̩/ |
| pharma'cology | /ˌfɑːməˈkɑlədʒi/ | 'digital | /ˈdɪdʒɪtəl/ |
| ana'lytical | /ˌænəˈlɪtɪkəl/ | micro'scopic | /ˌmaɪkrəˈskɒpɪk/ |

## Activity 5

◀ Listen to the examples:

Complete the columns below marking the primary stress in each word:

| Verb | Noun |
|------|------|
| pre'sent | 'present |
| e'xamine | exami'nation |
| pro'duce | pro'duction |
| in'sult | 'insult |
| re'cord | 'record |
| re'duce | re'duction |

| Noun | Adjective |
|------|-----------|
| 'history | hi'storical |
| 'secretary | secre'tarial |
| a'nalysis | ana'lytical |
| 'politics | po'litical |

## Activity 6

(a) loudspeaker
    bad-mannered
    cotton wool

(b) armchair /'ɑːmtʃeə/     keyboard /'kiːbɔːd/     microwave /'maɪkrəweɪv/
    doorbell /'dɔːbel/     first-class /fɜːs'klæs/     north-east /nɔː'θiːst/

## Activity 7

(a) (i) Intolerance is an unreasonable, unacceptable attitude
    (ii) Hyperactive children can undo the most careful plans.

(b) (i) ði ʌn'siːzn̩əl 'weðə 'siːmd tə 'brɪŋ ə'baut ə 'pɜːsə'nælɪti dɪs'ɔːdə ɪn 'sʌm 'piːpl̩
    (ii) ðə 'æksɪdənt 'left ðə 'mæn 'fiːlɪŋ 'helpləs.

# Chapter 10  Features of Connected Speech

## Key to Activities

### Activity 2

Content Words

Can you come to the office at six this evening.

Structure Words

### Activity 3

a. *Basic accentuation patterns*
   1. The <u>Queen</u> is <u>visiting Cairo</u> this <u>morning</u>.
   2. Do you <u>want</u> a <u>cup</u> of <u>coffee</u>?
   3. Can you <u>tell</u> her I <u>called</u>?
   4. I'm <u>sorry</u> to <u>trouble</u> you but it's <u>rather urgent</u>.

c. *New focus*
   A: What are you doing?
   B: I came to see Barbara.
   A: Well, Barbara's not here.
   B: I can see she's not here. Where is she?
   A: I don't know where she is.
   B: Not very friendly, are you.
   A: Neither are you!

b. *Focus*
   1. The film was brilliant!
   2. Are you coming on Saturday?
   3. Can you give it to him?
   4. I think I left it in the kitchen.

d. *Contrastive focus*
   1. A: David's funny.
      a. B: He isn't funny. He's strange.
   2. A: So the number is 493656.
      B: No, it's 492656.
   3. A: That's £10. 30 altogether.
      a. B: £10.13?
      b. A: No, £10.30.

### Activity 4

● · ● ·
(a) Let her take it.

● · · ● · · ●
(b) Show me the way to go home.

● ● · · · ● ·
(c) What's happened to the doctor?

● · · · ● · · · ● ·
(d) Meet me at the entrance to the station.

## Activity 5

(a)

| Words | Strong forms | Weak forms |
|-------|-------------|-----------|
| a | /æ/ /eɪ/ | /ə/ |
| and | /ænd/ | /ən/ /n/ |
| but | /bʌt/ | /bə(t)/* |
| that | /ðæt/ | /ðə(t)/* |
| the | /ði:/ | /ðə/ /ði/ |
| as | /æz/ | /əz/ |
| than | /ðæn/ | /ðən/ |

*Remember that final /t/ is frequently unexploded or unreleased in unstressed syllables.

(b)
   i. Stephen is younger <u>than</u> /ðən/ Matthew.
   ii. He left <u>as</u> /əz/ soon <u>as</u> /əz/ he could.
   iii. The director said <u>that</u> /ðət/ Tom <u>and</u> /ən/ Alan would do it.
   iv. That is not what <u>the</u> /ðə/ rest said <u>that</u> /ðət/ they wanted.
   v. Star Wars is good <u>but</u> /bət/ not <u>as</u> /əz/ good <u>a</u> /ə/ film <u>as</u> /əz/ people say

(c)
   i. He's' as fit as a fiddle
   ii. It's raining cats and dogs
   iii. Better late than never

## Activity 6

   (a) Have some more tea
   (b) Pass her a biscuit
   (c) Leave him alone
   (d) Her sister's at the door

## Activity 7

In 'good morning' the final alveolar /d/ of 'good; assimilates to the place of articulation of the following bilabial consonant /m/, so it becomes bilabial. In 'what said', the final /t/ consonant of 'what' and the initial /s/ of 'side' are both alveolar but the /t/ assimilates to the manner of articulation of the initial /s/ in 'side', becoming a fricative.

## Activity 8

/aɪv 'gɒtə 'sæmwɪtʃ ɪmaɪ 'hæmbæg

Did you see him /dɪd jə/ becomes /dɪdʒə/
Would you /wʊd jə/ becomes /wʊdʒə/
Did you tell her what you saw /'dɪdʒə 'tel ə 'wɒtʃə 'sɔː/

## Activity 9

A: wɒt 'wʊdʒə 'laɪk
B: ə 'kɒfi 'pliːz
A: dʒə 'wɒnə 'keɪk ə 'sʌmθɪŋ
B: aɪ də'nəʊ 'riːli 'ɜː
A: wɪl 'læt bi 'ɔːl ən
B: 'jes 'θæŋks

## Activity 10

Mark any elided vowels in these words and then transcribe the words:

| | |
|---|---|
| rectɵry | /'rektrɪ/ |
| preferable | /'prefrəbļ / |
| librɑry | /'laɪbrɪ/ |
| cɵrrect | /'krekt/ |
| bɑlloon | bļ,uːn/ (the /l/ tends to be syllabic here because of the elided vowel) |

## Activity 11

Mark any elided consonants in these words and then transcribe the words:

| | |
|---|---|
| 'conscrip̲ts | /'kɒnskrɪps/ |
| fac̲ts | /fæks/ |
| 'dus̲tmen | /'dʌsmən/ |
| cold̲ 'coffee | /kəʊl 'kɒfɪ/ |
| las̲t 'month | /lɑːs 'mʌnθ / |
| the 'fac̲t that | / ðə 'fæk ðət/ |

## Activity 12

1. He ~~has~~ got a cold.
2. Do you think she ~~has~~ finished?
3. Where ~~have~~ they been?
4. I have to go to work.

5. We ~~have~~ got to work hard.
6. She has four children.
7. Have you seen David?
8. I ~~have~~ never been to India.

## Activity 13

1. 'No, I 'do not 'think she 'has.
2. They ~~would~~ 'help you 'if they 'could.
3. 'No, I 'should not i'magine he 'is.
4. I am 'sure you 'are.

## Activity 14

1. Do you know if he is busy this afternoon

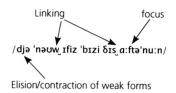

Linking           focus

/djə 'nəʊw‿ɪfiz 'bɪzi ðɪs‿ɑːftə'nuːn/

Elision/contraction of weak forms

2. If I had known about the party I would have come

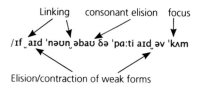

Linking   consonant elision  focus

/ɪf‿aɪd 'nəʊn‿əbaʊ ðə 'pɑːti aɪd‿əv 'kʌm/

Elision/contraction of weak forms

⇨

## Activity 14—Cont'd

3. I will ask him to come over as soon as possible

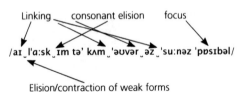

4. Do you want a sandwich or an apple

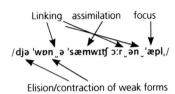

5. I do not know where he is actually

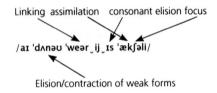

6. Will there be a message in case he is late?

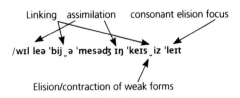

## Activity 15

1. Helen's machine stopped printing
2. Tom crept quietly away
3. Liz smiled gently
4. He passed his exam
5. Give me a break
6. I want to hold your hand

# Chapter 11 Intonation

## Key to Intonation Activities

---

### Activity 1

//that's **all**// from the ten o'clock **news** team// have a good week-**end**//

---

### Activity 2

The 'car was 'where I '**left** it

e.g.

tone unit    prehead    head    tonic tail

---

### Activity 3

The most likely tonic placement:

A: Where does she **work**?           B: At the **hospital**.
A: Are you **OK**?                    B. My **leg** hurts.
A: Would you like something to **drink**?  B: A cup of **coffee**, please.
A: Do you come here **often**?        B: Not **very** often.
A: Does she work in a **school**?     B: Yes, it's the **British** School
A: Does this bus go to the **station**?  B: Only on **weekdays**, I'm afraid.

---

### Activity 9

A: // it's five o'**clock**//
B: //‿ **mm**//
A: // ˎ**John**//
B: // ˏ **mm**//
A: // are you ˎ**hungry**//
B: // ˇ **mm**//
A: // piece of ˎ**chocolate** cake//
B: // ˆ **mm**//

## Activity 12

    a. // ˌ**Alfred** said//the boss is ˌ**stupid**//
    b. //I quite like ˌ**rice**// but I prefer ˌ**potatoes**//
    c. //His ˌ**phone** number is// 0116 252748 ˌ5//
    d. // ˌ**five**//plus seven minus ˌ**three**// ˌ**equals**// ˌ**nine**
    e. //Alison is leaving ˌ**work** //so I've been ˌ**told**//

## Activity 13

    (a) // Wheel your bike into the **shed** // (not the garage)
    (b) // Wheel your **bike** into the shed // (not that scooter)
    (c) // **Wheel** your bike into the shed // (don't try to carry it)
    (d) // Wheel **your** bike into the shed // (not my bike)

## Activity 14

Customer:   Can I have one chicken **sandwich** and two cheese **rolls**, please?
Waiter:      That's one **cheese** sandwich.
Customer:   **No**, one **chicken** sandwich.
Waiter:      Sorry that's **one** chicken sandwich and **two** cheese sandwiches.
Customer:   **No,** two cheese **rolls**.
Waiter:      Right. You did want **two** chicken sandwiches, didn't you?
Customer:   **No** I didn't. Just **one**.
Waiter:      I think I'd better write this **down**.

## Activity 18

Recording 1 -Transcript

    //I was 'born in 'nineteen 'forty ˌ**two**// - in - - ˌ**Salisbury**//ˌ**England** // - which is - 'south ˌ**west**// - and I was 'there because my ˌ**father**// was in the ˌ**army** //during the ˌ**war**/- and 'Salisbury ˌ**Plain** /- was the 'place where 'all the 'military **training**// -'went ˌ**on**// - and 'still ˌ**does**//

Recording 2 -Transcript

//er - my 'name is 'Jo ˌ**Clayton**// - I'm ˌ**British**//- at the 'moment I 'live in ˌ**Tulsa**// - in ˌ**Okla'homa** //- but I 'come from - - ˌ**Lancashire** 'actually// - I was 'born in ˌ**Lancashire**// - and 'then 'moved to ˌ**London** // - which is in the 'south of ˌ**England**// - ˌa'**bout**// - 'when I was a'boutˌ **twenty** //

Recording 3 -Transcript

//'when I was ˌ **sixteen** // - and I 'd 'taken my 'school ˌe'**xams**// - with a 'whole 'ˌ **bunch** of 'us// -'that's an **A'merican** ex'pression/ -ˌ **isn't** it// - ˌ **erm** // -- they 'didn't 'know 'what to ˌ**do** with us// - for the 'last 'twoˌ **weeks** //- at the ˌ **school**// - 'so they 'sent us 'all ˌ**off** //- on an archeo'logicalˌ **exca'vation**//- for 'twoˌ **weeks**//

Recording 4 -Transcript

// ˌO'**K**// - I'm a 'student from ˌ**Manchester** // - I was ˌ**born** // - and ˌ **raised** // - in ˌ**Manchester** // - erm -my 'dad'sˌ **Irish** //- my 'mum's ˌ**English** / -ˌ **erm** // - I 'studied in ˌ**Greece**// - for some ˌ**time** //- and I've 'travelled 'quite a ˌ**lot** //- ˌ**erm**// - I'm 'now 'doing my ˌ**masters**// - in ˌ**Dublin** //

# Chapter 12  Phonology Review 2

## Key to Activities

### Activity 2

1. Elision
   (a) 'kæm(ə)rə/
   (b) (ə)'ksu:z mi:
   (c) t(ə)'ma:təʊ
   (d) 'sekrət(ə)ri/
   (e) 'mem(ə)ri/

2. Assimilation
   (a) 'hæv ðə 'la:s 'keɪk
   (b) /'həʊl lə 'dɔ:
   (c) ɪts 'lʌnʃtaɪm
   (d) 'ðæ(t) wəz 'la:tʃɪə
   (e) ə 'gʊp 'pleɪs tə 'gəʊ

⇨

## Activity 2—Cont'd

3. Vowel reduction

   (a) hi 'ræn tə ðə 'tɒp ə ðə 'hɪl əz 'faːst əz ɪz 'legz wəd 'kærɪ ɪm

   (b) /aɪ 'wen(t) tə ði əʊ'tel ən 'bʊkt ə 'ruːm fə 'tuː 'naɪts fə maɪ 'faːðər ən hɪz 'bes(t) 'frend/

   (c) hɪl bɪ ə'raɪvɪŋ 'hɪə ɒn ði 'ɪiːvnɪŋ əv ðə 'tenθ

   (d) ʃiː 'ræn tə ðə 'steɪʃən

   (e) 'wʌn 'bɔɪ 'ræn tə ɪz 'mʌm tə 'tel ər ə'baʊ(t) ði 'æksɪdənt

Don't forget /iː/ is often reduced to /i/ when unstressed.

## Activity 3

1. I don't know where he's gone actually. I'm sure he was in the lecture earlier.
2. Excuse me, do you know if this coach goes to Sheffield?
3. I suppose the best thing is to ask her yourself.
4. Oh dear. You <u>are</u> in a bad mood, aren't you!
5. He could be right, I suppose, but she said it starts on Monday.

## Activity 4

   (a) // kən jə 'piːl ðə 'rest əv ðə 'kærəts // 'ðen 'wɒʃ ðə 'letɪs 'pliːz //

   (b) // aɪm ə'freɪd ðə 'nʌmbəz ɪŋ'geɪdʒd// kən jə 'traɪ ə'gen 'leɪtə//

   (c) // ə'pærəntli // ði 'ɪŋglən(d) 'tiːm wə 'luːzɪŋ əz 'juːʒuəl//

   (d) // 'pliːz 'dəʊm 'pænɪk// aɪm 'ʃʊə (or 'ʃɔː) ðə 'dɒktəz 'ɒn ɪz 'weɪ//

   (e) // kəd aɪ 'hæv ə 'prɔːn 'sæləd// ən ə 'glaːs ə 'spaːklɪŋ 'wɔːtə 'pliːz//

## Activity 5

A: The police have been asking questions again about the robbery

B: What robbery are you talking about?

A: The one on Saturday, from a shop in Main Street, I told you last night, remember

B: Oh yeah, sorry but I couldn't think what you were talking about

A: Apparently, the robbers got away with half a million

B: What – pounds?

A: No, pairs of shoes

A: // ðə pə'li:s əv 'bɪn 'æskɪŋ 'kwestʃənz ə'gen// ə'baʊt 'ðæt 'rɒbəri//
Notice the weak forms of 'the', 'have'.

B: // 'wɒt 'rɒbəri// ə jə 'tɔ:kɪŋ ə'baʊt//
Notice the reduction of unstressed 'are you'.

A: //ðə 'wʌn ɒn 'sætədi// frəm ə 'ʃɒp ɪm 'meɪn 'stri:t// aɪ 'təʊld jə 'lɑ:s 'naɪt // rɪ'membə//
Here, there is assimilation of /n/ to /m/ in 'in main street'; /j/ could also be assimilated to /ʒ/ in 'told you' ; elision of final /t/ in 'last' in 'last night', and weak forms for 'from' 'a' 'the' and 'you'.

B: //əʊ 'je // 'sɒri bət aɪ 'kʊdn̩t 'θɪŋk 'wɒt jə wə̰ 'tɔ:kɪŋ ə'baʊt//
Reduced forms occur in 'but', 'you', 'were'. Also note the syllabic consonant in 'couldn't'.

A: //'əpærəntli// ðə 'rɒbəz gɒt ə'weɪ wɪθ 'hɑ:f ə 'mɪljən//
Note the reduction of 'a' to / ə/.

B: // 'wɒ(t) // 'paʊnz/
The final plosive /t/ of 'what' is frequently unreleased in such positions.

A: // 'nəʊ// 'peəz ə 'ʃu:z//
Note the reduction of 'of' to / ə/.

# Activity 6

A: // 'weər əv jə 'bi:n//
B: aɪv bɪn 'weɪtɪŋ 'hɪə fər 'eɪʤɪz// 'dəʊn(t) 'tel mi ðə(t) 'pi:təz nɒt 'kʌmɪŋ ə'gen//
A: // 'dəʊm 'pænɪk // 'hɪz ɒn ɪz 'weɪ // hɪ 'sen(t) mɪ tə 'faɪnd ʒu// ən 'tel jə ðə(t) jə ʃəd 'teɪk ə 'tæksi// ən 'mi:t ɪm ə(t) 'mæksɪms//
B: // 'wɒts 'hæpn̩ŋ ə(t) 'mæksɪms//
A: // aɪ də'nəʊ // bə(t) ðə fu:dz 'gʊd//

Note the loss of /t/ word finally to avoid consonant clusters in many cases (eg 'don't tell me') Also, the assimilation of 'don't' to / dəʊm / before 'panic'. Similarly, the consonant cluster in 'find you' is assimilated to /faɪnʤu/. Also, notice the loss of /h/ in initial position in unstressed structure words like 'his way'

# Activity 7

Recording 1

//'my 'name is ˌTer'ese// - and I was 'born in ˏChi'cago // - I 'lived in the A'merican 'Mid ˌWest //- un'til 'twelve 'years ˌa'go// -when I 'emigrated to the U'nited ˏKingdom // -and 'settled in 'north ˏWales// - a 'few months ˏa'go//-I 'relocated toˏLeicester//- in the ˏmidlands//

## Activity 7—Cont'd

Recording 2

//'my 'name is ˌ**Simon** //- and I was 'born in ˌ**Tanza'nia //** - I 'grew 'up in 'many ˌ**'different** 'countries //- I have 'lived in the 'east ˌ**midlands** //for the 'past 'fifteenˌ **years**//

Recording 3

// my 'name's ˌ**Paul**// and I was 'born inˌ **Nort'hampton**//- in 'days when it was con'sidered ˌ**normal**// to 'stay in the same ˌ**city**// for one's 'wholeˌ **life** // but 'since 'going to ˌ**uni'versity** //I've had to 'move ˌ**a'round** //-and 'lived in ˌ**London** //- ˌ**Brighton**//- ˌ**Birmingham** // ˌ**Glasgow**// - ˌ**Oxford**// - and 'nowˌ **Leicester**// I'm 'rather 'hoping I can ˌ**stay** in 'Leicester now//ˌ **be'cause** //- there's been a 'lot of 'moving ˌ**a'round**// in myˌ **life**//

Recording 4

//I was 'born in ˌ**Jo'hannesburg**// - South ˌ**'Africa**// - which, as you may ˌ**know**//- is called ˌ**Jo'burg** //for ˌ**short**// all my 'schooling was under theˌ **British** 'system// - 'first I at'tended a ˌ**private**// - 'all ˌ**girls** 'school//- 'called St ˌ**Mary's**// in ˌ**Jo'burg**//- and 'then, at the 'age of ˌ**fifteen**//- I 'went to an 'Anglican ˌ**boarding** 'school //in a 'town called ˌ**Grahamstown**// - which is a'bout a 'thousand 'kilometres ˌ**south**//- of ˌ**Jo'burg**// - 'people 'always 'give me 'pitying ˌ**looks** //when I 'say I 'went to ˌ**boarding** 'school// - but 'actually it was ˌ**wonderful**//

Recording 5

//he'llo my 'name is ˌ**Sahm** //- I 'come from ˌ**Ghana**//- but 'currently 'live inˌ **England**// -- be'fore 'coming to the ˌ**UK**//- I 'worked as a ˌ**librarian**//- in a 'university ˌ**college**// - 'currently I 'work as a 'research as'sociate in ˌ**e-learning**// in the University of ˌ**Leicester**// and I'm - 'part of a project ˌ**team**// - working to de'velop 'open edu'cational ˌ**re'sources**// which are to be 'made 'freely and 'openly a'vailable toˌ **all**//

Recording 6

my 'name is ˌ**Ale'jandro**// - 'people 'call me - ˌ**Ale**// a'round ˌ**here**//- be'cause they 'find it 'hard to pro'nounce the - ˌ**/x/** //orˌ **'j'**//-- I was 'born in er- ˌ**Montevi'deo** //- ˌ**Uruguay**// but have 'lived and 'worked in the ˌ**U'K**// for the 'past 'sevenˌ **years**// my aca'demic ˌ**ca'reer**// has 'taken me to ˌ**Kent**//- ˌ**Manchester**// - and 'finally ˌ**Leicester**// -where I am based ˌ**now**// 'one of the 'things that I ˌ**miss**//- from ˌ**Montevi'deo**// is the **sea** // al'though I 'live on an ˌ**island** // - I'm a'lmost a 'hundred 'miles from theˌ **coast**//

# Chapter 13  Pronunciation in the Classroom

## Key to Activities

---

### Activity 2

d.  /b/p/ & /t/d/

Various 'tips' can be given here. For instance, place a piece of paper in front of mouth to demonstrate the difference between /p/ and /b/ in terms of aspiration. You could take a look at the BBC Learning English – 'pronunciation tips' website for more ideas http://www.bbc.co.uk/worldservice/learningenglish/grammar/pron/

Or look at the chapters on 'voicing' and 'aspiration ' in 'Speaking Clearly' Rogerson,P & Gilbert, J. (1990)

---

### Activity 3

(a) Examples of minimal pairs include:

| | |
|---|---|
| torn | turn |
| born | burn |
| form | firm |
| short | short |

(b) These are usually not too difficult to teach but as with any aspect of pronunciation is it important to consider if this is a priority area first. As you might expect this can be done by:

breaking diphthong into its component parts
practising each one in isolation
running them together, remembering that the first part receives the heavier stress
You could start by getting students to say the two vowels separately and then slowly putting them together, gradually speeding up

e.g.  boy = bɒ +ɪ
tower = tɑ+ʊ+ə

# Glossary of Key Terms

**accent**: a pronunciation variety used by a specific group of people.

**allophone**: different phonetic realizations of a phoneme.

**allophonic variation**: variations in how a phoneme is pronounced which do not create a meaning difference in words.

**alveolar**: a sound produced near or on the alveolar ridge.

**alveolar ridge**: the small bony ridge behind the upper front teeth.

**approximants**: obstruct the air flow so little that they could almost be classed as vowels if they were in a different context (e.g. /w/ or /j/).

**articulatory organs** – (or **articulators**): are the different parts of the vocal tract that can change the shape of the air flow.

**articulatory settings** or '**voice quality**': refers to the characteristic or long-term positioning of articulators by individual or groups of speakers of a particular language.

**aspirated**: phonemes involve an auditory plosion ('puff of air') where the air can be heard passing through the glottis after the release phase.

**assimilation**: a process where one sound is influenced by the characteristics of an adjacent sound.

**back vowels**: vowels where the back part of the tongue is raised (like 'two' and 'tar')

**bilabial**: a sound that involves contact between the two lips.

**breathy voice**: voice quality where whisper is combined with voicing.

**cardinal vowels**: a set of phonetic vowels used as reference points which do not relate to any specific language.

**central vowels**: vowels where the central part of the tongue is raised (like 'fur' and 'sun')

**centring diphthongs**: glide towards /ə/.

**citation form**: the way we say a word on its own.

**close vowel**: where the tongue is raised as close as possible to the roof of the mouth. For example, 'tea'.

**closed syllable**: a syllable which is closed by a final consonant such as 'seen' /si:n/, which has three phonemes (cvc).

**closing diphthongs**: glide towards closer/ higher vowels, either /ɪ/ or /ʊ/.

**coda**: the final consonant of a syllable (which is optional).

**comfortable intelligibility**: as a pronunciation goal is where speaker and listener can communicate effectively without undue stress or effort.

**complementary distribution**: when one allophone or variation of a phoneme operates in a separate context from another

**comprehensibility**: the understanding and interpretation of words and messages

**conflation**: pronunciation of two distinct phonemes as one (e.g. /s/ and /θ/).

**consonant**: is a phonological term referring to the way such sounds function in the language. For instance, consonants are typically found at the beginning and ends of syllables while vowels are typically found in the middle.

**consonant cluster**: a sequence of consonants at the beginning or end of a syllable.

**consonant deletion**: omission or elision of a sound (e.g. 'p(e)rhaps') or replacement by a glottal stop (e.g. 'but' – /bʌʔ/).

**continuant**: a sound which involves the continuous expulsion of air, as opposed to a stop sound where the air is blocked by one or more articulator.

**contoid**: is a phonetic term to describe those sounds which produce a significant obstruction to the flow of air through the vocal tract.

**contractions**: when elisions occur between weak forms, producing a contracted forms, for example 'he + will' = 'he'll'.

**creaky voice**: is created by a succession of glottal stops.

**dental**: sounds involving the the tip of the tongue and the front teeth, for example /ð/ in 'this' and /θ/ in 'thanks'.

**diacritic**: mark added to phonetic symbols to provide additional information, for example [ ˜ ] indicates nasalization.

**dialect**: refers to a variety of a language used by a group of people and distinguished by its grammar and lexis.

**diphthong**: a vowel requiring two articulations, a nucleus and a glide.

**egressive**: sounds created by expelling the air from the lungs out through the mouth or nose.

**elision or ellipsis**: the deletion of certain sounds in connected speech (e.g. 'last night' – /lɑːs ˈnaɪt/).

**epenthesis**: vowel insertion between two consonants to ease articulation (typically in clusters) (e.g. 'sport' – /səpɔːt/)

**final position**: the position of a sound at the end of a syllable or word.

**focus**: one content word within an utterance will typically receive greater stress than the others.

**fortis**: a fortis sound involves greater effort, that is, muscular tension, to produce and is usually voiceless.

**free variation**: when one allophone can be substituted for another in various contexts without changing the meaning

**frequency**: the speed of vibration of the vocal folds.

**fricative**: a term applied to the manner of articulation of consonants where the constriction of the air flow between articulators causes friction (e.g. /s/ /z/).

**front vowels**: vowels where the front part of the tongue is raised (like 'tea' and 'tan')

**full vs reduced vowels**: vowels in strong syllables are full and vowels in weak syllables are reduced.

**functional load**: this refers to the amount of work two phonemes do to distinguish word meaning, that is, the importance of phoneme distinctions in minimal pairs.

**function or grammatical words**: such as pronouns, auxiliary verbs, conjunctions, articles and prepositions which are frequently unstressed.

**glottal**: sounds made where the vocal folds are the articulators (e.g. /h/).

**glottal stop**: if the vocal folds are tightly closed (i.e. the glottis is tightly shut) a stop sound can be produced when pent up air behind the closure is suddenly released.

**glottis**: the space between the focal folds or cords.

**ingressive**: sounds created while breathing in or inhaling.

**initial position**: the position of a sound at the beginning of a syllable or word.

**intelligibility**: how much a listener actually understands.

**intervocalic**: a sound that comes between vowel sounds, as for the /t/ in butter.

**intonation**: the pitch pattern of speech.

**intrusive 'r'**: when it is possible to hear linking /r/ when there is no 'r' in the spelling of the word. For example, 'law and order' – 'lawrand order'.

**IPA**: stands for the International Phonetic Association.

**key**: the overall pitch height of a thought group, in relation to surrounding thought groups.

**labial**: a sound articulated with the lips.

**labiodental:** place of articulation involving the upper lip and the lower teeth, such as /f/.

**labio-dental:** sounds produced with the top teeth and bottom lip.

**larynx (also known as the voice-box):** an organ at the top of the windpipe, containing the vocal cords which produce voice.

**lateral:** describes a manner of articulation of consonants where contact between articulators restricts central air flow so that the air escapes around the sides or laterally, as in /l/.

**lax:** vowels require less muscular tension than tense vowels (e.g. 'bit').

**lenis:** a sound pronounced with less muscular tension than a fortis sound and usually voiced.

**lexical** or **content:** words are typically accented and include main verbs, adverbs, nouns, adjectives and demonstratives.

**linking** or **liaison:** in connected speech, words often blend together: this process is called linking.

**markedness:** relates to the degree of difference or distinctiveness of linguistic contrasts in a language in relation to universal preferences.

**medial position:** a consonant is in medial position (or intervocalic position) when it comes between vowel sounds, as the /t/ in butter.

**minimal pair:** contrasts is where sounds occurring in identical environments produce a difference in meaning, for example, curl vs girl.

**monophthongs:** or pure vowels: where the tongue remains in a relatively stable position throughout the articulation.

**nasal cavity:** the upper part of the vocal tract inside the nose.

**nasal:** a consonant sound, produced with the soft palate lowered so that air passes through the nasal cavity, such as /n/.

**non-rhotic:** accents are one where the /r/ phoneme is not pronounced after a vowel (e.g. car, horse) while in rhotic accents (e.g. General American, Canadian, Scottish, Irish) the post vocalic /r/ is pronounced.

**nucleus:** the most prominent syllable in the thought group (also known as the nuclear or tonic syllable or focus).

**onset:** the initial consonant of a syllable.

**open syllable:** a syllable which ends in a vowel, for example 'see' /si:/ which has a two phoneme (cv) syllable structure.

**open vowel:** when the tongue is lowered and the jaw is as open as possible, for example 'tap'.

**oral cavity:** the upper part of the vocal tract inside the mouth.

**overlapping stop:** where the first plosive is unexploded as the second begins before plosion can occur in the first (e.g. bagpipe).

**palatal:** sounds where the front of tongue is raised to the hard palate.

**palate:** the roof of the mouth which can be subdivided into the hard and the soft palate (velum).

**palato-alveolar:** describes sounds produced just behind the alveolar ridge.

**paragoge:** vowel insertion after a final consonant.

**peak:** the middle part of a syllable (normally a vowel).

**pharyngeal:** sounds with the root of the tongue raised to the pharynx.

**pharyngeal cavity:** the lower part of the vocal tract, where the throat or pharynx is.

**pharynx:** this is the airway in the throat behind the mouth which connects with the nasal cavity and the nose.

**phoneme:** an abstract unit representing the smallest distinctive speech sound that distinguishes one word from another, for example 'thin' and 'tin'.

**phonetics:** the scientific description of speech sounds across languages, unrelated to a specific language.

**phonological fluency:** 'sustained oral production in a natural context' (Pennington 1992).

**phonology:** the study of these sounds patterns within a particular language, such as Chinese or English, or in a variety of language, such as Cantonese Chinese or Indian English.

**phonotactics:** study of sequences of phonemes. every language has phonotactic rules, that is, restrictions on which phonemes can go together at the beginning, middle or end of syllables and native speakers know these rules subconsciously.

**pitch:** the perceived level of the voice, based on frequency.

**pitch range:** refers to the upper and lower limits of a speaker's vocal pitch.

**plosives:** sounds which make a complete stoppage of the air stream, for example, /p//t/.

**post-alveolar:** sounds where the tip of tongue falls just behind the gum ridge and before the hard palate, also termed palato-alveolar, for example, /ʃ/ in 'sheep'.

**proclaiming tones:** in Brazil (1977) description these are falling tones which carry unshared or new information.

**progressive assimilation:** the initial consonant (ci) of the second word is affected by the final consonant of the preceding word (cf).

**prominence:** has four key acoustic signals, that is, pitch frequency, duration, amplitude and quality.

**prosodic:** describes features of speech above the level of phonemes or segments, such as stress and intonation.

**prosody:** refers to the broader study of stress, rhythm and prominence.

**referring tones:** in Brazil (1977) description, these are typically rising tones which signal given or shared information.

**regressive assimilation:** where the final consonant ('consonant final' abbreviated to 'cf') of the first word assumes the phonetic characteristics of the following word's first consonant (i.e. 'consonant initial' or 'ci').

**retroflex:** sounds with the tip of the tongue curled back on to the hard palate.

**rhotic accents:** accents where /r/ is pronounced after a vowel that is, post-vocalic /r/.

**rhyme:** the combination of peak and coda in a syllable.

**RP:** Received Pronunciation – a term used to define a variety of southern English which is commonly used as the standard pronunciation model, despite the fact that few people speak it in its full form.

**schwa:** is the most frequently ocurring vowel in English. It only occurs in unstressed syllables.

**segmental phonology:** is concerned with describing individual phonemes or sound segments.

**sonorants:** a term covering nasals, approximants and vowels. The sonority of a sound is its inherent loudness or strength.

**sonority:** the loudness of a speech sound compared to other sounds.

**speech organs** or **speech mechanism:** the organs in the various parts of the speech mechanism which modify the air expelled from the lungs on its way through the throat, mouth and nose.

**Standard English:** this generally refers to the use of standard syntax or lexis. however, it does not necessarily imply standard pronunciation, so for instance Standard English could be spoken with a non-standard, regional accent, rather than RP.

**stress:** refers to the relative prominence of a syllable within a word (i.e. word stress), or a word within in a thought group (i.e. nuclear stress).

**stress-timed:** a type of speech rhythm with stressed syllables occurring at regular intervals, regardless of the number of unstressed syllables between them.

**strong form**: many function words (i.e. auxiliaries, determiners, pronouns, prepositions and conjunctions) can often be pronounced in two different ways; the strong form has full vowels while the weak form has reduced vowel (e.g. 'for' is /fɔ:/ in strong form and /fə/ in weak form).

**strong syllables**: either have a long vowel or a diphthong or end in two consonants.

**substitution**: the replacement of one phoneme by another (e.g. /l/ by /r/ by some Japanese learners).

**supralaryngeal**: above the larynx.

**suprasegmental phonology**: the study of these broader aspects of the sound system such as syllables, words and connected speech.

**syllabic consonant**: when a vowel occurring between one consonant and a final sonorant consonant is elided (e.g. sudden sʌdn̩). /l, n, m, ŋ, r/ all occur as syllabic consonants.

**syllable**: a phonological unit between a word and a phoneme which normally contains at least a single vowel as the nucleus.

**syllable timed**: a type of speech rhythm giving the impression of roughly equal length to each syllable regardless of stress.

**tense vowels**: require more muscular tension to produce (e.g. 'beat') than **lax** vowels.

**thought group** or **tone unit**: this is a melodic unit made up of a specific pitch contour segmenting the stretch of discourse into message blocks, often marked by pauses at its boundary.

**tone languages**: in some languages, changing the pitch level (e.g. high, mid, low) or contour (falling or rising) on a particular word can change the lexical meaning (e.g. in Chinese).

**tone**: the pitch pattern that begins on this nuclear syllable and continues through the rest of the thought group.

**tonic syllable**: the syllable within a tone unit that carries the most prominence.

**trachea**: otherwise known as the windpipe.

**triphthong**: a vowel composed of three sounds, a rapid glide from one sound to another and then to a third.

**unvoiced/voiceless sound**: describes sounds where the vocal cords do not vibrate.

**uvula**: this is the soft, fleshy hanging tip that falls from the base of the soft palate.

**uvular**: sounds articulated with the back of the tongue is against the uvula.

**velar**: a velar sound is produced at the velum, or the soft palate.

**velum**: the soft palate, that is, the part of the palate that is just behind the hard palate.

**vocal cords**: (or folds, or bands or voice box) – pair of muscular flaps in the larynx.

**vocalization**: a general term to explain the production of vocal sounds.

**vocal tract:** the part of the speech mechanism above the larynx.

**vocoid**: phonetic term describing sounds that do not obstruct the air flow – typically vowels.

**voiced sound**: a sound produced with vibration of the vocal cords.

**voiceless sound**: when the vocal folds are held wide apart, as in relaxed breathing, air passes through freely.

**vowel elision**: when a vowel is elided or disappears.

**vowel insertion**: involves adding an additional vowel to ease a difficult articulation.

**weak syllable**: a syllable which is unstressed and typically contains a short vowel or schwa.

**whisper**: a voice quality setting where the folds are brought close together but without vibration.

**word stress**: or 'accent' refers to the syllable or syllables of a word which stand out from the remainder by being more prominent.

**word-class pairs**: can operate as nouns or verbs. They can be distinguished by stress placement, for example, 'record (noun), re'cord (verb).

# Index

Page numbers in **bold** denote figures and tables.

CPSIA information can be obtained
at www.ICGtesting.com
Printed in the USA
LVOW09s1929021216
515537LV00009B/145/P